THE DIALOGIC IMAGINATION

UNIVERSITY OF TEXAS PRESS SLAVIC SERIES, NO. 1

Michael Holquist, General Editor

THE DIALOGIC IMAGINATION

Four Essays

by

M. M. BAKHTIN

Edited by
Michael Holquist

Translated by
Caryl Emerson and Michael Holquist

UNIVERSITY OF TEXAS PRESS
AUSTIN

Copyright © 1981 by the University of Texas Press
All rights reserved
Printed in the United States of America

Library of Congress Cataloging in Publication Data

Bakhtin, Mikhail Mikhaïlovich.
  The dialogic imagination.
  (University of Texas Press Slavic series; no. 1)
  Translation of Voprosy literatury i estetiki.
  Includes index.
    1. Fiction—Addresses, essays, lectures. 2. Literature—
  Addresses, essays, lectures. I. Holquist, J. Michael.
  II. Title. III. Series.
  PN3331.B2513   801'.953   80-15450
  ISBN 0-292-71527-7
  ISBN 0-292-71534-X (pbk.)

Requests for permission to reproduce material from this work should be
sent to Permissions, University of Texas Press, Box 7819, Austin, Texas
78712.

First Paperback Printing, 1982

The publication of this volume was assisted in part by a grant from the
National Endowment for the Humanities, an independent federal agency
whose mission is to award grants to support education, scholarship, media programming, libraries, and museums in order to bring the results of
cultural activities to the general public. Preparation was made possible
in part by a grant from the Translations Program of the endowment.

Dedication

There is nothing more fragile than the word, and Bakhtin's was almost lost. This translation is dedicated to those devoted Russian scholars who gave so generously of themselves to Mikhail Mikhailovich the man and to the cause of preserving dialogue.

CONTENTS

ACKNOWLEDGMENTS

Thanks are due first of all to the Executors of the Bakhtin Archives, Vadim Kožinov and Sergej Bočorov. Their devotion to Bakhtin is matched only by their generosity toward those who would study him. To I. R. Titunik we owe a special debt of gratitude. He read large parts of the first draft of this translation and if, as we hope, there were improvements in subsequent drafts, it is because we constantly had his image before us, the threat of one of his red-penciled "ughs" or "cute, but wrong, utterly wrong" in the margin. The high standard of scholarship as well as translation that he has established in his own work was a constant inspiration to us. He did not see the final version and therefore cannot be charged with any inaccuracies, all of which are our own responsibility. Thanks also to the many scholars from various departments who helped us in the task of identifying some of Bakhtin's more recherché examples: to Millicent Marcus in Italian; Robert Hill in French; James Wimsatt, Medievalist, in English; Robert Mollenauer in German; Michael Gagarin and Carl Rubino in Classics, all of the University of Texas. Thanks also to Vadim Liapunov of the Slavic Department, Indiana University, to whom we turned when all else failed. We are grateful as well to Ilya Levin and Sofia Nikonova who played the role of native speakers, with resource and wit.

Preparation of the manuscript was particularly complex due to the many languages, two sets of footnotes and so forth. We could not have done it without Elaine Hamilton. The person who has borne with this for three years now and still had the patience and dedication to come in on weekends when it was necessary to retype yet another version of some arcane passage is Gianna Kirtley. The National Endowment for the Humanities and the University Research Institute at the University of Texas provided generous grants to support this translation.

This book is also a sponsored activity of the Institute of Modern Russian Culture at Blue Lagoon, Texas.

Thanks as always to Katerina Clark, who was ready to give help whenever it was needed, whether it was a technical term in Russian or a word of encouragement in English. Thanks to Snugli Cottage Industries. Thanks finally to the anonymous donor whose Medician gesture made not only this book but the whole series in which it appears possible.

A NOTE ON TRANSLATION

The IPA transcription system is used in this book, except in those cases where a word or a name has entered general English usage via another system (i.e., Bakhtin, not Baxtin).

Bakhtin's footnotes are indicated by superscript numbers; the editor's footnotes are indicated by superscript letters.

This book contains four essays that originally appeared in *Voprosy literatury i estetiki* (Moscow, 1975). Two additional essays are not included here, because they either have already been translated into English or do not bear directly on the theme unifying the other four, the novel and its relation to language.

The "Translator's Note" to non-Russian versions of Bakhtin's works has become a genre in its own right. More often than not, the peculiarity of Bakhtin's Russian is invoked to justify a certain awkwardness in the translated text. We believe the matter is more complicated. Bakhtin himself provides the best context for perceiving the true nature of the problem in the distinction he draws between "style" and "language"—especially as it pertains to the "image of a language." We have sought to make a translation at the level of images of a whole language (*obraz jazyka*).

The translations are complete. Bakhtin is not an efficient writer, but we believe he pays his way.

* * *

Since junior members of team projects frequently receive less credit than is their due, I wish to emphasize that this translation is the result of a real dialogue: Caryl Emerson and I went over every word of Bakhtin's text together.

MICHAEL HOLQUIST

INTRODUCTION

I

Mikhail Mikhailovich Bakhtin is gradually emerging as one of
the leading thinkers of the twentieth century. This claim will
strike many as extravagant, since a number of factors have until
recently conspired to obscure his importance. Beyond the difficulties usually attending the careers of powerful but eccentric
thinkers, there are, in Bakhtin's case, complications that are
unique. Some of these inhere in his times: his two most productive periods occurred during the darkest years of recent Russian
history: the decade following 1917, when the country reeled under the combined effects of a lost war, revolution, civil war and
famine; and the following decade, the thirties, when Bakhtin was
in exile in Kazakhstan, and most of the rest of Russia was hud-
dling through the long Stalinist night. It was in these years that
Bakhtin wrote something on the order of nine large books on topics as major and varied as Freud, Marx and the philosophy of language. Only one of these (the Dostoevsky book) appeared under
his own name during these years. Three others were published
under different names (see section III of this introduction); some
were partially lost during his forced moves; some disappeared
when the Nazis burned down the publishing house that had accepted his large manuscript on the *Erziehungsroman*; some were
"delayed" forty-one years in their publication when journals that
had accepted manuscripts were shut down, as happened to the
Russian Contemporary in 1924; others, such as the Rabelais
book, were considered too aberrant for publication, due to their
emphasis on sex and body functions (see section II of this
introduction).

Another factor that has clouded perception of the scope of
Bakhtin's activity in the anglophone world, at least, is the tradi-

tion in which he was working. He was trained as a classicist during a period when the German model of philology dominated Russian universities; thus he inherited a certain heaviness of style and a predilection for abstraction that English or American readers, accustomed to a more essayistic prose, sometimes find heavy going. Bakhtin's style, while recognizably belonging to a Russian tradition of scholarly prose, is, nevertheless, highly idiosyncratic. Language in his texts works somewhat as language does in the novel, the genre that obsessed him all his life: according to Ian Watt (*The Rise of the Novel*), "the genre itself works by exhaustive presentation rather than by elegant concentration." The more we know about Bakhtin's life, the clearer it becomes that he was a supreme eccentric, of an order the Russians express better than we in their word *čudak*, which has overtones of such intense strangeness that it borders on *čudo*, a wonder. And this peculiarity is reflected not only in the strange history of his texts (why, ultimately, did he publish under so many names?), but in his style as well, if one may speak of a *single* style for one who was so concerned with "other-voicedness." Russians immediately sense this strangeness: again and again when we have gone to native speakers with questions about a peculiar usage of a familiar word or an unfamiliar coinage, the Russians have thrown up their hands or shaken their heads and smiled ruefully.

Another difficulty the reader must confront is the unfamiliar shadings Bakhtin gives to West European cultural history. He tends to ignore the available chapterization into familiar periods and -isms. It is not so much Periclean Athens or Augustan Rome that attracts him as it is the vagaries of the Hellenistic age. He is preoccupied by centuries usually ignored by others; and within these, he has great affection for figures who are even more obscure. A peculiar school of grammarians at Toulouse in the seventh century A.D. may appear to others as an obscure group working in a backwater during the darkest of the Dark Ages; for Bakhtin the work of these otherwise almost forgotten men constitutes an extremely important chapter in the human struggle to accommodate the mysteries of human language. He keeps returning to the Carolingian Revival or the interstitial periods between the Middle Ages and the Renaissance. When he does cite a familiar period, he often tends to isolate an otherwise obscure figure within it—thus his focusing on Pigres of Halicarnassus or Ion of Chios among the Greeks, on Varro among the Romans; when

dealing with the nineteenth century, it is the relatively unfamiliar Wezel or Musäus he cites.

Bakhtin throws a weird light on our received models of intellectual history. It is as if he set out to carnivalize—to use a verb
that has become modishly transitive due to his own work on
Rabelais—the normal periods and figures we use to define the re-
lay of culture. Clearly, one could make such a perverse undertaking pay its way only if possessed of two prerequisites: enormous
learning and a theory capable of sustaining a balance between
such an aberrant history and more conventional historical
models.

Of Bakhtin's preternatural erudition there can be no doubt—he
belongs to the tradition that produced Spitzer, Curtius, Auerbach
and, somewhat later, René Wellek. Many times when we have
consulted specialists in the various fields from which Bakhtin so
easily draws his recherché examples, it was only to be told that
such and such a work did not exist, or, if it did, it was not "characteristic." A few days later, however, after some more digging or
thinking, the same specialist would call to say that indeed there
was such a work, and, although little known even to most experts, it was the most precisely correct text for illustrating the
point Bakhtin sought to make by invoking it.

He has, then, a knowledge of West European civilization detailed enough to permit him to use traditional accounts as a dialogizing background to sustain the counter-model he will pro-
pose. And that counter-model is motivated by a theory that can
rationalize not only its own subversions, but the effects of mainstream traditions as well.

I say theory and not system—the two do not always go hand in
hand—because Bakhtin's motivating idea is in its essence opposed to any strict formalization. Other commentators, such as
Tsvetan Todorov in a forthcoming book devoted to Bakhtin, have
seen this as a weakness in his work. They have come to this conclusion, I believe, because they bring to Bakhtin's work expectations based on the kind of thinking characteristic of other major
theorists who engage the same issues as Bakhtin.

Bakhtin is constantly working with what is emerging as the
central preoccupation of our time—language. But unlike others
who have made substantial contributions to our understanding of
language in the twentieth century—Saussure, Hjelmslev, Ben-
veniste and, above all, Roman Jakobson (all of whom are system-

atic to an extraordinary degree)—Bakhtin is not. If you expect a
Jakobsonian order of systematicalness in Bakhtin, you are bound
to be frustrated. This does not mean, however, that he is without
a peculiar rigor of his own. It is rather that his concept of language stands in relation to others (of the sort that occupy linguists) much as the novel stands in opposition to other, more for-
malized genres. That is, the novel—as Bakhtin more than anyone
else has taught us to see—does not lack its organizing principles,
but they are of a different order from those regulating sonnets or
odes. It may be said Jakobson works with poetry because he has a
Pushkinian love of order; Bakhtin, on the contrary, loves novels
because he is a baggy monster.

At the heart of everything Bakhtin ever did—from what we
know of his very earliest (lost) manuscripts to the very latest (still
unpublished) work—is a highly distinctive concept of language.
The conception has as its enabling *a priori* an almost Manichean
sense of opposition and struggle at the heart of existence, a cease-
less battle between centrifugal forces that seek to keep things
apart, and centripetal forces that strive to make things cohere.
This Zoroastrian clash is present in culture as well as nature, and
in the specificity of individual consciousness; it is at work in the
even greater particularity of individual utterances. The most
complete and complex reflection of these forces is found in
human language, and the best transcription of language so understood is the novel.

Two things must immediately be added here. First, while language does serve to reflect this struggle, it is no passive stuff, no
mere yielding clay. Language itself is no less immune from the
effects of the struggle than anything else. Its nature as a system is
even *more* fraught with the contest, which may be why it occupies so central a place in the activity of mind. Bakhtin, need it
be said, is not working in this dichotomy of forces with the kind
of binary opposition that has proved so important in structuralist
linguistics (and so seductive to social scientists and humanists
lusting for a greater degree of systematicalness). That opposition
leads from human speech to computer language; it conduces, in
other words, to machines. Bakhtin's sense of a duel between
more widely implicated forces leads in the opposite direction and
stresses the fragility and ineluctably historical nature of language, the coming and dying of meaning that it, as a phenomenon, shares with that other phenomenon it ventriloquates, man.

Secondly, language must not be understood in these essays in the restricted sense in which it occupies professional linguists. As Bakhtin says (in "Discourse in the Novel"), "At any given moment . . . a language is stratified not only into dialects in the strict sense of the word (i.e., dialects that are set off according to formal linguistic [especially phonetic] markers), but is . . . stratified as well into languages that are socio-ideological: languages belonging to professions, to genres, languages peculiar to particular generations, etc. This stratification and diversity of speech [*raznorečivost'*] will spread wider and penetrate to ever deeper levels so long as a language is alive and still in the process of becoming."

The two contending tendencies are not of equal force, and each has a different kind of reality attaching to it: centrifugal forces are clearly more powerful and ubiquitous—theirs is the reality of actual articulation. They are always *in praesentia*; they determine the way we actually experience language as we use it—and are used by it—in the dense particularity of our everyday lives. Unifying, centripetal forces are less powerful and have a complex ontological status. Their relation to centrifugal operations is akin to the interworking that anthropologists nominate as the activity of culture in modeling a completely different order called nature. As Bakhtin says (again in "Discourse"): "A unitary language is not something that is given [*dan*], but is in its very essence something that must be posited [*zadan*]—at every moment in the life of a language it opposes the realities of heteroglossia [*raznorečie*], but at the same time the [sophisticated] ideal [or primitive delusion] of a single, holistic language makes the actuality of its presence felt as a force resisting an absolute heteroglot state; it posits definite boundaries for limiting the potential chaos of variety, thus guaranteeing a more or less maximal mutual understanding. . . ."

The term Bakhtin uses here, "heteroglossia" [*raznorečie*], is a master trope at the heart of all his other projects, one more fundamental than such other categories associated with his thought as "polyphony" or "carnivalization." These are but two specific ways in which the primary condition of heteroglossia manifests itself. Heteroglossia is Bakhtin's way of referring, in any utterance of any kind, to the peculiar interaction between the two fundamentals of all communication. On the one hand, a mode of transcription must, in order to do its work of separating out texts, be a more or less fixed system. But these repeatable features, on the other hand, are in the power of the particular context in which the utterance is made; this context can refract, add to, or, in some cases, even subtract from the amount and kind of meaning the utterance may be said to have when it is conceived only as a systematic manifestation independent of context.

This extraordinary sensitivity to the immense plurality of experience more than anything else distinguishes Bakhtin from other moderns who have been obsessed with language. I emphasize experience here because Bakhtin's basic scenario for modeling variety is two actual people talking to each other in a specific dialogue at a particular time and in a particular place. But these persons would not confront each other as sovereign egos capable of sending messages to each other through the kind of uncluttered space envisioned by the artists who illustrate most receiver-sender models of communication. Rather, each of the two persons would be a consciousness at a specific point in the history of defining itself through the choice it has made—out of all the possible existing languages available to it at that moment—of a discourse to transcribe its intention *in this specific exchange*.

The two will, like everyone else, have been born into an environment in which the air is already aswarm with names. Their development as individuals—and in this Bakhtin's thought parallels in suggestive ways that of Vygotsky in Russia (see Emerson, 1978) and Lacan in France (see Bruss, in Titunik's translation of Vološinov's *Freudianism*, 1976)—will have been prosecuted as a gradual appropriation of a specific mix of discourses that are capable of best mediating their own intentions, rather than those which sleep in the words they use before they use them. Thus each will seek, by means of intonation, pronunciation, lexical choice, gesture, and so on, to send out a message to the other with a minimum of interference from the otherness constituted by pre-existing meanings (inhering in dictionaries or ideologies) and the otherness of the intentions present in the other person in the dialogue.

Implicit in all this is the notion that all transcription systems—including the speaking voice in a living utterance—are inadequate to the multiplicity of the meanings they seek to convey. My voice gives the illusion of unity to what I say; I am, in fact, constantly expressing a plenitude of meanings, some intended, others of which I am unaware. (There is in this obsession with voice and speech a parallel with the attempts of two important recent thinkers—both in other ways very different from Bakhtin—to come to grips with the way intimacy with our own voice conduces to the illusion of presence: Husserl in the *Logical Investigations* and Derrida in his 1967 essay "Speech and Phenomenon.")

It is the need to confront this multiplicity in a principled way that impels Bakhtin to coin some of his more outré terms (the word "heteroglossia" itself, "word-with-a-loophole," "word-with-a-sidewards-glance," "intonational quotation marks" and so forth). He uses these rather than the more conventional terminology we associate with a linguistic concern for language first of all because traditional linguistics has taken little heed of the problem of alterity in language. Bakhtin, like Austin (*How to Do Things with Words,* 1962), Searle (*Speech Acts,* 1969) and particularly Grice (the legendary but still unpublished 1967 James lectures on Logic and Conversation), stresses the speech aspect of language, *utterance,* to emphasize the immediacy of the kind of meaning he is after. He does so as well to highlight his contention that language is never—except for certain linguists—what linguists say it is. There is no such thing as a "general language," a language that is spoken by a general voice, that may be divorced from a specific saying, which is charged with particular overtones. Language, when it *means,* is somebody talking to somebody else, even when that someone else is one's own inner addressee.

Bakhtin's theory of metalanguage is extremely complicated and deserves detailed study. I have merely alluded to it here in order to provide a context for the more particular subject matter unifying these four essays—the novel. I began with Bakhtin's insistence on the primacy of speech because what he has to say about novels is incomprehensible if the emphasis on utterance is not always kept in mind. In section IV we shall once again take up the relationship between Bakhtin's ideas about language and his distinctive theory of the novel's extraliterary importance.

II

Bakhtin was born 16 November 1895 in Orel into an old family of the nobility, dating from at least the fourteenth century, that no longer owned property at the time of his birth. Bakhtin's father was a bank official who worked in several cities as Mikhail

Mikhailovich was growing up. The early years of his childhood were spent in Orel, then in Vilnius (Lithuania) and finally Odessa, where he finished the gymnasium and entered the historical and philological faculty of the local university in 1913. He soon transferred to Petersburg University, where his brother Nikolaj (later professor of Greek and Linguistics at Birmingham University) was a student.

It was an exhilarating time to be in St. Petersburg. There was the stimulation of attacks and counterattacks by Symbolists, Acmeists and Futurists in poetry. Criticism, too, took on a new urgency and glamor: the very year Bakhtin came to the city Shklovsky published the article that was to be the first salvo in the battles that raged around the Formalists. The university was an especially exciting place to be, notably in the areas of Bakhtin's interests. D. K. Petrov, the distinguished Hispanist and student of Baudouin de Courtenay, the philosopher A. I. Vvedenskij and Aleksandr N. Veselovskij, a founder of the modern study of comparative literature, were teaching at this time. But Bakhtin was influenced particularly by the great classicist F. F. Zelinskij; some of Bakhtin's key concepts can be traced back to suggestions in Zelinskij's works, primarily those dealing with the Roman oratorical tradition. During these years Bakhtin laid the foundations of his prodigious knowledge of philosophy, especially classical and German thinkers. Vvedenskij was the leading Russian Kantian, and N. O. Losskij, another of Bakhtin's teachers, had studied under Windelband and Wundt. In 1918 Bakhtin finished the university and moved to Nevel', a west Russian city, where he taught school for two years.

It was here that the members of the first "Bakhtin Circle" (with the exception of P. N. Medvedev, who became associated with it in 1920 in Vitebsk) came together: Lev Pumpianskij, later professor in the Philological Faculty at Leningrad University; V. N. Vološinov, later a linguist, but at this time a musicologist and would-be Symbolist poet; M. V. Judina, later one of Russia's greatest concert pianists; I. I. Sollertinskij, later artistic director of the Leningrad Philharmonic; and B. M. Zubakin, archeologist, Mason and grand eccentric. There were others as well who attended discussions less frequently, but who shared the passionate interest of the group in threshing out literary, religious and political topics. But the most frequent topic of discussion, the subject of most burning concern for the majority of the group—certainly for

Bakhtin—was German philosophy. At this point Bakhtin thought of himself essentially as a philosopher and not as a literary scholar.

A very important member of the group for him, then, was Matvej Isaič Kagan, later an editor of the monumental *Encyclopedia of Soviet Energy Resources*, but at this time still a professional philosopher—a philosopher, moreover, who had just returned from Germany, where he had spent almost ten years studying at Marburg and Berlin. He had been close to the Marburg Neo-Kantians: he translated Natorp and was highly thought of by Hermann Cohen and Ernst Cassirer. Kagan was Bakhtin's best friend in these years, in some ways filling the personal and intellectual gap left by the departure of Bakhtin's brother, Nikolaj. We can see traces of Kagan's influence in the concern for such Neo-Kantian preoccupations as axiology and the need to rethink the mind/world opposition that are present in Bakhtin's first published work, "Art and Responsibility." This small 1919 piece is actually a *précis* of a major work on moral philosophy to which Bakhtin devoted himself while in Nevel' that was never published (except in portions, and then only sixty years later, in 1979).

In 1920 he moved to Vitebsk, in the same general area. Vitebsk was at that time a cultural boom town, an island of light in the dark currents of revolution and civil war, a refuge for such artists as El Lisitskij, Malevich and Marc Chagall. Several prominent scientists also lived in the Belorussian city at this time, as well as leading musicians from the former Mariinskij Theater who taught at the Conservatory. A lively journal, *Iskusstvo*, was started, and there were constant lectures and discussions.

Two events of great personal importance occurred during the Vitebsk period: in 1921 Bakhtin married Elena Aleksandrovna Okolovič, who was indispensable to him until her death in 1971; and in 1923 the bone disease that was to plague Bakhtin all his life—and that would lead to the amputation of a leg in 1938—made its first appearance. In 1924 Bakhtin moved back to Leningrad, working at the Historical Institute and consulting for the State Publishing House. Bakhtin was finally moved to let some of his work see the light of day.

In the fate of an early article we can see the emergence of a vicious pattern that was to repeat itself throughout his life: continually, Bakhtin's manuscripts were suppressed or actually lost, by chance or by the opposition of determined enemies. Just as Bakhtin's "On the Question of the Methodology of Aesthetics in Written Works" was about to appear, *Russkij sovremennik*, the journal that had commissioned the piece, ceased publication. Thus this seminal work was not published until fifty-one years later. These were nevertheless fruitful years for Bakhtin, during which he continued his constant discussions, now with a circle made up of such friends and followers as the poet N. A. Kljuev, the renowned biologist I. I. Kanaev, the experimental writers Konstantin Vaginov and Daniil Kharms, the Indologist M. I. Tubianskij.

Although Bakhtin had been studying and thinking ceaselessly during these years, his first major published work finally appeared only in 1929, the magisterial *Problems of Dostoevsky's Art*, in which Bakhtin's revolutionary concept of "dialogism" (polyphony) was first announced to the world. The book, controversial as only a radically new vision of an old topic can be, was nevertheless well received. Some (including the Minister of Education and the leading Party intellectual Anatoly Lunacharsky) even recognized it to be the revolutionary document that it has indeed proved to be. The impact of the book was muffled, however, because just as it appeared, Bakhtin was sent to the wilds of Kazakhstan. He spent the next six years in exile as a bookkeeper in the obscure town of Kustanaj. Several of his closest associates disappeared forever during the purges of the late 1930s. Bakhtin somehow continued to work even in Kustanaj, and several of his most important essays, such as "Discourse [*Slovo*] in the Novel," were written during these years. He was supplied books from the Saltykov-Shchedrin Library in Leningrad and the Lenin Library in Moscow by his friends.

In 1936 he was able to teach courses in the Mordovian Pedagogical Institute in Saransk and in 1937 moved to the town of Kimry, two hundred kilometers from Moscow, where he finished work on a major book devoted to the eighteenth-century German novel (*Erziehungsroman*). This manuscript was accepted by the Sovetskij Pisatel' Publishing House, but the only copy of it disappeared during the confusion of the German invasion—yet another example of the hex at work in Bakhtin's publishing career. The only other copy of this manuscript Bakhtin—an inveterate smoker—used as paper to roll his own cigarettes during the dark days of the German invasion (which gives some idea, perhaps, of how cavalierly Bakhtin regarded his own thoughts once they had already been thought through). It was only after the most strenuous arguments by Vadim Kožinov and Sergej Bočarov that Bakhtin could be persuaded first of all to reveal the whereabouts of what unpublished manuscripts he had (in a rat-infested woodshed in Saransk) and then to permit them to be retranscribed for publication.

From 1940 to the end of World War II Bakhtin lived in the environs of Moscow. In 1940 he had submitted a long dissertation on Rabelais, but it could not be defended until after the war was over. In 1946 and 1949 his defense of the dissertation split the Moscow scholarly world into two camps: the original and unorthodox manuscript was accepted by the official opponents appointed to preside over the defense, but other professors felt strongly enough about Bakhtin to intervene against its acceptance. There were several stormy meetings (one lasting seven hours) until the government finally stepped in: in the end the State Accrediting Bureau denied his doctorate. Thus *Rabelais and Folk Culture of the Middle Ages and Renaissance*, which has since gone through many editions in several languages, had to wait until 1965, nineteen years later, before it was published.

But Bakhtin's friends were no less determined than his enemies, and a group that had been attracted to him during his stay in Saransk in 1936 now invited him back to be the chairman of the General Literature Department. Thus began Bakhtin's long and affectionate relationship with the institution that, when it was upgraded from teacher's college to university in 1957, made him head of the expanded Department of Russian and World Literature. A beloved teacher himself (whenever he lectured the hall was sure to be crowded), he influenced generations of young people who went out to teach. In August of 1961 Bakhtin was forced to retire due to declining health. In 1969 he returned to Moscow for medical treatment, living in the city until his death on 7 March 1975.

These last years were busy and fulfilling for Bakhtin, finally bringing him the fame and influence he so long had been denied. A group of young scholars at Moscow University (under V. Turbin) and at the Gor'kij Institute, most notably V. Kožinov and S. Bočarov (yet another Bakhtin Circle), energetically took up his cause. He was also aided by the eminent linguist and theoretician, V. V. Ivanov. The Dostoevsky book was republished in 1963, largely due to the extraordinary efforts of Kožinov, whose role in this affair does him honor. Its appearance created a sensation that helped to rekindle interest in basic questions of literary study. In 1965 the Rabelais book was published following a series of programmatic articles in leading journals. In 1975 a collection of Bakhtin's major essays outlining a historical poetics for the novel, *Questions of Literature and Aesthetics* (from which the four essays in this volume are taken), came out soon after his death. Just before he died he learned that Yale University was trying to arrange for him to be awarded an honorary degree.

III

There is a great controversy over the authorship of three books that have been ascribed to Bakhtin: *Freudianism* (1927) and *Marxism and the Philosophy of Language* (1929; 2nd ed. 1930), both published under the name of V. N. Vološinov, and *The Formal Method in Literary Scholarship* (1928), published under the name of P. N. Medvedev. This is not the place to go into the arcana of Bakhtin's textology. The question is of a complexity that requires extended treatment on its own. The view of the present editor is that ninety percent of the text of the three books in question is indeed the work of Bakhtin himself.

IV

The most immediate contribution these essays make is to the theory of the novel, a particularly vexed area of literary scholarship.

The enormous success of the novel in the nineteenth century has obscured the fact that for most of its history it was a marginal genre, little studied and frequently denounced. Even in an age such as our own, when there is no dearth of books devoted to "the novel," there is very little agreement as to what the word means. Consider three examplary titles in which the substantive "novel" is preceded by the definite article: Lukács' *Theory of the Novel* (1920), Ian Watt's *The Rise of the Novel* (1957) and Lucien Goldmann's *Towards a Sociology of the Novel* (1964, English tr. 1975). These are all important books that have greatly advanced our understanding of certain kinds of novels, but each in its own way dramatizes the same shortcoming: they seek to elevate *one kind* of novel into a definition of the novel as such (as does René Girard in another very influential book, *Deceit, Desire and the Novel* [1961]). They lack a field theory capable of encompassing not only the texts nominated by the others as novels, but two millennia of long prose fictions preceding the seventeenth century—the period when, according to consensus, the novel experienced its "birth." (The same view holds that the novel "rose" in the eighteenth century and "triumphed" in the nineteenth—its "death" in the twentieth century is a foregone conclusion by the same historical logic.)

A major reason why so little powerfully syncretic work has been done in the area of novels, even by those who recognize the dilemma posed by excluding pre–seventeenth-century narrative such as Scholes and Kellogg (*The Nature of Narrative* [1966]), is that the absolute novelty of the novel has not been adequately recognized. Bakhtin's advantage over everyone else working on novel theory is that he is able to include more texts from the past in his scheme than anyone else—and this because, paradoxically, he more than others perceives the novel as new. Not new when it is said to have "arisen," but new *whenever* that kind of text made its appearance, as it has done since at least the ancient Greeks, a text that merely found its most comprehensive form in Cervantes and those who have come after. In order to see what kind of text might have so radical a novelty, we shall have to rethink the basic categories of genre and style.

Syncretic chronicles of such genres as the ode, the lyric or tragedy may be written extending back to classical times, because each such history will have as its subject a set of formal characteristics so fixed—from the earliest days of European culture—that nuanced modulations (in their surface features, at least) can be recognized with relative ease. It is probably for this reason that such discursively homogeneous genres accord so well with received ideas about the periodization of general history into such chapters as "classical antiquity," the "Age of Louis XIV" and so forth.

So militantly protean a form as the novel raises serious problems for those who seek to confine it to the linear shape of most histories. The difficulty is compounded if we recognize further that such histories usually begin by presupposing the very organizing categories that it is the nature of novels to resist. Histories are like novels in that they set out to provide more or less comprehensive accounts of social systems. Histories occupy themselves with relationships between the strata of legal codes, religious beliefs, economic organization, family structure and so forth, in order to create a series of moments in which the interaction of these forces can be seen in their simultaneity as well as their continuity. And novels, too, concern themselves more or less with such interrelationships, the particular assemblage of discourses that define specific cultures.

But histories differ from novels in that they insist on a homology between the sequence of their own telling, the form they impose to create a coherent explanation in the form of a narrative on the one hand, and the sequence of *what* they tell on the other. This templating of what is enunciated with the act of enunciation is a narrative consequence of the historian's professional desire to tell "wie es eigentlich gewesen ist." The novel, by contrast, dramatizes the gaps that always exist between what is told and the telling of it, constantly experimenting with social, discursive and narrative asymmetries (the formal teratology that led Henry James to call them "fluid puddings").

History has perhaps most often been compared with the novel because both presume a certain completeness of inventory. Each in its own way strives to give narrative shape to material of encyclopedic variety and plentitude. Thus, a good history of Russia, for instance, might very well seek to be what Belinsky said *Evgenij Onegin* was, "an encyclopedia of Russian life": like the novel, such a history would describe rank, manners, differences between the capital and the provinces and so forth. But as Bakhtin has said of Pushkin's work, it is not an encyclopedia that merely catalogs inert institutions, the brute *things* of everyday life: "Russian life speaks in all its voices [in *Evgenij Onegin*], in all the languages and styles of the era. Literary language is not represented in the novel [as it is in other genres] as a unitary, completely finished off, indubitably adequate language—it is represented precisely as a living mix of varied and opposing voices [*raznorečivost'*]."

The emphasis on social variety dramatized as contests between different voices speaking various intralanguages of the abstract system we call "the" Russian language is what defines the "devilish difference" [*djavol'skaja raznica*] making *Evgenij Onegin* a novel in verse, and not just a long poem. And insofar as *Evgenij*

Onegin is a dialogized system made up of the images of "languages, styles and consciousnesses that are concrete and inseparable from language," it is typical of all novels. It dramatizes in these features both the difficulty of defining the novel as a genre and the reason the question of its history is so fraught. Other genres are constituted by a set of formal features for fixing language that pre-exist any specific utterance within the genre. Language, in other words, is assimilated to form. The novel by contrast seeks to shape its form to languages; it has a completely different relationship to languages from other genres since it constantly experiments with new shapes in order to display the variety and immediacy of speech diversity. It is thus best conceived either as a supergenre, whose power consists in its ability to engulf and ingest all other genres (the different and separate languages peculiar to each), together with other stylized but non-literary forms of language; or not a genre in any strict, traditional sense at all. In either case it is obvious that the history of what might be called novels, when they are defined by their proclivity to display different languages interpenetrating each other, will be extremely complicated.

The only history of the novel adequate to such complexity has been proposed by Mikhail Bakhtin, whose definition of the genre as a consciously structured hybrid of languages I have used in the preceding remarks. Bakhtin has succeeded in forging a history capable of comprehending the very earliest classical texts (such as the *Margites* traditionally ascribed to Homer), Hellenistic and Roman texts and medieval romances, as well as the titles that are usually advanced in more traditional accounts of the genre, such as *Guzman Alfarache* and *Don Quixote*. It is a history that includes as well elements from the oral tradition of folklore going back to prehistoric times.

And Bakhtin has been able to do this because he has grasped that the novel cannot be studied with the same set of ideas about the relation of language to style that we bring to bear on other genres. Most versions of literary stylistics—whether Spitzer's or Vinogradov's—assume that language operates more or less as professional linguists tell us it does, both in our everyday lives and in literary texts. Literary texts simply intensify certain capabilities of language that are potential in spoken speech as well: "Poetry is violence practiced on ordinary speech," to paraphrase the young Jakobson. Style in this view means the sum of the operations performed by the poet in order to accomplish the violence necessary to mark the text off as literature.

Valuable work has been done in most genres by critics presuming style so understood. The reason is that not only most critics, but most genres begin with this assumption: the homogeneity of the genre corresponds to ideas about the privileged status of a unitary, centripetalizing language shared by its practitioners on the one hand and its students on the other.

The novel is utterly different from such genres because it presumes a completely other relationship to language. But, according to Bakhtin, this has not yet been perceived by its students who—if they are not utterly lost in the morass of gossipy "character analysis," ethical high-mindedness and watered-down psychology that frequently passes as novel criticism—continue to view the novel through the optic of a traditional stylistic that has proved so successful with other text types, but is quite inappropriate to novels.

The most recent form this approach has taken is a concern no longer for a Lansonian attention to the language of the text, but rather for the "language" of the plot—what, following Propp's ground-breaking work, has been called the morphology or syntagmatics of narrative. Attempts have been made to apply to the novel the kind of structural analysis that has been so remarkably successful with short formulaic forms such as folktales, detective stories and industrial folklore, that is, serial novels for children (*Tom Swift*, etc.). The work of men such as Greimas in France (*Du sens*, 1970) or Van Dijk in Holland (*Some Aspects of Text Grammars*, 1972) has led others (such as Meir Sternberg ["What Is Exposition?" in *The Theory of the Novel*, ed. John Halperin, 1974]) to conclude that the novel, too, might lend itself to tree diagrams and Freytag pyramids. Such critics forget what Eikhenbaum pointed out in 1925: that "the novel and the short story are forms not only different in kind but also inherently at odds. . . ." ("O. Henry and the Short Story"). The lugubrious results of these analyses serve to confirm what Bakhtin concluded long ago: "The utter inadequacy of [most existing] literary theory is exposed when it is forced to deal with the novel" (see "Epic and Novel"). The situation he decried in the thirties is no better in the seventies. This situation Bakhtin addresses in the four essays in this collection.

V

By the time Bakhtin came to write these essays he had completed the Dostoevsky book, which made what appeared at the time to be rather extravagant claims for that author's uniqueness. The second edition (1963) has attached to it new material that seeks rather to place the Dostoevskian novel into a tradition. The new material and the point of view that it entails are drawn from work on the history of the novel Bakhtin pursued during the thirty-four years that intervened between the two editions. In those years Bakhtin came to regard the Dostoevskian novel not so much as an absolutely unprecedented event in the history of the genre, but rather as the purest expression of what always had been implicit in it. Viewing the history of the novel through the optic of the Dostoevskian example had revolutionary consequences. The novel ceases to be "merely one genre among many" ("Epic and Novel"). It becomes not only "the leading hero in the drama of literary development in our time" ("Epic and Novel"), but the most significant force at work even in those early periods when most other scholars would argue that there were no novels being written at all.

Such scholars would, within their own terms, be correct in asserting that there were no novels in Plato's Athens or during the Middle Ages, or at least no novel as we have come to know it. But Bakhtin is clearly not referring to that concept of a novel that begins with Cervantes or Richardson. These books, and especially the nineteenth-century psychological novel that evolved from them, have become the canon of the genre-novel. The majority of literary scholars are most at home when dealing with canons, which is why Bakhtin said that literary theory is helpless to deal with the novel. Rather, "novel" is the name Bakhtin gives to whatever force is at work within a given literary system to reveal the limits, the artificial constraints of that system. Literary systems are comprised of canons, and "novelization" is fundamentally anticanonical. It will not permit generic monologue. Always it will insist on the dialogue between what a given system will admit as literature and those texts that are otherwise excluded from such a definition of literature. What is more conventionally thought of as the novel is simply the most complex and distilled expression of this impulse.

The history of the novel so conceived is very long, but it exists outside the bounds of what traditional scholars would think of as strictly *literary* history. Bakhtin's history would be charted, among other ways, in devaluation of a given culture's higher literary forms: the parodies of knightly romances (Cervantes), pastorals (Sorel), sentimental fictions (Sterne, Fielding). But these texts are merely late examples of a tendency that has been abroad at least since the ancient Greeks. Bakhtin comes very close to naming Socrates as the first novelist, since the gadfly role he played, and which he played out in the drama of precisely the dialogue, is more or less what the role of the novel always has been. That role has been assumed by such unexpected forms as the confession, the utopia, the epistle or the Menippean satire, in which Bakhtin is particularly interested. Even the drama (Ibsen and other Naturalists), the long poem (*Childe Harold* or *Don Juan*) or the lyric (as in Heine) become masks for the novel during the nineteenth century. As formerly distinct literary genres are subjected to the novel's intensifying antigeneric power, their systematic purity is infected and they become "novelized."

The first essay in this volume seeks to establish the distinctiveness of the novel by opposing it to the epic. What emerges is a definition of novels as peculiarly suited to our post-lapsarian, post-industrial civilization, since it thrives on precisely the kind of diversity the epic (and by extension, myth and all other traditional forms of narrative) sets out to purge from its world. The essay posits a novel defined by what could be called the rule of genre inclusiveness: the novel can include, ingest, devour other genres and still retain its status as a novel, but other genres cannot include novelistic elements without impairing their own identity as epics, odes or any other fixed genre.

This essay will inevitably be compared with the use Lukács, in his *Theory of the Novel*, makes of the same contrast, and will, no doubt, be compared as well to the way Auerbach (*Mimesis* [1946]) distinguishes between Homeric and Biblical texts. Bakhtin differs from Lukács in his evaluation of the novel's fallen state: just as his concept of heteroglossia is a happy redaction of the conditions otherwise so gloomily charted by Derrida's epigones as "differance," so his concept of the novel's relation to epic is an affirming version of what the pessimistic Lukács means when he says the novel is the characteristic text of an age of "Absolute sinfulness." Bakhtin differs from Auerbach (with whom he shares, otherwise, many suggestive parallels, both in his life and in his work) in that the Bible could never represent the novel in a contrast with epic, since *both*, Bible and epic, would share a presumption of authority, a claim to absolute language, utterly foreign to the novel's joyous awareness of the inadequacies of its own language. But since the novel is aware of the impossibility of full meaning, presence, it is free to exploit such a lack to its own hybridizing purposes.

The second essay, "From the Prehistory of Novelistic Discourse," is less conventional than the first, and outlines in a most economical way how a number of disparate texts from the distant past finally coalesced into what we now know as the modern novel. It is a thumbnail history of the force Bakhtin calls "novelness," an epistemological capability larger than any concrete expression of it before the novel as a text type emerges in its own right.

The third essay introduces one of Bakhtin's coinages in its title. "Chronotope" is a category that no brief introduction (much less glossary) can adequately adumbrate. The long essay uses the concept as yet another way to define the distinctiveness of the novel by means of its history, using differing ratios of time-space projection as the unit for charting changes.

The fourth essay in this volume, "Discourse in the Novel," is one of Bakhtin's most suggestive and, with the exception of certain chapters in *Marxism and the Philosophy of Language*, the most comprehensive statement of his philosophy of language. It has as its skeleton yet another model for a history of discourse that eventuates in the supreme self-consciousness (consciousness of the other) marked by the heteroglossia of the modern novel.

It will be clear from even so cursory an overview that the essays in this volume have been arranged in order of their complexity, with the simplest and most conventional appearing first, and the most difficult appearing last.

Bibliography of Bakhtin's Works and Selected Secondary Literature

Works: *Problemy tvorčestva Dostoevskogo* (L., 1929); *Problemy poetiki Dostoevskogo*, 2nd rev. and enl. ed. (M., 1963), 3rd ed. (M., 1972); *Tvorčestva Fransua Rable i narodnaja kul'turà srednevekov'ja i Renessansa* (M., 1965); *Voprosy literatury i estetiki* (M., 1975); *Estetika slovesnogo tvorčestva* (M., 1979). Translations into English: *Problems of Dostoevsky's Poetics*, translation of the 2nd edition (Ann Arbor, Mich., 1973); *Rabelais and His World* (Cambridge, Mass., 1968).

Books published under other names: V. N. Vološinov, *Freidizm* (L., 1927); V. N. Vološinov, *Marksizm i filosofija jazyka* (L., 1929, 1930); P. N. Medvedev, *Formal'nyj metod v literaturovedenii* (L., 1928). Translations into English: V. N. Vološinov, *Marxism and the Philosophy of Language* (N.Y., 1973); V. N. Vološinov, *Freudianism: A Marxist Critique* (N.Y., 1976); P. N. Medvedev, *The Formal Method in Literary Scholarship* (Baltimore, 1978).

References: V. Kožinov, "Literatura i literaturovedenie," *Literatura i žizn'*, No. 34 (16 March 1962); Julia Kristeva, "Bakhtine, le mot, le dialogue et le roman," *Critique*, No. 239 (April 1967), 438–465; Julia Kristeva, "Une poétique ruinée," in M. Bakhtine, *La Poétique de Dostoievsky* (Paris, 1970)—an English translation can be found in *Russian Formalism*, ed. Stephen Bann, John E. Bowlt (N.Y., 1973); G. M. Fridlender, B. S. Meilax, M. M. Žirmunskij, "Voprosy poetiki romana v rabotax M. M. Baxtina," *Izvestija AN SSSR*, Serija literatury i jazyka, vol. 30, fascicle 1 (1970); V. V. Ivanov, "Značenie idei M. M. Baxtina o znake, vyskazyvanii i dialoge dlja sovremennoj semiotiki," *Semiotika* [Trudy po znakovym sistemam], No. 6 (Tartu, 1973), 5–44—a translation of this article appears in *Semiotics and Structuralism: Readings from the Soviet Union*, ed. Henryk Baran (White Plains, N.Y., 1976), 310–367; V. Kožinov, S. Konkin, "M. M. Baxtin, kratkij očerk žizni i dejatel'nosti," *Problemy poetiki i istorii literatury* (Saransk, 1973); Irwin R. Titunik, "M. M. Baxtin (The Baxtin School) and Soviet Semiotics," *Dispositio* 1, No. 3 (1976), 327–338; Caryl Emerson, "The Outer Word and Inner Speech," *Cherez* (Spring 1978, Austin, Texas), 2–21; James M. Holquist, "M. M. Bakhtin," *Modern Encyclopedia of Russian and Soviet Literature*, Vol. 2 (1978), 52–59; Gary Saul Morson, "The Heresiarch of Meta," *PTL*, Vol. 3, No. 3 (October 1978); Michel Aucouturier, "Préface," M. Bakhtine, *Esthétique et théorie du roman* (Paris, 1978), 9–19; Krystyna Pomorska, "Mixail Baxtin and His Verbal Universe," *PTL*, Vol. 3, No. 2 (April 1978), 379–386.

THE DIALOGIC IMAGINATION

EPIC AND NOVEL
Toward a Methodology for the Study of the Novel

The study of the novel as a genre is distinguished by peculiar difficulties. This is due to the unique nature of the object itself: the novel is the sole genre that continues to develop, that is as yet uncompleted. The forces that define it as a genre are at work before our very eyes: the birth and development of the novel as a genre takes place in the full light of the historical day. The generic skeleton of the novel is still far from having hardened, and we cannot foresee all its plastic possibilities.

We know other genres, as genres, in their completed aspect, that is, as more or less fixed pre-existing forms into which one may then pour artistic experience. The primordial process of their formation lies outside historically documented observation. We encounter the epic as a genre that has not only long since completed its development, but one that is already antiquated. With certain reservations we can say the same for the other major genres, even for tragedy. The life they have in history, the life with which we are familiar, is the life they have lived as already completed genres, with a hardened and no longer flexible skeleton. Each of them has developed its own canon that operates in literature as an authentic historical force.

All these genres, or in any case their defining features, are considerably older than written language and the book, and to the present day they retain their ancient oral and auditory characteristics. Of all the major genres only the novel is younger than writing and the book: it alone is organically receptive to new forms of mute perception, that is, to reading. But of critical importance here is the fact that the novel has no canon of its own, as do other genres; only individual examples of the novel are historically active, not a generic canon as such. Studying other genres is analogous to studying dead languages; studying the novel, on the other hand, is like studying languages that are not only alive, but still young.

This explains the extraordinary difficulty inherent in formulating a theory of the novel. For such a theory has at its heart an object of study completely different from that which theory treats in other genres. The novel is not merely one genre among other genres. Among genres long since completed and in part already dead, the novel is the only developing genre. It is the only genre that was born and nourished in a new era of world history and therefore it is deeply akin to that era, whereas the other major genres entered that era as already fixed forms, as an inheritance, and only now are they adapting themselves—some better, some worse—to the new conditions of their existence. Compared with them, the novel appears to be a creature from an alien species. It gets on poorly with other genres. It fights for its own hegemony in literature; wherever it triumphs, the other older genres go into decline. Significantly, the best book on the history of the ancient novel—that by Erwin Rohde[a]—does not so much recount the history of the novel as it does illustrate the process of disintegration that affected all major genres in antiquity.

The mutual interaction of genres within a single unified literary period is a problem of great interest and importance. In certain eras—the Greek classical period, the Golden Age of Roman literature, the neoclassical period—all genres in "high" literature (that is, the literature of ruling social groups) harmoniously reinforce each other to a significant extent; the whole of literature, conceived as a totality of genres, becomes an organic unity of the highest order. But it is characteristic of the novel that it never enters into this whole, it does not participate in any harmony of the genres. In these eras the novel has an unofficial existence, outside "high" literature. Only already completed genres, with fully formed and well-defined generic contours, can enter into such a literature as a hierarchically organized, organic whole. They can mutually delimit and mutually complement each other, while yet preserving their own generic natures. Each is a unit, and all units are interrelated by virtue of certain features of deep structure that they all have in common.

---

a. Erwin Rohde (1845–1898), *Der Griechesche Roman und seine Vorläufer* (1876, but many later editions, most recently that published by F. Olds [Hildesheim, 1960]), one of the greatest monuments of nineteenth-century classical scholarship in Germany. It has never really ever been superseded. But see: Ben F. Perry, *The Ancient Romances* (Berkeley, 1967) and Arthur Heiserman, *The Novel before the Novel* (Chicago, 1977).

The great organic poetics of the past—those of Aristotle, Horace, Boileau—are permeated with a deep sense of the wholeness of literature and of the harmonious interaction of all genres contained within this whole. It is as if they literally hear this harmony of the genres. In this is their strength—the inimitable, all-embracing fullness and exhaustiveness of such poetics. And they all, as a consequence, ignore the novel. Scholarly poetics of the nineteenth century lack this integrity: they are eclectic, descriptive; their aim is not a living and organic fullness but rather an abstract and encyclopedic comprehensiveness. They do not concern themselves with the actual possibility of specific genres coexisting within the living whole of literature in a given era; they are concerned rather with their coexistence in a maximally complete anthology. Of course these poetics can no longer ignore the novel—they simply add it (albeit in a place of honor) to already existing genres (and thus it enters the roster as merely one genre among many; in literature conceived as a living whole, on the other hand, it would have to be included in a completely different way).

We have already said that the novel gets on poorly with other genres. There can be no talk of a harmony deriving from mutual limitation and complementariness. The novel parodies other genres (precisely in their role as genres); it exposes the conventionality of their forms and their language; it squeezes out some genres and incorporates others into its own peculiar structure, reformulating and re-accentuating them. Historians of literature sometimes tend to see in this merely the struggle of literary tendencies and schools. Such struggles of course exist, but they are peripheral phenomena and historically insignificant. Behind them one must be sensitive to the deeper and more truly historical struggle of genres, the establishment and growth of a generic skeleton of literature.

Of particular interest are those eras when the novel becomes the dominant genre. All literature is then caught up in the process of "becoming," and in a special kind of "generic criticism." This occurred several times in the Hellenic period, again during the late Middle Ages and the Renaissance, but with special force and clarity beginning in the second half of the eighteenth century. In an era when the novel reigns supreme, almost all the remaining genres are to a greater or lesser extent "novelized": drama (for example Ibsen, Hauptmann, the whole of Naturalist drama), epic poetry (for example, *Childe Harold* and especially Byron's *Don Juan*), even lyric poetry (as an extreme example, Heine's lyrical verse). Those genres that stubbornly preserve their old canonic nature begin to appear stylized. In general any strict adherence to a genre begins to feel like a stylization, a stylization taken to the point of parody, despite the artistic intent of the author. In an environment where the novel is the dominant genre, the conventional languages of strictly canonical genres begin to sound in new ways, which are quite different from the ways they sounded in those eras when the novel was *not* included in "high" literature.

Parodic stylizations of canonized genres and styles occupy an essential place in the novel. In the era of the novel's creative ascendency—and even more so in the periods of preparation preceding this era—literature was flooded with parodies and travesties of all the high genres (parodies precisely of genres, and not of individual authors or schools)—parodies that are the precursors, "companions" to the novel, in their own way studies for it. But it is characteristic that the novel does not permit any of these various individual manifestations of itself to stabilize. Throughout its entire history there is a consistent parodying or travestying of dominant or fashionable novels that attempt to become models for the genre: parodies on the chivalric romance of adventure (*Dit d'aventures*, the first such parody, belongs to the thirteenth century), on the Baroque novel, the pastoral novel (Sorel's *Le Berger extravagant*),[b] the Sentimental novel (Fielding, and *The Second Grandison*[c] of Musäus) and so forth. This ability of the novel to criticize itself is a remarkable feature of this ever-developing genre.

What are the salient features of this novelization of other genres

---

b. Charles Sorel (1599–1674), an important figure in the reaction to the *preciosité* of such figures as Honoré d'Urfé (1567–1625), whose *L'Astrée* (1607–1627), a monstrous 5,500-page volume overflowing with highflown language, is parodied in *Le Berger extravagant* (1627). The latter book's major protagonist is a dyed-in-the-wool Parisian who reads too many pastoral novels; intoxicated by these, he attempts to live the rustic life as they describe it—with predictably comic results.

c. Johann Karl August Musäus (1735–1787), along with Tieck and Brentano, one of the great collectors of German folktales and author of several *Kunstmärchen* of his own (translated into English by Carlyle). Reference here is to his *Grandison der Zweite* (1760–1762, rewritten as *Der deutsche Grandison*, 1781–1782), a satire on Richardson.

suggested by us above? They become more free and flexible, their language renews itself by incorporating extraliterary heteroglossia and the "novelistic" layers of literary language, they become dialogized, permeated with laughter, irony, humor, elements of self-parody and finally—this is the most important thing—the novel inserts into these other genres an indeterminacy, a certain semantic openendedness, a living contact with unfinished, still-evolving contemporary reality (the openended present). As we will see below, all these phenomena are explained by the transposition of other genres into this new and peculiar zone for structuring artistic models (a zone of contact with the present in all its openendedness), a zone that was first appropriated by the novel.

It is of course impossible to explain the phenomenon of novelization purely by reference to the direct and unmediated influence of the novel itself. Even where such influence can be precisely established and demonstrated, it is intimately interwoven with those direct changes in reality itself that also determine the novel and that condition its dominance in a given era. The novel is the only developing genre and therefore it reflects more deeply, more essentially, more sensitively and rapidly, reality itself in the process of its unfolding. Only that which is itself developing can comprehend development as a process. The novel has become the leading hero in the drama of literary development in our time precisely because it best of all reflects the tendencies of a new world still in the making; it is, after all, the only genre born of this new world and in total affinity with it. In many respects the novel has anticipated, and continues to anticipate, the future development of literature as a whole. In the process of becoming the dominant genre, the novel sparks the renovation of all other genres, it infects them with its spirit of process and inconclusiveness. It draws them ineluctably into its orbit precisely because this orbit coincides with the basic direction of the development of literature as a whole. In this lies the exceptional importance of the novel, as an object of study for the theory as well as the history of literature.

Unfortunately, historians of literature usually reduce this struggle between the novel and other already completed genres, all these aspects of novelization, to the actual real-life struggle among "schools" and "trends." A novelized poem, for example, they call a "romantic poem" (which of course it is) and believe that in so doing they have exhausted the subject. They do not see beneath the superficial hustle and bustle of literary process the major and crucial fates of literature and language, whose great heroes turn out to be first and foremost genres, and whose "trends" and "schools" are but second- or third-rank protagonists.

The utter inadequacy of literary theory is exposed when it is forced to deal with the novel. In the case of other genres literary theory works confidently and precisely, since there is a finished and already formed object, definite and clear. These genres preserve their rigidity and canonic quality in all classical eras of their development; variations from era to era, from trend to trend or school to school are peripheral and do not affect their ossified generic skeleton. Right up to the present day, in fact, theory dealing with these already completed genres can add almost nothing to Aristotle's formulations. Aristotle's poetics, although occasionally so deeply embedded as to be almost invisible, remains the stable foundation for the theory of genres. Everything works as long as there is no mention of the novel. But the existence of novelized genres already leads theory into a blind alley. Faced with the problem of the novel, genre theory must submit to a radical re-structuring.

Thanks to the meticulous work of scholars, a huge amount of historical material has accumulated and many questions concerning the evolution of various types of novels have been clarified—but the problem of the novel genre as a whole has not yet found anything like a satisfactory principled resolution. The novel continues to be seen as one genre among many; attempts are made to distinguish it as an already completed genre from other already completed genres, to discover its internal canon—one that would function as a well-defined system of rigid generic factors. In the vast majority of cases, work on the novel is reduced to mere cataloging, a description of all variants on the novel—albeit as comprehensive as possible. But the results of these descriptions never succeed in giving us as much as a hint of comprehensive formula for the novel as a genre. In addition, the experts have not managed to isolate a single definite, stable characteristic of the novel—without adding a reservation, which immediately disqualifies it altogether as a generic characteristic.

Some examples of such "characteristics with reservations" would be: the novel is a multi-layered genre (although there also exist magnificent single-layered novels); the novel is a precisely plotted and dynamic genre (although there also exist novels that push to its literary limits the art of pure description); the novel is a complicated genre (although novels are mass produced as pure and frivolous entertainment like no other genre); the novel is a love story (although the greatest examples of the European novel are utterly devoid of the love element); the novel is a prose genre (although there exist excellent novels in verse). One could of course mention a large number of additional "generic characteristics" for the novel similar to those given above, which are immediately annulled by some reservation innocently appended to them.

Of considerably more interest and consequence are those normative definitions of the novel offered by novelists themselves, who produce a specific novel and then declare *it* the only correct, necessary and authentic form of the novel. Such, for instance, is Rousseau's foreword to his *La Nouvelle Héloïse*, Wieland's to his *Agathon*,[d] Wezel's to his *Tobias Knouts*;[e] in such a category belong the numerous declarations and statements of principle by the Romantics on *Wilhelm Meister, Lucinda* and other texts. Such statements are not attempts to incorporate all the possible variants of the novel into a single eclectic definition, but are themselves part and parcel of the living evolution of the novel as a genre. Often they deeply and faithfully reflect the novel's struggle with other genres and with itself (with other dominant and fashionable variants of the novel) at a particular point in its development. They come closer to an understanding of the peculiar position of the novel in literature, a position that is not commensurate with that of other genres.

Especially significant in this connection is a series of statements that accompanied the emergence of a new novel-type in the eighteenth century. The series opens with Fielding's reflections on the novel and its hero in *Tom Jones*. It continues in Wie-

---

d. Christoph Martin Wieland (1733–1813) is the author of *Geschichte des Agathon* (1767, first of many versions), an autobiographical novel in the guise of a Greek romance, considered by many to be the first in the long line of German *Bildungsromane*.

e. Reference here is to Johann Carl Wezel (1747–1819), *Lebensgeschichte Tobias Knouts, des Weisen, sonst der Stammler genannt* (1773), a novel that has not received the readership it deserves. A four-volume reprint was published by Metzler (Stuttgart, Afterword by Viktor Lange) in 1971. Also see, Elizabeth Holzbeg-Pfenniger, *Der desorientierte Erzähler: Studien zu J. C. Wezels Lebensgeschichte des Tobias Knauts* (Bern, 1976).

land's foreword to *Agathon*, and the most essential link in the series is Blankenburg's *Versuch über den Roman*.[f] By the end of this series we have, in fact, that theory of the novel later formulated by Hegel. In all these statements, each reflecting the novel in one of its critical stages (*Tom Jones, Agathon, Wilhelm Meister*), the following prerequisites for the novel are characteristic: (1) the novel should not be "poetic," as the word "poetic" is used in other genres of imaginative literature; (2) the hero of a novel should not be "heroic" in either the epic or the tragic sense of the word: he should combine in himself negative as well as positive features, low as well as lofty, ridiculous as well as serious; (3) the hero should not be portrayed as an already completed and unchanging person but as one who is evolving and developing, a person who learns from life; (4) the novel should become for the contemporary world what the epic was for the ancient world (an idea that Blankenburg expressed very precisely, and that was later repeated by Hegel).

All these positive prerequisites have their substantial and productive side—taken together, they constitute a criticism (from the novel's point of view) of other genres and of the relationship these genres bear to reality: their stilted heroizing, their narrow and unlifelike poeticalness, their monotony and abstractness, the pre-packaged and unchanging nature of their heroes. We have here, in fact, a rigorous critique of the literariness and poeticalness inherent in other genres and also in the predecessors of the contemporary novel (the heroic Baroque novel and the Sentimental novels of Richardson). These statements are reinforced significantly by the practice of these novelists themselves. Here the novel—its texts as well as the theory connected with it—emerges consciously and unambiguously as a genre that is both critical and self-critical, one fated to revise the fundamental concepts of literariness and poeticalness dominant at the time. On the one hand, the contrast of novel with epic (and the novel's op-

---

f. Friedrich von Blankenburg (1744–1796), *Versuch über den Roman* (1774), an enormous work (over 500 pages) that attempts to define the novel in terms of a rudimentary psychology, a concern for *Tugend* in the heroes. A facsimile edition was published by Metzler (Stuttgart) in 1965. Little is known about Blankenburg, who is also the author of an unfinished novel with the imposing title *Beytrage zur Geschichte deutschen Reichs und deutschen Sitten*, the first part of which appeared a year after the *Versuch* in 1775.

position to the epic) is but one moment in the criticism of other literary genres (in particular, a criticism of epic heroization); but on the other hand, this contrast aims to elevate the significance of the novel, making of it the dominant genre in contemporary literature.

The positive prerequisites mentioned above constitute one of the high-points in the novel's coming to self-consciousness. They do not yet of course provide a theory of the novel. These statements are also not distinguished by any great philosophical depth. They do however illustrate the nature of the novel as a genre no less—if perhaps no more—than do other existing theories of the novel.

I will attempt below to approach the novel precisely as a genre-in-the-making, one in the vanguard of all modern literary development. I am not constructing here a functional definition of the novelistic canon in literary history, that is, a definition that would make of it a system of fixed generic characteristics. Rather, I am trying to grope my way toward the basic structural characteristics of this most fluid of genres, characteristics that might determine the direction of its peculiar capacity for change and of its influence and effect on the rest of literature.

I find three basic characteristics that fundamentally distinguish the novel in principle from other genres: (1) its stylistic three-dimensionality, which is linked with the multi-languaged consciousness realized in the novel; (2) the radical change it effects in the temporal coordinates of the literary image; (3) the new zone opened by the novel for structuring literary images, namely, the zone of maximal contact with the present (with contemporary reality) in all its openendedness.

These three characteristics of the novel are all organically interrelated and have all been powerfully affected by a very specific rupture in the history of European civilization: its emergence from a socially isolated and culturally deaf semipatriarchal society, and its entrance into international and interlingual contacts and relationships. A multitude of different languages, cultures and times became available to Europe, and this became a decisive factor in its life and thought.

In another work[1] I have already investigated the first stylistic

1. Cf. the article "From the Prehistory of Novelistic Discourse" in the present volume.

peculiarity of the novel, the one resulting from the active polyglossia of the new world, the new culture and its new creative literary consciousness. I will summarize here only the basic points.

Polyglossia had always existed (it is more ancient than pure, canonic monoglossia), but it had not been a factor in literary creation; an artistically conscious choice between languages did not serve as the creative center of the literary and language process. Classical Greeks had a feeling both for "languages" and for the epochs of language, for the various Greek literary dialects (tragedy is a polyglot genre), but creative consciousness was realized in closed, pure languages (although in actual fact they were mixed). Polyglossia was appropriated and canonized among all the genres.

The new cultural and creative consciousness lives in an actively polyglot world. The world becomes polyglot, once and for all and irreversibly. The period of national languages, coexisting but closed and deaf to each other, comes to an end. Languages throw light on each other: one language can, after all, see itself only in the light of another language. The naive and stubborn coexistence of "languages" within a given national language also comes to an end—that is, there is no more peaceful co-existence between territorial dialects, social and professional dialects and jargons, literary language, generic languages within literary language, epochs in language and so forth.

All this set into motion a process of active, mutual cause-and-effect and interillumination. Words and language began to have a different feel to them; objectively they ceased to be what they had once been. Under these conditions of external and internal interillumination, each given language—even if its linguistic composition (phonetics, vocabulary, morphology, etc.) were to remain absolutely unchanged—is, as it were, reborn, becoming qualitatively a different thing for the consciousness that creates in it.

In this actively polyglot world, completely new relationships are established between language and its object (that is, the real world)—and this is fraught with enormous consequences for all the already completed genres that had been formed during eras of closed and deaf monoglossia. In contrast to other major genres, the novel emerged and matured precisely when intense activization of external and internal polyglossia was at the peak of its activity; this is its native element. The novel could therefore assume leadership in the process of developing and renewing literature in its linguistic and stylistic dimension.

In the above-mentioned work I tried to elucidate the profound stylistic originality of the novel, which is determined by its connection with polyglossia.

Let us move on to the two other characteristics, both concerned with the thematic aspect of structure in the novel as a genre. These characteristics can be best brought out and clarified through a comparison of the novel with the epic.

The epic as a genre in its own right may, for our purposes, be characterized by three constitutive features: (1) a national epic past—in Goethe's and Schiller's terminology the "absolute past"—serves as the subject for the epic;[g] (2) national tradition (not personal experience and the free thought that grows out of it) serves as the source for the epic; (3) an absolute epic distance separates the epic world from contemporary reality, that is, from the time in which the singer (the author and his audience) lives.

We will deal in more detail with each of these constitutive features of the epic.

The world of the epic is the national heroic past: it is a world of "beginnings" and "peak times" in the national history, a world of fathers and of founders of families, a world of "firsts" and "bests." The important point here is not that the past constitutes the content of the epic. The formally constitutive feature of the epic as a genre is rather the transferral of a represented world into the past, and the degree to which this world participates in the past. The epic was never a poem about the present, about its own time (one that became a poem about the past only for those who came later). The epic, as the specific genre known to us today, has been from the beginning a poem about the past, and the authorial position immanent in the epic and constitutive for it (that is, the position of the one who utters the epic word) is the environment of a man speaking about a past that is to him inaccessible, the reverent point of view of a descendent. In its style, tone and manner of expression, epic discourse is infinitely far removed from discourse of a contemporary about a contemporary addressed to con-

---

g. Reference here is to "Über epische und dramatische Dichtung," co-signed by Schiller and Goethe, but probably written by the latter in 1797, although not published until 1827. The actual term used by Goethe for what Bakhtin is calling "absolute past" is *vollkommen vergangen*, which is opposed not to the novel, but to drama, which is defined as *vollkommen gegenwärtig*. The essay can be found in Goethe's *Sämtliche Werke* (Jubiläums-Ausgabe, Stuttgart and Berlin [1902–1907]), vol. 36, pp. 149–152.

temporaries ("Onegin, my good friend, was born on the banks of the Neva, where perhaps you were also born, or once shone, my reader. . . ."). Both the singer and the listener, immanent in the epic as a genre, are located in the same time and on the same evaluative (hierarchical) plane, but the represented world of the heroes stands on an utterly different and inaccessible time-and-value plane, separated by epic distance. The space between them is filled with national tradition. To portray an event on the same time-and-value plane as oneself and one's contemporaries (and an event that is therefore based on personal experience and thought) is to undertake a radical revolution, and to step out of the world of epic into the world of the novel.

It is possible, of course, to conceive even "my time" as heroic, epic time, when it is seen as historically significant; one can distance it, look at it as if from afar (not from one's own vantage point but from some point in the future), one can relate to the past in a familiar way (as if relating to "my" present). But in so doing we ignore the presentness of the present and the pastness of the past; we are removing ourselves from the zone of "my time," from the zone of familiar contact with me.

We speak of the epic as a genre that has come down to us already well defined and real. We come upon it when it is already completely finished, a congealed and half-moribund genre. Its completedness, its consistency and its absolute lack of artistic naiveté bespeak its old age as a genre and its lengthy past. We can only conjecture about this past, and we must admit that so far our conjectures have been rather poor. Those hypothetical primordial songs that preceded both the epic and the creation of a generic epic tradition, songs about contemporaries that directly echoed events that had just occurred—such songs we do not know, although we must presume they existed. We can only guess at the nature of those original aëdonic songs, or of the cantilenas. And we have no reason to assume that they are any more closely related to the later and better-known epic songs than to our topical feuilletons or popular ditties. Those heroicized epic songs about contemporaries that *are* available to us and that we *do* know existed arose only after the epic was already an established form, and arose on the basis of an already ancient and powerful epic tradition. These songs transfer to contemporary events and contemporaries the ready-made epic form; that is, they transfer to these events the time-and-value contour of the past, thus attaching them to the world of fathers, of beginnings and peak times—canonizing these events, as it were, while they are still current. In a patriarchal social structure the ruling class does, in a certain sense, belong to the world of "fathers" and is thus separated from other classes by a distance that is almost epic. The epic incorporation of the contemporary hero into a world of ancestors and founders is a specific phenomenon that developed out of an epic tradition long since completed, and that therefore is as little able to explain the origin of the epic as is, say, the neoclassical ode.

Whatever its origins, the epic as it has come down to us is an absolutely completed and finished generic form, whose constitutive feature is the transferral of the world it describes to an absolute past of national beginnings and peak times. The absolute past is a specifically evaluating (hierarchical) category. In the epic world view, "beginning," "first," "founder," "ancestor," "that which occurred earlier" and so forth are not merely temporal categories but *valorized* temporal categories, and valorized to an extreme degree. This is as true for relationships among people as for relations among all the other items and phenomena of the epic world. In the past, everything is good: all the really good things (i.e., the "first" things) occur *only* in this past. The epic absolute past is the single source and beginning of everything good for all later times as well.

In ancient literature it is memory, and not knowledge, that serves as the source and power for the creative impulse. That is how it was, it is impossible to change it: the tradition of the past is sacred. There is as yet no consciousness of the possible relativity of any past.

The novel, by contrast, is determined by experience, knowledge and practice (the future). In the era of Hellenism a closer contact with the heroes of the Trojan epic cycle began to be felt; epic is already being transformed into novel. Epic material is transposed into novelistic material, into precisely that zone of contact that passes through the intermediate stages of familiarization and laughter. When the novel becomes the dominant genre, epistemology becomes the dominant discipline.

The epic past is called the "absolute past" for good reason: it is both monochronic and valorized (hierarchical); it lacks any relativity, that is, any gradual, purely temporal progressions that might connect it with the present. It is walled off absolutely from all subsequent times, and above all from those times in which the singer and his listeners are located. This boundary, consequently, is immanent in the form of the epic itself and is felt and heard in its every word.

To destroy this boundary is to destroy the form of the epic as a genre. But precisely because it is walled off from all subsequent times, the epic past is absolute and complete. It is as closed as a circle; inside it everything is finished, already over. There is no place in the epic world for any openendedness, indecision, indeterminacy. There are no loopholes in it through which we glimpse the future; it suffices unto itself, neither supposing any continuation nor requiring it. Temporal and valorized definitions are here fused into a single inseparable whole (as they are also fused in the semantic layers of ancient languages). Everything incorporated into this past was simultaneously incorporated into a condition of authentic essence and significance, but therefore also took on conclusiveness and finality, depriving itself, so to speak, of all rights and potential for a real continuation. Absolute conclusiveness and closedness is the outstanding feature of the temporally valorized epic past.

Let us move on to tradition. The epic past, walled off from all subsequent times by an impenetrable boundary, is preserved and revealed only in the form of national tradition. The epic relies entirely on this tradition. Important here is not the fact that tradition is the factual source for the epic—what matters rather is that a reliance on tradition is immanent in the very form of the epic, just as the absolute past is immanent in it. Epic discourse is a discourse handed down by tradition. By its very nature the epic world of the absolute past is inaccessible to personal experience and does not permit an individual, personal point of view or evaluation. One cannot glimpse it, grope for it, touch it; one cannot look at it from just any point of view; it is impossible to experience it, analyze it, take it apart, penetrate into its core. It is given solely as tradition, sacred and sacrosanct, evaluated in the same way by all and demanding a pious attitude toward itself. Let us repeat: the important thing is not the factual sources of the epic, not the content of its historical events, nor the declarations of its authors—the important thing is this formal constitutive characteristic of the epic as a genre (to be more precise, the formal-substantive characteristic): its reliance on impersonal and sacrosanct tradition, on a commonly held evaluation and point of view— which excludes any possibility of another approach—and which therefore displays a profound piety toward the subject described and toward the language used to describe it, the language of tradition.

The absolute past as the subject for epic and sacrosanct tradition as its sole source also determine the nature of epic distance—that is, the third constitutive characteristic of the epic as a genre. As we have already pointed out, the epic past is locked into itself and walled off from all subsequent times by an impenetrable boundary, isolated (and this is most important) from that eternal present of children and descendents in which the epic singer and his listeners are located, which figures in as an event in their lives and becomes the epic performance. On the other hand, tradition isolates the world of the epic from personal experience, from any new insights, from any personal initiative in understanding and interpreting, from new points of view and evaluations. The epic world is an utterly finished thing, not only as an authentic event of the distant past but also on its own terms and by its own standards; it is impossible to change, to re-think, to re-evaluate anything in it. It is completed, conclusive and immutable, as a fact, an idea and a value. This defines absolute epic distance. One can only accept the epic world with reverence; it is impossible to really touch it, for it is beyond the realm of human activity, the realm in which everything humans touch is altered and re-thought. This distance exists not only in the epic material, that is, in the events and the heroes described, but also in the point of view and evaluation one assumes toward them; point of view and evaluation are fused with the subject into one inseparable whole. Epic language is not separable from its subject, for an absolute fusion of subject matter and spatial-temporal aspects with valorized (hierarchical) ones is characteristic of semantics in the epic. This absolute fusion and the consequent unfreedom of the subject was first overcome only with the arrival on the scene of an active polyglossia and interillumination of languages (and then the epic became a semiconventional, semimoribund genre).

Thanks to this epic distance, which excludes any possibility of activity and change, the epic world achieves a radical degree of completedness not only in its content but in its meaning and its values as well. The epic world is constructed in the zone of an absolute distanced image, beyond the sphere of possible contact with the developing, incomplete and therefore re-thinking and re-evaluating present.

The three characteristics of the epic posited by us above are, to a greater or lesser extent, also fundamental to the other high genres of classical antiquity and the Middle Ages. At the heart of all these already completed high genres lie the same evaluation of time, the same role for tradition, and a similar hierarchical distance. Contemporary reality as such does not figure in as an available object of representation in any of these high genres. Contemporary reality may enter into the high genres only in its hierarchically highest levels, already distanced in its relationship to reality itself. But the events, victors and heroes of "high" contemporary reality are, as it were, appropriated by the past as they enter into these high genres (for example, Pindar's odes or the works of Simonides); they are woven by various intermediate links and connective tissue into the unified fabric of the heroic past and tradition. These events and heroes receive their value and grandeur precisely through this association with the past, the source of all authentic reality and value. They withdraw themselves, so to speak, from the present day with all its inconclusiveness, its indecision, its openness, its potential for re-thinking and re-evaluating. They are raised to the valorized plane of the past, and assume there a finished quality. We must not forget that "absolute past" is not to be confused with time in our exact and limited sense of the word; it is rather a temporally valorized hierarchical category.

It is impossible to achieve greatness in one's own time. Greatness always makes itself known only to descendents, for whom such a quality is always located in the past (it turns into a distanced image); it has become an object of memory and not a living object that one can see and touch. In the genre of the "memorial," the poet constructs his image in the future and distanced plane of his descendents (cf. the inscriptions of oriental despots, and of Augustus). In the world of memory, a phenomenon exists in its own peculiar context, with its own special rules, subject to conditions quite different from those we meet in the world we see with our own eyes, the world of practice and familiar contact. The epic past is a special form for perceiving people and events in art. In general the act of artistic perception and representation is almost completely obscured by this form. Artistic representation here is representation *sub specie aeternitatis*. One may, and in fact one must, memorialize with artistic language only that which is worthy of being remembered, that which should be preserved in the memory of descendents; an image is created for descendents, and this image is projected on to their sublime and distant horizon. Contemporaneity for its own sake (that is to say, a contemporaneity that makes no claim on future memory) is molded in clay; contemporaneity for the future (for descendents) is molded in marble or bronze.

The interrelationship of times is important here. The valorized emphasis is not on the future and does not serve the future, no favors are being done it (such favors face an eternity outside time); what is served here is the future memory of a past, a broadening of the world of the absolute past, an enriching of it with new images (at the expense of contemporaneity)—a world that is always opposed in principle to any *merely transitory* past.

In the already completed high genres, tradition also retains its significance—although under conditions of open and personal creativity, its role becomes more conventionalized than in the epic.

In general, the world of high literature in the classical era was a world projected into the past, on to the distanced plane of memory, but not into a real, relative past tied to the present by uninterrupted temporal transitions; it was projected rather into a valorized past of beginnings and peak times. This past is distanced, finished and closed like a circle. This does not mean, of course, that there is no movement within it. On the contrary, the relative temporal categories within it are richly and subtly worked out (nuances of "earlier," "later," sequences of moments, speeds, durations, etc.); there is evidence of a high level of artistic technique in matters of time. But within this time, completed and locked into a circle, all points are equidistant from the real, dynamic time of the present; insofar as this time is whole, it is not localized in an actual historical sequence; it is not relative to the present or to the future; it contains within itself, as it were, the entire fullness of time. As a consequence all high genres of the classical era, that is, its entire high literature, are structured in the zone of the distanced image, a zone outside any possible contact with the present in all its openendedness.

As we have said, contemporaneity as such (that is, one that preserves its own living contemporary profile) cannot become an object of representation for the high genres. Contemporaneity was reality of a "lower" order in comparison with the epic past. Least of all could it serve as the starting point for artistic ideation or evaluation. The focus for such an idea of evaluation could only be found in the absolute past. The present is something transitory, it is flow, it is an eternal continuation without beginning or end; it is denied an authentic conclusiveness and consequently lacks an essence as well. The future as well is perceived either as an essentially indifferent continuation of the present, or as an end, a final destruction, a catastrophe. The temporally valorized categories of absolute beginning and absolute end are extremely significant in our sense of time and in the ideologies of past times. The beginning is idealized, the end is darkened (catastrophe, "the twilight of the gods"). This sense of time and the hierarchy of times described by us here permeate all the high genres of antiquity and the Middle Ages. They permeated so deeply into the basic foundation of these genres that they continue to live in them in subsequent eras—up to the nineteenth century, and even further.

This idealization of the past in high genres has something of an official air. All external expressions of the dominant force and truth (the expression of everything conclusive) were formulated in the valorized-hierarchical category of the past, in a distanced and distant image (everything from gesture and clothing to literary style, for all are symbols of authority). The novel, however, is associated with the eternally living element of unofficial language and unofficial thought (holiday forms, familiar speech, profanation).

The dead are loved in a different way. They are removed from the sphere of contact, one can and indeed must speak of them in a different style. Language about the dead is stylistically quite distinct from language about the living.

In the high genres all authority and privilege, all lofty significance and grandeur, abandon the zone of familiar contact for the distanced plane (clothing, etiquette, the style of a hero's speech and the style of speech about him). It is in this orientation toward completeness that the classicism of all non-novel genres is expressed.

Contemporaneity, flowing and transitory, "low," present—this "life without beginning or end" was a subject of representation only in the low genres. Most importantly, it was the basic subject matter in that broadest and richest of realms, the common people's creative culture of laughter. In the aforementioned work I tried to indicate the enormous influence exercised by this realm—in the ancient world as well as the Middle Ages—on the birth and formation of novelistic language. It was equally significant for all other historical factors in the novelistic genre, during their emergence and early formation. Precisely here, in popular laughter, the authentic folkloric roots of the novel are to be sought. The present, contemporary life as such, "I myself" and "my contemporaries," "my time"—all these concepts were originally the objects of ambivalent laughter, at the same time cheerful and annihilating. It is precisely here that a fundamentally new attitude toward language and toward the word is generated. Alongside direct representation—laughing at living reality—there flourish parody and travesty of all high genres and of all lofty models embodied in national myth. The "absolute past" of gods, demigods and heroes is here, in parodies and even more so in travesties, "contemporized": it is brought low, represented on a plane equal with contemporary life, in an everyday environment, in the low language of contemporaneity.

In classical times this elemental popular laughter gave rise directly to a broad and varied field of ancient literature, one that the ancients themselves expressively labeled *spoudogeloion*, that is, the field of "serio-comical." The weakly plotted mimes of Sophron,[h] all the bucolic poems, the fable, early memoir literature (the *Epidēmiai* of Ion of Chios,[i] the *Homilae* of Critias),[j] pamphlets all belong to this field; here the ancients themselves included the "Socratic dialogues" (as a genre), here belong Roman satire (Lucilius,[k] Horace, Persius,[l] Juvenal), the extensive literature of the

---

h. Sophron (fl. 5th century B.C.) was probably the first writer to give literary form to the mime. He was greatly admired by Plato. The mimes were written in rhythmic prose and took as their subject matter events of everyday life.

i. Ion of Chios (490–421 B.C.), a Greek poet who, when he won first for tragedy in the Great Dionysia, made a present of Chian wine to every Athenian. His memoirs have not come down to us, but Athenaeus (q.v.) gives long quotes, including the description of an evening Sophocles spent with him in his home on Chios. It has been said no other Greek before Socrates has been presented so vividly. The title of these *Epidēmiai* probably refers to the visits of distinguished Athenians who came to see Ion on Chios.

j. Critias (460–403 B.C.), one of the Thirty Tyrants, also active as a writer. He wrote mostly elegies and tragedies. Fragments of *Homilai* ("discussions") have come down to us; Galen is cited by the editors of the Pauly-Wissowa (vol. II of the 1910 ed., p. 1910) as calling the two books of the original *Homilai* "aimless discussions" (*zwanglose Unterhaltungen*).

k. Lucilius Gaius (?–102 B.C.), member of one of the greatest Roman families, author of several important satires, chiefly remarkable for the personal, almost autobiographical tone he introduces into them.

l. Persius, Flaccus Aulus (A.D. 34–62), satirist heavily influenced by Stoic philosophy.

"Symposia" and finally Menippean satire (as a genre) and dialogues of the Lucianic type. All these genres, permeated with the "serio-comical," are authentic predecessors of the novel. In addition, several of these genres are thoroughly novelistic, containing in embryo and sometimes in developed form the basic elements characteristic of the most important later prototypes of the European novel. The authentic spirit of the novel as a developing genre is present in them to an incomparably greater degree than in the so-called Greek novels (the sole ancient genre bearing the name). The Greek novel [Greek romance] had a powerful influence on the European novel precisely in the Baroque era, that is, precisely at that time when novel theory was beginning to be reworked (Abbé Huet)[m] and when the very term "novel" was being tightened and made more precise. Out of all novelistic works of antiquity, the term "novel" was, therefore, attached to the Greek novel alone. Nevertheless, the serio-comical genres mentioned above anticipate the more essential historical aspects in the development of the novel in modern times, even though they lack that sturdy skeleton of plot and composition that we have grown accustomed to demand from the novel as a genre. This applies in particular to the Socratic dialogues, which may be called—to rephrase Friedrich Schlegel—"the novels of their time," and also to Menippean satire (including the *Satyricon* of Petronius), whose role in the history of the novel is immense and as yet inadequately appreciated by scholarship. These serio-comical genres were the first authentic and essential step in the evolution of the novel as the genre of becoming.

Precisely what is this novelistic spirit in these serio-comical genres, and on what basis do we claim them as the first step in the development of the novel? It is this: contemporary reality serves as their subject, and—even more important—it is the starting point for understanding, evaluating and formulating such genres. For the first time, the subject of serious literary representation (although, it is true, at the same time comical) is portrayed without any distance, on the level of contemporary reality, in a

---

m. Abbé Huet (1630–1721), bishop of Avranches, learned scholar who wrote numerous works on a wide variety of subjects. His *Traité de l'origine des romans* (1670) was first published as an introduction to Mme. de La Fayette's *Zaïde*, a novel written while its author was still influenced by ideas of the *précieux* society.

zone of direct and even crude contact. Even where the past or myth serves as the subject of representation in these genres there is no epic distance, and contemporary reality provides the point of view. Of special significance in this process of demolishing distance is the comical origin of these genres: they derive from folklore (popular laughter). It is precisely laughter that destroys the epic, and in general destroys any hierarchical (distancing and valorized) distance. As a distanced image a subject cannot be comical; to be made comical, it must be brought close. Everything that makes us laugh is close at hand, all comical creativity works in a zone of maximal proximity. Laughter has the remarkable power of making an object come up close, of drawing it into a zone of crude contact where one can finger it familiarly on all sides, turn it upside down, inside out, peer at it from above and below, break open its external shell, look into its center, doubt it, take it apart, dismember it, lay it bare and expose it, examine it freely and experiment with it. Laughter demolishes fear and piety before an object, before a world, making of it an object of familiar contact and thus clearing the ground for an absolutely free investigation of it. Laughter is a vital factor in laying down that prerequisite for fearlessness without which it would be impossible to approach the world realistically. As it draws an object to itself and makes it familiar, laughter delivers the object into the fearless hands of investigative experiment—both scientific and artistic—and into the hands of free experimental fantasy. Familiarization of the world through laughter and popular speech is an extremely important and indispensable step in making possible free, scientifically knowable and artistically realistic creativity in European civilization.

The plane of comic (humorous) representation is a specific plane in its spatial as well as its temporal aspect. Here the role of memory is minimal; in the comic world there is nothing for memory and tradition to do. One ridicules in order to forget. This is the zone of maximally familiar and crude contact; laughter means abuse, and abuse could lead to blows. Basically this is uncrowning, that is, the removal of an object from the distanced plane, the destruction of epic distance, an assault on and destruction of the distanced plane in general. In this plane (the plane of laughter) one can disrespectfully walk around whole objects; therefore, the back and rear portion of an object (and also its innards, not normally accessible for viewing) assume a special importance. The object is broken apart, laid bare (its hierarchical ornamentation is removed): the naked object is ridiculous; its "empty" clothing, stripped and separated from its person, is also ridiculous. What takes place is a comical operation of dismemberment.

One can play games with the comical (that is, contemporize it); serving as the objects of the game we have the primordial artistic symbols of space and time—above, below, in front of, behind, earlier, later, first, last, past, present, brief (momentary), long and so forth. What reigns supreme here is the artistic logic of analysis, dismemberment, turning things into dead objects.

We possess a remarkable document that reflects the simultaneous birth of scientific thinking and of a new artistic-prose model for the novel. These are the Socratic dialogues. For our purposes, everything in this remarkable genre, which was born just as classical antiquity was drawing to a close, is significant. Characteristically it arises as *apomnemoneumata*,[n] that is, as a genre of the memoir type, as transcripts based on personal memories of real conversations among contemporaries;[2] characteristic, also, is the fact that a speaking and conversing man is the central image of the genre. Characteristic, too, is the combination of the image of Socrates, the central hero of the genre, wearing the popular mask of a bewildered fool (almost a *Margit*)[o] with the image of a wise man of the most elevated sort (in the spirit of legends about seven wise men); this combination produces the ambivalent image of wise ignorance. Characteristic also is the ambivalent self-praise in the Socratic dialogue: I am wiser than everyone, because I know that I know nothing. In the image of Socrates one can detect a new type of prose heroization. Around this image, carnivalized legends spring up (for example, Socrates' relationship

2. "Memory" in memoirs and autobiographies is of a special sort: it is memory of one's own contemporaneity and of one's own self. It is a de-heroizing memory; there is an element of the mechanical in it, of mere transcription (nonmonumental). What results is personal memory without pre-existing chronological pattern, bounded only by the termini of a single personal life (there are no fathers or generations). This "memoir quality" was already inherent in the Socratic dialogue.

n. *Apomnemoneumata*, or *Hypomnemata* (literally, "recollections"). It is thought by some that a work of this title ascribed to Ion of Chios may be identical with the *Epidēmiai* (cf. note 9).

o. *Margit*, Greek "fool," subject of a work frequently cited by Bakhtin, the *Margites* (q.v.).

with Xanthippe); the hero turns into a jester (compare the more recent carnivalization of legends surrounding Dante, Pushkin,[p] etc.).

Characteristic, even canonic, for the genre is the spoken dialogue framed by a dialogized story. Characteristic also is the proximity of its language to popular spoken language, as near as was possible for classical Greece; these dialogues in fact opened the path to Attic prose, and are connected with the essential renovation of the literary-prose language—and with a shift in languages in general. Characteristically this genre is at the same time a rather complex system of styles and dialects, which enter it as more-or-less parodied models of languages and styles (we have before us therefore a multi-styled genre, as is the authentic novel). Moreover the figure of Socrates himself is characteristic for the genre—he is an outstanding example of heroization in novelistic prose (so very different from epic heroization). It is, finally, profoundly characteristic—and for us this is of utmost importance—that we have laughter, Socratic irony, the entire system of Socratic degradations combined with a serious, lofty and for the first time truly free investigation of the world, of man and of human thought. Socratic laughter (reduced to irony) and Socratic degradations (an entire system of metaphors and comparisons borrowed from the lower spheres of life—from tradespeople, from everyday life, etc.) bring the world closer and familiarize it in order to investigate it fearlessly and freely. As our starting point we have contemporary reality, the living people who occupy it together with their opinions. From this vantage point, from this contemporary reality with its diversity of speech and voice, there comes about a new orientation in the world and in time (including the "absolute past" of tradition) through personal experience and investigation. It is canonical for the genre that even an accidental and insignificant pretext can ordinarily and deliberately

---

p. A good example of what Bakhtin has in mind here is provided by the leader of the *Oberiuty*, Daniil Kharms (1905–1942), "Anecdotes about Pushkin." They are difficult to appreciate in translation, but are all similar to the following: "Pushkin loved to throw rocks. As soon as he saw a rock, he would throw it. Sometimes he became so excited that he stood, all red in the face, waving his arms, throwing rocks, simply something awful."—from *Russia's Lost Literature of the Absurd*, tr. and ed. by George Gibian (New York, 1974), p. 67.

serve as the external and most immediate starting point for a dialogue; the "todayness" of the day was emphasized in all its randomness (accidental encounters, etc.).

In other serio-comical genres we will come upon other aspects, nuances and consequences of this radical shift of the temporally valorized center of artistic orientation, and of the revolution in the hierarchy of times. A few words now about Menippean satire. Its folklore roots are identical with those of the Socratic dialogue, to which it is genetically related (it is usually considered a product of the disintegration of the Socratic dialogue). The familiarizing role of laughter is here considerably more powerful, sharper and coarser. The liberty to crudely degrade, to turn inside out the lofty aspects of the world and world views, might sometimes seem shocking. But to this exclusive and comic familiarity must be added an intense spirit of inquiry and a utopian fantasy. Nothing is left of the distant epic image of the absolute past; the entire world and everything sacred in it is offered to us without any distancing at all, in a zone of crude contact, where we can grab at everything with our own hands. In this world, utterly familiarized, the subject moves with extreme and fantastic freedom; from heaven to earth, from earth to the nether world, from the present into the past, from the past into the future. In the comic afterlife visions of Menippean satire, the heroes of the absolute past, real-life figures from various eras of the historic past (for example, Alexander of Macedonia) and living contemporaries jostle one another in a most familiar way, to talk, even to brawl; this confrontation of times from the point of view of the present is extremely characteristic. In Menippean satire the unfettered and fantastic plots and situations all serve one goal—to put to the test and to expose ideas and ideologues. These are experimental and provocative plots.

The appearance of the utopian element in this genre is symptomatic, although it is, to be sure, timid and shallow. The inconclusive present begins to feel closer to the future than to the past, and begins to seek some valorized support in the future, even if this future is as yet pictured merely as a return to the Golden Age of Saturn (in Roman times, Menippean satire was closely associated with the Saturnalia and with the freedom of Saturnalian laughter).

Menippean satire is dialogic, full of parodies and travesties, multi-styled, and does not fear elements of bilingualism (in Varro^q and especially in Boethius' *The Consolation of Philosophy*). The *Satyricon* of Petronius is good proof that Menippean satire can expand into a huge picture, offering a realistic reflection of the socially varied and heteroglot world of contemporary life.

For almost all the above-mentioned genres, the "serio-comical" is characterized by a deliberate and explicit autobiographical and memoirist approach. The shift of the temporal center of artistic orientation, which placed on the same temporally valorized plane the author and his readers (on the one hand) and the world and heroes described by him (on the other), making them contemporaries, possible acquaintances, friends, familiarizing their relations (we again recall the novelistic opening of *Onegin*), permits the author, in all his various masks and faces, to move freely onto the field of his represented world, a field that in the epic had been absolutely inaccessible and closed.

The field available for representing the world changes from genre to genre and from era to era as literature develops. It is organized in different ways and limited in space and time by different means. But this field is always specific.

The novel comes into contact with the spontaneity of the inconclusive present; this is what keeps the genre from congealing. The novelist is drawn toward everything that is not yet completed. He may turn up on the field of representation in any authorial pose, he may depict real moments in his own life or make allusions to them, he may interfere in the conversations of his heroes, he may openly polemicize with his literary enemies and so forth. This is not merely a matter of the author's image appearing within his own field of representation—important here is the fact that the underlying, original formal author (the author of the authorial image) appears in a new relationship with the represented world. Both find themselves now subject to the same temporally valorized measurements, for the "depicting" authorial language now lies on the same plane as the "depicted" language of the hero, and may enter into dialogic relations and hybrid combina-

---

q. Marcus Terentius Varro (fl. 1st century B.C.), politician and scholar, a pupil of Stilo—the first Roman philologist—who had made himself known through research on the genuineness of Plautus' comedies. Varro wrote numerous works on the Latin language, but Bakhtin refers to him as author of the lost work *Statuarum Menippearum libri*, humorous essays in the Menippean style satirizing the luxury of his age.

tions with it (indeed, it cannot help but enter into such relations).

It is precisely this new situation, that of the original formally present author in a zone of contact with the world he is depicting, that makes possible at all the appearance of the authorial image on the field of representation. This new positioning of the author must be considered one of the most important results of surmounting epic (hierarchical) distance. The enormous formal, compositional and stylistic implications this new positioning of the author has for the specific evolution of the novel as a genre require no further explanation.

Let us consider in this connection Gogol's *Dead Souls*. The form of his epic Gogol modeled on the *Divine Comedy*; it was in this form that he imagined the greatness of his work lay. But what in fact emerged was Menippean satire. Once having entered the zone of familiar contact he was unable to leave it, and he was unable to transfer into this sphere distanced and positive images. The distanced images of the epic and the images of familiar contact can never meet on the same field of representation; pathos broke into the world of Menippean satire like a foreign body, affirmative pathos became abstract and simply fell out of the work. Gogol could not manage the move from Hell to Purgatory and then to Paradise with the same people and in the same work; no continuous transition was possible. The tragedy of Gogol is to a very real extent the tragedy of a genre (taking genre not in its formalistic sense, but as a zone and a field of valorized perception, as a mode for representing the world). Gogol lost Russia, that is, he lost his blueprint for perceiving and representing her; he got muddled somewhere between memory and familiar contact—to put it bluntly, he could not find the proper focus on his binoculars.

But as a new starting point for artistic orientation, contemporaneity by no means excludes the depiction of a heroic past, and without any travesty. As an example we have Xenophon's *Cyropaedia*[1] (not, of course, a serio-comical work, but one that does lie on the borderline). Its subject is the past, its hero is Cyrus the Great. But the starting point of representation is Xenophon's

---

1. Xenophon (428–354 B.C.), *Cyropaedia*, a text that haunts the history of thinking about novels from Julian the Apostate's citation of it as a model to be avoided (cf. Perry, *Ancient Romances*, p. 78) to Boileau, who, in his *Dialogue sur les héros des romans* (1664) attacks Mme. de Scudéry's monstrous *Artamène, ou le grand Cyrus* (1649–1653).

own contemporary reality; it is that which provides the point of view and value orientation. It is characteristic that the heroic past chosen here is not the national past but a foreign and barbaric past. The world has already opened up; one's own monolithic and closed world (the world of the epic) has been replaced by the great world of one's own plus "the others." This choice of an alien heroism was the result of a heightened interest, characteristic for Xenophon's time, in the Orient—in Eastern culture, ideology and sociopolitical forms. A light was expected from the East. Cultural interanimation, interaction of ideologies and languages had already begun. Also characteristic was the idealization of the oriental despot, and here one senses Xenophon's own contemporary reality with its idea (shared widely by his contemporaries) of renovating Greek political forms in a spirit close to oriental autocracy. Such an idealization of oriental autocracy is of course deeply alien to the entire spirit of Hellenic national tradition. Characteristic and even extremely typical for the time was the concept of an individual's upbringing: this was to become one of the most important and productive themes for the new European novel. Also characteristic is the intentional and completely explicit transfer onto the image of Cyrus the Great of the features of Cyrus the Younger, a contemporary of Xenophon in whose campaign Xenophon participated. And one also senses here the personality of another contemporary and close friend of Xenophon, Socrates; thus are elements of the memoir introduced into the work. As a final characteristic we might mention the form of the work itself—dialogues framed by a story. In such a way, contemporary reality and its concerns become the starting point and center of an artistic ideological thinking and evaluating of the past. This past is given us without distancing, on the level of contemporary reality, although not (it is true) in its low but in its high forms, on the level of its most advanced concerns. Let us comment upon the somewhat utopian overtones in this work that reflect a slight (and uncertain) shift of its contemporaneity from the past toward the future. *Cyropaedia* is a novel, in the most basic sense of the word.

The depiction of a past in the novel in no sense presumes the modernization of this past (in Xenophon there are, of course, traces of such modernization). On the contrary, only in the novel have we the possibility of an authentically objective portrayal of the past as the past. Contemporary reality with its new experiences is retained as a way of seeing, it has the depth, sharpness, breadth and vividness peculiar to that way of seeing, but should not in any way penetrate into the already portrayed content of the past, as a force modernizing and distorting the uniqueness of that past. After all, every great and serious contemporaneity requires an authentic profile of the past, an authentic other language from another time.

The revolution in the hierarchy of times outlined above makes possible a radical revolution in the structuring of the artistic image as well. The present, in its so-called "wholeness" (although it is, of course, never whole) is in essence and in principle inconclusive; by its very nature it demands continuation, it moves into the future, and the more actively and consciously it moves into the future the more tangible and indispensable its inconclusiveness becomes. Therefore, when the present becomes the center of human orientation in time and in the world, time and world lose their completedness as a whole as well as in each of their parts. The temporal model of the world changes radically: it becomes a world where there is no first word (no ideal word), and the final word has not yet been spoken. For the first time in artistic-ideological consciousness, time and the world become historical: they unfold, albeit at first still unclearly and confusedly, as becoming, as an uninterrupted movement into a real future, as a unified, all-embracing and unconcluded process. Every event, every phenomenon, every thing, every object of artistic representation loses its completedness, its hopelessly finished quality and its immutability that had been so essential to it in the world of the epic "absolute past," walled off by an unapproachable boundary from the continuing and unfinished present. Through contact with the present, an object is attracted to the incomplete process of a world-in-the-making, and is stamped with the seal of inconclusiveness. No matter how distant this object is from us in time, it is connected to our incomplete, present-day, continuing temporal transitions, it develops a relationship with our unpreparedness, with our present. But meanwhile our present has been moving into an inconclusive future. And in this inconclusive context all the semantic stability of the object is lost; its sense and significance are renewed and grow as the context continues to unfold. This leads to radical changes in the structuring of the artistic image. The image acquires a specific actual existence. It acquires a relationship—in one form or another, to one degree or another—to the ongoing event of current life in which we, the author and readers, are intimately participating. This creates the radically new zone for structuring images in the novel, a zone of maximally close contact between the represented object and contemporary reality in all its inconclusiveness—and consequently a similarly close contact between the object and the future.

Prophecy is characteristic for the epic, prediction for the novel. Epic prophecy is realized wholly within the limits of the absolute past (if not in a given epic, then within the limits of the tradition it encompasses); it does not touch the reader and his real time. The novel might wish to prophesize facts, to predict and influence the real future, the future of the author and his readers. But the novel has a new and quite specific problematicalness: characteristic for it is an eternal re-thinking and re-evaluating. That center of activity that ponders and justifies the past is transferred to the future.

This "modernity" of the novel is indestructible, and verges on an unjust evaluation of times. Let us recall the re-evaluation of the past that occurred during the Renaissance ("the darkness of the Gothic Age"), in the eighteenth century (Voltaire) and that is inherent in positivism (the exposure of myth, legend, heroization, a maximum departure from memory and a maximum reduction of the concept of "knowledge," even to the point of empiricism, a mechanical faith in "progress" as the highest criterion).

* * *

Let us now touch upon several artistic features related to the above. The absence of internal conclusiveness and exhaustiveness creates a sharp increase in demands for an *external* and *formal* completedness and exhaustiveness, especially in regard to plot-line. The problems of a beginning, an end, and "fullness" of plot are posed anew. The epic is indifferent to formal beginnings and can remain incomplete (that is, where it concludes is almost arbitrary). The absolute past is closed and completed in the whole as well as in any of its parts. It is, therefore, possible to take any part and offer it as the whole. One cannot embrace, in a single epic, the entire world of the absolute past (although it is unified from a plot standpoint)—to do so would mean a retelling of the whole of national tradition, and it is sufficiently difficult to embrace even a significant portion of it. But this is no great loss, because the structure of the whole is repeated in each part, and each part is complete and circular like the whole. One may begin the story at almost any moment, and finish at almost any moment.

The *Iliad* is a random excerpt from the Trojan cycle. Its ending (the burial of Hector) could not possibly be the ending from a novelistic point of view. But epic completedness suffers not the slightest as a result. The specific "impulse to end"—How does the war end? Who wins? What will happen to Achilles? and so forth—is absolutely excluded from the epic by both internal and external motifs (the plot-line of the tradition was already known to everyone). This specific "impulse to continue" (what will happen next?) and the "impulse to end" (how will it end?) are characteristic only for the novel and are possible only in a zone where there is proximity and contact; in a zone of distanced images they are impossible.

In distanced images we have the whole event, and plot interest (that is, the condition of not knowing) is impossible. The novel, however, speculates in what is unknown. The novel devises various forms and methods for employing the surplus knowledge that the author has, that which the hero does not know or does not see. It is possible to utilize this authorial surplus in an external way, manipulating the narrative, or it can be used to complete the image of an individual (an externalization that is peculiarly novelistic). But there is another possibility in this surplus that creates further problems.

The distinctive features of the novelistic zone emerge in various ways in various novels. A novel need not raise any problematic questions at all. Take, for example, the adventuristic "boulevard" romance. There is no philosophy in it, no social or political problems, no psychology. Consequently none of these spheres provides any contact with the inconclusive events of our own contemporary reality. The absence of distance and of a zone of contact are utilized here in a different way: in place of our tedious lives we are offered a surrogate, true, but it is the surrogate of a fascinating and brilliant life. We can experience these adventures, identify with these heroes; such novels almost become a substitute for our own lives. Nothing of the sort is possible in the epic and other distanced genres. And here we encounter the specific danger inherent in the novelistic zone of contact: we ourselves may actually enter the novel (whereas we could never enter an epic or other distanced genre). It follows that we might substitute for our own life an obsessive reading of novels, or dreams based on novelistic models (the hero of [Dostoevsky's] *White Nights*); Bovaryism becomes possible, the real-life appearance of fashionable heroes taken from novels—disillusioned, demonic and so forth. Other genres are capable of generating such phenomena only after having been novelized, that is, after having been transposed to the novelistic zone of contact (for example, the verse narratives of Byron).

Yet another phenomenon in the history of the novel—and one of extreme importance—is connected with this new temporal orientation and with this zone of contact: it is the novel's special relationship with extraliterary genres, with the genres of everyday life and with ideological genres. In its earliest stages, the novel and its preparatory genres had relied upon various extraliterary forms of personal and social reality, and especially those of rhetoric (there is a theory that actually traces the novel back to rhetoric). And in later stages of its development the novel makes wide and substantial use of letters, diaries, confessions, the forms and methods of rhetoric associated with recently established courts and so forth. Since it is constructed in a zone of contact with the incomplete events of a particular present, the novel often crosses the boundary of what we strictly call fictional literature—making use first of a moral confession, then of a philosophical tract, then of manifestos that are openly political, then degenerating into the raw spirituality of a confession, a "cry of the soul" that has not yet found its formal contours. These phenomena are precisely what characterize the novel as a developing genre. After all, the boundaries between fiction and nonfiction, between literature and nonliterature and so forth are not laid up in heaven. Every specific situation is historical. And the growth of literature is not merely development and change within the fixed boundaries of any given definition; the boundaries themselves are constantly changing. The shift of boundaries between various strata (including literature) in a culture is an extremely slow and complex process. Isolated border violations of any given specific definition (such as those mentioned above) are only symptomatic of this larger process, which occurs at a great depth. These symptoms of change appear considerably more often in the novel than they do elsewhere, as the novel is a developing genre; they are sharper and more significant because the novel is in the vanguard of change. The novel may thus serve as a document for gauging the lofty and still distant destinies of literature's future unfolding.

But the changes that take place in temporal orientation, and in the zone where images are constructed, appear nowhere more profoundly and inevitably than in the process of re-structuring the image of the individual in literature. Within the bounds of the present article, however, I can touch on this great and complex question only briefly and superficially.

The individual in the high distanced genres is an individual of the absolute past and óf the distanced image. As such he is a fully finished and completed being. This has been accomplished on a lofty heroic level, but what is complete is also something hopelessly ready-made; he is all there, from beginning to end he coincides with himself, he is absolutely equal to himself. He is, furthermore, completely externalized. There is not the slightest gap between his authentic essence and its external manifestation. All his potential, all his possibilities are realized utterly in his external social position, in the whole of his fate and even in his external appearance; outside of this predetermined fate and predetermined position there is nothing. He has already become everything that he could become, and he could become only that which he has already become. He is entirely externalized in the most elementary, almost literal sense: everything in him is exposed and loudly expressed: his internal world and all his external characteristics, his appearance and his actions all lie on a single plane. His view of himself coincides completely with others' views of him—the view of his society (his community), the epic singer and the audience also coincide.

In this context, mention should be made of the problem of self-praise that comes up in Plutarch and others. "I myself," in an environment that is distanced, exists not *in* itself or for *itself* but for the self's descendents, for the memory such a self anticipates in its descendents. I acknowledge myself, an image that is my own, but on this distanced plane of memory such a consciousness of self is alienated from "me." I see myself through the eyes of another. This coincidence of forms—the view I have of myself as self, and the view I have of myself as other—bears an integral, and therefore naive, character—there is no gap between the two. We have as yet no confession, no exposing of self. The one doing the depicting coincides with the one being depicted.[3]

3. Epic disintegrates when the search begins for a new point of view on one's own self (without any admixture of others' points of view). The expressive novelistic gesture arises as a departure from a norm, but the "error" of this norm immediately reveals how important it is for subjectivity. First there is a departure from a norm, and then the problematicalness of the norm itself.

He sees and knows in himself only the things that others see and know in him. Everything that another person—the author—is able to say about him he can say about himself, and vice versa. There is nothing to seek for in him, nothing to guess at, he can neither be exposed nor provoked; he is all of a piece, he has no shell, there is no nucleus within. Furthermore, the epic hero lacks any ideological initiative (heroes and author alike lack it). The epic world knows only a single and unified world view, obligatory and indubitably true for heroes as well as for authors and audiences. Neither world view nor language can, therefore, function as factors for limiting and determining human images, or their individualization. In the epic, characters are bounded, preformed, individualized by their various situations and destinies, but not by varying "truths." Not even the gods are separated from men by a special truth: they have the same language, they all share the same world view, the same fate, the same extravagant externalization.

These traits of the epic character, shared by and large with other highly distanced genres, are responsible for the exclusive beauty, wholeness, crystal clarity and artistic completedness of this image of man. But at the same time such traits account for his limitations and his obvious woodenness under conditions obtaining in a later period of human existence.

The destruction of epic distance and the transferral of the image of an individual from the distanced plane to the zone of contact with the inconclusive events of the present (and consequently of the future) result in a radical re-structuring of the image of the individual in the novel—and consequently in all literature. Folklore and popular-comic sources for the novel played a huge role in this process. Its first and essential step was the comic familiarization of the image of man. Laughter destroyed epic distance; it began to investigate man freely and familiarly, to turn him inside out, expose the disparity between his surface and his center, between his potential and his reality. A dynamic authenticity was introduced into the image of man, dynamics of inconsistency and tension between various factors of this image; man ceased to coincide with himself, and consequently men ceased to be exhausted entirely by the plots that contain them. Of these inconsistencies and tensions laughter plays up, first of all, the comic sides (but not only the comic sides); in the serio-comical genres of antiquity, images of a new order emerge—for example, the imposing, newly and more complexly integrated heroic image of Socrates.

Characteristic here is the artistic structuring of an image out of durable popular masks—masks that had great influence on the novelistic image of man during the most important stages of the novel's development (the serio-comical genres of antiquity, Rabelais, Cervantes). Outside his destiny, the epic and tragic hero is nothing; he is, therefore, a function of the plot fate assigns him; he cannot become the hero of another destiny or another plot. On the contrary, popular masks—Maccus, Pulcinello, Harlequin—are able to assume any destiny and can figure into any situation (they often do so within the limits of a single play), but they cannot exhaust their possibilities by those situations alone; they always retain, in any situation and in any destiny, a happy surplus of their own, their own rudimentary but inexhaustible human face. Therefore these masks can function and speak independent of the plot; but, moreover, it is precisely in these excursions outside the plot proper—in the Atellan *trices*,[s] in the *lazzi*[t] of Italian comedy—that they best of all reveal a face of their own. Neither an epic nor a tragic hero could ever step out in his own character during a pause in the plot or during an intermission: he has no face for it, no gesture, no language. In this is his strength and his limitation. The epic and tragic hero is the hero who, by his very nature, must perish. Popular masks, on the contrary, never perish: not a single plot in Atellan, Italian or Italianized French comedies provides for, or could ever provide for, the actual death of a Maccus, a Pulcinello or a Harlequin. However, one frequently witnesses their fictive comic deaths (with subsequent resurrections). These are heroes of free improvisation and not heroes of tradition, heroes of a life process that is imperishable and forever renewing itself, forever contemporary—these are not heroes of an absolute past.

These masks and their structure (the noncoincidence with themselves, and with any given situation—the surplus, the inexhaustibility of their self and the like), have had, we repeat, an enormous influence on the development of the novelistic image

---

s. *Trices* are thought to have been interludes in the action of the Atellanae during which the masks often stepped out of character.

t. *Lazzi* were what we might now call "routines" or "numbers" that were not part of the ongoing action of the plot.

of man. This structure is preserved even in the novel, although in a more complex, deeply meaningful and serious (or serio-comical) form.

One of the basic internal themes of the novel is precisely the theme of the hero's inadequacy to his fate or his situation. The individual is either greater than his fate, or less than his condition as a man. He cannot become once and for all a clerk, a landowner, a merchant, a fiancé, a jealous lover, a father and so forth. If the hero of a novel actually becomes something of the sort—that is, if he completely coincides with his situation and his fate (as do generic, everyday heroes, the majority of secondary characters in a novel)—then the surplus inhering in the human condition is realized in the main protagonist. The way in which this surplus will actually be realized grows out of the author's orientation toward form and content, that is, the ways he sees and depicts individuals. It is precisely the zone of contact with an inconclusive present (and consequently with the future) that creates the necessity of this incongruity of a man with himself. There always remains in him unrealized potential and unrealized demands. The future exists, and this future ineluctably touches upon the individual, has its roots in him.

An individual cannot be completely incarnated into the flesh of existing sociohistorical categories. There is no mere form that would be able to incarnate once and forever all of his human possibilities and needs, no form in which he could exhaust himself down to the last word, like the tragic or epic hero; no form that he could fill to the very brim, and yet at the same time not splash over the brim. There always remains an unrealized surplus of humanness; there always remains a need for the future, and a place for this future must be found. All existing clothes are always too tight, and thus comical, on a man. But this surplus of un-fleshed-out humanness may be realized not only in the hero, but also in the author's point of view (as, for example, in Gogol). Reality as we have it in the novel is only one of many possible realities; it is not inevitable, not arbitrary, it bears within itself other possibilities.

The epic wholeness of an individual disintegrates in a novel in other ways as well. A crucial tension develops between the external and the internal man, and as a result the subjectivity of the individual becomes an object of experimentation and representation—and first of all on the humorous familiarizing plane. Coordination breaks down between the various aspects: man for himself alone and man in the eyes of others. This disintegration of the integrity that an individual had possessed in epic (and in tragedy) combines in the novel with the necessary preparatory steps toward a new, complex wholeness on a higher level of human development.

Finally, in a novel the individual acquires the ideological and linguistic initiative necessary to change the nature of his own image (there is a new and higher type of individualization of the image). In the antique stage of novelistic development there appeared remarkable examples of such hero-ideologues—the image of Socrates, the image of a laughing Epicurus in the so-called "Hypocratic" novel, the deeply novelized image of Diogenes in the thoroughly dialogized literature of the cynics and in Menippean satire (where it closely approximates the image of the popular mask) and, finally, the image of Menippius in Lucian. As a rule, the hero of a novel is always more or less an ideologue.

What all this suggests is a somewhat abstract and crude schematization for re-structuring the image of an individual in the novel.

We will summarize with some conclusions.

The present, in its all openendedness, taken as a starting point and center for artistic and ideological orientation, is an enormous revolution in the creative consciousness of man. In the European world this reorientation and destruction of the old hierarchy of temporalities received its crucial generic expression on the boundary between classic antiquity and Hellenism, and in the new world during the late Middle Ages and Renaissance. The fundamental constituents of the novel as a genre were formed in these eras, although some of the separate elements making up the novel were present much earlier, and the novel's roots must ultimately be sought in folklore. In these eras all other major genres had already long since come to completion, they were already old and almost ossified genres. They were all permeated from top to bottom with a more ancient hierarchization of temporalities. The novel, from the very beginning, developed as a genre that had at its core a new way of conceptualizing time. The absolute past, tradition, hierarchical distance played no role in the formation of the novel as a genre (such spatiotemporal categories did play a role, though insignificant, in certain periods of the novel's development, when it was slightly influenced by the epic—for example in the Baroque novel). The novel took shape precisely at the point when epic distance was disintegrating, when both the world and man were assuming a degree of comic familiarity, when the object of artistic representation was being degraded to the level of a contemporary reality that was inconclusive and fluid. From the very beginning the novel was structured not in the distanced image of the absolute past but in the zone of direct contact with inconclusive present-day reality. At its core lay personal experience and free creative imagination. Thus a new, sober artistic-prose novelistic image and a new critical scientific perception came into being simultaneously. From the very beginning, then, the novel was made of different clay than the other already completed genres; it is a different breed, and with it and in it is born the future of all literature. Once it came into being, it could never be merely one genre among others, and it could not erect rules for interrelating with others in peaceful and harmonious co-existence. In the presence of the novel, all other genres somehow have a different resonance. A lengthy battle for the novelization of the other genres began, a battle to drag them into a zone of contact with reality. The course of this battle has been complex and tortuous.

The novelization of literature does not imply attaching to already completed genres a generic canon that is alien to them, not theirs. The novel, after all, has no canon of its own. It is, by its very nature, not canonic. It is plasticity itself. It is a genre that is ever questing, ever examining itself and subjecting its established forms to review. Such, indeed, is the only possibility open to a genre that structures itself in a zone of direct contact with developing reality. Therefore, the novelization of other genres does not imply their subjection to an alien generic canon; on the contrary, novelization implies their liberation from all that serves as a brake on their unique development, from all that would change them along with the novel into some sort of stylization of forms that have outlived themselves.

I have developed my various positions in this essay in a somewhat abstract way. There have been few illustrations, and even these were taken only from an ancient period in the novel's development. My choice was determined by the fact that the significance of that period has been greatly underestimated. When people talk about the ancient period of the novel they have traditionally had in mind the "Greek novel" alone. The ancient period of the novel is enormously significant for a proper understanding of the genre. But in ancient times the novel could not really develop all its potential; this potential came to light only in the modern world. We indicated that in several works of antiquity, the inconclusive present begins to sense a greater proximity to the future than to the past. The absence of a temporal perspective in ancient society assured that this process of reorientation toward a real future could not complete itself; after all, there was no real concept of a future. Such a reorientation occurred for the first time during the Renaissance. In that era, the present (that is, a reality that was contemporaneous) for the first time began to sense itself not only as an incomplete continuation of the past, but as something like a new and heroic beginning. To reinterpret reality on the level of the contemporary present now meant not only to degrade, but to raise reality into a new and heroic sphere. It was in the Renaissance that the present first began to feel with great clarity and awareness an incomparably closer proximity and kinship to the future than to the past.

The process of the novel's development has not yet come to an end. It is currently entering a new phase. For our era is characterized by an extraordinary complexity and a deepening in our perception of the world; there is an unusual growth in demands on human discernment, on mature objectivity and the critical faculty. These are features that will shape the further development of the novel as well.

FROM THE PREHISTORY
OF NOVELISTIC DISCOURSE

I

The stylistic study of the novel began only very recently. Classicism of the seventeenth and eighteenth centuries did not recognize the novel as an independent poetic genre and classified it with the mixed rhetorical genres. The first theoreticians of the novel—Abbé Huet (*Essay* [*Traité*] *sur l'origine des romans*, 1670), Wieland (in his celebrated preface to *Agathon*, 1766–1767), Blankenburg (*Versuch über den Roman*, 1774, published anonymously) and the Romantics (Friedrich Schlegel, Novalis) barely touched upon questions of style.[1] In the second half of the nineteenth century there was an intensification of interest in the theory of the novel, as it had become the leading European genre[2]— but scholarship was concentrated almost exclusively on questions of composition and thematics.[3] Questions of stylistics were touched upon only in passing and then in a manner that was completely unsystematic.

Beginning with the 1920s, this situation changed rather abruptly: there appeared a large number of works dealing with the sty-

---

1. The Romantics maintained that the novel was a mixed genre (a mixture of verse and prose), incorporating into its composition various genres (in particular the lyrical)—but the Romantics did not draw any stylistic conclusions from this. Cf., for example, Friedrich Schlegel's *Brief über den Roman*.

2. In Germany, in a series of works by Spielhagen (which began to appear in 1864) and especially with R. Riemanns' work, *Goethes Romantechnik* (1902); in France, beginning in the main with Brunetière and Lanson.

3. Literary scholars studying the technique of framing ("Ramenerzählung") in literary prose and the role of the storyteller in the epic (Käte Friedemann, *Die Rolle des Erzählers in der Epik* [Leipzig, 1910]) came close to dealing with this fundamental problem of the plurality of styles and levels characteristic of the novel as a genre, but this problem remained unresolved on the stylistic plane.

listics of individual novelists and of individual novels. These works are often rich in valuable observations.[4] But the distinctive features of novelistic discourse, the stylistic *specificum* of the novel as a genre, remained as before unexplored. Moreover, the problem of this *specificum* itself, its full significance, has to this day not yet been posed. Five different stylistic approaches to novelistic discourse may be observed: (1) the author's portions alone in the novel are analyzed, that is, only direct words of the author more or less correctly isolated—an analysis constructed in terms of the usual, direct poetic methods of representation and expression (metaphors, comparisons, lexical register, etc.); (2) instead of a stylistic analysis of the novel as an artistic whole, there is a neutral linguistic description of the novelist's language;[5] (3) in a given novelist's language, elements characteristic of his particular literary tendency are isolated (be it Romanticism, Naturalism, Impressionism, etc.);[6] (4) what is sought in the language of the novel is examined as an expression of the individual personality, that is, language is analyzed as the individual style of the given novelist;[7] (5) the novel is viewed as a rhetorical genre, and its devices are analyzed from the point of view of their effectiveness as rhetoric.[8]

All these types of stylistic analysis to a greater or lesser degree are remote from those peculiarities that define the novel as a genre, and they are also remote from the specific conditions under which the word lives in the novel. They all take a novelist's language and style not as the language and style of a *novel* but merely as the expression of a specific individual artistic personality, or as the style of a particular literary school or finally as a phenomenon common to poetic language in general. The individual artistic personality of the author, the literary school, the gen-

4. Of special value is the work by H. Hatzfeld, *Don-Quijote als Wortkunstwerk* (Leipzig-Berlin, 1927).
5. Such, for example, is L. Sainéan's book, *La Langue de Rabelais* (Paris, vol. 1, 1922; vol. 2, 1923).
6. Such, for example, as G. Loesch's book, *Die impressionistische Syntax der Goncourts* (Nuremberg, 1919).
7. Of such a type are the works by the Vosslerians devoted to style: we should mention as especially worthwhile the works of Leo Spitzer on the stylistics of Charles-Louis Philippe, Charles Péguy and Marcel Proust, brought together in his book *Stilstudien* (vol. 2, *Stilsprachen*, 1928).
8. V. V. Vinogradov's book *On Artistic Prose* [O xudožestvennoj proze] (Moscow-Leningrad, 1930) assumes this position.

eral characteristics of poetic language or of the literary language of a particular era all serve to conceal from us the genre itself, with the specific demands it makes upon language and the specific possibilities it opens up for it. As a result, in the majority of these works on the novel, relatively minor stylistic variations— whether individual or characteristic of a particular school—have the effect of completely covering up the major stylistic lines determined by the development of the novel as a unique genre. And all the while discourse in the novel has been living a life that is distinctly its own, a life that is impossible to understand from the point of view of stylistic categories formed on the basis of poetic genres in the narrow sense of that term.

The differences between the novel (and certain forms close to it) and all other genres—*poetic* genres in the narrow sense—are so fundamental, so categorical, that all attempts to impose on the novel the concepts and norms of *poetic* imagery are doomed to fail. Although the novel does contain poetic imagery in the narrow sense (primarily in the author's direct discourse), it is of secondary importance for the novel. What is more, this direct imagery often acquires in the novel quite special functions that are not direct. Here, for example, is how Pushkin characterizes Lensky's poetry [*Evgenij Onegin*, 2. 10, 1–4]:

He sang love, he was obedient to love,
And his song was as clear
As the thoughts of a simple maid,
As an infant's dream, as the moon. . . .[a]

(a development of the final comparison follows).

The poetic images (specifically the metaphoric comparisons) representing Lensky's "song" do not here have any direct poetic significance at all. They cannot be understood as the direct poetic images of Pushkin himself (although formally, of course, the characterization is that of the author). Here Lensky's "song" is characterizing itself, in its own language, in its own poetic manner. Pushkin's direct characterization of Lensky's "song"—which we find as well in the novel—sounds completely different [6. 23, 1]:

Thus he wrote gloomily and *languidly*. . . .

---

a. These lines and the following citations from *Eugene Onegin* are taken from Walter Arndt's translation (New York: Dutton, 1963), slightly modified in places to correspond with Bakhtin's remarks about particular words used.

In the four lines cited by us above it is Lensky's song itself, his voice, his poetic style that sounds, but it is permeated with the parodic and ironic accents of the author; that is the reason why it need not be distinguished from authorial speech by compositional or grammatical means. What we have before us is in fact an *image* of Lensky's song, but not an image in the narrow sense; it is rather a *novelistic* image: the image of another's [*čužoj*] language, in the given instance the image of another's poetic style (sentimental and romantic). The poetic metaphors in these lines ("as an infant's dream," "as the moon" and others) in no way function here as the *primary means of representation* (as they would function in a direct, "serious" song written by Lensky himself); rather they themselves have here become the object of representation, or more precisely of a representation that is parodied and stylized. This novelistic image of another's style (with the direct metaphors that it incorporates) must be taken in *intonational quotation marks* within the system of direct authorial speech (postulated by us here), that is, taken as if the image were parodic and ironic. Were we to discard intonational quotation marks and take the use of metaphors here as the direct means by which the author represents himself, we would in so doing destroy the novelistic image [*obraz*] of another's style, that is, destroy precisely that image that Pushkin, as novelist, constructs here. Lensky's represented poetic speech is very distant from the direct word of the author himself as we have postulated it: Lensky's language functions merely as an *object* of representation (almost as a material thing); the author himself is almost completely outside Lensky's language (it is only his parodic and ironic accents that penetrate this "language of another").

Another example from *Onegin* [1. 46, 1–7]:

He who has lived and thought can never
Look on mankind without disdain;
He who has felt is haunted ever
By days that will not come again;
No more for him enchantment's semblance,
On him the serpent of remembrance
Feeds, and remorse corrodes his heart.

One might think that we had before us a direct poetic maxim of the author himself. But these ensuing lines:

All this is likely to impart
An added charm to conversation

(spoken by the posited author to Onegin) already give an objective coloration to this maxim. Although it is part of authorial speech, it is structured in a realm where Onegin's voice and Onegin's style hold sway. We once again have an example of the novelistic image of another's style. But it is structured somewhat differently. All the images in this excerpt become in turn the object of representation: they are represented as Onegin's style, Onegin's world view. In this respect they are similar to the images in Lensky's song. But unlike Lensky's song these images, being the object of representation, at the same time represent themselves, or more precisely they express the thought of the author, since the author agrees with this maxim to a certain extent, while nevertheless seeing the limitations and insufficiency of the Onegin-Byronic world view and style. Thus the author (that is, the direct authorial word we are postulating) is considerably closer to Onegin's "language" than to the "language" of Lensky: he is no longer merely outside it but in it as well; he not only represents this "language" but to a considerable extent he himself speaks in this "language." The hero is located in a zone of potential conversation with the author, in a zone of *dialogical contact*. The author sees the limitations and insufficiency of the Oneginesque language and world view that was still fashionable in his (the author's) time; he sees its absurd, atomized and artificial face ("A Muscovite in the cloak of a Childe Harold," "A lexicon full of fashionable words," "Is he not really a parody?"); at the same time however the author can express some of his most basic ideas and observations only with the help of this "language," despite the fact that as a system it is a historical dead end. The image of another's language and outlook on the world [*čužoe jazyk-mirovozzrenie*], simultaneously represented *and* representing, is extremely typical of the novel; the greatest novelistic images (for example, the figure of Don Quixote) belong precisely to this type. These descriptive and expressive means that are direct and poetic (in the narrow sense) retain their direct significance when they are incorporated into such a figure, but at the same time they are "qualified" and "externalized," shown as something historically relative, delimited and incomplete—in the novel they, so to speak, criticize themselves.

They both illuminate the world and are themselves illuminated. Just as all there is to know about a man is not exhausted by his situation in life, so all there is to know about the world is not exhausted by a particular discourse about it; every available style is restricted, there are protocols that must be observed.

The author represents Onegin's "language" (a period-bound language associated with a particular world view) as an image that speaks, and that is therefore preconditioned [*ogovorennij govorjaščij*]. Therefore, the author is far from neutral in his relationship to this image: to a certain extent he even polemicizes with this language, argues with it, agrees with it (although with conditions), interrogates it, eavesdrops on it, but also ridicules it, parodically exaggerates it and so forth—in other words, the author is in a dialogical relationship with Onegin's language; the author is actually *conversing* with Onegin, and such a conversation is the fundamental constitutive element of all novelistic style as well as of the controlling image of Onegin's language. The author represents this language, carries on a conversation with it, and the conversation penetrates into the interior of this language-image and dialogizes it from within. And all essentially novelistic images share this quality: they are internally dialogized images—of the languages, styles, world views of another (all of which are inseparable from their concrete linguistic and stylistic embodiment). The reigning theories of poetic imagery are completely powerless to analyze these complex internally dialogized images of whole languages.

Analyzing *Onegin*, it is possible to establish without much trouble that in addition to the images of Onegin's language and Lensky's language there exists yet another complex language-image, a highly profound one, associated with Tatiana. At the heart of this image is a distinctive internally dialogized combination of the language of a "provincial miss"—dreamy, sentimental, Richardsonian—with the folk language of fairy tales and stories from everyday life told to her by her nurse, together with peasant songs, fortune telling and so forth. What is limited, almost comical, old-fashioned in Tatiana's language is combined with the boundless, serious and direct truth of the language of the folk. The author not only represents this language but is also in fact speaking in it. Considerable sections of the novel are presented in Tatiana's voice-zone (this zone, as is the case with zones of all other characters, is not set off from authorial speech in any formally compositional or syntactical way; it is a zone demarcated purely in terms of style).

In addition to the character-zones, which take up a considerable portion of authorial speech in the novel, we also find in

Onegin individual parodic stylizations of the languages associated with various literary schools and genres of the time (such as a parody on the neoclassical epic formulaic opening, parodic epitaphs, etc.). And the author's lyrical digressions themselves are by no means free of parodically stylized or parodically polemicizing elements, which to a certain degree enter into the zones of the characters as well. Thus, from a stylistic point of view, the lyrical digressions in the novel are categorically distinct from the direct lyrics of Pushkin. The former are not lyrics, they are the novelistic image of lyrics (and of the poet as lyricist). As a result, under careful analysis almost the entire novel breaks down into images of languages that are connected to one another and with the author via their own characteristic dialogical relationships. These languages are, in the main, the period-bound, generic and common everyday varieties of the epoch's literary language, a language that is in itself ever evolving and in process of renewal. All these languages, with all the direct expressive means at their disposal, themselves become the object of representation, are presented as images of whole languages, characteristically typical images, highly limited and sometimes almost comical. But at the same time these represented languages themselves do the work of representing to a significant degree. The author participates in the novel (he is omnipresent in it) with *almost no direct language of his own*. The language of the novel is a *system* of languages that mutually and ideologically interanimate each other. It is impossible to describe and analyze it as a single unitary language.

We pause on one more example. Here are four excerpts from different sections of *Onegin*:

(1) Thus a young [*molodoj*] good-for-nothing muses. . . .
 [1. 2, 1]
(2) . . . Our youthful [*mladoj*] singer
 Has gone to his untimely end! . . . [6. 31, 10–11]
(3) I sing of a young [*mladoj*] friend, his checkered
 Career in fortune's cruel coil. [7. 55, 6–7]
(4) What if your pistol-shot has shattered
 The temple of a dear young [*molodoj*] boy. . . .
 [6. 34, 1–2]

We see here in two instances the Church Slavonic form *mladoj* and in two instances the Russian metathesized form *molodoj*. Could it be said that both forms belong to a single authorial language and to a single authorial style, one or the other of them being chosen, say, "for the meter"? Any assertion of the sort would be, of course, barbaric. Certainly it *is* the author speaking in all four instances. But analysis shows us that these forms belong to different stylistic systems of the novel.

The words *"mladoj pevec"* [youthful singer] (the second excerpt) lie in Lensky's zone, are presented in his style, that is, in the somewhat archaicized style of Sentimental Romanticism. The words *"pet'"* [to sing] in the sense of *pisat' stixi* [to write verses] and *"pevec"* [singer] and *"poet"* [poet] are used by Pushkin in Lensky's zone or in other zones that are parodied and objectified (in his own language Pushkin himself says of Lensky: "Thus he wrote. . . ."). The scene of the duel and the "lament" for Lensky ("My friends, you mourn the poet. . . ." [6. 36, 1], etc.) are in large part constructed in Lensky's zone, in his poetic style, but the realistic and soberminded authorial voice is forever breaking in; the orchestration in this section of the novel is rather complex and highly interesting.

The words "I sing of a young friend" (third excerpt) involve a parodic travesty on the formulaic opening of the neoclassical epic. The stylistically crude link-up of the archaic, high word *mladoj* with the low word *prijatel'* [acquaintance, friend] is justified by the requirements of parody and travesty.

The words *molodoj povesa* [young good-for-nothing] and *molodoj prijatel'* [young friend] are located on the plane of direct authorial language, consistent with the spirit of the familiar, conversational style characteristic of the literary language of the era.

Different linguistic and stylistic forms may be said to belong to different systems of languages in the novel. If we were to abolish all the intonational quotation marks, all the divisions into voices and styles, all the various gaps between the represented "languages" and direct authorial discourse, then we would get a conglomeration of *heterogeneous* linguistic and stylistic forms lacking any real sense of style. It is impossible to lay out the languages of the novel on a single plane, to stretch them out along a single line. It is a system of intersecting planes. In *Onegin*, there is scarcely a word that appears as Pushkin's direct word, in the unconditional sense that would for instance be true of his lyrics or romantic poems. Therefore, there is no unitary language or style in the novel. But at the same time there does exist a center of language (a verbal-ideological center) for the novel. The author (as creator of the novelistic whole) cannot be found at any one of the novel's language levels: he is to be found at the center of organization where all levels intersect. The different levels are to varying degrees distant from this authorial center.

Belinsky called Pushkin's novel "an encyclopedia of Russian life." But this is no inert encyclopedia that merely catalogues the things of everyday life. Here Russian life speaks in all its voices, in all the languages and styles of the era. Literary language is not represented in the novel as a unitary, completely finished-off and indisputable language—it is represented precisely as a living mix of varied and opposing voices [*raznorečivost'*], developing and renewing itself. The language of the author strives to overcome the superficial "literariness" of moribund, outmoded styles and fashionable period-bound languages; it strives to renew itself by drawing on the fundamental elements of folk language (which does not mean, however, exploiting the crudely obvious, vulgar contradictions between folk and other languages).

Pushkin's novel is a self-critique of the literary language of the era, a product of this language's various strata (generic, everyday, "currently fashionable") mutually illuminating one another. But this interillumination is not of course accomplished at the level of linguistic abstraction: images of language are inseparable from images of various world views and from the living beings who are their agents—people who think, talk, and act in a setting that is social and historically concrete. From a stylistic point of view we are faced with a complex system of languages of the era being appropriated into one unitary dialogical movement, while at the same time separate "languages" within this system are located at different distances from the unifying artistic and ideological center of the novel.

The stylistic structure of *Evgenij Onegin* is typical of all authentic novels. To a greater or lesser extent, every novel is a dialogized system made up of the images of "languages," styles and consciousnesses that are concrete and inseparable from language. Language in the novel not only represents, but itself serves as the object of representation. Novelistic discourse is always criticizing itself.

In this consists the categorical distinction between the novel and all straightforward genres—the epic poem, the lyric and the drama (strictly conceived). All directly descriptive and expressive means at the disposal of these genres, as well as the genres themselves, become upon entering the novel an object of representation within it. Under conditions of the novel every direct word—

epic, lyric, strictly dramatic—is to a greater or lesser degree made into an object, the word itself becomes a bounded [*ograničennij*] image, one that quite often appears ridiculous in this framed condition.

The basic tasks for a stylistics in the novel are, therefore: the study of specific images of languages and styles; the organization of these images; their typology (for they are extremely diverse); the combination of images of languages within the novelistic whole; the transfers and switchings of languages and voices; their dialogical interrelationships.

The stylistics of direct genres, of the direct poetic word, offer us almost no help in resolving these problems.

We speak of a special novelistic discourse because it is only in the novel that discourse can reveal all its specific potential and achieve its true depth. But the novel is a comparatively recent genre. Indirect discourse, however, the representation of another's word, another's language in intonational quotation marks, was known in the most ancient times; we encounter it in the earliest stages of verbal culture. What is more, long before the appearance of the novel we find a rich world of diverse forms that transmit, mimic and represent from various vantage points another's word, another's speech and language, including also the languages of the direct genres. These diverse forms prepared the ground for the novel long before its actual appearance. Novelistic discourse has a lengthy prehistory, going back centuries, even thousands of years. It was formed and matured in the genres of familiar speech found in conversational folk language (genres that are as yet little studied) and also in certain folkloric and low literary genres. During its germination and early development, the novelistic word reflected a primordial struggle between tribes, peoples, cultures and languages—it is still full of echoes of this ancient struggle. In essence this discourse always developed on the boundary line between cultures and languages. The prehistory of novelistic discourse is of great interest and not without its own special drama.

In the prehistory of novelistic discourse one may observe many extremely heterogeneous factors at work. From our point of view, however, two of these factors prove to be of decisive importance: one of these is *laughter*, the other *polyglossia* [*mnogojazyčie*]. The most ancient forms for representing language were organized by laughter—these were originally nothing more than the ridiculing of another's language and another's direct discourse. Polyglossia and the *interanimation of languages* associated with it elevated these forms to a new artistic and ideological level, which made possible the genre of the novel.

These two factors in the prehistory of novelistic discourse are the subject of the present article.

II

One of the most ancient and widespread forms for representing the direct word of another is *parody*. What is distinctive about parody as a form?

Take, for example, the parodic *sonnets* with which *Don Quixote* begins. Although they are impeccably structured as sonnets, we could never possibly assign them to the sonnet genre. In *Don Quixote* they appear as part of a novel—but even the isolated parodic sonnet (outside the novel) could not be classified generically as a sonnet. In a parodied sonnet, the sonnet form is not a genre at all; that is, it is not the form of a whole but is rather *the object of representation*: the sonnet here is the *hero of the parody*. In a parody on the sonnet, we must first of all recognize a sonnet, recognize its form, its specific style, its manner of seeing, its manner of selecting from and evaluating the world—the world view of the sonnet, as it were. A parody may represent and ridicule these distinctive features of the sonnet well or badly, profoundly or superficially. But in any case, what results is not a sonnet, but rather the *image of a sonnet*.

For the same reasons one could not under any circumstances assign to the genre of "epic poem" the parodic epic "War between the Mice and the Frogs."[b] This is an *image of the Homeric style*. It is precisely style that is the true hero of the work. We would have to say the same of Scarron's *Virgil travesti*.[c] One could like-

---

b. The *Batrachomyomachia*, a still extant parody of Homer thought to have been written about 500 B.C., but with many later interpolations. It is now usually ascribed to Pigres of Halicarnassus (brother-in-law of Mausoleus, whose tomb was one of the seven wonders of the ancient world). The *Margites* (cf. note z) has also been ascribed to Pigres.

c. This work, comprised of seven books (1638–1653), was considered the masterpiece of Paul Scarron (1610–1660) in his day. Scarron is now best remembered for his picaresque novel, *Le Roman comique* (2 vol., 1651–1657, unfinished, 3rd vol. by other hands, 1659).

wise not include the fifteenth-century *sermons joyeux*[d] in the genre of the sermon, or parodic "Pater nosters" or "Ave Marias" in the genre of the prayer and so forth.

All these parodies on genres and generic styles ("languages") enter the great and diverse world of verbal forms that ridicule the straightforward, serious word in all its generic guises. This world is very rich, considerably richer than we are accustomed to believe. The nature and methods available for ridiculing something are highly varied, and not exhausted by parodying and travestying in a strict sense. These methods for making fun of the straightforward word have as yet received little scholarly attention. Our general conceptions of parody and travesty in literature were formed as a scholarly discipline solely by studying very late forms of literary parody, forms of the type represented by Scarron's *Énéide travestie*,[e] or Platen's "Verhängnisvolle Gabel,"[f] that is, the impoverished, superficial and historically least significant forms. These impoverished and limited conceptions of the nature of the parodying and travestying word were then retroactively applied to the supremely rich and varied world of parody and travesty in previous ages.

The importance of parodic-travestying forms in world literature is enormous. Several examples follow that bear witness to their wealth and special significance.

Let us first take up the ancient period. The "literature of erudition" of late antiquity—Aulus Gellius,[g] Plutarch[h] (in his *Mo-*

---

d. These were mock sermons originally given in the churches of medieval France as part of the *Fête des fous*; later they were expelled from the church and became a secular genre in their own right, satires in verse form, often directed against women. The humor consisted in pious passages intermingled with ribaldry.

e. Cf. note c.

f. "Die verhängnissvolle Gabel" (1826), a parody of Romantic "fate tragedies" by August, Graf von Platen-Hallermünde (1796–1835), who was concerned to re-establish classical norms in the face of what he saw as the excesses of the *Stürmer und Dränger* (see his Venetian sonnets [1825]).

g. Aulus Gellius (c. 130–c. 180 A.D.), author of the *Noctes Atticae* in twenty books, a collection of small chapters dealing with a great variety of topics: literary criticism, the law, grammar, history, etc. His Latin is remarkable for its mixture of classical purity and affected archaism.

h. The *Moralia* of Plutarch (translated in fourteen volumes by F. C. Babbitt et al. [1927–1959]) are essays and dialogues on a wide variety of literary, historical and ethical topics, with long sections of quotations from the ancient dramatists.

ralia), Macrobius[i] and, in particular, Athenaeus[j]—provide sufficiently rich data for judging the scope and special character to the parodying and travestying literature of ancient times. The commentaries, citations, references and allusions made by these "erudites" add substantially to the fragmented and random material on the ancient world's literature of laughter that has survived. The works of such literary scholars as Dietrich,[k] Reich,[l] Cornford[m] and others have prepared us for more correct assessment of the role and significance of parodic-travestying forms in the verbal culture of ancient times.

It is our conviction that there never was a single strictly straightforward genre, no single type of direct discourse—artistic, rhetorical, philosophical, religious, ordinary everyday—that did not have its own parodying and travestying double, its own comic-ironic *contre-partie*. What is more, these parodic doubles and laughing reflections of the direct word were, in some cases, just as sanctioned by tradition and just as canonized as their elevated models.

I will deal only very briefly with the problem of the so-called "fourth drama," that is, the satyr play. In most instances this drama, which follows upon the tragic trilogy, developed the same narrative and mythological motifs as had the trilogy that preceded it. It was, therefore, a peculiar type of parodic-travestying *contre-partie* to the myth that had just received a tragic treat-

---

i. Ambrosius Theodosius Macrobius (a figure variously identified with several Macrobii), author of the *Saturnalia*, a symposium presented in the form of a dialogue in seven books, drawing heavily on Aulus Gellius (cf. note g).

j. Atheneus (fl. 200 A.D.), author of *Deipnosophistai* (*Doctors at Dinner*, or as it is sometimes translated, *Experts on Dining*). This is a work of fifteen books filled with all kinds of miscellaneous information on medicine, literature, the law, etc., intermingled with anecdotes and quotations from a large number of other authors, many of whose works are otherwise lost or unknown.

k. A. Dietrich, author of *Pulcinella: Pompeyanische Wandbilder und Römische Satyrspiele* (Leipzig, 1897), a book that played a major role in shaping some of Bakhtin's early ideas about the role of fools in history.

l. Hermann Reich, author of *Der Mimus* (Berlin, 1903), a theoretical attempt to reconstruct the reasons for the mime's importance in ancient Greece.

m. F. M. Cornford (1874–1943), from whose many works Bakhtin here has in mind *The Origin of Attic Comedy* (London, 1914).

ment on the stage; it showed the myth in a different aspect.

These parodic-travestying counter-presentations of lofty national myths were just as sanctioned and canonical as their straightforward tragic manifestations. All the tragedians—Phrynicous,[n] Sophocles, Euripides—were writers of satyr plays as well, and Aeschylus, the most serious and pious of them all, an initiate into the highest Eleusinian Mysteries, was considered by the Greeks to be the greatest master of the satyr play. From fragments of Aeschylus' satyr play *The Bone-Gatherers*[o] we see that this drama gave a parodic, travestying picture of the events and heroes of the Trojan War, and particularly the episode involving Odysseus' quarrel with Achilles and Diomedes, where a stinking chamber pot is thrown at Odysseus' head.

It should be added that the figure of "comic Odysseus," a parodic travesty of his high epic and tragic image, was one of the most popular figures of satyr plays, of ancient Doric farce and pre-Aristophanic comedy, as well as of a whole series of minor comic epics, parodic speeches and disputes in which the comedy of ancient times was so rich (especially in southern Italy and Sicily). Characteristic here is that special role that the motif of madness played in the figure of the "comic Odysseus": Odysseus, as is well known, donned a clown's fool's cap (*pileus*) and harnessed his horse and ox to a plow, pretending to be mad in order to avoid participation in the war. It was the motif of madness that switched the figure of Odysseus from the high and straightforward plane to the comic plane of parody and travesty.[9]

But the most popular figure of the satyr play and other forms of the parodic travestying word was the figure of the "comic Hercules." Hercules, the powerful and simple servant to the cowardly, weak and false king Euristheus; Hercules, who had conquered death in battle and had descended into the nether world; Hercules the monstrous glutton, the playboy, the drunk and

9. Cf. J. Schmidt, *Ulixes comicus.*

n. Phrynicous, one of the originators of Greek tragedy. He was first to introduce the feminine mask, and was greatly admired by Aristophanes. His first victory was in 511 B.C. Some of his titles are *Pleuroniae, Aegyptii, Alcestis, Acteon;* he wrote several other plays as well.

o. The *Ostologoi* may have been part of a tetralogy with *Penelope,* deriving its title from the hungry beggars in the palace at Ithaca who collected bones hurled at them by the suitors.

scrapper, but especially Hercules the madman—such were the motifs that lent a comic aspect to his image. In this comic aspect, heroism and strength are retained, but they are combined with laughter and with images from the material life of the body.

The figure of the comic Hercules was extremely popular, not only in Greece but also in Rome, and later in Byzantium (where it became one of the central figures in the marionette theater). Until quite recently this figure lived on in the Turkish game of "shadow puppets." The comic Hercules is one of the most profound folk images for a cheerful and simple heroism, and had an enormous influence on all of world literature.

When taken together with such figures as the "comic Odysseus" and the "comic Hercules," the "fourth drama," which was an *indispensable* conclusion to the tragic trilogy, indicates that the literary consciousness of the Greeks did not view the parodic-travestying reworkings of national myth as any particular profanation or blasphemy. It is characteristic that the Greeks were not at all embarrassed to attribute the authorship of the parodic work "War between the Mice and the Frogs" to Homer himself. Homer is also credited with a comic work (a long poem) about the fool *Margit*. For any and every straightforward genre, any and every direct discourse—epic, tragic, lyric, philosophical—may and indeed must itself become the object of representation, the object of a parodic travestying "mimicry." It is as if such mimicry rips the word away from its object, disunifies the two, shows that a given straightforward generic word—epic or tragic—is one-sided, bounded, incapable of exhausting the object; the process of parodying forces us to experience those sides of the object that are not otherwise included in a given genre or a given style. Parodic-travestying literature introduces the permanent corrective of laughter, of a critique on the one-sided seriousness of the lofty direct word, the corrective of reality that is always richer, more fundamental and most importantly *too contradictory and heteroglot* to be fit into a high and straightforward genre. The high genres are monotonic, while the "fourth drama" and genres akin to it retain the ancient binary tone of the word. Ancient parody was free of any nihilistic denial. It was not, after all, the heroes who were parodied, nor the Trojan War and its participants; what was parodied was only its epic heroization; not Hercules and his exploits but their tragic heroization. The genre itself, the style, the language are all put in cheerfully irreverent quotation marks, and they are perceived against a backdrop of a contradictory reality that cannot be confined within their narrow frames. The direct and serious word was revealed, in all its limitations and insufficiency, only after it had become the laughing image of that word—but it was by no means discredited in the process. Thus it did not bother the Greeks to think that Homer himself wrote a parody of Homeric style.

Evidence from Roman literature casts additional light on the problem of the "fourth drama." In Rome its functions were filled by the Atellan literary farces. When, beginning with the period of Sulla, the Atellan farces were reworked for literature and fixed in texts, they were staged after the tragedy, during the exodium.[p] Thus the Atellan farces[q] of Pomponius[r] and Novius[s] were performed after the tragedies of Accius.[t] The strictest correspondence was observed between the Atellan farces and the tragedies. The insistence upon a single source for both the serious and the comic material was more strict and sustained in Rome than had been the case in Greece. At a later date, the Atellan farces that had been performed during the tragedic exodium were replaced by mimes: apparently they also travestied the material of the preceding tragedy.

The attempt to accompany every tragic (or serious) treatment of material with a parallel comic (parodic-travestying) treatment also found its reflection in the graphic arts of the Romans. In the so-called "consular diptychs," comic scenes in grotesque masks were usually depicted on the left, while on the right were found tragic scenes. An analogous counterposing of scenes can also be

---

p. The exodium was, in Greek drama, the end or catastrophe of a play, but is used here by Bakhtin as it applied in Roman plays, where the word means a comic interlude or farce following something more serious. Its function is comparable with the satyr play in Athenian tetralogies. (Not to be confused with *exodos*, the portion near the end of Greek plays where the chorus leaves the stage.)

q. First-century B.C. farces that emphasized crude physiological details and bawdy jokes.

r. Lucius Pomponius of Bononia (fl. 100–85 B.C.), author of at least seventy Atellan farces.

s. Novius (fl. 95–80 B.C.), younger contemporary of Pomponius, and author of forty-three farces.

t. Lucius Accius (170–90 B.C.), historian of literature, but cited here by Bakhtin because he was generally regarded as the last real tragedian of Rome.

observed in the mural paintings in Pompeii. Dieterich, who made use of the Pompeiian paintings to unlock the secret of ancient comic forms, describes, for example, two frescoes arranged facing each other: on the one we see Andromeda being rescued by Perseus, on the opposite wall is a picture of a naked woman bathing in a pond with a serpent wrapped around her; peasants are trying to come to her aid with sticks and stones.[10] This is an obvious parodic travesty of the first mythological scene. The plot of the myth is relocated in a specifically prosaic reality; Perseus himself is replaced by peasants with rude weapons (compare the knightly world of Don Quixote translated into Sancho's language).

From a whole series of sources, and particularly from the fourteenth book of Atheneus, we know of the existence of an enormous world of highly heterogeneous parodic-travestying forms; we know, for instance, of the performances of phallophors[u] and deikelists[v] [mimers] who on the one hand travestied national and local myths and on the other mimicked the characteristically typical "languages" and speech mannerisms of foreign doctors, procurers, hetaerae, peasants, slaves and so forth. The parodic-travestying literature of southern Italy was especially rich and varied. Comic parodic plays and riddles flourished there, as did parodies of the speeches of scholars and judges, and forms of parodic and agonic dialogues, one of whose variants became a structural component of Greek comedy. Here the word lived an utterly different life from that which it lived in the high, straightforward genres of Greece.

It is worth remembering that the most primitive mime, that is, a wandering actor of the most banal sort, always had to possess, as a professional minimum, two skills: the ability to imitate the voices of birds and animals, and the ability to mimic the speech, facial expressions and gesticulation of a slave, a peasant, a procurer, a scholastic pedant and a foreigner. To this very day this is

10. Cf. A. Dieterich, *Pulcinella: Pompeyanische Wandbilder und römische Satyrspiele* (Leipzig, 1897), p. 131.

---

u. Phallophors, "phallus bearers," the figures who carried carved *phalloi* in religious processions and whose role was to joke and cavort obscenely.

v. Deikelists, from the Greek *deikeliktas*, simply "one who represents," but according to Athenaeus (cf. note j), in book 14 of the *Deipnosophistai*, they were actors who specialized in burlesque parts.

still the stock-in-trade for the farcical actor-impersonators at annual fairs.

The culture of laughter was no less rich and diverse in the Roman world than it had been in the Greek. Especially characteristic for Rome was the stubborn vitality of ritualistic ridicule. Everyone is familiar with the soldiers' sanctioned ritualistic ridicule of the commander returning in triumph, or the ritualistic laughter at Roman funerals and the license granted the laughter of the mime; there is no need to expand further on the Saturnalia. What is important for us here is not the ritual roots of this laughter, but rather the literature it produced, and the role played by Roman laughter in the ultimate destinies of discourse. Laughter proved to be just as profoundly productive and deathless a creation of Rome as Roman law. This laughter broke through the grim atmosphere of seriousness of the Middle Ages to fertilize the great creations of Renaissance literature; up to this day it continues to resonate in many aspects of European literature.

The literary and artistic consciousness of the Romans could not imagine a serious form without its comic equivalent. The serious, straightforward form was perceived as only a fragment, only half of a whole; the fullness of the whole was achieved only upon adding the comic *contre-partie* of this form. Everything serious had to have, and indeed did have, its comic double. As in the Saturnalia the clown was the double of the ruler and the slave the double of the master, so such comic doubles were created in all forms of culture and literature. For this reason Roman literature, and especially the low literature of the folk, created an immense number of parodic-travestying forms: they provided the matter for mimes, satires, epigrams, table talk, rhetorical genres, letters, various types of low comic folk art. It was oral tradition preeminently that transmitted many of these forms to the Middle Ages, transmitting as well the very style and logic of Roman parody, a logic that was bold and consistent. It was Rome that taught European culture how to laugh and ridicule. But of the rich heritage of laughter that was part of the written tradition of Rome only a miniscule quantity has survived: those upon whom the transmission of this heritage depended were agelasts[w] who elected the se-

---

w. Agelasts, from the Greek "without-laughter," is an example of Bakhtin's often rarified vocabulary. The word implies grim ideologues.

rious word and rejected its comic reflections as a profanation (as happened, for example, with the numerous parodies on Virgil).

Thus we see that alongside the great and significant models of straightforward genres and direct discourses, discourses with no conditions attached, there was created in ancient times a rich world of the most varied forms and variations of parodic-travesty-ing, indirect, conditional discourse. Of course our term "parodic-travestying discourse" far from expresses the full richness of types, variants and nuances of the laughing word. But the question arises: what unifies all these diverse forms of laughter, and what relationship do they bear to the novel?

Some forms of parodic-travestying literature issue directly from the form of the genres being parodied—parodic poems, tragedies (Lucian's *Tragopodagra*[x] ["Gout-Tragedy"], for example), parodic judicial speeches and so forth. This is a parody and travesty in the narrow sense of the word. In other cases we find special forms of parody constituted as genres—satyr-drama, improvised comedy, satire, plotless dialogue [*bessjužetnyj dialog*] and others. As we have said above, parodied genres do not belong to the genres that they parody; that is, a parodic poem is not a poem at all. But the particular genres of the parodic-travestying word of the sort we have enumerated here are unstable, compositionally still un-shaped, lacking a firm or definite generic skeleton. It can be said, then, that in ancient times the parodic-travestying word was (generically speaking) homeless. All these diverse parodic-trav-estying forms constituted, as it were, a special extra-generic or inter-generic world. But this world was unified, first of all, by a common purpose: to provide the corrective of laughter and crit-icism to all existing straightforward genres, languages, styles, voices; to force men to experience beneath these categories a dif-ferent and contradictory reality that is otherwise not captured in them. Such laughter paved the way for the impiety of the novelis-tic form. In the second place, all these forms are unified by virtue of their shared subject: language itself, which everywhere serves as a means of direct expression, becomes in this new context the image of language, the image of the direct word. Consequently this extra-generic or inter-generic world is internally unified and even appears as its own kind of totality. Each separate element in

x. Cf. note z.

it—parodic dialogue, scenes from everyday life, bucolic humor, etc.—is presented as if it were a fragment of some kind of unified whole. I imagine this whole to be something like an immense novel, multi-generic, multi-styled, mercilessly critical, soberly mocking, reflecting in all its fullness the heteroglossia and multiple voices of a given culture, people and epoch. In this huge novel—in this mirror of constantly evolving heteroglossia—any direct word and especially that of the dominant discourse is reflected as something more or less bounded, typical and characteristic of a particular era, aging, dying, ripe for change and renewal. And in actual fact, out of this huge complex of parodically reflected words and voices the ground was being prepared in ancient times for the rise of the novel, a genre formed of many styles and many images. But the novel could not *at that time* gather unto itself and make use of all the material that language images had made available. I have in mind here the "Greek romance," and Apuleius and Petronius. The ancient world was apparently not capable of going further than these.

These parodic-travestying forms prepared the ground for the novel in one very important, in fact decisive, respect. They liberated the object from the power of language in which it had become entangled as if in a net; they destroyed the homogenizing power of myth over language; they freed consciousness from the power of the direct word, destroyed the thick walls that had imprisoned consciousness within its own discourse, within its own language. A distance arose between language and reality that was to prove an indispensable condition for authentically realistic forms of discourse.

Linguistic consciousness—parodying the direct word, direct style, exploring its limits, its absurd sides, the face specific to an era—constituted itself *outside* this direct word and outside all its graphic and expressive means of representation. A new mode developed for working creatively with language: the creating artist began to look at language from the outside, with another's eyes, from the point of view of a potentially different language and style. It is, after all, precisely in the light of another potential language or style that a given straightforward style is parodied, travestied, ridiculed. The creating consciousness stands, as it were, on the boundary line between languages and styles. This is, for the creating consciousness, a highly peculiar position to find itself in with regard to language. The aedile or rhapsode experienced himself in his own language, in his own discourse, in an utterly different way from the creator of "War between the Mice and the Frogs," or the creators of *Margites*.[y]

One who creates a direct word—whether epic, tragic or lyric—deals only with the subject whose praises he sings, or represents, or expresses, and he does so in his own language that is perceived as the sole and fully adequate tool for realizing the word's direct, objectivized meaning. This meaning and the objects and themes that compose it are inseparable from the straightforward language of the person who creates it: the objects and themes are born and grow to maturity in this language, and in the national myth and national tradition that permeate this language. The position and tendency of the parodic-travestying consciousness is, however, completely different: it, too, is oriented toward the object—but toward another's word as well, a parodied word *about* the object that in the process becomes *itself* an image. Thus is created that distance between language and reality we mentioned earlier. Language is transformed from the absolute dogma it had been within the narrow framework of a sealed-off and impermeable monoglossia into a working hypothesis for comprehending and expressing reality.

But such a full and complete transformation can occur only under certain conditions, namely, under the condition of thoroughgoing *polyglossia*. Only polyglossia fully frees consciousness from the tyranny of its own language and its own myth of language. Parodic-travestying forms flourish under these conditions, and only in this milieu are they capable of being elevated to completely new ideological heights.

Roman literary consciousness was bilingual. The purely national Latin genres, conceived under monoglotic conditions, fell into decay and did not achieve the level of literary expression. From start to finish, the creative literary consciousness of the Romans functioned against the background of the Greek language and Greek forms. From its very first steps, the Latin literary word viewed itself in the light of the Greek word, *through the eyes of* the Greek word; it was from the very beginning a word "with a sideways glance," a stylized word enclosing itself, as it were, in its own piously stylized quotation marks.

---

y. An early satirical epic, traditionally ascribed to Homer, but to Pigres as well (cf. note c).

Latin literary language in all its generic diversity was created in the light of Greek literary language. Its national distinctiveness and the specific verbal thought process inherent in it were realized in creative literary consciousness in a way that would have been absolutely impossible under conditions of monoglossia. After all, it is possible to objectivize one's own particular language, its internal form, the peculiarities of its world view, its specific linguistic habitus, only in the light of another language belonging to someone else, which is almost as much "one's own" as one's native language.

In his book on Plato, Wilamowitz-Moellendorff writes: "Only knowledge of a language that possesses another mode of conceiving the world can lead to the appropriate knowledge of one's own language. . . ."[11] I do not continue the quotation, for it primarily concerns the problem of understanding one's own language in purely cognitive linguistic terms, an understanding that is realized only in the light of a different language, one not one's own; but this situation is no less pervasive where the literary imagination is conceiving language in actual artistic practice. Moreover, in the process of literary creation, languages interanimate each other and objectify precisely that side of one's own (and of the other's) language *that pertains to its world view*, its inner form, the axiologically accentuated system inherent in it. For the creating literary consciousness, existing in a field illuminated by another's language, it is not the phonetic system of its own language that stands out, nor is it the distinctive features of its own morphology nor its own abstract lexicon—what stands out is precisely that which makes language concrete and which makes its world view ultimately untranslatable, that is, precisely the *style of the language as a totality*.

For a creative, literary bilingual consciousness (and such was the consciousness of the literary Roman) language taken as a whole, that is, able to comprehend the language *I* call *my* own [*svoj-rodnoj*] as well as the language that someone else calls *his* own [*svoj-čužoj*]—was a concrete *style*, but not an abstract linguistic system. It was extremely characteristic for the literary Roman to perceive all of language, from top to bottom, as style—a conception of language that is somewhat cold and "exteriorizing." Speaking as well as writing, the Roman *stylized*, and not

11. U. Wilamowitz-Moellendorff, *Platon*, vol. 1 (Berlin, 1920), p. 290.

without a certain cold sense of alienation from his own language. For this reason the objective and expressive *directness* of the Latin literary word was always somewhat conventionalized (as indeed is every sort of stylization). An element of stylizing is inherent in all the major straightforward genres of Roman literature; it is even present in such a great Roman creation as the *Aeneid.*

But we have to do here not only with the cultural *bi*lingualism of literary Rome. Roman literature at the outset was characterized by *tri*lingualism. "Three souls" lived in the breast of Ennius. But three souls—three language-cultures—lived in the breast of all the initiators of Roman literary discourse, all the translator-stylizers who had come to Rome from lower Italy, where the boundaries of three languages and cultures intersected with one another—Greek, Oscan and Roman. Lower Italy was the home of a specific kind of hybrid culture and hybrid literary forms. The rise of Roman literature is connected in a fundamental way with this trilingual cultural home; this literature was born in the interanimation of three languages—one that was indigenously its own, and two that were other but that were *experienced* as indigenous.

From the point of view of polyglossia, Rome was merely the concluding phase of Hellenism, a phase whose final gesture was to carry over into the barbarian world of Europe a radical polyglossia, and thus make possible the creation of a new type of medieval polyglossia.

For all the barbarian peoples who came in contact with it, Hellenism provided a powerful and illuminating model of other-languagedness. This model played a fateful role in national, straightforward forms of artistic discourse. It overwhelmed almost all of the tender shoots of national epic and lyric, born in an environment muffled by a dense monoglossia; it turned the direct word of barbarian peoples—their epic and lyric word—into a discourse that was somewhat conventional, somewhat stylized. And this greatly facilitated the development of all forms of parodic-travestying discourse. On Hellenistic and Helleno-Roman soil there became possible a maximal distance between the speaker (the creating artist) and his language, as well as a maximal distance between language itself and the world of themes and objects. Only under such conditions could Roman laughter have developed so powerfully.

A complex polyglossia was, as we have seen, characteristic of Hellenism. But the Orient, which was itself always a place of many languages and many cultures, crisscrossed with the intersecting boundary lines of ancient cultures and languages, was anything but a naive monoglotic world, passive in its relationship to Greek culture. The Orient was itself bearer of an ancient and complex polyglossia. Scattered throughout the entire Hellenistic world were centers, cities, settlements where several cultures and languages directly cohabited, interweaving with one another in distinctive patterns. Such, for instance, was Samosata, Lucian's[z] native city, which has played such an immense role in the history of the European novel. The original inhabitants of Samosata were Syrians who spoke Aramaic. The entire literary and educated upper classes of the urban population spoke and wrote in Greek. The official language of the administration and chancellery was Latin, all the administrators were Romans, and there was a Roman legion stationed in the city. A great thoroughfare passed through Samosata (strategically very important) along which flowed the languages of Mesopotamia, Persia and even India. Lucian's cultural and linguistic consciousness was born and shaped at this point of intersection of cultures and languages. The cultural and linguistic environment of the African Apuleius and of the writers of Greek novels—who were for the most part Hellenized barbarians—is analogous to Lucian's.

In his book on the history of the Greek novel,[12] Erwin Rohde analyzes the dissolution of the Greek national myth on Hellenistic soil, and the concomitant decline and diminution of the epic and drama forms—forms that can be sustained only on the basis of a unitary national myth that perceives itself as a totality. Rohde does not have much to say on the role of polyglossia. For him, the Greek novel was solely a product of the decay of the major straightforward genres. In part this is true: everything new is born out of the death of something old. But Rohde was no dialec-

12. Cf. Erwin Rohde, *Der griechische Roman und seine Vorläufer* (n.p., 1896).

---

z. Lucian (c. 120–180 A.D.), greatest of all the second-century Sophists, is one of Bakhtin's favorites. Lucian is the author of some 130 works, most of them dialogues that hold up to ridicule the pretensions of his age, such as the *Lexiphanes*, an attack on the stilted Atticists who larded their works with polysyllabic, obsolete words.

tician. It was precisely what was new in all this that he failed to see.[aa] He did define, more or less correctly, the significance of a unitary and totalizing national myth for the creation of the major forms of Greek epic, lyric and drama. But the disintegration of this national myth, which was so fatal for the straightforward monoglotic genres of Hellenism, proved productive for the birth and development of a new prosaic, novelistic discourse. The role of polyglossia in this slow death of the myth and the birth of novelistic matter-of-factness is extremely great. Where languages and cultures interanimated each other, language became something entirely different, its very nature changed: in place of a single, unitary sealed-off Ptolemaic world of language, there appeared the open Galilean world of many languages, mutually animating each other.

Unfortunately the Greek novel only weakly embodied this new discourse that resulted from polyglot consciousness. In essence this novel-type resolved only the problem of plot, and even that only partially. What was created was a new and large multi-genred genre, one which included in itself various types of dialogues, lyrical songs, letters, speeches, descriptions of countries and cities, short stories and so forth. It was an encyclopedia of genres. But this multi-generic novel was almost exclusively cast in a single style. Discourse was partially conventionalized, stylized. The stylizing attitude toward language, characteristic of all forms of polyglossia, found its paradigmatic expression in such novels. But semiparodic, travestying and ironic forms were present in them as well; there were probably many more such forms than literary scholars admit. The boundaries between semi-stylized and semiparodic discourse were very unstable: after all, one need only emphasize ever so slightly the conventionality in stylized discourse for it to take on a light overtone of parody or irony, a sense that words have "conditions attached to them": it is not, strictly speaking, *I* who speak; I, perhaps, would speak quite differently. But images of languages that are capable of reflecting

---

aa. Compare Mandelstam's insight: "Just as there are two geometries, Euclid's and Lobachevsky's, there may be two histories of literature, written in different keys: one that speaks only of acquisitions, another only of losses, and both would be speaking of one and the same thing" ("About the Nature of the Word," in *Osip Mandelstam: Selected Essays*, tr. Sidney Monas, [Austin, Tx., 1977], p. 67).

in a polyglot manner speakers of the era are almost entirely absent in the Greek novel. In this respect certain varieties of Hellenistic and Roman satire are incomparably more "novelistic" than the Greek novel.

At this point it becomes necessary to broaden the concept of polyglossia somewhat. We have been speaking so far of the interanimation of major national languages (Greek, Latin), each of which was in itself already *fully formed* and *unitary*, languages that had already passed through a lengthy phase of comparatively stable and peaceful monoglossia. But we saw that the Greeks, even in their classical period, had at their disposal a very rich world of parodic-travestying forms. It is hardly likely that such a wealth of images of language would arise under conditions of a deaf, sealed-off monoglossia.

It must not be forgotten that monoglossia is always in essence relative. After all, one's own language is never a single language: in it there are always survivals of the past and a potential for other-languagedness that is more or less sharply perceived by the working literary and language consciousness.

Contemporary scholarship has accumulated a mass of facts that testify to the intense struggle that goes on between languages and within languages, a struggle that preceded the relatively stable condition of Greek as we know it. A significant number of Greek roots belong to the language of the people who had settled the territory before the Greeks. In the Greek literary language we encounter behind each separate genre the consolidation of a particular dialect. Behind these gross facts a complex trial-at-arms is concealed, a struggle between languages and dialects, between hybridizations, purifications, shifts and renovations, the long and twisted path of struggle for the unity of a literary language and for the unity of its system of genres. This was followed by a lengthy period of relative stabilization. But the memory of these past linguistic disturbances was retained, not only as congealed traces in language but also in literary and stylistic figuration—and preeminently in the parodying and travestying verbal forms.

In the historical period of ancient Greek life—a period that was, linguistically speaking, stable and monoglotic—all plots, all subject and thematic material, the entire basic stock of images, expressions and intonations, arose from within the very heart of the native language. Everything that entered from outside (and that was a great deal) was assimilated in a powerful and confident environment of closed-off monoglossia, one that viewed the polyglossia of the barbarian world with contempt. Out of the heart of this confident and uncontested monoglossia were born the major straightforward genres of the ancient Greeks—their epic, lyric and tragedy. These genres express the centralizing tendencies in language. But alongside these genres, especially among the folk, there flourished parodic and travestying forms that kept alive the memory of the ancient linguistic struggle and that were continually nourished by the ongoing process of linguistic stratification and differentiation.

Closely connected with the problem of polyglossia and inseparable from it is the problem of heteroglossia *within* a language, that is, the problem of internal differentiation, the stratification characteristic of any national language. This problem is of primary importance for understanding the style and historical destinies of the modern European novel, that is, the novel since the seventeenth century. This latecomer reflects, in its stylistic structure, the struggle between two tendencies in the languages of European peoples: one a centralizing (unifying) tendency, the other a decentralizing tendency (that is, one that stratifies languages). The novel senses itself on the border between the completed, dominant literary language and the extraliterary languages that know heteroglossia; the novel either serves to further the centralizing tendencies of a new literary language in the process of taking shape (with its grammatical, stylistic and ideological norms), or—on the contrary—the novel fights for the renovation of an antiquated literary language, in the interests of those strata of the national language that have remained (to a greater or lesser degree) outside the centralizing and unifying influence of the artistic and ideological norm established by the dominant literary language. The literary-artistic consciousness of the modern novel, sensing itself on the border between two languages, one literary, the other extraliterary, each of which now knows heteroglossia, also senses itself on the border of time: it is extraordinarily sensitive to time in language, it senses time's shifts, the aging and renewing of language, the past and the future—and all in language.

Of course all these processes of shift and renewal of the national language that are reflected *by* the novel do not bear an abstract linguistic character *in* the novel: they are inseparable from social and ideological struggle, from processes of evolution and of the renewal of society and the folk.

The speech diversity within language thus has primary importance for the novel. But this speech diversity achieves its full creative consciousness only under conditions of an active polyglossia. Two myths perish simultaneously: the myth of a language that presumes to be the only language, and the myth of a language that presumes to be completely unified. Therefore even the modern European novel, reflecting intra-language heteroglossia as well as processes of aging and renewal of the literary language and its generic types, was prepared for by the polyglossia of the Middle Ages—which was experienced by all European peoples— and by that intense interanimation of languages that took place during the Renaissance, during that shifting away from an ideological language (Latin) and the move of European peoples toward the critical monoglossia characteristic of modern times.

III

The laughing, parodic-travestying literature of the Middle Ages was extremely rich. In the wealth and variety of its parodic forms, the Middle Ages was akin to Rome. It must in fact be said that in a whole series of ways the medieval literature of laughter appears to be the direct heir to Rome, and the Saturnalian tradition in particular continued to live in altered form throughout the Middle Ages. The Rome of the Saturnalia, crowned with a fool's cap— "pileata Roma" (Martial)[bb]—successfully retained its force and its fascination, even during the very darkest days of the Middle Ages. But the original products of laughter among the European peoples, which grew out of local folklore, were also important.

One of the more interesting stylistic problems during the Hellenistic period was the problem of quotation. The forms of direct, half-hidden and completely hidden quoting were endlessly varied, as were the forms for framing quotations by a context, forms of intonational quotation marks, varying degrees of alienation or assimilation of another's quoted word. And here the prob-

---

bb. Martial (Marcus Valerius Martialis), famous for his epigrams, many of which contain vivid, almost novelistic details of everyday life in Rome (i.e., sausage vendors, wounded slaves, etc.).

lem frequently arises: is the author quoting with reverence or on the contrary with irony, with a smirk? Double entendre as regards the other's word was often deliberate.

The relationship to another's word was equally complex and ambiguous in the Middle Ages. The role of the other's word was enormous at that time: there were quotations that were openly and reverently emphasized as such, or that were half-hidden, completely hidden, half-conscious, unconscious, correct, intentionally distorted, unintentionally distorted, deliberately reinterpreted and so forth. The boundary lines between someone else's speech and one's own speech were flexible, ambiguous, often deliberately distorted and confused. Certain types of texts were constructed like mosaics out of the texts of others. The so-called *cento*[cc] (a specific genre) was, for instance, composed exclusively out of others' verse-lines and hemistichs. One of the best authorities on medieval parody, Paul Lehmann, states outright that the history of medieval literature and its Latin literature in particular "is the history of the appropriation, re-working and imitation of someone else's property" ["eine Geschichte der Aufnahme, Verarbeitung und Nachahmung fremden Gutes"][13]— or as we would say, of another's language, another's style, another's word.

The primary instance of appropriating another's discourse and language was the use made of the authoritative and sanctified word of the Bible, the Gospel, the Apostles, the fathers and doctors of the church. This word continually infiltrates the context of medieval literature and the speech of educated men (clerics). But how does this infiltration occur, how does the receiving context relate to it, in what sort of intonational quotation marks is it enclosed? Here a whole spectrum of possible relationships toward this word comes to light, beginning at one pole with the pious and inert quotation that is isolated and set off like an icon, and ending at the other pole with the most ambiguous, disrespectful, parodic-travestying use of a quotation. The transitions

13. Cf. Paul Lehmann, *Die Parodie im Mittelalter* (Munich, 1922), p. 10.

cc. *Cento* (Latin, "patchwork"), a poetic compilation made up of passages selected from the work of great poets of the past. A recent example of what a *cento* might be is provided by Andrew Field's collection of writings by modern Russian critics: *The Complection of Russian Literature: A Cento* (London, 1971).

between various nuances on this spectrum are to such an extent flexible, vacillating and ambiguous that it is often difficult to decide whether we are confronting a reverent use of a sacred word or a more familiar, even parodic playing with it; if the latter, then it is often difficult to determine the degree of license permitted in that play.

At the very dawning of the Middle Ages there appeared a whole series of remarkable parodic works. Among them is the well-known *Cena Cypriani* or *Cyprian Feasts,*[dd] a fascinating gothic symposium. But how was it constituted? The entire Bible, the entire Gospel was as it were cut up into little scraps, and these scraps were then arranged in such a way that a picture emerged of a grand feast at which all the personages of sacred history from Adam and Eve to Christ and his Apostles eat, drink and make merry. In this work a correspondence of all details to Sacred Writ is strictly and precisely observed, but at the same time the entire Sacred Writ is transformed into carnival, or more correctly into Saturnalia. This is "pileata Biblia."

But what purpose motivates the author of this work? What was his attitude toward Holy Writ? Scholars answer this question in various ways. All are agreed, of course, that some sort of play with the sacred word figures in here, but the degree of license enjoyed by this play and its larger sense are evaluated in different ways. There are those scholars who insist that the purpose of such play is innocent, that is, purely mnemonic: to teach through play. In order to help those believers (who had not long before been pagans) better remember the figures and events of Sacred Writ, the author of the *Feasts* wove out of them the mnemonic

---

dd. The *Cena* seem to have been composed to be recited at table, following the advice given by Bishop Zeno of Verona (in his tract *ad neophytos post baptisma*) that instruction be provided in this pleasant way. The work is a narrative concerning the marriage feast of King Johel at Cana of Galilee. All kinds of persons from both the Old and the New Testament are invited. The work was popular enough to be set to verse during the Carolingian Revival by John the Deacon, a contemporary of Charles the Bald. The verse redaction was intended to amuse Pope John VIII, to whom it is dedicated. F. J. E. Raby, the great expert on medieval Latin, says somewhat sententiously of this version that, "while puerile in itself, it might serve the purpose of instruction, if it did not rather move those who heard it recited to unseemly laughter" (*A History of Secular Latin Poetry in the Middle Ages*, 2 vols. [Oxford, 1934], vol. 1, p. 220).

pattern of a banquet. Other scholars see the *Feasts* as straightforward blasphemous parody.

We mention these scholarly opinions only as an example. They testify to the complexity and ambiguity of the medieval treatment of the sacred word as another's word. *Cyprian Feasts* is not, of course, a mnemonic device. It is parody, and more precisely a parodic travesty. But one must not transfer contemporary concepts of parodic discourse onto medieval parody (as one also must not do with ancient parody)[In modern times the functions of parody are narrow and unproductive. Parody has grown sickly, its place in modern literature is insignificant.]We live, write and speak today in a world of free and democratized language; the complex and multi-leveled hierarchy of discourses, forms, images, styles that used to permeate the entire system of official language and linguistic consciousness was swept away by the linguistic revolutions of the Renaissance. European *literary* languages—French, German, English—came into being while this hierarchy was in the process of being destroyed, and while the laughing, travestying genres of the late Middle Ages and Renaissance—novellas, Mardi Gras, *soties*, farces and finally novels— were in the process of shaping these languages. The language of French literary prose was created by Calvin and Rabelais—but Calvin's language, the language of the middle classes ("of shopkeepers and tradesmen") was an intentional and conscious lowering of, almost a travesty on, the sacred language of the Bible. The middle strata of national languages, while being transformed into the language of the higher ideological spheres and into the language of Sacred Writ, were perceived as a denigrating travesty of these higher spheres. For this reason these new languages provided only very modest space for parody: these languages hardly knew, and now do not know at all, sacred words, since they themselves were to a significant extent born out of a parody of the sacred word.

However, in the Middle Ages the role of parody was extremely important: it paved the way for a new literary and linguistic consciousness, as well as for the great Renaissance novel.

Cyprian Feasts is an ancient and excellent example of medieval "parodia sacra," that is, sacred parody—or to be more accurate, parody on sacred texts and rituals. Its roots go deep into ancient ritualistic parody, ritual degrading and the ridiculing of higher powers. But these roots are distant; the ancient ritualistic element in them has been re-interpreted; parody now fulfills the new and highly important functions of which we spoke above.

We must first of all take into account the recognized and legalized freedom then enjoyed by parody. The Middle Ages, with varying degrees of qualification, respected the freedom of the fool's cap and allotted a rather broad license to laughter and the laughing word. This freedom was bounded primarily by feast days and school festivals. Medieval laughter is holiday laughter. The parodic-travestying "Holiday of Fools"[ee] and "Holiday of the Ass" are well known, and were even celebrated in the churches themselves by the lower clergy. Highly characteristic of this tendency is *risus paschalis*, or paschal laughter. During the paschal days laughter was traditionally permitted in church. The preacher permitted himself risqué jokes and gay-hearted anecdotes from the church pulpit in order to encourage laughter in the congregation—this was conceived as a cheerful rebirth after days of melancholy and fasting. No less productive was "Christmas laughter" (*risus natalis*); as distinct from *risus paschalis* it expressed itself not in stories but in songs. Serious church hymns were sung to the tunes of street ditties and were thus given a new twist. In addition a huge store of special Christmas carols existed in which reverent nativity themes were interwoven with folk motifs on the cheerful death of the old and the birth of the new. Parodic-travestying ridicule of the old often became dominant in these songs, especially in France, where the "Noël," or Christmas carol, became one of the most popular generic sources for the revolutionary street song (we recall Pushkin's "Noël," with its parodic-travestying use of the nativity theme). To holiday laughter, almost everything was permitted.

Equally broad were the rights and liberties enjoyed by the school festivals, which played a large role in the cultural and literary life of the Middle Ages. Works created for these festivals were predominantly parodies and travesties. The medieval monastic pupil (and in later times the university student) ridiculed with a clear conscience during the festival everything that had been the subject of reverent studies during the course of the year—every-

---

ee. Reference here is to the *festa stultorum*, a form of *ludus* in which everything is reversed, even clothing: trousers were worn on the head, for instance, an operation that symbolically reflects in some measure the jongleurs, who are depicted in miniatures head-downward.

thing from Sacred Writ to his school grammar. The Middle Ages produced a whole series of variants on the parodic-travestying Latin grammar. Case inflection, verbal forms and all grammatical categories in general were reinterpreted either in an indecent, erotic context, in a context of eating and drunkenness or in a context ridiculing church and monastic principles of hierarchy and subordination. Heading this unique grammatical tradition is the seventh-century work of Virgilius Maro Grammaticus.^{ff} This is an extraordinarily learned work, stuffed with an incredible quantity of references, quotations from all possible authorities of the ancient world including some that had never existed; in a number of cases even the quotations themselves are parodic. Interwoven with serious and rather subtle grammatical analysis is a sharp parodic exaggeration of this very subtlety, and of the scrupulousness of scholarly analyses; there is a description, for example, of a scholarly discussion lasting two weeks on the question of the vocative case of *ego*, that is, the vocative case of "I." Taken as a whole, Virgilius Grammaticus' work is a magnificent and subtle parody of the formalistic-grammatical thinking of late antiquity. It is grammatical Saturnalia, *grammatica pileata*.

Characteristically, many medieval scholars apparently took this grammatical treatise completely seriously. And even contemporary scholars are far from unanimous in their evaluation of the character and degree of the parodic impulse in it. This is additional evidence, were it needed, for just how flexible the boundaries were between the straightforward and the parodically refracted word in medieval literature.

Holiday and school-festival laughter was fully legalized laugh-

---

ff. Virgilius Maro the Grammarian lived in Toulouse in the seventh century and wrote a number of remarkable meditations on the secrets of Latin grammar (*Opera*, ed. J. Heumer [Teubner], 1886). Bakhtin has two of these in mind, apparently, the *Epist. de verbo* and *Epist. de pron.* Helen Waddell (*The Wandering Scholars* [New York, 1927]) says of this dark age that "the grammarians of Toulouse argue over the vocative of *ego* amid the crash of empires" (p. 8), but she singles Virgilius Maro the Grammarian out as a bright (?) spot: "It was low tide on the continent of Europe, except for one deep pool at Toulouse, where the grammarian Virgilius Maro agitated strangely on the secret tongues of Latin, and told his story of the two scholars who argued for fifteen days and nights without sleeping or eating on the frequentative of the verb *to be*, till it almost came to knives, rather like the monsters one expects to find stranded in an ebb" (p. 28).

ter. In those days it was permitted to turn the direct sacred word into a parodic-travestying mask; it could be born again, as it were, out of the grave of authoritative and reverential seriousness. Under these conditions, the fact that *Cyprian Feasts* could enjoy enormous popularity even in strict church circles becomes understandable. In the ninth century the severe abbot of Fulda, Raban Maur,[gg] put the work into verse: the *Feasts* were read at the banquet tables of kings, and were performed during the paschal festivals by pupils of monastic schools.

The great parodic literature of the Middle Ages was created in an atmosphere of holidays and festivals. There was no genre, no text, no prayer, no saying that did not receive its parodic equivalent. Parodic liturgies have come down to us—liturgies of drunks[hh] and gamblers, liturgies about money. Numerous evangelical readings have also survived, readings that began with the traditional "ab illo tempore," that is, "in former times . . ." and that often included highly indiscreet stories. A great number of parodic prayers and hymns are intact as well. In his dissertation, "Parodies des thèmes pieux dans la poésie française du moyen age" [Helsinki, 1914], the Finnish scholar Eero Ilvoonen published the texts of six parodies on the "Pater noster," two on the "Credo" and one on the "Ave Maria," but he gives only the macaronic Latin-French texts. One cannot begin to conceive of the huge number of parodic Latin and macaronic prayers and hymns in medieval manuscript codices. In his *Parodia Sacra*, F. Novati surveys but a small part of this literature.[14] The stylistic devices employed in this parodying, travestying, reinterpreting and re-accentuating are extremely diverse. These devices have so far been very little studied, and such studies as there are have lacked the necessary stylistic depth.

14. F. Novati, *Parodia sacra nelle letterature moderne* (see: "Novatis Studi critici e letterari," Turin, 1889).

---

gg. Magnentius Raban Maur (780–856) was the greatest ecclesiastic of his age, generally regarded as the first in the still unbroken line of German theologians. His reputation for severity is caught in Raby's description: "Strict, and not too sympathetic by nature; he ruled the Abbey well, caring little for politics and testing all things by a high standard of duty" (*A History of Christian Latin Poetry* [Oxford, 1927], p. 179).

hh. Liturgies for drunks constitute a whole medieval genre, the *missa potatorum*.

Alongside the specific "parodia sacra" we find a diverse parodying and travestying of the sacred word in other comic genres and in literary works of the Middle Ages—for example, in the comic beast epics.

The sacred, authoritative, direct word in another's language—that was the hero of this entire grand parodic literature, primarily Latin, but in part macaronic. This word, its style and the way it means, became an object of representation; both word and style were transformed into a bounded and ridiculous image. The Latin "parodia sacra" is projected against the background of the vulgar national language. The accentuating system of this vulgar language penetrates to the very heart of the Latin text. In essence Latin parody is, therefore, a bilingual phenomenon: although there is only one language, this language is structured and perceived in the light of another language, and in some instances not only the accents but also the syntactical forms of the vulgar language are clearly sensed in the Latin parody. Latin parody is an intentional bilingual hybrid. We now come upon the problem of the *intentional hybrid.*

Every type of parody or travesty, every word "with conditions attached," with irony, enclosed in intonational quotation marks, every type of indirect word is in a broad sense an intentional hybrid—but a hybrid compounded of two orders: one linguistic (a single language) and one stylistic. In actual fact, in parodic discourse two styles, two "languages" (both intra-lingual) come together and to a certain extent are crossed with each other: the language being parodied (for example, the language of the heroic poem) and the language that parodies (low prosaic language, familiar conversational language, the language of the realistic genres, "normal" language, "healthy" literary language as the author of the parody conceived it). This second parodying language, against whose background the parody is constructed and perceived, does not—if it is a strict parody—enter as such into the parody itself, but is invisibly present in it.

It is the nature of every parody to transpose the values of the parodied style, to highlight certain elements while leaving others in the shade: parody is always biased in some direction, and this bias is dictated by the distinctive features of the parodying language, its accentual system, its structure—we feel its presence in the parody and we can recognize that presence, just as we at other times recognize clearly the accentual system, syntactic construction, tempi and rhythm of a specific vulgar language within purely Latin parody (that is, we recognize a Frenchman or a German as the author of the parody). Theoretically it is possible to sense and recognize in any parody that "normal" language, that "normal" style, in light of which the given parody was created. But in practice it is far from easy and not always possible.

Thus it is that in parody two languages are crossed with each other, as well as two styles, two linguistic points of view, and in the final analysis two speaking subjects. It is true that only one of these languages (the one that is parodied) is present in its own right; the other is present invisibly, as an actualizing background for creating and perceiving. Parody is an intentional hybrid, but usually it is an intra-linguistic one, one that nourishes itself on the stratification of the literary language into generic languages and languages of various specific tendencies.

Every type of intentional stylistic hybrid is more or less dialogized. This means that the languages that are crossed in it relate to each other as do rejoinders in a dialogue; there is an argument between languages, an argument between styles of language. But it is not a dialogue in the narrative sense, nor in the abstract sense; rather it is a dialogue between points of view, each with its own concrete language that cannot be translated into the other.

Thus every parody is an intentional dialogized hybrid. Within it, languages and styles actively and mutually illuminate one another.

Every word used "with conditions attached," every word enclosed in intonational quotation marks, is likewise an intentional hybrid—if only because the speaker insulates himself from this word as if from another "language," as if from a style, when it sounds to him (for example) too vulgar, or on the contrary too refined, or too pompous, or if it bespeaks a specific tendency, a specific linguistic manner and so forth.

But let us return to the Latin "parodia sacra." It is an intentional dialogized hybrid, but a hybrid of different languages. It is a dialogue between languages, although one of them (the vulgar) is present only as an actively dialogizing backdrop. What we have is a never-ending folkloric dialogue: the dispute between a dismal sacred word and a cheerful folk word, a dispute that resembles the well-known medieval dialogues between Solomon and the cheerful rogue Marcolph—except that Marcolph argued with Solomon in Latin, and here the arguments are carried on in various languages.[ii] Another's sacred word, uttered in a foreign language, is degraded by the accents of vulgar folk languages, re-evaluated and reinterpreted against the backdrop of these languages, and congeals to the point where it becomes a ridiculous image, the comic carnival mask of a narrow and joyless pedant, an unctious hypocritical old bigot, a stingy and dried-up miser. This manuscript tradition of "parodia sacra," prodigious in scope and almost a thousand years long, is a remarkable and as yet poorly read document testifying to an intense struggle and interanimation among languages, a struggle that occurred everywhere in Western Europe. This was a language drama played out as if it were a gay farce. It was linguistic Saturnalia—*lingua sacra pileata.*

The sacred Latin word was a foreign body that invaded the organism of the European languages. And throughout the Middle Ages, national languages, as organisms, repulsed this body. It was not, however, the repelling of a *thing,* but rather of a conceptualizing discourse that had made a home for itself in all the higher reaches of national ideological thought processes. The repulsion of this foreign-born sacred word was a dialogized operation, and was accomplished under cover of holiday and festival merrymaking; it was precisely the old ruler, the old year, the winter, the fast that was driven out. Such was the "parodia sacra."

But the remainder of medieval Latin literature was also in its essence a great and complex dialogized hybrid. It is no wonder that Paul Lehmann defines it as the appropriation, reworking and imitation of someone else's property, that is, of someone else's word. This reciprocal orientation of each word to the other occurs across the entire spectrum of tones—from reverent acceptance to parodic ridicule—so that it is often very difficult to establish precisely where reverence ends and ridicule begins. It is exactly like the modern novel, where one often does not know where the direct authorial word ends and where a parodic or stylized playing with the characters' language begins. Only here, in the Latin liter-

---

ii. Reference here is to the *Dialogus Salomonis et Marcolphus,* available in the edition of W. Benary (Heidelberg, 1914). See also Piero Camporesi, *La Maschera di Bertoldo* (Turin, 1976). A re-edition, with a re-publication of the first printed vernacular version (Venice, 1502) is contained in an appendix to Giulio Cesare Croce, *La Sottilissime astuzie di Bertoldo: Le piacevoli ridicoloso simplicita di Bertoldino* (Turin, 1978).

ature of the Middle Ages, the complex and contradictory process of accepting and then resisting the other's word, the process of reverently heeding it while at the same time ridiculing it, was accomplished on a grand scale throughout all the Western European world, and left an irradicable mark on the literary and linguistic consciousness of its peoples.

In addition to Latin parody there also existed, as we have already mentioned, macaronic parody. This is an already fully developed, intentionally dialogized bilingual (and sometimes trilingual) hybrid. In the bilingual literature of the Middle Ages we also find all possible types of relationships to the other's word— from reverence to merciless ridicule. In France, for example, the so-called "épîtres farcies" were widespread. Here, a verse of Sacred Writ (part of the Apostolic Epistles read during the mass) is accompanied by lines of octo-syllabic verse in French that piously translate and paraphrase the Latin text. The French language functioned in such a pious and commentating way in a whole series of macaronic prayers. Here, for example, is an excerpt from a macaronic "Pater noster" of the thirteenth century (the beginning of the final stanza):

Sed libera nos, mais delivre nous, Sire,
a malo, de tout mal et de cruel martire.

In this hybrid the French portion piously and affirmatively translates and completes the Latin portion.

But here is the beginning of a "Pater noster" of the fourteenth century describing the disasters of war:

Pater noster, tu n'ies pas foulz
Quar tu t'ies mis en grand repos
Qui es montés haut in celis.[15]

Here the French portion sharply ridicules the sacred Latin word. It interrupts the opening words of the prayer and gives a picture of life in heaven as something peaceful and marvelous compared to our earthly woes. The style of the French portion does not correspond to the high style of the prayer, as it does in the first example; high style is in fact deliberately vulgarized. This is a crude earthly rejoinder to the other-wordly pomposity of the prayer.

15. Cf. Eero Ilvoonen, *Parodies des thèmes pieux dans la poésie française du moyen âge* (Helsinki, 1914).

There are an extraordinarily large number of macaronic texts of varying degrees of piety and parody. The macaronic verse from *Carmina burana* is universally known. We might also recall the macaronic language of liturgical dramas. There, national languages often serve as a comic rejoinder, lowering the lofty Latin · portions of the drama.

The macaronic literature of the Middle Ages is likewise an extremely important and interesting document in the struggle and interanimation among languages.

There is no need to expand upon the great parodic-travestying · literature of the Middle Ages that exists in national folk languages. This literature constituted a fully articulated superstructure of laughter, erected over all serious straightforward genres. Here, as in Rome, the tendency was toward a laughing double for every serious form. We recall the role of medieval clowns, those professional creators of the "second level," who with the doubling effect of their laughter insured the wholeness of the serio-laughing word. We recall all the different kinds of comic intermedia and entr'actes that played a role in the "fourth drama" of Greece and in the cheerful exodium of Rome. A clear example of just this doubling effect of laughter can be found at the second level, the level of the fool, in the tragedies and comedies of Shakespeare. Echoes of this comic parallelism can still be heard today—for example, in the rather common doubling by a circus clown of the serious and dangerous numbers of a program, or in the half-joking role of our masters of ceremonies.

All the parodic-travestying forms of the Middle Ages, and of the ancient world as well, modeled themselves on folk and holiday merrymaking, which throughout the Middle Ages bore the character of carnival and still retained in itself ineradicable traces of Saturnalia.

At the waning of the Middle Ages and during the Renaissance the parodic-travestying word broke through all remaining boundaries. It broke through into all strict and closed straightforward genres; it reverberated loudly in the epics of the *Spielmänner* and *cantastorie*;[jj] it penetrated the lofty chivalric romance. Devilry

---

jj. *Cantastorie* were the medieval singers of the Carolingian epic in Tuscany. Although the battle between Christians and Moors is still the subject, the dignified Charlemagne is less important in the rhymes of the *cantastorie* than erotic love stories and improbable adventures. They are an important source for the *Orlando Furioso*.

almost completely overwhelmed the mystery rites, of which devilry was originally only a part. Such major and extremely important genres as the *sotie*[kk] made their appearance. And there arrived on the scene, at last, the great Renaissance novel—the
novels of Rabelais and Cervantes. It is precisely in these two
works that the novelistic word, prepared for by all the forms analyzed above as well as by a more ancient heritage, revealed its full
potential and began to play such a titanic role in the formulation
of a new literary and linguistic consciousness.

In the Renaissance, this interanimation of languages that was
working to destroy bilingualism reached its highest point. It became, in addition, extraordinarily more complex. In the second
volume of his classic work, Ferdinand Bruno,[ll] the historian of the
French language, poses the question: why was the task of transition to a national language accomplished precisely during the Renaissance, that period whose tendencies were otherwise overwhelmingly toward the classical? And the answer he provides is
absolutely correct: the very attempt of the Renaissance to establish the Latin language in all its classical purity inevitably transformed it into a dead language. It was impossible to sustain the
classic Ciceronian purity of Latin while using it in the course of
everyday life and in the world of objects of the sixteenth century,
that is, while using it to express concepts and objects from the
contemporary scene. The re-establishment of a classically pure
Latin restricted its area of application to essentially the sphere of
stylization alone. It was as if the language were being measured
against a new world. And the language could not be stretched to
fit. At the same time classical Latin illuminated the face of medieval Latin. This face, as it turned out, was hideous; but this face
could only be seen in the light of classical Latin. And thus there
came about that remarkable image of a language—*The Letters of
Obscure People.*[mm]

---

kk. *Sotie,* a type of French comic play of the fifteenth and sixteenth centuries, differing from the farce essentially because of its political and social
satire. Twenty of these are still extant, the best known of which is Pierre
Gringoire's *La Sottie du Prince des Sots* (1512), directed against Pope Julius II.
See E. Picot, *La Sottie en France* (Paris, 1878).

ll. Ferdinand Bruno, author of the magisterial *Histoire de la langue française des origines à 1900* (Paris, 1924–).

mm. *Letters of Obscure People,* or *Epistolae obscurorum virorum* (1515), a
collection of satirical letters making fun of the obscurantist enemies of the

This satire is a complex intentional linguistic hybrid. The language of obscure people is parodied; that is, it coalesces into a stereotype, it is exaggerated, reduced to a type—when measured against the standard of the proper and correct Latin of the humanists. At the same time, beneath the Latin language of these obscure people their native German tongue shines distinctly through: they take the syntactical constructions of the German language and fill them with Latin words, and they even translate specific German expressions literally into Latin; their intonation is coarse, Germanic. From the point of view of the obscure people this hybrid is not intentional; they write in the only way they can. But this Latin-German hybrid is intentionally exaggerated and highlighted by the parodying intention of the authors of the satire. One must note, however, that this linguistic satire has something of the air of the study about it, a somewhat abstract and grammatical character.

The poetry of the macaronics was also complex linguistic satire, but it was not a parody on kitchen Latin; it was a travesty that aimed at lowering the Latin used by the Ciceronian purists with their lofty and strict lexical norms. The macaronics worked with correct Latin constructions (as distinct from the obscure people), but into these constructions they introduced an abundance of words from their native vulgar tongue (Italian), having given them an external Latin formulation. The Italian language and the style of the low genres—the facetious tales and so forth—functioned as an actualizing backdrop against which macaronic poetry could be perceived, with the themes of body and material emphasized and thereby degraded. The language of the Ciceronians featured a high style; it was, in essence, a style rather than a language. It was this style that the macaronics parodied.

In the linguistic satires of the Renaissance (*The Letters of Obscure People*, the poetry of the macaronics) three languages thus animate one another: medieval Latin, the purified and rigorous Latin of the humanists and the national vulgar tongue. At the same time two worlds are animating each other: a medieval one and a new folk-humanist one. We also hear the same old folkloric

---

great humanist Johann Reuchlin (1455–1522) by two of his younger—and more irreverent—supporters, Crotus Rubianus and Ulrich von Hutten. The letters were ordered burnt by Pope Adrian. See David Friedrich Strauss, *Ulrich von Hutten*, tr. G. Sturge (London, 1874), pp. 120–140.

quarrel of old with new; we hear the same old folkloric disgracing and ridiculing of the old—old authority, old truth, the old word.

The Letters of Obscure People, the poetry of the macaronics and a series of other analogous phenomena indicate to what extent this process of interanimation of languages, the measuring of them against their current reality and their epoch, was a conscious process. They indicate further to what extent forms of language, and forms of world view, were inseparable from each other. And they indicate, finally, to what extent the old and new worlds were characterized precisely by their own peculiar languages, by the image of language that attached to each. Languages quarreled with each other, but this quarrel—like any quarrel among great and significant cultural and historical forces—could not pass on to a further phase by means of abstract and rational dialogue, nor by a purely dramatic dialogue, but only by means of complexly dialogized hybrids. The great novels of the Renaissance were such hybrids, although stylistically they were monoglot.

In the process of this linguistic change, the dialects within national languages were also set into new motion. Their period of dark and deaf co-existence came to an end. Their unique qualities began to be sensed in a new way, in the light of the evolving and centralizing norm of a national language. Ridiculing dialectological peculiarities, making fun of the linguistic and speech manners of groups living in different districts and cities throughout the nation, is something that belongs to every people's most ancient store of language images. But during the Renaissance this mutual ridiculing of different groups among the folk took on a new and fundamental significance—occurring as it did in the light of a more general interanimation of languages, and when a general, national norm for the country's language was being created. The parodying images of dialects began to receive more profound artistic formulation, and began to penetrate major literature.

Thus in the commedia dell'arte, Italian dialects were knit together with the specific types and masks of the comedy. In this respect one might even call the commedia dell'arte a comedy of dialects. It was an intentional dialectological hybrid.

Thus did the interanimation of languages occur in the very epoch that saw the creation of the European novel. Laughter and polyglossia had paved the way for the novelistic discourse of modern times.

*　*　*

In our essay we have touched upon only two factors that were at work in the prehistory of novelistic discourse. There remains before us the very important task of studying speech genres—primarily the familiar strata of folk language that played such an enormous role in the formulation of novelistic discourse and that, in altered form, entered into the composition of the novel as a genre. But this already takes us beyond the boundaries of our present study. Here, at the conclusion, we wish only to emphasize that the novelistic word arose and developed not as the result of a narrowly literary struggle among tendencies, styles, abstract world views—but rather in a complex and centuries-long struggle of cultures and languages. It is connected with the major shifts and crises in the fates of various European languages, and of the speech life of peoples. The prehistory of the novelistic word is not to be contained within the narrow perimeters of a history confined to mere literary styles.

FORMS OF TIME AND OF THE CHRONOTOPE IN THE NOVEL
Notes toward a Historical Poetics

The process of assimilating real historical time and space in literature has a complicated and erratic history, as does the articulation of actual historical persons in such a time and space. Isolated aspects of time and space, however—those available in a given historical stage of human development—have been assimilated, and corresponding generic techniques have been devised for reflecting and artistically processing such appropriated aspects of reality.

We will give the name *chronotope* (literally, "time space") to the intrinsic connectedness of temporal and spatial relationships that are artistically expressed in literature. This term [space-time] is employed in mathematics, and was introduced as part of Einstein's Theory of Relativity. The special meaning it has in relativity theory is not important for our purposes; we are borrowing it for literary criticism almost as a metaphor (almost, but not entirely). What counts for us is the fact that it expresses the inseparability of space and time (time as the fourth dimension of space). We understand the chronotope as a formally constitutive category of literature; we will not deal with the chronotope in other areas of culture.[1]

In the literary artistic chronotope, spatial and temporal indicators are fused into one carefully thought-out, concrete whole. Time, as it were, thickens, takes on flesh, becomes artistically visible; likewise, space becomes charged and responsive to the movements of time, plot and history. This intersection of axes and fusion of indicators characterizes the artistic chronotope.

The chronotope in literature has an intrinsic *generic* signifi-

---

1. In the summer of 1925, the author of these lines attended a lecture by A. A. Uxtomskij on the chronotope in biology; in the lecture questions of aesthetics were also touched upon.

cance. It can even be said that it is precisely the chronotope that defines genre and generic distinctions, for in literature the primary category in the chronotope is time. The chronotope as a formally constitutive category determines to a significant degree the image of man in literature as well. The image of man is always intrinsically chronotopic.[2]

As we have said, the process of assimilating an actual historical chronotope in literature has been complicated and erratic; certain isolated aspects of the chronotope, available in given historical conditions, have been worked out, although only certain specific forms of an actual chronotope were reflected in art. These generic forms, at first productive, were then reinforced by tradition; in their subsequent development they continued stubbornly to exist, up to and beyond the point at which they had lost any meaning that was productive in actuality or adequate to later historical situations. This explains the simultaneous existence in literature of phenomena taken from widely separate periods of time, which greatly complicates the historico-literary process.

In the notes we are offering here toward a historical poetics, we will try to illustrate this process, taking our examples from the various histories of generic heterogeneity in the European novel, beginning with the so-called "Greek romance" and ending with the Rabelaisian novel. The relative typological stability of the novelistic chronotopes that were worked out in these periods permits us to glance ahead as well, at various novel types in succeeding periods.

We do not pretend to completeness or precision in our theoretical formulations and definitions. Here and abroad, serious work on the study of space and time in art and literature has only just begun. Such work will in its further development eventually supplement, and perhaps substantially correct, the characteristics of novelistic chronotopes offered by us here.

---

2. In his "Transcendental Aesthetics" (one of the main sections of his *Critique of Pure Reason*) Kant defines space and time as indispensable forms of any cognition, beginning with elementary perceptions and representations. Here we employ the Kantian evaluation of the importance of these forms in the cognitive process, but differ from Kant in taking them not as "transcendental" but as forms of the most immediate reality. We shall attempt to show the role these forms play in the process of concrete artistic cognition (artistic visualization) under conditions obtaining in the genre of the novel.

I. The Greek Romance

Three basic types of novels developed in ancient times, and there are consequently three corresponding methods for artistically fixing time and space in these novels—in short, there were three novelistic chronotopes. These three types turned out to be extraordinarily productive and flexible, and to a large degree determined the development of the adventure novel up to the mid-eighteenth century. One must therefore begin with a detailed analysis of these three ancient types, in order to uncover the variants on them that are found in the European novel, and in order to discover the new element that was eventually brought forth on European soil.

In the analyses that follow, we will devote our entire attention to the problem of time (the dominant principle in the chronotope) and to those things, and only those things, that have a direct and unmediated relationship to time. We will bypass all questions dealing with the origin of these types in history.

We will call, provisionally, the first type of ancient novel (not first in the chronological sense) the "adventure novel of ordeal." This type would include all the so-called "Greek" or "Sophist" novels written between the second and sixth centuries A.D.

The following examples have come down to us intact, and exist in Russian translation: *An Ethiopian Tale* or *Aethiopica* of Heliodorus,[a] *Leucippe and Clitophon* of Achilles Tatius,[b] *Chareas and Callirhoë* of Chariton,[c] the *Ephesiaca* of Xenophon of

---

a. The *Aethiopica* is the longest—and by many considered to be the best—of the still extant Greek novels, or *erōtika pathēmata* (tales of suffering from love). The author, Heliodorus (fl. 220–250 A.D.) is variously associated with several figures, but it cannot be doubted he was heavily influenced by the cult of Helios. The novel was exceptionally influential even in modern times: Scaliger and Tasso admired him; Calderón (*Los Hijos de la fortuna*) and Cervantes (the unfortunate *Persiles y Sigismunda*) imitated it.

b. Achilles Tatius (fl. second century A.D.), *Leucippe and Clitophon*, in eight books, remarkable for its many *coups de théâtre* and the free and easy attitude of its heroine toward sex. Byzantine critics admired Achilles' pure Attic diction, but were scandalized by his licentiousness. Arthur Heiserman (*The Novel before the Novel* [Chicago, 1977]) interprets this text as a parodic send-up of Greek novels.

c. Chariton (fl. no later than the second century A.D.) is now thought to be perhaps the earliest of the Greek romancers, although very little is known about him. The novel is exceptionally well made as the romances go, with fewer irrelevant digressions.

Ephesus,[d] *Daphnis and Chloë* of Longus.[e] Several other characteristic examples have survived in excerpts and paraphrases.[3]

In these novels we find a subtle and highly developed type of *adventure-time*, with all its distinctive characteristics and nuances. This adventure-time and the technique of its use in the novel is so perfected, so full, that in all subsequent evolution of the *purely* adventure novel nothing essential has been added to it down to the present day. The distinctive features of adventure-time are thus best illustrated with material from these novels.

The plots of these romances (like those of their nearest and most immediate successors, the Byzantine novels) are remarkably similar to each other, and are in fact composed of the very same elements (motifs): individual novels differ from each other only in the number of such elements, their proportionate weight within the whole plot and the way they are combined. One can easily construct a typical composite schema of this plot, taking into account the most important individual deviations and variations. Such a schema would go something like this.

There is a boy and a girl of *marriageable* age. Their lineage is *unknown, mysterious* (but not always: there is, for example, no such instance in Tatius). They are remarkable for their *exceptional beauty*. They are also exceptionally *chaste*. They meet each other *unexpectedly*, usually during some festive *holiday*. A *sudden* and *instantaneous* passion flares up between them that is as irresistible as fate, like an incurable disease. However, the marriage cannot take place straightway. They are confronted with obstacles that *retard* and delay their union. The lovers are *parted*, they seek one another, find one another; again they lose each

3. *Marvels beyond Thule*, by Antonius Diogenes, the Ninus novel, the Princess Chio novel and others.

---

d. The *Ephesiaca* (also known as *Anthia and Habracomes*) is the clumsiest of the romances; while it contains all the obligatory shipwrecks and enslavements, they are more than ordinarily disjointed. Nothing is known about Xenophon of Ephesus, and he has been assigned dates from the second to the fifth century A.D., depending on which expert you read.

e. No more about Longus is known (the very name is suspect) than of Xenophon of Ephesus, but in Longus' case we care; we *want* to know more, since *Daphnis and Chloë* is psychologically the most sophisticated of all the romances (if the bucolic atmosphere is a bit laid on and oppressive). The great Willamowitz accused Longus of pandering to "die Naturschwärmerei des Salonmenschen."

other, again they find each other. There are the usual obstacles and adventures of lovers: the abduction of the bride on the eve of the wedding, the *absence of parental consent* (if parents exist), a different bridegroom and bride intended for either of the lovers (*false couples*), the flight of the lovers, their journey, a storm at sea, a *shipwreck*, a miraculous rescue, an attack by *pirates, captivity* and *prison*, an attempt on the innocence of the hero and heroine, the offering-up of the heroine as a purifying sacrifice, wars, battles, *being sold into slavery, presumed deaths, disguising one's identity*, recognition and failures of recognition, presumed betrayals, attempts on chastity and fidelity, false accusations of crimes, court trials, court inquiries into the chastity and fidelity of the lovers. The heroes find their parents (if unknown). Meetings with unexpected friends or enemies play an important role, as do fortune-telling, prophecy, prophetic dreams, premonitions and sleeping potions. The novel ends happily with the lovers united in marriage. Such is the schema for the basic components of the plot.

The action of the plot unfolds against a very broad and varied geographical background, usually in three to five countries separated by seas (Greece, Persia, Phoenicia, Egypt, Babylon, Ethiopia and elsewhere). There are descriptions, often very detailed, of specific features of countries, cities, structures of various kinds, works of art (pictures, for example), the habits and customs of the population, various exotic and marvelous animals and other wonders and rarities. The novel also contains fairly wide ranging discussions on various religious, philosophical, political and scientific topics (on fate, omens, the power of Eros, human passions, tears and so forth). Large portions of these novels are taken up with speeches of the characters—relevant or otherwise—constructed in accordance with all the rules of a later rhetoric. Compositionally, therefore, the Greek romance strives for a certain encyclopedic quality, a quality that is characteristic of the genre.

All the aspects of the novel we listed above (in their abstract form) are, without exception, in no way new—neither in their plot nor in their descriptive and rhetorical aspects. They had all been encountered before and were well developed in other genres of ancient literature: love motifs (first meeting, sudden passion, melancholy) had been worked out in Hellenistic love poetry; certain other motifs (storms, shipwrecks, wars, abductions) were developed in the ancient epic; several other of these motifs (such as recognition) had played an essential role in tragedy; descriptive motifs had already been well developed in the ancient geographical novel and in historiographic works (for example, in Herodotus); deliberations and speeches had occurred in rhetorical genres. The significance of such genres as the love elegy, the geographical novel, rhetoric, drama, the historiographic genre in the genesis of the Greek romance may be variously assessed, but one cannot deny a very real syncretism of these generic features. The Greek romance utilized and fused together in its structure almost all genres of ancient literature.

But all these elements, derived from various different genres, are fused and consolidated into a new—specifically novelistic— unity, of which the constitutive feature is adventure—novel- time. The elements derived from various other genres assumed a new character and special functions in this completely new chronotope—"an alien world in adventure-time"—and ceased to be what they had been in other genres.

What then is the essence of this adventure-time in the Greek romance?

The first meeting of hero and heroine and the sudden flareup of their passion for each other is the starting point for plot movement; the end point of plot movement is their successful union in marriage. All action in the novel unfolds between these two points. These points—the poles of plot movement—are themselves crucial events in the heroes' lives; in and of themselves they have a biographical significance. But it is not around these that the novel is structured; rather, it is around that which lies (that which takes place) *between* them. But *in essence* nothing need lie between them. From the very beginning, the love between the hero and heroine is not subject to doubt; this love remains *absolutely unchanged* throughout the entire novel. Their chastity is also preserved, and their marriage at the end of the novel is *directly conjoined* with their love—that same love that had been ignited at their first meeting at the outset of the novel; it is as if absolutely nothing had happened between these two moments, as if the marriage had been consummated on the day after their meeting. Two adjacent moments, one of biographical life, one of biographical time, are directly conjoined. The gap, the pause, the hiatus that appears between these two strictly adjacent biographical moments and in which, as it were, the entire novel is constructed is not contained in the biographical time-sequence, it lies outside biographical time; it changes nothing in the life of the heroes, and introduces nothing into their life. It is, precisely, an extratemporal hiatus between two moments of biographical time.

If the situation were otherwise—had, for example, the initial instantaneous passion of the heroes grown stronger as a result of their adventures and ordeals; had that passion been tested in action, thereby acquiring new qualities of a stable and tried love; had the heroes themselves matured, come to know each other better—then we would have an example of a much later European novel-type, one that would not be an adventure novel at all, and certainly not a Greek romance. Although the poles of the plot would have remained the same (passion at the beginning, marriage at the end), the events that retard the marriage would have acquired in themselves a certain biographical or at least psychological significance; they would give the appearance of being stretched along the real time-line of the heroes' lives, and of effecting change in both the heroes and in the events (the key events) of their lives. But this is precisely what is lacking in the Greek romance; in it there is a sharp hiatus between two moments of biographical time, a hiatus that leaves no *trace* in the life of the heroes or in their personalities.

All the events of the novel that fill this hiatus are a pure digression from the normal course of life; they are excluded from the kind of real duration in which additions to a normal biography are made.

This Greek romance-time does not have even an elementary biological or maturational duration. At the novel's outset the heroes meet each other at a marriageable age, and at the same marriageable age, no less fresh and handsome, they consummate the marriage at the novel's end. Such a form of time, in which they experience a most improbable number of adventures, is not measured off in the novel and does not add up; it is simply days, nights, hours, moments clocked in a technical sense within the limits of each separate adventure. This time—adventure-time, highly intensified but undifferentiated—is not registered in the slightest way in the age of the heroes. We have here an extratemporal hiatus between two biological moments—the arousal of passion, and its satisfaction.

When Voltaire, in his *Candide*, parodied the type of Greek adventure novel that was popular in the seventeenth and eighteenth centuries (the so-called "Baroque novel"), he took into account the real time that would have been required in such romances for the hero to experience the customary dose of adventures and "turns of fate." With all obstacles overcome at the novel's end, his heroes (Candide and Cunegonde) consummate the obligatory happy marriage. But, alas, they have already grown old, and the wondrous Cunegonde resembles some hideous old witch. Consummation follows upon passion, but only when it is no longer biologically possible.

It goes without saying that Greek adventure-time lacks any natural, everyday cyclicity—such as might have introduced into it a temporal order and indices on a human scale, tying it to the repetitive aspects of natural and human life. No matter where one goes in the world of the Greek romance, with all its countries and cities, its buildings and works of art, there are absolutely no indications of historical time, no identifying traces of the era. This also explains the fact that scholarship has yet to establish the precise chronology of Greek romances, and until quite recently scholarly opinion as to the dates of origin of individual novels has differed by as much as five or six centuries.

Thus all of the action in a Greek romance, all the events and adventures that fill it, constitute time-sequences that are neither historical, quotidian, biographical, nor even biological and maturational. Actions lie outside these sequences, beyond the reach of that force, inherent in these sequences, that generates rules and defines the measure of a man. In this kind of time, nothing changes: the world remains as it was, the biographical life of the heroes does not change, their feelings do not change, people do not even age. This empty time leaves no traces anywhere, no indications of its passing. This, we repeat, is an extratemporal hiatus that appears between two moments of a real time sequence, in this case one that is biographical.

Such is adventure-time as an entity. But what is it like on the inside?

It is composed of a series of short segments that correspond to separate adventures; within each such adventure, time is organized from without, technically. What is important is to be able to escape, to catch up, to outstrip, to be or not to be in a given place at a given moment, to meet or not to meet and so forth. Within the limits of a given adventure, days, nights, hours, even minutes and seconds add up, as they would in any struggle or any active external undertaking. These time segments are introduced and intersect with specific link-words: "suddenly" and "at just that moment."

"Suddenly" and "at just that moment" best characterize this type of time, for this time usually has its origin and comes into its own in just those places where the normal, pragmatic and pre-meditated course of events is interrupted—and provides an opening for sheer chance, which has its own specific logic. This logic is one of *random contingency* [*sovpadenie*], which is to say, chance *simultaneity* [meetings] and *chance rupture* [nonmeetings], that is, a logic of random *disjunctions* in time as well. In this random contingency, "earlier" and "later" are crucially, even decisively, significant. Should something happen a minute earlier or a minute later, that is, should there be no chance simultaneity or chance disjunctions in time, there would be no plot at all, and nothing to write a novel about.

"I had reached my nineteenth year, and my father had arranged a marriage for me the following year when *Fate began her game*," Clitophon tells us (*Leucippe and Clitophon*, part 1, 3).[4]

This "game of fate," its "suddenlys" and "at just that moments" make up the entire contents of the novel.

War broke out unexpectedly between the Thracians and the Byzantines. In the novel nothing is said about the causes of the war, but thanks to it Leucippe turns up in the home of Clitophon's father. "As soon as I saw her, I perished on the spot," Clitophon relates.[f]

But Clitophon's father had already chosen another bride for him. The father begins to hurry the wedding along, sets it for the *following day* and prepares the preliminary sacrifices. "When I heard about this I considered myself doomed, and began to devise some clever trick to postpone the wedding. While occupied with this, a voice *unexpectedly* rang out in the men's half of the house" (part 2, 12). As it happened, an eagle had carried off the sacrificial meat that Clitophon's father had prepared. This was a bad omen, and the wedding had to be postponed for several days.

---

4. *Leucippe and Clitophon* by Achilles Tatius; citations from Achilles Tatius of Alexandria, *Leucippe and Clitophon* (Moscow, 1925).

---

f. The passages from *Leucippe and Clitophon* are taken from *The Greek Romances* (London: G. Bell, 1901).

But just at that moment, thanks to chance, Clitophon's intended bride was abducted—taken by mistake for Leucippe.

Clitophon resolves to steal into Leucippe's bedroom. "*As soon as* I entered the girl's bedchamber, the following *strange thing happened* to her mother. She was alarmed by a dream" (part 2, 23). She enters the bedchamber and finds Clitophon there, but he manages to slip away unrecognized. The next day, however, everything is in danger of being exposed, and Clitophon and Leucippe must flee. The entire escape is built on a chain of random "suddenlys" and "at just that moments" that benefit the heroes. "One must admit that Conops, who kept watch over us, had just *happened that day* to be gone from the house, on some errand for his mistress. . . . We were lucky: having gotten as far as the port of Berytus, we found a ship setting sail, whose mooring-lines had *already* been prepared for unfurling."

On board ship, "A young man turned up alongside us quite *by chance*" (part 2, 31–32). He befriends them and plays a significant role in subsequent adventures.

Then follows the traditional storm and shipwreck. "On the third day of our voyage, a *sudden* fog spread over the clear sky and dimmed the light of day" (part 3, 1).

During the shipwreck everyone perishes except the heroes, who are saved thanks to good fortune. "And here, just as the ship was sinking, some kindly deity preserved for us a portion of its cargo." They are cast up on the shore: "*Thanks to our good fortune* we were delivered to Pelusium towards evening, and joyfully came out on dry land. . . ." (part 3, 5).

It later turns out that all other characters who were thought to have perished during the shipwreck were also saved, thanks to good fortune. When in the course of the novel the heroes need emergency help, these persons manage to be in just the right place at just the right time. Convinced that Leucippe has been abducted by bandits as a sacrificial offering, Clitophon decides to commit suicide: "I took up the sword, in order to end my life on the very spot of Leucippe's immolation. *Suddenly* I see—it was a moonlit night—two people . . . running directly toward me . . . they turn out to be Menelaus and Satyrus. Although seeing my friends alive was very *unexpected*, I did not embrace them and was not overwhelmed with joy" (part 3, 17). Of course the friends prevent the suicide and announce that Leucippe is alive.

Toward the end of the novel, Clitophon is sentenced to death on a false accusation and before his death is to be tortured. "They chained me down, took off my clothes, hung me on the rack; some of the torturers brought whips, others a noose, and a fire was kindled. Klinius let out a howl and began to invoke the gods—when *suddenly*, in full view of all, a priest of Artemis approached, crowned with laurel. His approach signified the arrival of a festive procession in honor of the goddess. When this happens, an execution must be postponed for several days until the participants in the procession have finished their sacrificial offerings. In such a way was I then released from my chains" (part 7, 12).

Several days after the postponement, everything is cleared up, and events take yet another turn, not of course without a number of new random coincidences and interruptions. Leucippe, it turns out, is alive. The novel ends with happy marriages.

As we see (and we have cited here only an insignificant number of random contingencies), adventure-time lives a rather fraught life in the romance; one day, one hour, even one minute earlier or later have everywhere a decisive and fatal significance. The adventures themselves are strung together in an extratemporal and in effect infinite series: this series can be extended as long as one likes; in itself it has no necessary internal limits. Greek romances are comparatively short. In the seventeenth century, the length of similarly constructed novels increases by ten to fifteen times.[5] There are no internal limits to this increase. For all the days, hours, minutes that are ticked off within the separate adventures are not united into a real time series, they do not become the days and hours of a human life. These hours and days leave no trace, and therefore, one may have as many of them as one likes.

All moments of this infinite adventure-time are controlled by one force—*chance*. As we have seen, this time is entirely composed of contingency—of chance meetings and failures to meet. Adventuristic "chance time" is the specific time during which irrational forces intervene in human life; the intervention of Fate (Tyche), gods, demons, sorcerers or—in later adventure novels—

5. Here are some of the best-known novels of the seventeenth century: D'Urfé's *L'Astrée*—five volumes, in all over six thousand pages; La Calprenède's *Cléopâtre*—twelve volumes, more than five thousand pages; Caspar von Lohenstein's *Arminius and Tusnelda*—two huge volumes, over three thousand pages.

those novelistic villains who as villains use chance meetings or failures to meet for their own purposes: they "lie in wait," they "bide their time," we have a veritable downpour of "suddenlys" and "at just that moments."

Moments of adventuristic time occur at those points when the normal course of events, the normal, intended or purposeful sequence of life's events is interrupted. These points provide an opening for the intrusion of nonhuman forces—fate, gods, villains—and it is precisely these forces, and not the heroes, who in adventure-time take all the initiative. Of course the heroes themselves act in adventure-time—they escape, defend themselves, engage in battle, save themselves—but they act, as it were, as merely physical persons, and the initiative does not belong to them. Even love is unexpectedly sent to them by all-powerful Eros. In this time, persons are forever having things happen *to* them (they might even "happen" to win a kingdom); a purely adventuristic person is a person of chance. He enters adventuristic time as a person to whom something happens. But the initiative in this time does not belong to human beings.

We may take it for granted that moments of adventure-time, all these "suddenlys" and "at just that moments," cannot be foreseen with the help of analysis, study, wise foresight, experience, etc., alone. Such things are better understood through fortune-telling, omens, legends, oracular predictions, prophetic dreams and premonitions. Greek romances are indeed filled with all these. Hardly had "Fate begun her game" with Clitophon when he had a prophetic dream revealing his future meeting with Leucippe and their adventures. The novel is subsequently filled with similar events. Fate and the gods hold all initiative in their hands, and they merely inform people of their will. "At night the gods frequently like to reveal the future to people," says Achilles Tatius through his Clitophon, "and not that they may be spared suffering—for they cannot control what fate has decreed—but that they may bear their sufferings more easily" (part 1, 3).

Whenever Greek adventure-time appears in the subsequent development of the European novel, initiative is handed over to chance, which controls meetings and failures to meet—either as an impersonal, anonymous force in the novel or as fate, as divine foresight, as romantic "villains" or romantic "secret benefactors." Examples of the latter one can still find in Walter Scott's historical novels. Alongside chance (in its various guises) a number of other types of predictions inevitably figure in the novel, prophetic dreams and premonitions in particular. It is not mandatory, of course, for an entire novel to be constructed in adventure-time of the Greek type. One need only have a certain admixture of these time-elements to other time-sequences for its special accompanying effects to appear.

In the seventeenth century, the fates of nations, kingdoms and cultures were also drawn into this adventure-time of chance, gods and villains, a time with its own specific logic. This occurs in the earliest European historical novels, for example in de Scudéry's *Artamène, or the Grand Cyrus*,[g] in Lohenstein's *Arminius and Tusnelda*[h] and in the historical novels of La Calprenède.[i] Pervading these novels is a curious "philosophy of history" that hands over the settling of historical destinies to an extratemporal hiatus that exists between two moments of a real time sequence.

Through the connecting link of the "Gothic novel," this sequence of moments in a historical Baroque novel also survives into the historical novel of Walter Scott, determining several of its characteristics: undercover activities of secret benefactors and villains, the specific role of chance, various sorts of predictions and premonitions. In Walter Scott's novels these moments are not, of course, the dominant ones.

Let us hasten to add that we are not talking here of *chance tak-*

---

g. Madeleine de Scudéry's (1607–1701) ten-volume novel (1649–1653) is enormous; it is remembered as a primary example of the *roman à clef*, and because it was attacked by Boileau in his *Dialogue sur les héros des romans* (1687). Although it purports to be about the Persian conqueror of the fourth century B.C., it is mostly about love as it was conceived among the *précieux* at the Hôtel de Rambouillet, whose manners were imitated in Mme. de Scudéry's salon.

h. Caspar von Lohenstein (1635–1683), *Arminius und Tusnelda* (1689–1690), an endless novel covering most of the history of Germany's encounter with ancient Rome, larded with disquisitions on ladies' makeup, Syrian and Chinese history, whales, diamonds and so forth.

i. Gautier de La Calprenède (1614–1663) wrote several historical novels of great length; they were the delight of the *précieuses*. He marks the end of the vogue for pastorals and the beginning of an interest in novels devoted to heroes who are gallant nobles in historical settings. *Cassandre* (1642–1645) tells the destruction of the Persian Empire in ten volumes, *Faramond* the decline of the Merovingian Empire in twelve volumes (it was finally completed in 1670 by Vaumorière). There is also a *Cléopâtre* (1647–1658) in twelve volumes.

ing any specific initiative in Greek adventure-time, nor of chance in general. In general, chance is but one form of the principle of necessity and as such has a place in any novel, as it has its place in life itself. Even in human time-sequences that are more real (that are of varying degrees of reality) corresponding to moments of Greek initiative-generated chance, there are moments (one cannot of course even speak in a general way of their *strict* correspondence) of human error, crime (sometimes even in the Baroque novel), fluctuations and choice, decisions made on the basis of human initiative.

To conclude our analysis of adventure-time in the Greek romance, we must deal with one more general aspect, namely, individual motifs that are included as constituent elements in novelistic plots. Such motifs as meeting/parting (separation), loss/acquisition, search/discovery, recognition/nonrecognition and so forth enter as constituent elements into plots, not only of novels of various eras and types but also into literary works of other genres: epic, dramatic, even lyric. By their very nature these motifs are chronotopic (although it is true the chronotope is developed in different ways in the various genres). We shall discuss here only one motif, but the one that is probably the most important—the motif of meeting.

As we have already shown in our analysis of the Greek romance, in any meeting the temporal marker ("at one and the same time") is inseparable from the spatial marker ("in one and the same place"). In the negative motif ("they did not meet," "they were parted") the chronotopicity is retained but one or another member of the chronotope bears a negative sign: they did not meet because they did not arrive at the given place at the same time, or at the same time they were in different places. The inseparable unity of time and space markers (a unity without a merging) gives to the chronotope of meeting an elementary clear, formal, almost mathematical character. But this character is of course highly abstract. The motif of meeting is after all impossible in isolation: it always enters as a constituent element of the plot into the concrete unity of the entire work and, consequently, is part of the concrete chronotope that subsumes it; in our case, it enters adventure-time and a foreign (but not alien) country. In different works the motif of meeting may have different nuances depending on concrete associations, such as the emotional evaluation of meetings (a meeting may be desirable or undesirable, joyful or sad, sometimes terrifying, perhaps even ambivalent). In various contexts the motif of meeting may, of course, be expressed by various verbal stratagems. It may assume a multiply metaphoric or singly metaphoric meaning and may, finally, become a symbol (one that is sometimes very profound). Quite frequently in literature the chronotope of meeting fulfills architectonic functions: it can serve as an opening, sometimes as a culmination, even as a denouement (a finale) of the plot. A meeting is one of the most ancient devices for structuring a plot in the epic (and even more so in the novel). Of special importance is the close link between the motif of meeting and such motifs as *parting, escape, aquisition, loss, marriage* and so forth, which are similar to the motif of meeting in their unity of space and time markers. Of special importance is the close link between the motif of meeting and the chronotope of the road ("the open road"), and of various types of meetings on the road. In the chronotope of the road, the unity of time and space markers is exhibited with exceptional precision and clarity. The importance of the chronotope of the road in literature is immense: it is a rare work that does not contain a variation of this motif, and many words are directly constructed on the road chronotope, and on road meetings and adventures.[6]

The motif of meeting is also closely related to other important motifs, especially the motif of recognition/nonrecognition, which plays an enormous role in literature (for example, in ancient tragedy).

The motif of meeting is one of the most universal motifs, not only in literature (it is difficult to find a work where this motif is completely absent) but also in other areas of culture and in various spheres of public and everyday life. In the scientific and technical realm where purely conceptual thinking predominates, there are no motifs as such, but the concept of *contact* is equivalent in some degree to the motif of meeting. In mythological and religious realms the motif of meeting plays a leading role, of course: in sacred legends and Holy Writ (both in Christian works such as the Gospels and in Buddhist writings) and in religious rituals. The motif of meeting is combined with other motifs, for example that of apparition ("epiphany") in the religious realm. In

6. We will give a more fully developed characterization of this chronotope in the concluding section of the present work.

those areas of philosophy that are not strictly scientific, the motif of meeting can be of considerable importance (in Schelling, for example, or in Max Scheler and particularly in Martin Buber).

A real-life chronotope of meeting is constantly present in organizations of social and governmental life. Everyone is familiar with organized social meetings of all possible sorts, and how important they are. In the life of the state, meetings are also very important. Let us mention here only diplomatic encounters, always strictly regulated, where the time, place and makeup of these encounters are dependent upon the rank of the person being met. And finally, everyone knows the importance of meetings (sometimes the entire fate of a man may depend on them) in life, and in the daily affairs of any individual.

Such is the chronotopic motif of meeting. We shall return to the more general question of chronotopes and chronotopicity at the end of our essay. But we shall now resume our analysis of the Greek romance.

In what sort of space is the adventure-time of Greek romances realized?

For Greek adventure-time to work, one must have an *abstract* expanse of space. The world of the Greek romance is of course chronotopic, but the link between space and time has, as it were, not an organic but a purely technical (and mechanical) nature. In order for the adventure to develop it needs space, and plenty of it. The contingency that governs events is inseparably tied up with space, measured primarily by *distance* on the one hand and by *proximity* on the other (and varying degrees of both). To prevent Clitophon's suicide, his friends must turn up in that place where he is planning to commit it; to *manage* this, that is to be the right *time* in the *right* place, they *run*, that is they overcome *spatial distance*. In order for Clitophon to be saved at the end of the novel, the procession led by the priest of Artemis must arrive at the place of execution before the execution takes place. Abduction presumes a *rapid* removal of the abducted to a *distant* and *unknown place*. *Pursuit* presumes overcoming distance, as well as other *spatial obstacles*. *Captivity* and *prison* presume *guarding* and *isolating* the hero in a *definite spot in space*, impeding his subsequent spatial movement toward his goal, that is, his subsequent pursuits and searches and so forth. Abductions, escape, pursuit, search and captivity all play an immense role in the Greek romance. It, therefore, requires large spaces, land and seas, different countries. The world of these romances is large and diverse. But this size and diversity is utterly abstract. For a shipwreck one must have a sea, but which particular sea (in the geographical and historical sense) makes no difference at all. For escape it is important to go to another country; for kidnappers it is important to transport their victim to another country—but which particular country again makes no difference at all. The adventuristic events of the Greek romance have no essential ties with any particular details of individual countries that might figure in the novel, with their social or political structure, with their culture or history. None of these distinctive details contribute in any way to the event as a determining factor; the event is determined by chance alone, by random contingency in a given spatial locus (a given country, city and so forth). The nature of a given place does not figure as a component in the event; the place figures in solely as a naked, abstract expanse of space.

All adventures in the Greek romance are thus governed by an interchangeability of space; what happens in Babylon could just as well happen in Egypt or Byzantium and vice versa. Separate adventures, complete in themselves, are also interchangeable in time, for adventure-time leaves no defining traces and is therefore in essence reversible. The adventure chronotope is thus characterized by a *technical, abstract connection between space and time*, by the *reversibility* of moments in a temporal sequence, and by their *interchangeability* in space.

In this chronotope all initiative and power belongs to chance. Therefore, the degree of *specificity* and *concreteness* of this world is necessarily very limited. For any concretization—geographic, economic, sociopolitical, quotidian—would fetter the freedom and flexibility of the adventures and limit the absolute power of chance. Every concretization, of even the most simple and everyday variety, would introduce its own *rule-generating force*, its own *order*, its *inevitable ties* to human life and to the time specific to that life. Events would end up being interwoven with these rules, and to a greater or lesser extent would find themselves participating in this order, subject to its ties. This would critically limit the power of chance; the movement of the adventures would be organically localized and tied down in time and space. But if one were to depict one's own native world, the indigenous reality surrounding one, such specificity and concretization would be absolutely unavoidable (at least to some degree). A depiction of one's own world—no matter where or what it is—could never achieve that degree of abstractness necessary for Greek adventure-time.

Therefore, the world of the Greek romance is an *alien world*: everything in it is indefinite, unknown, foreign. Its heroes are there for the first time; they have no organic ties or relationships with it; the laws governing the sociopolitical and everyday life of this world are foreign to them, they do not know them; in this world, therefore, they can experience only random contingency.

But in the Greek romance the alien quality of this world is not emphasized and we cannot therefore call it exotic. Exoticism presupposes a deliberate *opposition of what is alien to what is one's own*, the otherness of what is foreign is emphasized, savored, as it were, and elaborately depicted against an implied background of one's own ordinary and familiar world. There is none of this in the Greek romance. In it everything is foreign, including the heroes' homeland (the hero and the heroine usually have different homelands); there is no implied native, ordinary, familiar world (the native country of the author and his readers) against whose background the otherness and foreignness of what is foreign might be clearly projected. Of course there is in these romances a minimal degree of some presumed native, ordinary, normal world (the world of the author and his readers); there are some indices for perceiving the wonders and rarities of this other world. But this degree is so minuscule that scholarship has been almost entirely unable to devise a method for analyzing in these romances the presumed "real world" and "real era" of their authors.

The world of Greek romances is an *abstract-alien* world, and furthermore one utterly and exclusively other, since the native world *from which the author came* and from which he is now watching is nowhere to be found in it. Therefore, nothing in this world limits the absolute power of chance, and for that reason all these abductions, escapes, captivities and liberations, alleged deaths and resurrections and other adventures follow upon each other with such remarkable speed and ease.

But as we have already indicated, many items and events in this abstract-alien world are described in minute detail. How can this be reconciled with the principle of abstraction? The abstraction is still there, because every feature described in Greek romances is described as if it were *isolated, single* and *unique*. Nowhere are we given a description of the country as a whole, with its distinctive characteristics, with the features that distinguish it from other countries, within a matrix of relationships. Only separate structures are described, without any connection to an encompassing whole; we have isolated natural phenomena—for example, the strange animals that breed in a given country. The customs and everyday life of the folk are nowhere described; what we get instead is a description of some strange isolated quirk, connected to nothing. This isolation and disconnectedness permeates all the objects described in the novel. Thus the sum total of these objects does not equal the countries that are depicted (or more precisely, enumerated) in the novel, but rather each object is sufficient unto itself.

All these isolated things described in the novel are unusual, strange, rare: that is precisely why they are described. In *Leucippe and Clitophon*, for example, one finds a description of a strange beast called a "Nile horse" (a hippopotamus). "It happened that the warriors caught a *noteworthy* river beast." Thus begins the description. Further on, an elephant is described and one hears of "*remarkable things* pertaining to its appearance on the earth" (part 4, 2–4). Elsewhere a crocodile is described: "I saw another Nile beast, even more *extraordinarily strong* than the river horse. It was called a crocodile" (part 4, 14).

Since there is no scale for measuring these items and events, no clear background of the usual, of one's own world, against which to perceive unusual things, they take on the nature of curiosities, wonders, rarities.

Thus in the Greek romance, the spaces of an *alien world* are filled with isolated curiosities and rarities that bear no connection to each other. These self-sufficient items—curious, odd, wondrous—are just as random and unexpected as the adventures themselves: they are made of the same material, they are congealed "suddenlys," adventures turned into things, offspring of the same chance.

As a result, the chronotope of Greek romances—an alien world in adventure-time—possesses its own peculiar consistency and unity. It has its own ineluctable logic that defines all its characteristics. Although in the abstract its motifs taken separately are not, as we have said above, new—they had already been well developed in other genres preceding the Greek romance—still, when combined in this new chronotope, they become subject to its ineluctable logic and thus acquire an utterly new meaning and special functions.

In other genres these motifs were connected with different, more concrete and condensed chronotopes. In Alexandrine poetry the love motifs (first meeting, sudden love, lovers' melancholy, first kiss and so forth) were developed in large part within a bucolic-pastoral-idyllic chronotope. This is a small but very concrete and condensed lyric-epic chronotope that has played no small role in world literature. A specific and cycled (but not, strictly speaking, cyclical) idyllic time functions here, a blend of natural time (cyclic) and the everyday time of the more or less pastoral (at times even agricultural) life. This time possesses its own definite semicyclical rhythm, but it has fused bodily with a specific insular idyllic landscape, one worked out in meticulous detail. This is a dense and fragrant time, like honey, a time of intimate lovers' scenes and lyric outpourings, a time saturated with its own strictly limited, sealed-off segment of nature's space, stylized through and through (we will not deal here with other variations of the love-idyllic chronotope in Hellenic and Roman poetry). In the Greek romance, of course, nothing of this chronotope remains. A single exception exists, and it is an oddity: Longus' *Daphnis and Chloë*. At its center we have a pastoral-idyllic chronotope, but a chronotope riddled with decay, its compact isolation and self-imposed limits destroyed, surrounded on all sides by an alien world and itself already half-alien; natural-idyllic time is no longer as dense, it is cut through by shafts of adventure-time. Longus' idyll cannot, of course, be definitively categorized as a Greek adventure romance. And this work gives rise to its own line of descendents in the further historical development of the novel.

Those factors in a Greek romance (of *compositional* as well as narrative interest) associated with travel through foreign countries had already been well developed in the ancient novel of travel. The world of the travel novel bears no resemblance to the alien world of the Greek romance. First and foremost we have at the center of the travel novel's world the *author's own real homeland*, which serves as organizing center for the point of view, the scales of comparison, the approaches and evaluations determining how alien countries and cultures are seen and understood (it is not compulsory that the native country be evaluated positively, but it must absolutely provide us with a scale and a background). In the novel of travel, this sense of a native country in itself—that is, as an internal organizing center for seeing and depicting that is located "at home"—radically changes the entire picture of a foreign world. Furthermore, the hero in such a novel is the *public* and *political* man of ancient times, a man governed by his sociopolitical, philosophical and utopian interests. In addition, the factor of the journey itself, the *itinerary*, is an actual one: it imparts to the temporal sequence of the novel a real and essential organizing center. In such novels, finally, biography is the crucial organizing principle for time. (We will not discuss here the various possible forms a novel of travel might assume; the adventure factor is regularly associated with one such form, but it does not serve as the dominant organizing principle in such a novel. It plays quite another role.)

This is not the place to investigate in detail the other chronotopes of other genres of ancient literature, including the major genres of epic and drama. We will merely point out that at their heart lies folk-mythological time, in which ancient historical time (with its specific constraints) begins to come into its own. The time of ancient epic and drama was profoundly localized, absolutely inseparable from the concrete features of a characteristically Greek natural environment, and from the features of a "man-made environment," that is, of specifically Greek administrative units, cities and states. In every aspect of his natural world the Greek saw a trace of mythological time; he saw in it a condensed mythological event that would unfold into a mythological scene or tableau. Historical time was equally concrete and localized—in epic and tragedy it was tightly interwoven with mythological time. These *classical* Greek chronotopes are more or less the antipodes of the alien world as we find it in Greek romances.

Thus the various motifs and factors (of a narrative as well as a compositional nature), worked out and still alive in other ancient genres, bore in them completely different character and functions from those obtaining in the Greek adventure-romance, under conditions characteristic of the romance's *specific chronotope*. In the romance they entered into a new and unique artistic unity, one, moreover, that was far from being a mere mechanical mélange of various ancient genres.

Now that we better understand the specific character of the Greek romance, we can consider the problem of *portraying an individual* in such novels. The distinctive features of all the narrative devices in the novel will also become clear in the course of our discussion.

How indeed can a human being be portrayed in the "adventure-time" that we have outlined above, where things occur simultaneously by chance and also *fail* to occur simultaneously by chance, where events have no consequences, where the initiative belongs everywhere exclusively to chance? It goes without saying that in this type of time, an individual can be nothing other than completely *passive*, completely *unchanging*. As we have said earlier, to such an individual things can merely *happen*. He himself is deprived of any initiative. He is merely the physical subject of the action. And it follows that his actions will be by and large of an elementary-spatial sort. In essence, all the character's actions in Greek romance are reduced to *enforced movement through space* (escape, persecution, quests); that is, to a change in spatial location. Human movement through space is precisely what provides the basic *indices* for measuring space and time in the Greek romance, which is to say, for its chronotope.

It is nevertheless a *living human being* moving through space and not merely a physical body in the literal sense of the term. While it is true that his life may be completely passive—"Fate" runs the game—he nevertheless *endures* the game fate plays. And he not only endures—he *keeps on being the same person* and emerges from this game, from all these turns of fate and chance, with his *identity* absolutely unchanged.

This *distinctive correspondence of an identity with a particular self* is the *organizing center* of the human image in the Greek romance. And one must not underestimate the significance, the profound ideological implications raised by this factor of human identity. In this way the Greek romance reveals its strong ties with a *folklore that predates class distinctions*, assimilating one of the essential elements in the folkloric concept of a man, one that survives to the present in various aspects of folklore, especially in folktales. No matter how impoverished, how denuded a human identity may become in a Greek romance, there is always preserved in it some precious kernel of folk humanity; one always senses a faith in the indestructible power of man in his struggle with nature and with all inhuman forces.

If we carefully examine the narrative and compositional aspects of Greek romance, we will be impressed by the enormous role played by such devices as *recognition*, *disguise*, temporary changes of dress, presumed death (with subsequent resurrection), *presumed betrayal* (with subsequent confirmation of unswerving fidelity) and finally the basic compositional (that is, organizing) motif of *a test of the heroes' integrity, their selfhood.* In all these instances the narrative plays directly with *traits of human identity.* Even this basic complex of motifs—meeting/separation, search/find—is but another narrative expression reflecting this same concern for individual human identity.

Let us first consider the compositional-organizing device of *testing* the heroes. At the beginning of this essay we defined the earliest type of ancient novel as an adventure *novel of ordeal.* The term "novel of ordeal" (*Prüfungsroman*) has long been applied primarily to the seventeenth-century Baroque novel by literary historians, who view it as the furthest extent of the European development of the Greek novel.

The shaping force of the idea of trial stands out with extraordinary clarity in the Greek romance—in fact, the general theme of trial literally takes on judicial and legal expression.

The majority of adventures in a Greek romance are organized precisely as trials of the hero and heroine, especially trials of their chastity and mutual fidelity. But other things may also be tested: their nobility, courage, strength, fearlessness, and—more rarely—their intelligence. Chance strews the path of our heroes not merely with dangers but also with temptations of every possible sort; they are placed in the most ticklish situations, but they always emerge with their honor intact. In the artful fabrication of such extremely complex situations, one sees evidence in a Greek romance of the overly ingenious casuistry of the Second Sophistic. For this reason the trials are somewhat external and formal, and rather judicial and rhetorical as well.

What is important here is not only the organization of separate adventures. The novel as a whole is conceived precisely as a test of the heroes. Greek adventure-time, as we already know, leaves no traces—neither in the world nor in human beings. No changes of any consequence occur, internal or external, as a result of the events recounted in the novel. At the end of the novel that initial equilibrium that had been destroyed by chance is restored once again. Everything returns to its source, everything returns to its own place. The result of this whole lengthy novel is that—the hero marries his sweetheart. And yet people and things have gone *through* something, something that did not, indeed, change them but that did (in a manner of speaking) affirm what they, and precisely they, were as individuals, something that did verify and establish their identity, their durability and continuity. The hammer of events shatters nothing and forges nothing—it merely tries the durability of an already finished product. And the product passes the test. Thus is constituted the artistic and ideological meaning of the Greek romance.

No artistic genre can organize itself around suspense alone, for the very good reason that to be suspenseful there must be matters of substance to engage. And only a human life, or at least something directly touching it, is capable of evoking such suspense. This human factor must be revealed in some substantial aspect, however slight; that is, it must possess some degree of living *reality.*

The Greek romance is a very malleable instance of the novelistic genre, one that possesses an enormous life-force. It is precisely the use of the trial as a compositional idea that has proved especially productive in the history of the novel. We encounter it in the medieval courtly romance, in its early and—especially—later manifestation. It is to a significant degree the organizing principle behind *Amadis*[j] and *Palmerin of England.*[k] We have already referred to its influence on the Baroque novel, where the idea of testing is enriched with specific ideological content—where a set of specific ideals emerge embodied in "the hero undergoing a trial"—"the knight without fear and above reproach." This absolute irreproachability of the heroes results in a certain stiltedness, leading Boileau to sharply criticize the Baroque novel in his Lucianic *Dialogue sur les héros des romans.*[l]

In the period following the Baroque, the organizational importance of the trial diminishes sharply. But it does not die out entirely, and is retained as one of the organizing ideas of the novel in all subsequent eras. It is filled with varied ideological content, and the trial *qua* trial increasingly leads to negative results—as in the nineteenth and early twentieth century, when we encounter just such variations on the theme of the trial. One meets especially often the kind of trial that seeks to identify the hero's

---

j. *Amadis de Gaula* (fourteenth century), the Spanish chivalric romance that is the primary target for Cervantes' satire in *Don Quixote.* Based loosely on the Arthurian cycle, it was enormously popular.

k. *Palmerin de Inglaterra* (1547), one of a whole series (*Palmerin de Oliva* [1511], *Primaleon* [1512]) of Amadis imitations.

l. Cf. footnote g.

calling, his "chosenness," his genius. We see one such variant in the testing of the Napoleonic parvenu in the French novel. Another version would be the testing of the hero's physical health and his ability to cope successfully with life. And finally, we have later variants on the theme of the trial in that mass of third-rate novels that deal with the testing of a moral reformer, a Nietzschean, an immoralist, an emancipated woman and so forth.

But all these European variants on the novel of ordeal, whether pure or mixed in form, depart significantly from that test of identity (in its lapidary, yet forceful, expression) that is present in the Greek romance. It is true that certain aspects of this preoccupation with human identity are retained—such as the motifs of recognition, presumed death and so on—but they have been made more complex, and have lost their original lapidary force. The link of these motifs with folklore in the Greek romance—although it is already sufficiently remote from folklore—is nevertheless more unmediated.

To fully understand the human image in a Greek romance and the distinctive features of its identity (and consequently the distinctive way its identity is put to the test) we must take into consideration the fact that human beings in such works—as distinct from all classical genres of ancient literature—are *individuals*, *private persons*. This feature corresponds to the *abstract-alien world* of the Greek romance: in such a world, a man can *only* function as an isolated and private individual, deprived of any organic connection with his country, his city, his own social group, his clan, even his own family. He does not feel himself to be a part of the social whole. He is a solitary man, lost in an alien world. And he has no mission in this world. Privacy and isolation are the essential features of the human image in a Greek romance, and they are inevitably linked up with the peculiarities of adventure-time and abstract space. It is for this reason that the human being in a Greek romance differs in principle so sharply from the *public* figure of the more ancient genres and, in particular, from that *public* and *political* man we see in the novel of travel.

But at the same time this private and isolated man of the Greek romance quite often behaves, on the surface, like a public man, and precisely like the public man of the rhetorical and historical genres. He delivers long speeches that are rhetorically structured and in which he seeks to enlighten us with the private and intimate details of his love life, his exploits and adventures—but all this not in the form of an intimate confession—rather in the form of a *public accounting*. Finally, in the majority of these novels legal procedures play a critical role: they serve to sum up the adventures of the heroes and provide a legal and judicial affirmation of their identity, especially in its most crucial aspect—the lovers' fidelity to each other (and in particular the chastity of the heroine). As a result, all the major moments of the novel are publicly and rhetorically highlighted and justified (an *apologia*) and all those moments, taken as a whole, receive a final legal and judicial stamp of approval. If, in the final analysis, we should ask what, more than anything else, defines the *unity of the human image* in a Greek romance, we would have to answer that this unity is characterized precisely by what is *rhetorical* and *judicial* in it.

These rhetorical, judicial and public moments, however, assume an external form that is *not consistent* with the internal and authentic content of an individual man. His internal content is *absolutely private*: the basic givens of his life, the goals by which he is guided, all his trials and exploits are of an exclusively personal sort and have no social or political significance at all. After all, the pivot around which content is organized is the main characters' love for each other and those internal and external trials to which this love is subjected. All other events have meaning in the novel only by virtue of their relationship to this pivot. Characteristically, even such events as *war* have meaning only (and exclusively) at the level of the heroes' love activities. In *Leucippe and Clitophon*, for example, the action begins with a war between the Byzantines and the Thracians—for the sole purpose of enabling Leucippe to end up in Clitophon's father's house, thus making possible their first meeting. This war is mentioned again at the end of the novel, so that its conclusion might be celebrated by the religious procession honoring Artemis that motivates Clitophon's release from torture and execution.

Characteristically it is not private life that is subjected to and interpreted in light of social and political events, but rather the other way around—social and political events gain meaning in the novel only thanks to their connection with private life. And such events are illuminated in the novel only insofar as they relate to private fates; their essence as purely social and political events remains outside the novel.

Thus, the public and rhetorical unity of the human image is to be found in the contradiction between it and its purely private content. This contradiction is highly characteristic of the Greek romance. It is also characteristic—as we will see below—of several later rhetorical genres, in particular of autobiography.

In general, the ancient world did not succeed in generating forms and unities that were adequate to the private individual and his life. Although personal life had already become private and persons individualized, although this sense of the private had begun to infiltrate literature in ancient times, still, it was able to develop forms adequate to itself only in the minor, lyrico-epic genres and in the small everyday genres, the comedy and novella of common life. In the major genres the private life of an individualized person was only externally and inadequately arrayed, and, therefore, in forms that were inorganic and formalistic, either public and bureaucratic or public and rhetorical.

This public and rhetorical side of the individual, which is responsible for his unity and which he bears with him throughout his adventures, also has an external, formalistic and conventional nature in the Greek romance. In general, the homogenization of all that is heterogeneous in a Greek romance (in the history of its origins as well as in its essence as a genre), a homogenization that results in a huge, almost encyclopedic genre, is achieved only at the cost of the most extreme abstraction, schematization and a denuding of all that is concrete and merely local. The chronotope of the Greek romance is the most abstract of all novelistic chronotopes.

This most abstract of all chronotopes is also the most static. In such a chronotope the world and the individual are finished items, absolutely immobile. In it there is no potential for evolution, for growth, for change. As a result of the action described in the novel, nothing in its world is destroyed, remade, changed or created anew. What we get is a mere affirmation of the identity between what had been at the beginning and what is at the end. Adventure-time leaves no trace.

Such is the first type of ancient novel. We will have to return to isolated aspects of it in connection with the further development of methods for expressing time in the novel. As we have suggested above, this novelistic type, and several of its defining characteristics in particular (especially adventure-time itself), exhibit great liveliness and flexibility in the subsequent history of the novel.

II. Apuleius and Petronius

Let us now pass to the second type of ancient novel, which we will provisionally call the *adventure novel of everyday life*. In a strict sense only two works belong to this category: the *Satyricon* of Petronius (which has come down to us in comparatively few fragments) and *The Golden Ass* of Apuleius (which has survived in its entirety). But the characteristic features of this type occur in other genres as well, primarily in satires and in the Hellenistic diatribe, as well as in several works from early Christian literature on the lives of saints (a sinful life, filled with temptation, followed by crisis and rebirth).

The key to our analysis of this second type of ancient novel is Apuleius' *The Golden Ass*. We will also mention some of the distinctive features of other surviving examples of this type.

In this second type, what strikes us first of all is the mix of adventure-time with everyday time—a quality we sought to express in our provisional designation of the type as an "adventure-everyday novel." Of course a merely mechanical mix of these two different times is out of the question. Both adventure- and everyday time change their essential forms in this combination, as they are subject to the conditions of the completely new chronotope created by this novel. Thus there emerges a new type of adventure-time, one sharply distinct from Greek adventure-time, one that is a special sort of everyday time.

The plot [*sjužet*] of *The Golden Ass* is in no sense an extratemporal hiatus between two adjacent moments of real-life sequence. On the contrary, it is precisely the course of the hero's (Lucius') life in its critical moments that makes up the plot of the novel. But two special prerequisites are essential to the portrayal of this life, which define the peculiar nature of *time* in this novel.

These prerequisites are: (1) that the course of Lucius' life be given to us sheathed in the context of a "metamorphosis," and (2) that the course of his life must somehow correspond to an *actual course of travel, to the wanderings* of Lucius throughout the world in the shape of an ass.

The basic plot of the novel—the life story of Lucius—is presented as the course of a life sheathed in a metamorphosis—as is also the case in the inserted novella about Cupid and Psyche, which turns out to be a parallel semantic variant of the basic plot.

The themes of *metamorphosis* (*transformation*)—particularly human transformation—and *identity* (particularly human identity) are drawn from the treasury of pre-class world folklore. The folkloric image of man is intimately bound up with transformation and identity. This combination may be seen with particular clarity in the popular folktale [*skazka*]. The folktale image of man—throughout the extraordinary variety of folkloric narratives—always orders itself around the motifs of *transformation* and *identity* (no matter how varied in its turn the concrete expression of these motifs might be). The motifs of transformation and identity, which began as matters of concern for the individual, are transferred to the entire human world, and to nature, and to those things that man himself has created. We will discuss later those distinctive features of popular-folktale time where this transformation-identity motif is revealed in the image of man, in connection with Rabelais.

In ancient times the idea of metamorphosis underwent an extremely complex and multi-branched path of development. One of the branches on this path is Greek philosophy, where the idea of transformation—along with that of identity—plays an enormous role: in fact the central *mythological sheath* of these ideas is retained as late as Democritus and Aristophanes (and even they did not succeed in casting it off completely).

Another branch would be the cultic development of the idea of metamorphosis (transformation) in ancient mysteries, especially the Eleusinian Mysteries. In the later stages of their development these ancient mysteries increasingly succumbed to the influence of oriental cults, which had their own specific forms of metamorphosis. The original forms of the Christian cult would be included in this line of development. We should also add to this group those crude magical forms of metamorphosis that were exceedingly widespread in the first and second century A.D., forms that were practiced by charlatans of various sorts and occupied a permanent place in the everyday life of the era.

A third branch would be the continuing presence of transformation motifs in purely popular folklore. This folklore has not, of course, come down to us in its pure form, but we know of its existence through the influence it exercised: its reflection in literature (for example, in Apuleius' novella about Cupid and Psyche).

And finally, a fourth branch is the development of the idea of metamorphosis in literature proper. Only this branch concerns us in the present context.

It is of course obvious that the literary development of this idea did not take place in isolation from all those other forms that the theme assumed and that we have enumerated above. One need only mention the influence of the Eleusinian Mystery tradition on Greek tragedy. Philosophical forms of transformation undoubtedly had an effect on literature, as did the influence of folklore referred to above.

Metamorphosis or transformation is a mythological sheath for the idea of development—but one that unfolds not so much in a straight line as spasmodically, a line with "knots" in it, one that therefore constitutes a distinctive type of *temporal sequence.* The makeup of this idea is extraordinarily complex, which is why the types of temporal sequences that develop out of it are extremely varied.

If we look closely at the ways Hesiod (in both his *Works and Days* and his *Theogony*) took this complex mythological theme and with great artistry broke it down into a variety of sequences, we observe the following: a specific genealogical series unfolding, a distinctive sequence of shifts in ages and generations (the myth of the five ages: Golden, Silver, Bronze, "Trojan" or Heroic and Iron), an irreversible theogonic sequence of metamorphosis in nature, including the cyclical series of metamorphosis for grain and an analogical series of metamorphosis in the vine of the grape. What is more, for Hesiod even the cyclical sequence of everyday agricultural labor is structured, in its own way, like a "metamorphosis of the farmer." With all the above we are still far from exhausting all the temporal sequences Hesiod generated that use the idea of *metamorphosis* as their mythological aetiology. All these series have in common the fact of sequentiality (items that follow upon one another), but a sequentiality whose units assume extremely varied forms (or images), forms utterly different from one another. Thus, in the theogonic process the Era of Zeus replaces the Era of Cronos; as the ages change (Golden, Silver, etc.) so do the generations of men, while in another series it is the seasons that replace each other.

The images we are given of various eras, generations, seasons and phases of agricultural labor differ profoundly from one another. But amid all this diversity the unity of the theogonic process, of the historical process, of nature and of agricultural life is preserved.

The conception of metamorphosis in Hesiod, as in other early philosophical systems and classical mysteries, has far-reaching implications: the word "metamorphosis" itself, in Hesiod, is not used in the specific sense of a miraculous, instantaneous transformation of one being into another (a definition bordering on the magical); this definition the word acquired only in the Roman and Hellenistic era. The word appeared with this meaning only at a later stage in the development of the metamorphosis theme.

Ovid's *Metamorphoses* is typical of this later stage. Here the general idea of metamorphosis has already become the private metamorphosis of individual, isolated beings and is already acquiring the characteristics of an external, miraculous transformation. The idea of representing the whole world of cosmogonic and historical process from the point of view of metamorphosis—beginning with the creation of the cosmos out of chaos and ending with the transformation of Caesar into a star—is retained. But this idea is now actualized through a selection of metamorphoses taken from the whole of the mythological and literary tradition, of which separate instances are superficially vivid but without connection to one another. They are metamorphoses only in the narrower sense of the word, changes that are deployed in a series lacking any internal unity. Each such metamorphosis suffices unto itself and constitutes in itself a closed, poetic whole. The mythological sheath of metamorphosis is no longer able to unite those temporal sequences that are major and essential. Time breaks down into isolated, self-sufficient temporal segments that mechanically arrange themselves into no more than single sequences. One can observe this same disintegration of the mythological unity of ancient temporal sequences in Ovid's *Fasti* (a work of great importance for studying the sense of time in the Roman and Hellenistic era).

In Apuleius, metamorphosis acquires an even more personal, isolated and quite openly magical nature. Almost nothing remains of its former breadth and force. Metamorphosis has become a vehicle for conceptualizing and portraying personal, individual fate, a fate cut off from both the cosmic and the historical whole. Nevertheless, the idea of metamorphosis retains enough energy (thanks to the influence of an unmediated folklore tradition) to comprehend the *entire life-long destiny of a man*, at all its critical *turning points*. Herein lies its significance for the genre of the novel.

This is not the place for an in-depth analysis of the essence of the metamorphosis itself—Lucius' transformation into an ass, his reverse transformation into a man and his mystical purification. Such an analysis is not necessary for our purposes. Furthermore, the genesis of the theme "metamorphosis into an ass" is itself very complex. Apuleius' treatment of the theme is also complex, and to this day it has not been fully explicated. For our immediate purposes all this is of no essential importance. We are concerned only with the functions of this metamorphosis in the structure of a novel of the second type.

Metamorphosis serves as the basis for a method of portraying the whole of an individual's life in its more important moments of *crisis*: for showing *how an individual becomes other than what he was*. We are offered various sharply differing images of one and the same individual, images that are united in him as various epochs and stages in the course of his life. There is no evolution in the strict sense of the word; what we get, rather, is crisis and rebirth.

This is what essentially distinguishes the Apuleian plot from the plots of the Greek romance. The events that Apuleius describes determine the life of the hero; they define his *entire* life. But of course his entire life, from childhood through old age and death, is not laid out for us. This is not, therefore, a *biographical life* in its entirety. In the crisis-type of portrayal we see only one or two moments that decide the fate of a man's life and determine its entire disposition. In keeping with this principle, the novel provides us with two or three different images of the same individual, images that have been disjoined and rejoined through his crisis and rebirths. In the major plot, Apuleius presents three images of Lucius: Lucius before his transformation into an ass, Lucius the Ass and Lucius mysteriously purified and renewed. In the parallel plot we have only two images of Psyche: before she is purified by redemptive suffering, and after. But here the progression of the heroine's rebirth is not broken down into three sharply differentiated images of her, as in the case of Lucius.

In early Christian *crisis hagiographies* belonging to this type, we also have as a rule only two images of an individual, images that are separated and reunited through crisis and rebirth: the image of the sinner (before rebirth) and the image of the holy man or saint (after crisis and rebirth). Three-image sequences are sometimes met with, especially where there is a particular emphasis and development of that portion of the saint's life devoted to *askesis*, or to purification through suffering, to a struggle with oneself (corresponding to the segment of time Lucius spends as an ass).

From what has been said, it should be clear that a novel of this type does not, strictly speaking, unfold in *biographical time*. It depicts only the *exceptional*, utterly *unusual* moments of a man's life, moments that are very short compared to the whole length of a human life. But these moments *shape the definitive image of the man, his essence, as well as the nature of his entire subsequent life*. But the further course of that life, with its biographical pace, its activities and labors, stretches out after the rebirth and consequently already lies beyond the realm of the novel. Thus, Lucius, having passed through three initiations, enters upon his biographical life as a rhetorician and a priest.

These, then, are the constitutive features of adventure-time of the second type. It is not the time of a Greek romance, a time that leaves no traces. On the contrary, it leaves a deep and irradicable mark on the man himself as well as on his entire life. It is, nevertheless, decidedly adventure-time: a time of exceptional and unusual events, events determined by chance, which, moreover, manifest themselves in fortuitous encounters (temporal junctures) and fortuitous nonencounters (temporal disjunctions).

But in the second type of adventure-time this logic of chance is subordinated to another and higher logic that contains it, in the literal sense. The witch's maid Fotis *accidentally* took the wrong box and in place of a cream for transforming men into birds gave Lucius the cream for turning men into asses. It was an *accident* that *at that moment* the roses necessary to reverse this transformation were not to be found in the house. It was an *accident* that *on that very* night robbers attacked the house and drove away the ass. And in all subsequent adventures of the ass itself, and of its various masters as well, chance continues to play a major role. Time and again, it is chance that prevents the reverse transformation from ass back into man. But the power of chance and the initiative that lies with it is limited; it can act only within the limits of that area marked out for it. It is not chance but voluptuousness, youthful frivolity and "prurient curiosity" that urged Lucius on to that dangerous entanglement with witchcraft. *He himself is guilty.* He undoes the game of chance by his own prurience. The *primary initiative*, therefore, belongs to *the hero himself* and to his own *personality*. It is true that this initiative is *not positive in a creative sense* (but this is not very important); what we have is *guilt, moral weakness, error* (and in its Christian hagiographic variant, sin) as initiating forces. The first image of the hero is characterized by this negative initiative—youthful, frivolous, unrestrained: a voluptuary, curious in a careless way. He attracts the power of chance to himself. The initial link of the adventure sequence is thus determined not by chance, but by the hero himself and by the nature of his personality.

The final link—the conclusion of the entire adventure sequence—is likewise not determined by chance. Lucius is saved by the goddess Isis, who shows him what he must do to regain human form. The goddess Isis functions here not as a synonym for "good fortune" (as do the gods in a Greek romance), but as Lucius' patroness, directing him to his purification, demanding from him highly detailed purifying rituals and *askesis*. Characteristically, visions and dreams have a very different meaning in Apuleius from what they had in a Greek romance. In the Greek romance, dreams and visions make men aware of the will of the gods or of chance; they could not be used as a means for avoiding the blows of fate or for taking measures against such a fate, but were granted rather "that men may bear their sufferings more easily" (Achilles Tatius). Dreams and visions, therefore, do not incite the heroes to any activity. In Apuleius, on the contrary, dreams and visions provide instructions to the heroes, telling them what to do, how to act in order to change their fate; that is, they force the heroes to take definite steps, to act.

Thus both the initial and the final links in the chain of adventures lie beyond the power of chance. As a consequence the nature of the entire chain is altered. It becomes more active, it changes the hero himself and his fate. The series of adventures that the hero undergoes does not result in a simple affirmation of his identity, but rather in the construction of a new image of the hero, a man who is now purified and reborn. Therefore, the chance governing within the limits of separate adventures must be interpreted in a new way.

In this connection, the speech delivered by the priest of Isis after Lucius' purification is characteristic (*The Golden Ass*, book 11):[m]

---

m. Lines quoted from Apuleius are taken from: Apuleius, *The Golden Ass*, tr. William Adlington and ed. Harry C. Schnur (New York: Collier, 1962).

Here you are, Lucius, after so many misfortunes *sent you by fate*, after having endured so many tempests, have you finally reached a peaceful haven, the altars of mercy. Neither your noble lineage, nor your position, nor learning itself in which you so excelled, could avail you, but because you had become a *slave of voluptuousness*, owing to the passion of your youthful years, *you have received a fateful retribution* for your prurient curiosity. But *blind fate*, tormenting you with the worst possible dangers, *herself not knowing how, led you to your present blessedness*. She must now go and rage somewhere else, she must seek out another victim on whom to practice her cruelty. For among those who have dedicated their lives to our supreme goddess *there is no place for ruinous chance*. How did subjecting you to thieves, to wild beasts, to slavery, to cruel choices at every turn, to a daily expectation of death—benefit fate? For now another fate has taken you under her protection, one not blind but *one who can see*, and the light of her radiance illuminates even the other gods.

What is emphasized here is Lucius' *individual guilt*, which delivered him over to the power of chance ("blind fate"). We also see a clear opposition of "blind fate" and "ruinous chance" to "a seeing fate," that is, to the hegemony of the goddess who had saved Lucius. And here, finally, the essential meaning of "blind fate" is revealed to us, a fate whose power is limited on the one hand by Lucius' individual guilt and on the other by the power of "a seeing fate," that is, the protection of the goddess. This essential meaning is contained in the *fateful retribution* and the *path to present blessedness* to which this "blind fate," "herself not knowing how," had led Lucius. Thus the entire adventure sequence must be interpreted as *punishment* and *redemption*.

The adventure-folktale sequence in the parallel subplot (the novella about Cupid and Psyche) is organized in precisely the same way. The individual guilt of Psyche serves as the initial link in the sequence, and the final link is the protection of the gods. Psyche's own adventures and folktale tribulations are interpreted as punishment and retribution. The role of chance, of "blind fate," is here even more circumscribed and subordinated.

Thus we see that the adventure sequence, governed as it is by chance, is here utterly subordinated to the other sequence that encompasses and interprets it: guilt⟶punishment⟶redemption⟶blessedness. This sequence is governed by a completely different logic, one that has nothing to do with adventure logic. It is an active sequence, determining (as its first priority) the very metamorphosis itself, that is, the shifting appearance of the hero.

Thus a frivolous and fecklessly curious Lucius beomes Lucius the Ass, and after his suffering he becomes Lucius purified and enlightened. Furthermore, a definite shape and degree of ineluctability is essential to this sequence, whereas in the Greek adventure sequence there was no hint of either. Retribution *must* follow guilt, purification and blessedness *must* follow upon the retribution of the hero. And furthermore, this ineluctability is human; it is not mechanical or depersonalized. Guilt is a function of individual personality itself; so is retribution, which is just as essential a force for purifying and improving the individual. This entire sequence is grounded in *individual responsibility.* Finally, the shifting appearance of one and the same individual gives this sequence its essential humanness.

The above considerations demonstrate the indisputable advantages such a sequence has in comparison with Greek adventure-time. Beginning with the purely mythological conception of metamorphosis, we have devised a means more legitimately to express some of the more critical and realistic characteristics of time. Here time is not merely technical, not a mere distribution of days, hours, moments that are reversible, transposable, unlimited internally, along a straight line; here the temporal sequence is an integrated and *irreversible whole.* And as a consequence, the abstractness so characteristic of Greek adventure-time falls away. Quite the contrary, this new temporal sequence demands precisely concreteness of expression.

But along with these progressive aspects some crucial limitations remain. As in a Greek romance, the individual is *private* and *isolated.* Therefore, his guilt, retribution, purification and blessedness are private and individual: it is the *personal* business of a *discrete, particular* individual. Such an individual's potential for initiating actions is, however, not creative; it is realized only negatively, in rash and hasty acts, in mistakes, in guilt. Therefore, the working of the entire sequence is limited by the particular shape of the individual and his fate. As in a Greek romance, this temporal sequence leaves no traces in the surrounding world. Therefore, the connection between an individual's fate and his world is *external.* The individual changes and undergoes metamorphosis completely independent of the world; the world itself remains unchanged. Therefore, metamorphosis has a merely personal and unproductive character.

Thus, the basic temporal sequence of the novel—although it is, as we have said, irreversible and integral—is nevertheless a closed circuit, isolated, not localized in historical time (that is, it does not participate in the irreversible historical sequence of time, because the novel does not yet know such a sequence).

Such is the basic adventure-time of this type of novel. But everyday time is present in it as well. What is *it* like, and how does it mesh with that distinctive adventure-time characterized by us above in such a way as to form one novelistic whole?

The most characteristic thing about this novel is the way it fuses the course of an individual's life (at its major turning points) with his actual spatial course or road—that is, with his wanderings. Thus is realized the metaphor "the path of life." The path itself extends through familiar, native territory, in which there is nothing exotic, alien or strange. Thus a unique novelistic chronotope is created, one that has played an enormous role in the history of the genre. At its heart is folklore. Various means for realizing the metaphor "the path of life" play a large role in all aspects of folklore. One can even go as far as to say that in folklore a road is almost never merely a road, but always suggests the whole, or a portion of, "a path of life." The choice of a real itinerary equals the choice of "the path of life." An intersection always signifies some turning point in the life of the folklore character; setting out on the road from one's birthplace, returning home, are usually plateaus of *age* in the life of the individual (he sets out as a youth, returns a man). Road markers are indicators of his fate and so on. Thus this novelistic chronotope of the road is specific, organic and deeply infused with folklore motifs.

An individual's movement through space, his pilgrimages, lose that abstract and technical character that they had in the Greek romance, where it was merely a mannered enchaining of coordinates both spatial (near/far) and temporal (at the *same* time/at *different* times). Space becomes more concrete and saturated with a time that is more substantial: space is filled with real, living meaning, and forms a crucial relationship with the hero and his fate. This type of space so saturates this new chronotope that such events as meeting, separation, collision, escape and so forth take on a new and markedly more concrete chronotopic significance.

The concreteness of this chronotope of the road permits *everyday life* to be realized within it. But this life is, so to speak, spread out along the edge of the road itself, and along the sideroads. The main protagonist and the major turning points of his life are to be found *outside everyday life.* He merely observes this life, meddles in it now and then as an alien force; he occasionally even dons a common and everyday mask—but in essence he does not participate in this life and is not determined by it.

The hero experiences *events that are exclusively extraordinary,* defined by the sequence of guilt—▸retribution—▸redemption—▸blessedness. Such was the experience of Lucius. But in passing from retribution to redemption—that is, precisely during the process of metamorphosis—Lucius must descend to low everyday life, and he must play the most humiliating role in that setting, not even the role of a slave, but of an ass. As an ass, a beast of burden, he descends to the very depths of common life, life among muleteers, hauling a millstone for the miller, serving a gardener, a soldier, a cook, a baker. He suffers constant beatings and is persecuted by shrewish wives (the muleteer's wife, the baker's wife). But in all these situations Lucius performs not as Lucius but as an ass. At the end of the novel he casts off the appearance of an ass and in a triumphant ceremony re-enters the highest, most privileged spheres of life, a life outside ordinary events. We might add further that the time spent by Lucius in everyday life coincides with his presumed death (his family considers him dead), and his leaving that life is his resurrection. The ancient folkloric core of Lucius' metamorphosis is in fact precisely death: the passage to the nether regions and resurrection. In this instance everyday life corresponds to the nether regions, to the grave. (Corresponding mythological equivalents might be found for all the narrative motifs in *The Golden Ass.*)

This stance of the hero vis-à-vis everyday life is a distinctive feature of this second type of ancient novel, and it is one of extreme importance. This feature is preserved (although of course with variations) throughout the entire subsequent history of the type. It is always the case that the hero cannot, by his very nature, be a part of everyday life; he passes through such life as would a man from another world. Most often this hero is a rogue, a man who changes his everyday personalities as he pleases and who occupies no fixed place in everyday life, who plays with life and does not take it seriously. The hero might also be a wandering actor disguised as an aristocrat, or a high-born gentleman ignorant of his lineage (a "foundling"). Everyday life is that lowest sphere of existence from which the hero tries to liberate himself, and with which he will never internally fuse himself. The course of his life is uncommon, outside everyday life; one of its stages just happens to be a progression through the everyday sphere.

Playing the lowest role in the lowest level of society, Lucius does not participate internally in that life and is, therefore, in an even better position to observe it and study all its secrets. For him this is the *experience* of studying and understanding human beings. "I myself," says Lucius, "remember my sojourn as an ass with great gratitude, for having suffered *the turns of fate under cover of this animal's skin* I have become, if not wiser, at least *more experienced.*"

The position of an ass is a particularly convenient one for observing the secrets of everyday life. The presence of an ass embarrasses no one, all open up completely. "And in my oppressive life only one consolation remained to me: to indulge that curiosity which is my native bent, since people never took my presence into consideration and talked and acted as freely as they wished" (book 9).

The ass has an additional advantage in this respect: his ears. "And I—although distraught at Fotis' mistake which had turned me into an ass instead of a bird—found consolation in my pathetic transformation in this fact alone, that thanks to my huge ears I could hear excellently, even those things that happened far away" (book 9).

This extraordinary positioning of the ass in the novel is a feature of extreme importance.

The everyday life that Lucius observes and studies is an *exclusively personal and private life.* By its very nature there can be nothing *public* about it. All its events are the personal affairs of isolated people: they could not occur "in the eyes of the world," publicly, in the presence of a *chorus.* These events are not liable to public reckoning on the open square. Events acquire a public significance as such only when they become crimes. The *criminal act* is a moment of private life that becomes, as it were, *involuntarily* public. The remainder of this life is made up of bedroom secrets (infidelities on the part of shrewish wives, husbands' impotence and so forth), secret profiteering, petty everyday fraud, etc.

By its very nature this private life does not create a place for the contemplative man, for that "third person" who might be in a position to meditate on this life, to judge and evaluate it. This life takes place between four walls and for only two pairs of eyes. On the other hand public life—any event that has any social significance—tends toward making itself public (naturally), necessarily presuming an observer, a judge, an evaluator; and a place is always created for such a person in the event, he is in fact an indispensable and obligatory participant *in* the event. The public man always lives and acts in the world, and each moment of his life, in principle and in essence, will avail itself to being made public. Public life and public man are by their very essence *open, visible* and *audible*. Public life adopts the most varied means for making itself public and accounting for itself (as does its literature). Therefore, the particular positioning of a person who could observe or eavesdrop on this life (a "third person") presents no special problem, nor do the particular forms necessary for making that life public. For this reason the problem was unknown in classical ancient literature, which was a literature of public life and public men.

But when the private individual and private life entered literature (in the Hellenistic era) these problems inevitably were bound to arise. *A contradiction developed between the public nature of the literary form and the private nature of its content.* The process of working out *private genres* began. But this process remained incomplete in ancient times.

This problem was especially critical in connection with larger epic forms (the "major epic"). In the process of resolving this problem, the ancient novel emerged.

The quintessentially private life that entered the novel at this time was, by its very nature and as opposed to public life, *closed.* In essence one could only *spy* and *eavesdrop* on it. The literature of private life is essentially a literature of snooping about, of overhearing "how others live." This life may be exposed and made public in a criminal trial, either directly, by inserting the trial into the novel (along with searches and investigations), by inserting criminal activities into private life, or circumstantially and conditionally, in a half-hidden way, by utilizing eyewitness accounts, confessions of the accused, court documents, evidence, investigative hunches and so forth. And finally we encounter those forms of self-revelation that occur in the ordinary course of our everyday lives: the personal letter, the intimate diary, the confession.

We have already seen how the Greek romance resolved this problem of portraying the personal life and the private individual. It tried to fit the content of a private life into external, inadequate public and rhetorical forms—forms that were by that time already stiff and dead; this was possible only in the context of Greek adventure-time and the extreme abstractness through which it was portrayed. In addition, on such a rhetorical basis the Greek romance introduces as well the criminal trial, as something that plays a crucial role in the novel. The Greek romance also frequently makes use of everyday forms such as the epistle.

In the subsequent history of the novel, the *criminal trial*—in its direct and oblique forms—and legal-criminal categories in general have an enormous organizational significance. Crimes play a correspondingly huge and significant role in the actual content of such novels. Various forms and varieties of the novel make use of these manifold legal and criminal categories in different ways. It suffices to mention, on the one hand, the adventure-detective novel (the investigation, clues, piecing-together of events with the help of these clues) and on the other hand, the novels of Dostoevsky (*Crime and Punishment* and *The Brothers Karamazov*).

The significance of legal-criminal categories in the novel, and the various ways they are used—as specific forms for uncovering and making private life public—is an interesting and important problem in the history of the novel.

The criminal aspect plays a large role in Apuleius' *The Golden Ass*. Several of the inserted novellas are structured precisely as stories about criminal acts (the sixth, seventh, eleventh and twelfth novellas). But the criminal material itself is not essential for Apuleius; what matters are the everyday secrets of private life that lay bare human nature—that is, everything that can be only spied and eavesdropped upon.

For the spying and eavesdropping on private life, the position of Lucius the Ass is most advantageous. For this reason, tradition has reinforced such a position, and we encounter it in a multitude of variations in the later history of the novel. What is preserved of the metamorphosis-into-ass is precisely this specific placement of the hero as a "third person" in relation to private everyday life, permitting him to spy and eavesdrop. Such is the positioning of the *rogue* and the *adventurer*, who do not participate internally in everyday life, who do not occupy in it any definite fixed place, yet who at the same time pass through that life and are forced to study its workings, all its secret cogs and wheels. This is particularly true of the positioning of the *servant* who goes from one master to the other. The servant is the eternal "third man" in the private life of his lords. Servants are the most privileged witnesses to private life. People are as little embarrassed in a servant's presence as they are in the presence of an ass, and at the same time the servant is called upon to participate in all intimate aspects of personal life. Thus, servants replace the ass in the later history of the adventure novel of the second type (that is, the adventure novel of everyday life). The picaresque novel, from *Lazarillo de Tormes* to *Gil Blas*, makes extensive use of the servant's role. But other aspects and motifs from *The Golden Ass* live on in this classical (pure) picaresque novel—first of all, they share the same chronotope. In a more complicated, no longer pure variant on the adventure novel of everyday life, the figure of the servant retreats into the background but his significance remains the same. And in other types of novels as well (indeed, in other genres too) the servant has this same essential significance (cf. Diderot's *Jacques le fataliste*, Beaumarchais' dramatic trilogy and other works). The servant is that distinctive, embodied point of view on the world of private life without which a literature treating private life could not manage.

The *prostitute* and *courtesan* occupy a place in the novel analogous (in their functions) to that of the servant (cf. for example, Defoe's *Moll Flanders* and *Roxanne*). Their position is likewise extremely convenient for spying and eavesdropping on private life with its secrets and intimacies. The *procurer* has the same significance in the novel, although he is a minor character; most often he functions as the storyteller. In *The Golden Ass*, for instance, the ninth inserted novella is narrated by an old procuress. I call to the reader's attention the magnificent story by an old procuress in Sorel's *Francion*,[n] almost equal to Balzac in the power with which it realistically portrays private life, and incomparably superior to analogous passages in Zola.

Finally, as we have said, the *adventurer* (in the broad sense of the term) and in particular the *parvenu* fulfill analogous functions in the novel. The role of the adventurer and parvenu is the role of one who has not yet found a definite or fixed place in life, but who seeks personal success—building a career, accumulating

---

n. Reference is to *La vraie Histoire comique de Francion* (1623) by Charles Sorel (1599–1674), a book somewhat reminiscent of *Gil Blas*. It is a relatively realistic portrait of the conditions under which poor students and would-be authors lived in seventeenth-century Paris.

wealth, winning glory (always out of personal interest, "for himself"); this role impels him to study personal life, uncover its hidden workings, spy and eavesdrop on its most intimate secrets. And so he begins his journey "to the depths" (where he rubs shoulders with servants, prostitutes, pimps, and from them learns about life "as it really is"): such a character can climb upward (usually via the courtesan route) and thus reach the high peaks of private life—or can suffer a reversal on the road or can remain to the very end a lowly adventurer (an adventurer of the slum world). The position of such characters is admirably suited to exposing and portraying all layers and levels of private life. Thus, the role of the adventurer or the parvenu can be said to determine the structure of the more complicated type of adventure novels of everyday life: we have an adventurer, in the broad sense, in Sorel's *L'Histoire comique de Francion*[o] (although of course he is no parvenu); the heroes of Scarron's *Comical Romance*[p] (seventeenth century) are likewise adventurers; *Captain Singleton* and *Colonel Jack*, the heroes of Defoe's "picaresque" novels (the word is used loosely) are also adventurers; parvenus first appear with Marivaux (*Le Paysan parvenu*)[q] and adventurers with the heroes of Smollett. Rameau's nephew in Diderot embodies and distills in himself, in a wonderfully complete and profound way, all the specific attributes of an ass, a rogue, a tramp, a servant, an adventurer, a parvenu, an actor: he offers us a remarkably strong and deep example of the *philosophy of the third person in private life*. This is the philosophy of a person who knows only private life and craves it alone, but who does not participate in it, who has no place in it—and therefore sees it in sharp focus, as a whole, in all its nakedness, playing out all its roles but not fusing his identity with any one of them.

In the complex, synthesizing novel of the great French realists Stendhal and Balzac, the positioning of the adventurer and the parvenu retains in full its organizing significance. All kinds of

---

o. Cf. footnote n.

p. *Le Roman comique* (1651) by Paul Scarron (1610–1660) recounts the adventures of itinerant actors, with satirical cameos of provincial life.

q. *Le Paysan parvenu* (1735–1736) by Pierre Marivaux (1688–1763), like Marivaux's other novel, *La Vie de Marianne* (1731–1741), is essentially a psychological study of the new middle class who seek—and find—happiness and success through their financial dealings.

other "third-person" representatives of private life—courtesans, prostitutes, pimps, servants, clerks, pawnbrokers, doctors—live and move in the background of their novels.

In classic English realism—Dickens and Thackeray—the role of the adventurer and parvenu is less important. In their works such characters play secondary roles (the exception is Becky Sharp in Thackeray's *Vanity Fair*).

I note in passing that in all the examples we have analyzed, the factor of metamorphosis is preserved, to a certain extent and in one or another form: the rogue's change of roles or masks, the transformation of the beggar into the rich man, the homeless tramp into the wealthy aristocrat, the thief and pickpocket into the kind and repentant Christian and so forth.

In addition to the figures of rogue, servant, adventurer, pimp, the novel devised other means for spying and eavesdropping on private life—and while these other means are at times very clever and subtle, they became neither typical nor essential to the genre as such. For example: the Lame Devil in Lesage (in his novel *Le Diable boiteux*)[1] removes the roofs from houses and exposes personal life at those moments when a "third person's" presence would not be permitted. In Smollett's *Peregrine Pickle* the hero makes the aquaintance of the Englishman Cadwallader, a man who is completely deaf, in whose presence no one is embarrassed to speak on any topic whatever (as has been the case with Lucius the Ass); later on it turns out that Cadwallader is not deaf at all, but has only pretended to be so in order to eavesdrop on the secrets of private life.

Such, then, is the extraordinarily important position Lucius the Ass occupies as an observer of private life. In what sort of time does this private life unfold?

In *The Golden Ass* and other examples of the ancient adventure novel of everyday life, "everyday time" is in no sense cyclical. In general, such novels offer few instances of repetition as such, of a periodic return of one and the same features (phenomena). The only cyclical time known to ancient literature was an idealized, agricultural, everyday time, one interwoven with

---

1. *Le Diable boiteux* (1797) by Alain Lesage (1668–1747) is an adaptation of Guevara's *El Diablo cojuelo* (1641), but has most of all to do with bourgeois life at the beginning of the eighteenth century.

the times of nature and myth (the basic stages of its development are Hesiod, Theocritus and Virgil). Novelistic everyday time differs sharply from all these variants of cyclical time. First and foremost, novelistic time is thoroughly cut off from nature and from natural and mythological cycles. This alienation of the everyday plane from nature is actually emphasized. Nature motifs turn up in Apuleius only in the sequence guilt→redemption→blessedness (cf., for example, the seashore scene before Lucius' return trip). Everyday life is the nether world, the grave, where the sun does not shine, where there is no starry firmament. For this reason, everyday life is presented to us as the underside of real life. At its center is obscenity, that is, the seamier side of sexual love, love alienated from reproduction, from a progression of generations, from the structures of the family and the clan. Here everyday life is priapic, its logic is the logic of obscenity. But around this sexual nucleus of common life (infidelity, sexually motivated murder, etc.) are distributed other everyday aspects: violence, thievery, various types of fraud, beatings.

In this everyday maelstrom of personal life, time is deprived of its unity and wholeness—it is chopped up into separate segments, each encompassing a single episode from everyday life. The separate episodes—and this is especially true of the inserted novellas dealing with everyday life—are rounded-off and complete, but at the same time are isolated and self-sufficient. The everyday world is scattered, fragmented, deprived of essential connections. It is not permeated with a single temporal sequence, which has its own specific systematization and ineluctability. These temporal segments of episodes from everyday life are, therefore, arranged, as it were, perpendicular to the pivotal axis of the novel, which is the sequence guilt→punishment→redemption→purification→blessedness (precisely at the moment of punishment—redemption). Everyday time is not parallel to this basic axis and not interwoven with it, but separate segments of this time—those parts into which everyday time breaks down—are perpendicular to this basic axis and intersect with it at right angles.

Despite all the fragmentariness and naturalistic quality of this everyday time, it is not absolutely without effect. Taken as a whole it is perceived as a punishment that purifies Lucius; taken in its separate episodic moments it serves Lucius as *experience*, revealing to him human nature. The everyday world itself is *static* in Apuleius, it has no "becoming": this is precisely the reason why there is no *single* everyday time. But it does reveal *social heterogeneity*. Social *contradictions* have not yet become apparent in this heterogeneity, but the situation is fraught with them. If such contradictions were to surface, then the world would start to move, it would be shoved into the future, time would receive a fullness and a historicity. But this process was not brought to completion in ancient times, and certainly not with Apuleius.

It is true that this process was advanced somewhat in Petronius. In his world, socially heterogeneous elements come close to being contradictory. As a result his world bears witness to the distinguishing features of a particular era, the earliest traces of historical time. But in his works as well the process is nevertheless far from completed.

The *Satyricon* of Petronius belongs, as we have already said, to the same type of everyday adventure novel. But in this work adventure-time is tightly interwoven with everyday time (therefore, the *Satyricon* is closer to the European type of picaresque novel). Underlying the wanderings and adventures of its heroes (Encolpius and others) there is no clearly defined metamorphosis nor any specific sequence of guilt→retribution→redemption. This theme is replaced, it is true, by an analogous motif: persecution by the infuriated god Priapus—although the motif is muffled and parodied (it is also a parody on the precedent-setting epic wanderings of Odysseus and Aeneas). But the location of the heroes vis-à-vis the everydayness of ordinary private life is in all respects the same as it was for Lucius the Ass. They pass through the everyday sphere of private life but do not participate internally in it. These rogues are spies, charlatans and parasites, spying and eavesdropping on all the cynical aspects of private life. That life is here even more priapic. But, we repeat, traces of historical time (however unstable) turn up in the social heterogeneity of this private-life world. The image of Trimalchio's feast and the way it is described serve to bring out the distinguishing features of the era: that is, we have to some extent a *temporal whole* that encompasses and unifies the separate episodes of everyday life.

In hagiographic examples of the everyday-type adventure, the factor of metamorphosis is foregrounded (a sinful life→crisis→redemption→sainthood). The everyday-plane adventure is given in the form of an exposure of a sinful life, or of a repentant confession. These forms—and particularly the latter—already border on a third type of ancient novel.

III. Ancient Biography and Autobiography

Moving on to the third type of ancient novel, we must from the outset make one crucial reservation. By this third type we have in mind a *biographical novel*, although antiquity did not produce the kind of novel that we (in our terminology) would call a "novel," that is, a large fiction influenced by biographical models. Nevertheless a series of autobiographical and biographical forms was worked out in ancient times that had a profound influence not only on the development of European biography, but also on the development of the European novel as a whole. At the heart of these ancient forms lies a new type of *biographical time* and a human image constructed to new specifications, that of an individual who passes through the course of a whole life.

From the point of view made available by this type of time and new human image, we will briefly survey ancient autobiographical and biographical forms. In our survey we will not pretend to any completeness of the data, nor to an exhaustive analysis of it. We will select only those details that bear a direct relationship to our subject of inquiry.

We note two essential types of autobiography in classical Greece.

Provisionally we will call the first type *Platonic*, since it found its earliest and most precise expression in such works of Plato as the *Apology* of Socrates and the *Phaedo*. This type, involving an individual's autobiographical self-consciousness, is related to the stricter forms of metamorphosis as found in mythology. At its heart lies the chronotope of "the life course of one seeking true knowledge." The life of such a seeker is broken down into precise and well-marked epochs or steps. His course passes from self-confident ignorance, through self-critical scepticism, to self-knowledge and ultimately to authentic knowing (mathematics and music).

This early Platonic scheme of "the seeker's path" is made more complex in Hellenistic and Roman times by the addition of various highly important motifs: the seeker's passage through a series of philosophical schools with their various tests, and the marking of this path by temporal divisions determined by their own biographical projects. We will return later to this more complex scheme, for it is one of great importance.

In the Platonic scheme there is also a moment of crisis and rebirth (the words of the oracle as a turning point in the course of Socrates' life). The specific nature of this "seeker's path" is all the more clearly revealed when contrasted with an analogous scheme: the course of the soul's ascent toward a perception of the Forms (the *Symposium*, the *Phaedra* and others). In such works the mythological and mystery-cult bases of the scheme are clearly in evidence. Such sources reinforce the kinship between this scheme and those "conversion stories" we discussed in the previous section. Socrates' life course, as it is revealed to us in the *Apology*, is a public and rhetorical expression of the same metamorphosis. Real biographical time is here almost entirely dissolved in the ideal (and even abstract) time of metamorphosis. What is important about the figure of Socrates is therefore not to be found in this idealized-biographical scheme.

The second Greek type is the *rhetorical* autobiography and biography.

At the base of this type lies the "encomium"—the civic funeral and memorial speech that had replaced the ancient "lament" (*trenos*). The form of the encomium also determined the first autobiography of ancient times, the advocatory speech of the Attic orator Isocrates.

When speaking of this classic type one must above all keep the following in mind. These classical forms of autobiography and biography were not works of a literary or bookish nature, kept aloof from the concrete social and political act of noisily making themselves public. On the contrary, such forms were completely determined by events: either verbal praise of civic and political acts, or real human beings giving a public account of themselves. Therefore, the important thing here is not only, and not so much, their internal chronotope (that is, the time-space of their represented life) as it is rather, and preeminently, that exterior real-life chronotope in which the representation of one's own or someone else's life is realized either as verbal praise of a civic-political act or as an account of the self. It is precisely under the conditions of this real-life chronotope, in which one's own or another's life is laid bare (that is, made public), that the limits of a human image and the life it leads are illuminated in all their specificity.

This real-life chronotope is constituted by the public square (the *agora*). In ancient times the autobiographical and biographical self-consciousness of an individual and his life was first laid bare and shaped in the public square.

When Pushkin said that the art of the theater was "born in the public square,"[s] the square he had in mind was that of "the common people," the square of bazaars, puppet theaters, taverns, that is the square of European cities in the thirteenth, fourteenth and subsequent centuries. He also had in mind the fact that the state and "official" society (that is, the privileged classes), with their "official" arts and sciences, were located by and large beyond the square. But the square in earlier (ancient) times itself constituted a state (and more—it constituted the entire state apparatus, with all its official organs), it was the highest court, the whole of science, the whole of art, the entire people participated in it. It was a remarkable chronotope, in which all the most elevated categories, from that of the state to that of revealed truth, were realized concretely and fully incarnated, made visible and given a face. And in this concrete and as it were all-encompassing chronotope, the laying bare and examination of a citizen's whole life was accomplished, and received its public and civic stamp of approval.

It is fully understandable that in such a "biographized" individual (in such an image of a man) there was not, nor could there be, anything intimate or private, secret or personal, anything relating solely to the individual himself, anything that was, in principle, solitary. Here the individual is open on all sides, he is all surface, there is in him nothing that exists "for his sake alone," nothing that could not be subject to public or state control and evaluation. Everything here, down to the last detail, is entirely public.

It is fully understandable that under such conditions there could not in principle be any difference between the approach one took to another's life and to one's own, that is, between the biographical and autobiographical points of view. Only later, in the Hellenistic and Roman era, when the public unity of the individual began to disintegrate, did Tacitus, Plutarch and various rhetoricians specifically pose the question: is it permissible to write

---

s. The line occurs in Pushkin's unpublished 1830 essay in response to Pogodin's new play, "On National [narodnaja] Drama and on Marfa Posadnitsa": "We saw that national tragedy was born in the public square, that it developed there, and only later was called to aristocratic society. . . . How can our tragedy, written on the Racinian model, unaccustom itself to aristocratic habits? How is it to shift from its measured, pompous and fastidious conversation to the crude frankness of folk [narodnaja] passions, to the license that is granted statements on the public square?"

an appraisal of one's own self? This question was resolved in the affirmative. Plutarch, by selecting material going back to Homer (whose heroes glorified themselves) established the permissibility of self-glorification and indicated those forms by which it should be molded, so as to avoid anything offensive. A second-rank rhetorician, Aristides, likewise sorted through a wide body of material on this question and concluded that proud self-glorification was a pure Hellenistic trait, and as such was fully permissible and correct.

But it is highly significant that such a question should arise at all. Self-glorification, after all, is but the most sharply focused, most vivid distinctive feature of a biographical and autobiographical approach to life. Thus there lurks beneath the specific question of the propriety of glorifying oneself a more general question, namely, the legitimacy of taking the same approach to one's own life as to another's life, to one's own self as to another self. The very posing of such a question is evidence that the classical *public wholeness* of an individual had broken down, and a differentiation between biographical and autobiographical forms had begun.

But there could be no talk of such a differentiation under the conditions of the Greek public square, where the self-consciousness of the individual originated. There was as yet no internal man, no "man for himself" (I for myself), nor any individualized approach to one's own self. An individual's unity and his self-consciousness were exclusively public. Man was completely *on the surface*, in the most literal sense of the word.

This utter exteriority is a very important feature of the human image as we find it in classical art and literature. It manifests itself in many ways, and by the most varied means. I will mention here only one familiar example.

Already by Homer's time, Greeks as reflected in their literature were individuals who behaved in a most unrestrained manner. Homer's heroes express their feelings vividly and noisily. We are particularly struck by how often and how loudly they sob and weep. In the familiar scene with Priam, Achilles weeps so noisily in his tent that his moans are heard throughout the entire Greek camp. This trait has been variously explained: it has been attributed to the peculiarities of a primitive psychology, to the arbitrary prerequisites of literary canon, to the particular nature of Homer's language—in which varying degrees of emotion could be transmitted only by indicating the varying degrees of its *exter-*

nal expression; or allusion is sometimes made to general "relativity" of methods for expressing emotions (it is well known, for instance, that people of the eighteenth century—the rational men of the Enlightenment themselves—wept often and willingly). But what is important is the fact that this is not an isolated feature in the ancient hero: it fits harmoniously with his other features and is rooted in a principle that is larger than is usually supposed. This feature is but one manifestation of that complete exteriority of public man we have been discussing.

For the classical Greek, every aspect of existence could be *seen* and *heard*. In principle (in essence) he did not know an invisible and mute reality. This applied to existence as a whole, but preeminently to human existence. A mute internal life, a mute grief, mute thought, were completely foreign to the Greek. All this— that is, his entire internal life—could exist only if manifested externally in audible or visible form. Plato, for example, understood thought as a conversation that a man carries on with himself (the *Theaetetus*, the *Sophist*). The concept of silent thought first appeared only with the mystics, and this concept had its roots in the Orient. Moreover, in Plato's understanding of the process, thought conceived as a "conversation with oneself" did not entail any special relationship to one's self (as distinct from one's relationship to others); conversation with one's own self turns directly into conversation with someone else, without a hint of any necessary boundaries between the two.

There is no mute or invisible core to the individual himself: he is entirely visible and audible, all on the surface. But in general there are no mute or invisible spheres of existence either, of the sort in which a man might take part and by which he might be shaped (the Platonic realm of Forms is thoroughly visible and audible). To locate the basic controlling nodes of human life in centers that are mute and invisible was even further from the classical Greek world view. This is the defining characteristic of the remarkable and immediate exteriority we find in the classical individual and in his life.

It is only with the Hellenistic and Roman epochs that we have the beginnings of a translation of whole spheres of existence— within the individual himself, as well as in the world outside him—onto a *mute register*, and into something that is in principle invisible. But this process was also far from completed in ancient times. It is significant that even today one cannot read St.

Augustine's *Confessions* "to oneself"; it must be declaimed aloud—to such an extent is the spirit of the Greek public square still alive in it, that square upon which the self-consciousness of European man first coalesced.

When we speak of the utter exteriority of Greek man we do so, of course, from our own point of view. It is precisely our distinction between internal and external which the Greek did not know, therefore he did not acknowledge the categories "mute" and "invisible." Our "internal" was, for the Greek's conception of man, laid out on the same axis as our "external," that is, it was just as visible and audible and it existed on the surface, for others as well as for oneself. Therefore, all aspects of the human image were related to one another.

But this utter exteriority of the individual did not exist in empty space ("under a starry sky, on the bare earth") but rather in an organic human collective, "in the folk." For that reason this "surface," on which the entire man existed and was laid bare, was not something alien and cold ("the desert of the world")—it was his own native folk. To be exterior meant to be for others, for the collective, for one's own people. A man was utterly exteriorized, but within a human element, in the human medium of his own people. Therefore, the *unity* of a man's externalized wholeness was of a *public* nature.

This explains the unrepeatable distinctiveness of the human image in classical art and literature. In it, everything corporeal and external is made more high-spirited and intense, while everything that is (from our point of view) spiritual and internal is made corporeal and externalized. This image had "neither core nor shell," neither an inner nor an outer, and was similar to nature as Goethe saw it (it was in fact just this image that provided the *Urphaenomenon*). In this it differs profoundly from the concept of man held in succeeding epochs.

In following epochs, man's image was distorted by his increasing participation in the mute and invisible spheres of existence. He was literally drenched in muteness and invisibility. And with them entered loneliness. The personal and detached human being—"the man who exists for himself"—lost the unity and wholeness that had been a product of his public origin. Once having lost the popular chronotope of the public square, his self-consciousness could not find an equally real, unified and whole chronotope; it therefore broke down and lost its integrity, it became abstract and idealistic. A vast number of new spheres of consciousness and objects appeared in the private life of the private individual that were not, in general, subject to being made public (the sexual sphere and others), or were subject only to an intimate, conditional, closeted expression. The human image became multi-layered, multi-faceted. A core and a shell, an inner and an outer, separated within it.

We will show below that the most remarkable experiment to re-establish the fully exteriorized individual in world literature—although without the stylization of the ancient model—was made by Rabelais.

Another attempt to resurrect the ancient wholeness and exteriority, but on an entirely different basis, was made by Goethe.

But let us return to the Greek encomium and the first autobiography. As we have analyzed it, the defining characteristic of the ancient world's peculiar consciousness of self was the fact that biographical and autobiographical approaches to life were identical, and were, therefore, both necessarily public. But in the encomium the image of man is extremely simple and pre-formed; in it there is almost no quality of "becoming." The starting point for an encomium is the idealized image of a definite life type, a specific profession—that of military commander, ruler, political figure. This idealized form is nothing but an accumulation of all the attributes adhering to a given profession: a commander should be *like this*, followed by an enumeration of all the qualities and virtues of a commander. All these idealized qualities and virtues are then discovered in the life of the man being eulogized. The ideal is fused together with the figure of the deceased. The figure of the eulogized man is one that is already formed, and the figure is usually given us at the moment of its greatest maturity and fullness of life.

It was on the basis of biographical schemes developed for the encomium that the first autobiography arose, in the form of an advocatory oration: the autobiography of Isocrates, which was to have an enormous influence on all of world literature (and especially on Italian and English humanists). This was a public accounting of a man's own life, in the form of an *apologia*. Human image in such a form was shaped by the same principles as shaped the image of the deceased in the encomium. At its heart was the ideal of a rhetorician. Isocrates glorifies rhetorical activity as the loftiest of life's activities. Isocrates' professional self-consciousness is fully particularized. He gives us the details of his material circumstances, even mentioning how much money he makes as a rhetorician. Elements which are (from our point of view) purely personal, or (again from our point of view) narrowly professional, or matters relating to society and the state, or even philosophical ideas, are all laid out in one detailed series, tightly interwoven. All these elements are perceived as completely homogeneous, and they come together to form a single human image that is both complete and fully formed. The individual's consciousness of himself in such cases relies exclusively upon those aspects of his personality and his life that are turned outward, that exist for others in the same way they exist of the individual himself; in those aspects alone can self-consciousness seek its support and integrity; it knows of no aspects other than these, aspects that might be intimately personal, unrepeatably individual, charged with self.

Such is the normative and pedagogical character of this earliest autobiography. At its conclusion a formative and educational moral is baldly stated. But this same normative and pedagogical quality suffuses the entire autobiography.

One must not forget, however, that the epoch that produced the first autobiography witnessed as well the initial stages in the breakdown of the Greek public wholeness of the human image (a wholeness that had manifested itself in epic and tragedy). Thus, this autobiography is still somewhat formal, rhetorical and abstract.

Another real-life chronotope is responsible for Roman autobiographies and memoirs. Both sprang from the soil of the Roman *family*. Such autobiographies are documents testifying to a family-clan consciousness of self. But on such family-clan soil, autobiographical self-consciousness does not become private or intimately personal. It retains a deeply public character.

The Roman patrician family—which was not a bourgeois family—is the symbol for all that can be private and intimate. The Roman family, precisely as a family, fuses directly with the state. Certain functions the state usually fulfills are entrusted to the heads of families. The religious cults of the family or clan (whose role was enormous) function as a direct extension of the cults of the state. The national ideal is represented by ancestors. Self-consciousness organizes itself around the particularized memory of a clan and ancestors, while at the same time looking toward future descendants. The traditions of the family and clan had to be passed down from father to son. Thus every family had its own archive, in which written documents on all links in the clan were kept. Autobiography "writes itself" in the orderly process of passing clan and family traditions from link to link, and these were preserved in the archive. This made even autobiographical consciousness public and historical, national.

The specific historicity that Rome gave to autobiographical self-consciousness distinguishes it from its Greek counterpart, which was oriented toward living contemporaries, toward those who were actually there on the public square. Roman self-consciousness felt itself to be primarily a link between, on the one hand, deceased ancestors, and on the other, descendents who had not yet entered political life. Such self-consciousness is thus not as pre-formed as in the Greek model, but it is more thoroughly saturated with time.

Another specific peculiarity of Roman autobiography (and biography) is the role of the *prodigia*, that is, of various auguries and their interpretations. In this context they are not an external feature of the narrative (as they become in seventeenth-century novels), but an important means for motivating and shaping autobiographical material. Tightly tied up with them is the important, and purely Roman, autobiographical category of "fortune" (*fortuna*).

In the *prodigia*, that is, in the auguries of a man's fate—his separate acts and undertakings as well as his life as a whole—individualized and personal elements indissolubly fuse with state and public elements. The *prodigia* are an important moment at the beginning and at the completion of all state acts and undertakings; the state takes no step without having first read the omens. The *prodigia* are indicators of the fate of the state, predicting for it either fortune or misfortune. From the state level they move to the individual personality of the dictator or military commander, whose fate is indissolubly bound up with the destinies of the state, and readings of the *prodigia* for the state fuse with his personal destiny. The dictator of the lucky arm (Sulla) and of the lucky star (Caesar) appear. In this context the category of luck has a distinctive life-shaping significance. It becomes the form for expressing a personal identity and the course of a whole life ("faith in one's own star"). Such is the origin of Sulla's consciousness of self in his autobiography. But, we repeat, in the good fortune of a

Sulla or a Caesar, the destinies of the state and of single persons fuse into a single whole. There can be no question of anything narrowly personal, any private luck. This is, after all, a luck measured in deeds, in projects of state, in wars. This good fortune is absolutely inseparable from deeds, creative activity, labor—from objective, public and state-oriented content. Thus this concept of good fortune includes as well our concepts of "talent," "intuition" and that specific understanding of "genius"[7] that was so important in the philosophy and aesthetics of the late eighteenth century (Young, Hamann, Herder, the *Stürmer und Dränger*). In succeeding centuries this category of good fortune became more fragmented and private. Good fortune lost all its creative, public and state attributes—and came to represent a principle that was private, personal, and one that was ultimately unproductive.

Hellenistic Greek autobiographical traditions functioned alongside these specifically Roman ones. In Rome the ancient laments (*naenia*) were likewise replaced by funeral speeches, the so-called *laudatiae*. Here Greek and Hellenistic rhetorical schemas reigned supreme.

Works "on one's own writings" emerged as an authentic autobiographical form in the Roman-Hellenistic context. As we have shown above, this form reflected the crucial influence of the Platonic schema, that of the life course of a seeker after knowledge. But an entirely different objective support was found for it in this new context. What we get is a catalog of a man's works, an exposition of their themes, a record of their successes with the public, autobiographical commentary on them (Cicero, Galen and others). It is the sequence of one's own works that provides solid support for perceiving the passage of time in one's own life. The continuity of one's works provides a critical sequential marker for biographical time, its objectification. And furthermore, consciousness of self in this context is not revealed to some general "someone," but rather to a specific circle of readers, the readers of one's works. The autobiography is constructed for them. The autobiographical concentration on oneself and one's own life acquires here a certain minimum of essential "publicness," but of

---

7. In this concept of luck, the ideas of genius and success are fused together; thus an unrecognized genius was a *contradictio in adjecto* [a contradiction in terms].

a completely new type. St. Augustine's *Retractationes*[t] belong to this autobiographical type. In more recent times a whole series of humanistic works (for example, Chaucer) could be included in this type, but in later periods this type is reduced to a single stage (albeit very important) in artistic biographies (for example, in Goethe).

Such are the types of ancient autobiography, which might all be called forms for depicting the *public self-consciousness of a man*.

We will briefly touch upon the mature biographical forms of the Roman-Hellenistic epoch. Here one must note, first and foremost, the influence of Aristotle on the distinctive methods of the ancient biographers, and in particular his doctrine of entelechy as the ultimate purpose of development that is at the same time its first cause. This Aristotelian identification of ultimate purpose with origin inevitably had a crucial effect on the distinctive nature of biographical time. From here it follows that a character at its most mature is the authentic origin of development. It is here that we get that unique "inversion in a character's development" that excludes any authentic "becoming" in character. A man's entire youth is treated as nothing but a preliminary to his maturity. The familiar element of "movement" is introduced into biography solely as a struggle of opposing impulses, as fits of passion or as an exercise in virtue—in order to invest this virtue with permanence. Such struggles and exercises serve to strengthen qualities of character that are already present, but create nothing new. The base remains the stable essence of an already completed character.

Two models for structuring ancient biography were created on this base.

The first may be called the "energetic" type. At its heart lies the Aristotelian concept of *energia*: the full existence, the essence of a man is realized not by his condition, but by his activity, his active force ("energy"). This "energy" manifests itself as the unfolding of his character in deeds and statements. And these acts, words and other expressions of a man are not merely external manifestations (that is, for others, for a "third person") of

---

t. In his *Retractiones* (427 A.D.) Augustine criticizes his own superabundant output of ninety-three works from a religious point of view he felt he had only recently achieved, although he had sought to conform to it most of his adult life.

some internal essence of character existing apart from its effects, predating them and located outside them. The manifestations themselves constitute the character's being, which outside its energy simply does not exist. Apart from its surface manifestations, its ability to express itself, its visibility and audibility, character possesses no fullness of reality, no fullness of being. The greater the power of self-expression, the fuller the being.

Therefore human life (*bios*) and character may no longer be portrayed by means of an analytical enumeration of the characterological qualities of the man (his vices and virtues) and through their unification into a single stable image of him—but rather, one must portray him by means of his deeds, his speeches and other extensions and expressions of the man.

This energetic type of biography was first established by Plutarch, who has had an enormous influence on world literature (and not only on biography).

Biographical time in Plutarch is specific. It is a time that discloses character, but is not at all the time of a man's "becoming" or growth.[8] It is true that outside this disclosure, this "manifestation," there is no character—but in keeping with the principle of "entelechy," character is predetermined and may be disclosed only in a single defined direction. Historical reality itself, in which disclosure of character takes place, serves merely as a means for the disclosure, it provides in words and deeds a vehicle for those manifestations of character: but historical reality is deprived of any determining influence on character as such, it does not shape or create it, it merely manifests it. Historical reality is an arena for the disclosing and unfolding of human characters— nothing more.

Biographical time is not reversible vis-à-vis the events of life itself, which are inseparable from historical events. But with regard to character, such time *is* reversible: one or another feature of character, taken by itself, may appear earlier or later. Features of character are themselves excluded from chronology: their instancing can be shifted about in time. Character itself does not grow, does not change, it is merely *filled in*: at the beginning it is incomplete, imperfectly disclosed, fragmentary; it becomes *full* and well rounded only at the end. Consequently, the process of

8. Time is phenomenal; the essence of character is outside time. It is therefore not time that gives a character its substantiality.

disclosing character does not lead to a real change or "becoming" in historical reality, but rather solely to a *fulfillment*, that is, to a filling-in of that form sketched at the very outset. Such is the Plutarchian biographical type.

The second type of biography may be called *analytic*. At its heart we have a scheme with well-defined rubrics, beneath which all biographical material is distributed: social life, family life, conduct in war, relationships with friends, memorable sayings, virtues, vices, physical appearance, habits and so forth. Various features and qualities of character are selected out from the various happenings and events that occur *at different times in the hero's life*, but these are arranged according to the prescribed rubrics. To prove the rubric valid, only one or two examples from the life of a given personality need be provided.

In this way, the temporal progression of the biographical sequence is broken up: one and the same rubric subsumes moments selected from widely separate periods of a life. Here as well, what governs from the outset is the *whole* of the character; and from such a point of view time is of no importance at all, nor is the order in which various parts of this whole make their appearance. From the very first strokes (the first manifestations of character) the firm contours of the whole are already predetermined, and everything that comes later distributes itself within these already existing contours—in the temporal order (the first, energetic Plutarchian type) as well as in the systematic (the second, atemporal, type).

The major representative of this second ancient type of biography was Suetonius.[u] If Plutarch had exercised a profound influence on literature, especially on the drama (for the energetic type of biography is essentially dramatic), then Suetonius primarily influenced the narrowly biographical genre, particularly during the Middle Ages. Biography structured by rubrics survives to our very day: the biography of "a human being," "a writer," "a family man," "an intellectual" and so forth.

The forms that we have mentioned so far, autobiographical as well as biographical (and there was no distinction, in principle, between the approaches toward the individual adopted by each), had an essentially public character. We must now touch upon

---

u. Reference here is to *De viris illustribus*, written during the reign of Trajan, and consisting of biographies of Roman literary men arranged according to classes, such as "De grammaticus et rhetoribus," etc.

those autobiographical forms in which the breakdown of this public exteriority of a man is already evident, where the detached and singular individual's private self-consciousness begins to force itself through and bring to the surface the private spheres of his life. In the area of autobiography as well, we get in ancient times only the beginning of the process by which a man and his life become private. New forms for autobiographical expression of a *singular self-consciousness* were therefore not developed. Instead there ensued merely specific modifications of already available public and rhetorical forms. We will note three basic kinds of modifications.

The first modification consists of a satirico-ironic or humorous treatment, in satires and diatribes, of one's self and one's life. Special note should be taken of the familiar ironic autobiographies and self-characterizations in verse by Horace, Ovid and Propertius, which include an element of the parodying of public and heroic forms. Here personal and private topics, unable to find a positive form for their expression, are clothed in *irony* and *humor*.

A second modification, and one that has had important historical resonance, is represented by Cicero's letters to Atticus.

Public and rhetorical forms expressing the unity of the human image had begun to ossify, had become official and conventional; heroization and glorification (as well as self-glorification) were felt to be stereotyped and stilted. Moreover, the available public and rhetorical genres could not by their very nature provide for the expression of life that was private, a life of activity that was increasingly expanding in width and depth and retreating more and more into itself. Under such conditions the forms of *drawing-room rhetoric* acquired increasing importance, and the most significant form was the *familiar letter*. In this intimate and familiar atmosphere (one that was, of course, semiconventionalized) a new private sense of self, suited to the drawing room, began to emerge. A whole series of categories involving self-consciousness and the shaping of a life into a biography—success, happiness, merit—began to lose their public and state significance and passed over to the private and personal plane. Even nature itself, drawn into this new private and drawing-room world, begins to change in an essential way. "Landscape" is born, that is, nature conceived as horizon (what a man sees) and as the environment (the background, the setting) for a completely private, singular individual who does not interact with it. Nature of this kind differs sharply from nature as conceived in a pastoral idyll or georgic—to say nothing of nature in an epic or tragedy. Nature enters the drawing-room world of private individuals only as picturesque "remnants," while they are taking a walk, or relaxing or glancing randomly at the surrounding view. These picturesque remnants are woven together in the unstable unity of a cultured Roman's private life; but they did not come together to form a single, powerful, animating independent nature complex, such as we see in epic or in tragedy (nature as it functions in *Prometheus Bound*, for instance). These picturesque remnants can exist only in the isolation created by closed verbal landscapes that surround them. Other categories as well undergo analogous transformations in this new little private drawing-room world. Numerous petty details of private life begin to take on an importance; in them, the individual feels himself "at home," his private sense of self begins to take its bearings from these petty details. The human begins to shift to a space that is closed and private, the space of private rooms where something approaching intimacy is possible, where it loses its monumental formedness and exclusively public exteriority.

Such is the characteristic space of the letters to Atticus. There is, nevertheless, a great deal in them that is still public and rhetorical, conventionalized and ossified—as well as much that is still vital and dynamic. It is as if the old public and rhetorical unity of the human image had been drenched with fragments of a future, thoroughly private man.

The third and final modification we will call the *stoic* type of autobiography. First and foremost, we must include in this group the so-called "consolationes" (consolations). These consolations were constructed in the form of a dialogue with Philosophy the Consoler. For our first example (one which has not survived) we must take the *Consolatio* of Cicero, which he wrote after the death of his daughter. Cicero's *Hortensius* belongs here as well. In succeeding epochs we meet such consolations in Augustine, Boethius and finally in Petrarch.

We must also include in this third modification Seneca's letters, Marcus Aurelius' autobiographical book ("To Myself")[v] and, finally, *The Confessions* and other autobiographical works of St. Augustine.

---

v. The reference is obscure here, but must be to the *Meditations* that Marcus Aurelius originally jotted down in notebooks for his own guidance. Only later, after his death, were they transcribed.

Typical of all the above-named works is the advent of a new form for relating to one's self. One might best characterize this new relationship by using Augustine's term "Soliloquia," that is, "solitary conversations with oneself." Conversations with Philosophy the Consoler in the consolations are, of course, also examples of such solitary conversations.

This is a new relationship to one's own self, to one's own particular "I"—with no witnesses, without any concessions to the voice of a "third person," whoever it might be. Here the self-consciousness of a solitary individual seeks support and more authoritative reading of its fate in its own self, without mediation, in the sphere of ideas and philosophy. There is even a place here for struggle with "another's" point of view—for example, in Marcus Aurelius. The point of view that "another" takes toward us— which we take into account, and by which we evaluate ourselves—functions as the source of vanity, vain pride, or as the source of offense. It clouds our self-consciousness and our powers of self-evaluation; we must free ourselves from it.

Another distinctive feature of this third modification is a sharp increase in the weight of events pertaining to one's own personal and intimate life; events enormously important in the private life of a given individual have no importance at all for others, and almost no larger social or political significance—for example, the death of a daughter (in Cicero's *Consolatio*); in such events a man feels himself to be preeminently alone. In events that have a public significance, however, the personal side of these events now begins to be accentuated. As part of this process, such issues as the transitoriness of all that is good, man's mortality, become very prominent; in general, the theme of personal death (and diverse variants on that theme) begins to play a crucial role in an individual's autobiographical self-consciousness (in public self-consciousness its role had been, of course, reduced almost to zero).

Despite these new features, even this third modification remains to a significant extent public and rhetorical. There is, as yet, nothing of that authentically solitary individual who makes his appearance only in the Middle Ages and henceforth plays such an enormous role in the European novel. Solitude, here, is still a very relative and naive thing. A sense of self is still rooted firmly in the public sphere, although this influence is well on the way to being ossified. The very Marcus Aurelius who excluded "another's point of view" (in his struggle to overcome his sensitivity to insult) is, nevertheless, filled with a profound respect for his own public dignity, and he is haughtily grateful to fate and to other men for his virtues. And the very form assumed by autobiography in this third modification bears a public and rhetorical stamp. We have already said that even Augustine's *Confessions* require a noisy declamation.

Such are the basic forms of ancient autobiography and biography. They were to exercise enormous influence on the development of similar forms in European literature, as well as on the development of the novel.

IV. The Problem of Historical Inversion and the Folkloric Chronotope

In concluding our survey of ancient forms of the novel, we will note some general characteristics of the methods used to express time in these works.

How is the fullness of time treated in the ancient novel? We have already seen that in any temporal representation some minimum sense of time's fullness is inevitable (and literature's primary mode of representation *is* temporal). Moreover, there can be no question of reflecting an epoch outside of the passage of time, outside any contact with past or future, outside time's fullness. Where there is no passage of time there is also no *moment* of time, in the full and most essential meaning of the word. If taken outside its relationship to past and future, the present loses its integrity, breaks down into isolated phenomena and objects, making of them a mere abstract conglomeration.

Even the ancient novel had a certain minimum fullness of time peculiar to it alone. Such time is, so to speak, minimal in the Greek novel, and only slightly more important in the adventure novel of everyday life. In the ancient novel, this fullness of time has a dual character. In the first place, its roots are in a popular and mythological understanding of time's fullness. But these fixed, temporal forms were already in decay and, under conditions of sharp social differentiation beginning to be felt at that time, they could not of course incorporate and adequately shape new content. But these folkloric forms for expressing the fullness of time nevertheless functioned in the ancient novel.

On the other hand, the ancient novel also contained the feeble first efforts at *new* forms for expressing time's fullness—forms related to the uncovering of social contradictions. Every such uncovering inevitably pushes time into the future. The more profoundly these contradictions are uncovered and the riper they become in consequence, the more authentic and comprehensive becomes time's fullness as the artist represents it. We have seen the first beginnings of such a real-life unity of time in the adventure novel of everyday life. But these first efforts were too feeble to stave off the collapse of the major epic forms into novelness.

Here it is imperative to pause on a distinctive feature of that feeling for time that exercised an enormous and determining influence on the development of literary forms and images.

This distinctive feature manifests itself preeminently in what might be called a *historical inversion*. The essence of this inversion is found in the fact that mythological and artistic thinking locates such categories as purpose, ideal, justice, perfection, the harmonious condition of man and society and the like in the *past*. Myths about paradise, a Golden Age, a heroic age, an ancient truth, as well as the later concepts of a "state of nature," of natural, innate rights and so on, are all expressions of this historical inversion. To put it in somewhat simplified terms, we might say that a thing that could and in fact must only be realized exclusively in the *future* is here portrayed as something out of the *past*, a thing that is in no sense part of the past's reality, but a thing that is in its essence a purpose, an obligation.

This peculiar "trans-positioning," this "inversion" of time typical of mythological and artistic modes of thought in various eras of human development, is characterized by a special concept of time, and in particular of future time. [The present and even more the past are enriched at the expense of the future.] The force and persuasiveness of reality, of real life, belong to the present and the past alone—to the "is" and the "was"—and to the future belongs a reality of a different sort, one that is more ephemeral, a reality that when placed in the future is deprived of that materiality and density, that real-life weightiness that is essential to the "is" and "was." The future is not homogeneous with the present and the past, and no matter how much time it occupies it is denied a basic concreteness, it is somehow empty and fragmented—since everything affirmative, ideal, obligatory, desired has been shifted, via the inversion, into the past (or partly into the present); en route, it has become weightier, more authentic and persuasive. In order to endow any ideal with authenticity, one need only conceive of its once having existed in its "natural state" in some Golden Age, or perhaps existing in the present but somewhere at the other end of the world, east of the sun and west of the moon, if not on earth then underground, if not underground then in heaven. There is a greater readiness to build a superstructure for reality (the present) along a vertical axis of upper and lower than to move forward along the horizontal axis of time. Should these vertical structurings turn out as well to be other-worldly, idealistic, eternal, outside time, then this extratemporal and eternal quality is perceived as something simultaneous with a given moment in the present; it is something contemporaneous, and that which already exists is perceived as better than the future (which does not yet exist and which never did exist). From the point of view of a present reality, historical inversion (in the strict sense of the word) prefers the past—which is more weighty, more fleshed out—to such a future. And these vertical, other-worldly structurings prefer to such a past that which is eternal and outside time altogether, yet which functions as if it were indeed real and contemporary. In its own way each of these forms empties out the future, dissects and bleeds it white, as it were. The historical inversion in philosophical structures is characterized by a corresponding assumption of "beginnings" as the crystal-clear, pure sources of all being, of eternal values and modes of existence that are ideal and outside time.

Another form that exhibits a like relationship to the future is eschatology. Here the future is emptied out in another way. The future is perceived as the end of everything that exists, as the end of all being (in its past and present forms). In this respect it makes no difference at all whether the end is perceived as catastrophe and destruction pure and simple, as a new chaos, as a Twilight of the Gods, as the advent of God's Kingdom—it matters only that the end effect everything that exists, and that this end be, moreover, relatively close at hand. Eschatology always sees the segment of a future separating the present from the end as lacking value; this separating segment of time loses its significance and interest, it is merely an unnecessary continuation of an indefinitely prolonged present.

Such are the specific characteristics of a mythological and literary relationship to the future. In all forms that partake of this relationship, the real future is drained and bled of its substance. But within the limits of each form, concrete variants of differing degrees of value are possible.

But before we deal with these individual variants, we must define in more detail the relationship between these forms and an actual future. For even in these forms, after all, everything must lead into a real future, into precisely that which does not yet exist but which at some point must exist. In essence these forms strive to make actual that which is presumed obligatory and true, to infuse it with being, to join it to time, to counterpose it—as something that actually exists and is at the same time true—to the available reality, which also exists, but which in contrast is bad, not true.

Images of this future were inevitably located in the past, or transferred to some Land of Cockaigne, beyond the seven seas; their dissimilarity to a cruel and evil present-day reality was measured by temporal and spatial distancing. But such images were not taken out of time as such, they were not torn out of the real and material world of the here-and-now. On the contrary, one might even say that all the energy of this presumed future served only to deepen and intensify images of material here-and-now reality, and above all the image of the living, corporeal human being: a man grew up at the future's expense, became a bogatyr compared with the present generation ("You are no bogatyrs"),[w] he had access to unseen physical strength and great capacity for work; his struggle with nature was portrayed as heroic, his sober-minded and pragmatic intelligence was heroic, even his healthy appetite and his thirst became heroic. In such works symbolic size, strength and a man's symbolic significance were never separated from spatial dimensions and temporal duration. A great man was physically a big man as well, with a huge stride, requiring an enormity of space and living a long time over the course of a real physical lifespan. It is true that in several folkloric forms such a great man may undergo a process of metamorphosis—during which he may indeed be small, and not realize his full potential in space and time (like the sun, he sets; he descends into the nether regions, into the earth)—but in the end he always realizes his full potential, spatially and temporally, becoming once again big and long-lived. We are simplifying somewhat this feature of

---

w. Stanza 2, line 3, of Lermontov's *Borodino* (1837).

authentic folklore, but it is important to emphasize that such a folklore did not know a system of ideals separate from embodiment of that system in time and space. In the final analysis everything that carries significance can and must also be significant in terms of space and time. Folkloric man demands space and time for his full realization; he exists entirely and fully in these dimensions and feels comfortable in them. A deliberate opposition between ideational significance and physical dimensions (in the broad sense of the word) is utterly foreign to folklore, as is the accommodation of the ideal to temporally and spatially skimpy forms (which would have the effect of playing down the importance time and space have). Here we must stress one additional feature characteristic of authentic folklore: in it a character is great in his own right, not on some other account; he himself is tall and strong, he alone is able to triumphantly repel enemy troops (as did Cuchulainn during the winter hibernation of the Ulads). He is the very antithesis of "a little tsar ruling a great Folk": folkloric man *is* the great folk, great in his own right. The only thing he enslaves is Nature; and he himself is served only by wild beasts (and even these are not his *slaves* [a social category, tr.]).

This spatial and temporal growth of a man, calibrated in forms of here-and-now (material) reality, appears in folklore not only as the above-mentioned features of external growth and strength, but in other highly diverse and subtle forms as well. Nevertheless the logic is everywhere the same: it is a direct and straightforward growth of a man in his own right and in the real world of the here-and-now, a growth process without any inauthentic debasing, without any idealized compensation in the form of weakness and need [which would be there only to offset his greatness, tr.]. We will discuss in some detail other forms for expressing the growth of a man in connection with our analysis of Rabelais' great novels.

Therefore, the fantastic in folklore is a *realistic* fantastic: in no way does it exceed the limits of the real, here-and-now material world, and it does not stitch together rents in that world with anything that is idealistic or other-worldly; it works with the ordinary expanses of time and space, and experiences these expanses and utilizes them in great breadth and depth. Such a fantastic relies on the real-life possibilities of human development— possibilities not in the sense of a program for immediate practical action, but in the sense of the needs and possibilities of men, those eternal demands of human nature that will not be denied. These demands will remain forever, as long as there are men; they will not be suppressed, they are real, as real as human nature itself, and therefore sooner or later they will force their way to a full realization.

Thus folkloric realism proves to be an inexhaustible source of realism for all written literature, including the novel. This source of realism had a special significance for the Middle Ages, and in particular for the Renaissance. But we will return again to this question in connection with our analysis of Rabelais.

V. The Chivalric Romance

We will touch very briefly on the distinctive features of time—and consequently of the chronotope as well—in the chivalric romance (we must refrain from an analysis of individual works).

The chivalric romance functions with adventure-time of the basically Greek type—although in certain novels time is closer to the everyday adventure type used by Apuleius (this is particularly true of Wolfram von Eschenbach's *Parzival*). Time breaks down into a sequence of adventure-fragments, within which it is organized abstractly and technically; the connection of time to space is also merely technical. We encounter here the same simultaneities and disjunctions in time, the same play with distance and proximity, the same retardations. The chronotope of this novel is also close to Greek romance—the "otherness" of its world is portrayed in a variety of ways, and has a somewhat abstract character. A testing of the identity of heroes (and things)—basically, their fidelity in love and their faithfulness to the demands of the chivalric code—plays the same organizing role. Inevitably there also appear moments crucial to identity: presumed deaths, recognition/nonrecognition, a change of names and the like (and also a more complex play with the issue of identity, such as the two Isoldes, the beloved and the unloved, in *Tristan*). We also find oriental and fairy-tale motifs that are ultimately linked to the issue of identity: enchantments of every sort, which temporarily take a man out of the ordinary course of events and transport him to a strange world.

But alongside this, a radically new element appears in the adventure-time of the chivalric romance (which in turn pervades everything in its chronotope).

Any adventure-time will contain a mixture of chance, fate, the gods and so forth. Indeed, this type of time emerges only at points of rupture (when some hiatus opens up) in normal, real-life, "law-abiding" temporal sequences, where these laws (of whatever sort) are *suddenly* violated and events take an unexpected and unforeseen turn. This "suddenly" is normalized, as it were, in chivalric romances; it becomes something generally applicable, in fact, almost ordinary. The whole world becomes miraculous, so the miraculous becomes ordinary without ceasing at the same time to be miraculous. Even "unexpectedness" itself—since it is always with us—ceases to be something unexpected. The unexpected, and only the unexpected, is what is expected. The entire world is subject to "suddenly," to the category of miraculous and unexpected chance. The hero of Greek romances, on the other hand, had striven to establish some "systematicalness," to reunite the sundered links in the normal course of life's events, to escape from the game of fate and to return to ordinary, normal life (which of course exists outside the limits of the novel); he endured adventures as if they were calamities sent from above—but he was not an adventurer *per se*, he himself did not seek out adventures (he was deprived of any initiative in this respect). The hero of a chivalric romance, on the other hand, plunges headfirst into adventures as if they were his native element; for him, the world exists exclusively under the sign of the miraculous "suddenly"; it is the normal condition of his world. He is an adventurer, but a disinterested one (he is not, of course, an adventurer in the later sense of the word, that is, in the sense of a man who coldbloodedly pursues his own greedy goals by extraordinary means). By his very nature he can live only in this world of miraculous chance, for only it preserves his identity. And the very code by which he measures his identity is calibrated precisely to this world of miraculous chance.

Moreover, the very coloration chance takes on—the fortuitous simultaneities and equally fortuitous disjunctions in time—is, in the chivalric romance, quite different from the Greek novel. In the Greek novel the mechanics of temporal partings and comings-together are unadorned, they take place in an abstract space filled with rarities and curiosities. In the chivalric romance, by contrast, chance has all the seductiveness of the miraculous and the mysterious; it is personified by good and evil fairies, good and evil magicians; in enchanted groves, in castles and elsewhere it lies in wait. In the majority of cases the hero does not endure real "misfortunes"—which intrigue only the reader—rather, he lives "miraculous adventures," which are interesting and attractive to him as well. "Adventure" takes on a new tone in the context of this completely miraculous world in which it occurs.

Furthermore, in this miraculous world heroic deeds are performed by which the heroes *glorify themselves*, and *glorify* others (their liege lord, their lady). The heroic deed is the feature that sharply distinguishes the chivalric romance from a Greek one, and brings it closer to *epic adventure*. *Glory* and *glorification* are features completely alien to the Greek romance, and this fact heightens the similarity between the chivalric romance and the epic.

In contrast to the heroes of Greek romance, the heroes of chivalric romance are *individualized*, yet at the same time *symbolic*. The heroes of different Greek romances resemble each other, although they bear different names; only one novel can be written about each such hero; cycles, variants, series of novels by different authors cannot be created around such heroes. The hero of such a novel is the private property of its author and belongs to him as might a thing. As we have seen, all such heroes represent nothing and no one beyond themselves; they simply exist as such. In contrast to this, the different heroes of chivalric romances in no way resemble each other, neither in their physical appearance nor in their diverse fates. Lancelot in no way resembles Parzival, Parzival does not resemble Tristan. But several novels have been created around each of these figures. Strictly speaking these are not heroes of individual novels (in general there are no *individual*, self-contained chivalric romances)—what we get is heroes of *cycles*. They cannot, therefore, belong to individual novelists as their private property (of course, we do not have in mind author's copyright and such notions)—like epic heroes, they belong to a common storehouse of images, although this is an international storehouse and not, as in the epic, one that is merely national.

Finally, both the hero and the miraculous world in which he acts are of a piece, there is no separation between the two. This world is not, to be sure, his national homeland; it is everywhere equally "other" (but this "otherness" is not emphasized)—the hero moves from country to country, comes into contact with various masters, crosses various seas—but everywhere the world is one, it is filled with the same concept of glory, heroic deed and disgrace; throughout this world the hero is able to bring glory on himself and on others; everywhere the same names resound and are glorious.

In this world the hero is "at home" (although he is not in his homeland); he is every bit as miraculous as his world. His lineage is miraculous, as are the conditions of his birth, his childhood and youth, his physique and so forth. He is flesh of the flesh and bone of the bone of this miraculous world, its best representative.

All these distinctive features of the chivalric adventure romance set it off sharply from the Greek romance and bring it closer to the epic. In fact the early chivalric romance in verse lies on the boundary between epic and novel. It is this that determined its place in the history of the novel. The above-mentioned features also determine the unique chronotope of this type of novel—*a miraculous world in adventure-time*.

In its own way this chronotope is very organic and internally consistent. It is no longer filled with rarities and curiosities, but with the miraculous; everything in it—weapons, clothing, a spring or bridge—either has something miraculous about it or is outright bewitched. There is also a great deal of symbolizing in this world, but not of a sort that is crudely rebus-like; it is rather of a type closer to the oriental fairy tale.

In the chivalric romance, adventure-time itself is structured by this tendency toward the miraculous. In the Greek novel, adventure-time was technically true-to-life within the limits of individual adventures; a day was equal to a day, an hour to an hour. In the chivalric romance, on the contrary, time itself becomes to a certain extent miraculous. There appears a hyperbolization of time typical of the fairy tale: hours are dragged out, days are compressed into moments, it becomes possible to bewitch time itself. Time begins to be influenced by dreams; that is, we begin to see the peculiar distortion of temporal perspectives characteristic of dreams. Dreams no longer function merely as an element of the content, but begin to acquire a form-generating function, in the same way that "visions" are made analogous to dreams (in medieval literature, "visions" are a very important organizing form).[9]

---

9. Antiquity also knew, of course, the external form of structuring events in the guise of a dream or dream-like vision. It suffices to mention Lucian and his "Dream" (an autobiographical account of the turning point in his life in the form of a dream). But a specific, internal dream logic is missing.

In general the chivalric romance exhibits a *subjective playing with time*, an emotional and lyrical stretching and compressing of it (excepting those fairy-tale and dream-vision deformations mentioned above); whole events disappear as if they had never been (thus in *Parzival* the episode in Montsalvat—when the hero fails to recognize the king—disappears, turns into a nonevent) and so on. Such a subjective playing with time is utterly foreign to antiquity. In fact, time—at least within the boundaries of individual adventures—was characterized in the Greek romance by a dry and considered precision. Antiquity treated time with great respect (it was sanctioned by myths) and did not permit itself the liberty of any subjective playing around with time.

The chronotope of the miraculous world, which is characterized by this subjective playing with time, this violation of elementary temporal relationships and perspectives, has a corresponding subjective playing with space, in which elementary spatial relationships and perspectives are violated. In the majority of cases, moreover, there is no trace of the "free" relationship of a man to space that is affirmed in folklore and fairy tales—what we get rather is an emotional, subjective distortion of space, which is in part symbolic.

Such is the chivalric romance. In its subsequent development the almost epic wholeness and unity characterizing the chronotope of the miraculous world disintegrates (this occurs in the later prose forms of the chivalric romance, in which Greek elements have more force)—and this wholeness and unity are never again to be resurrected in their epic fullness. But separate aspects of this highly distinctive chronotope—in particular the subjective playing with spatial and temporal perspectives—now and then re-emerge in the subsequent history of the novel (of course, with somewhat changed functions): among the Romantics (for example, Novalis' *Heinrich von Ofterdingen*), the Symbolists, the Expressionists (for example, the very subtle psychological playing with time in Meyrink's *Golem*)[x] and occasionally among the Surrealists as well.

Toward the end of the Middle Ages, a special sort of work begins to appear: encyclopedic (and synthetic) in its content, and which is structured as a "vision." We have in mind here *Roman*

---

x. Gustav Meyrink (pseudonym of Gustav Meyer, 1868–1932), a strange figure sometimes compared to Kafka. His *Der Golem* was published in 1915.

de la Rose (Guillaume de Lorris) and its continuation (Jean de Meung), *Piers Plowman* (Langland) and, finally, *The Divine Comedy.*

These works are of great interest in their treatment of time, but we can touch only on the most basic features common to them all.

Here the influence of the medieval, other-worldly, vertical axis is extremely strong. The entire spatial and temporal world is subject to symbolic interpretation. One might even say that in such works time is utterly excluded from action. This is a "vision," after all, and visions in real time are very brief; indeed the meaning of what is seen is itself extratemporal (although it does have some connection with time). In Dante, the real time of the vision—as well as the point at which it intersects with two other types of time, the specific biographical moment (the time of a human life) and historical time—has a purely symbolic character. All that is spatial and temporal, the images of people and objects, as well as actions, have either an allegorical significance (especially in *Roman de la Rose*), or a symbolic one (occasionally in Langland and to a very high degree in Dante).

What is most remarkable in these works is the fact that—especially in our last two examples—there lies at their heart an acute feeling for the epoch's contradictions, long overripe; this is, in essence, a feeling for the end of an epoch. From this springs that striving toward as full as possible an exposition of all the contradictory multiplicity of the epoch. And the manifold contradictions must be posited and portrayed by means of a single feature.

In a meadow during the plague Langland gathers together, around the image of Piers Plowman, representatives of all social classes and levels of feudal society from king to pauper, representatives of all professions and all ideological persuasions, and all of them take part in a symbolic deed (coming to Piers Plowman in a pilgrimage after truth, to help him in his agricultural labors, etc.). In both Langland and Dante this contradictory multiplicity is profoundly historical. But Langland and even more Dante stack up these many contradictions and stretch them out along a vertical axis. Literally, and with the consistency and force of genius, Dante realizes this stretching-out of the world—a historical world, in essence—along a vertical axis.

He structures a picture of the world remarkable for its architectonics—a world that has its life and movement tensely strung along a vertical axis: nine circles of Hell beneath the earth, seven circles of Purgatory above them and above that ten circles of Paradise. Below, a crude materiality of people and things; above, only the Light and the Voice. The temporal logic of this vertical world consists in the sheer simultaneity of all that occurs (or "the coexistence of everything in eternity"). Everything that on earth is divided by time, here, in this verticality, coalesces into eternity, into pure simultaneous coexistence. Such divisions as time introduces—"earlier" and "later"—have no substance here; they must be ignored in order to understand this vertical world; everything must be perceived as being within *a single time*, that is, in the synchrony of a single moment; one must see this entire world as simultaneous. Only under conditions of pure simultaneity—or, what amounts to the same thing, in an environment outside time altogether—can there be revealed the true meaning of "that which was, and which is and which shall be": and this is so because the force (time) that had divided these three is deprived of its authentic reality and its power to shape thinking. To "synchronize diachrony," to replace all temporal and historical divisions and linkages with purely interpretative, extratemporal and hierarchicized ones—such was Dante's form-generating impulse, which is defined by an image of the world structured according to a pure verticality.

But at the same time, the human beings who fill (populate) this vertical world are profoundly historical, they bear the distinctive marks of time; on all of them, the traces of the epoch are imprinted. Furthermore, Dante's historical and political conceptions, his understanding of both progressive and reactionary forces of historical development (an understanding that was very profound) are drawn into this vertical hierarchy. Therefore, the images and ideas that fill this vertical world are in their turn filled with a powerful desire to escape this world, to set out along the historically productive horizontal, to be distributed not upward, but forward. Each image is full of historical potential, and therefore strains with the whole of its being toward participation in historical events—toward participation in a temporal-historical chronotope. But the artist's powerful will condemns it to an eternal and immobile place on the extratemporal vertical axis. Now and then these temporal possibilities are realized in separate stories, which are complete and rounded-off like novellas. It is as if such stories as Francesca and Paolo, or Count Ugolino and the Archbishop Ruggieri, are horizontal time-saturated branches at right angles to the extratemporal vertical of the Dantesque world.

This is the source of the extraordinary tension that pervades all of Dante's world. It is the result of a struggle between living historical time and the extratemporal other-worldly ideal. The vertical, as it were, compresses within itself the horizontal, which powerfully thrusts itself forward. There is a contradiction, an antagonism between the form-generating principle of the whole and the historical and temporal form of its separate parts. The form of the whole wins out. The artistic resolution of precisely this struggle is what gives rise to the tension and provides Dante's work with its extraordinary power to express its epoch, or more precisely, the boundary line *between* two epochs.

In the subsequent history of literature, the Dantesque vertical chronotope never again appears with such rigor and internal consistency. But there are frequent attempts to resolve, so to speak, historical contradictions "along the vertical"; attempts to deny the essential thought-shaping power of "earlier" or "later," that is, to deny temporal divisions and linkages (from this point of view, all essentials can exist simultaneously). There are no attempts to lay open the world as a cross-section of pure simultaneity and coexistence (a rejection of the inability to see the whole of time that is implicit in any *historical* interpretation). After Dante, the most profound and consistent attempt to erect such a verticality was made by Dostoevsky.

VI. The Functions of the Rogue, Clown and Fool in the Novel

Simultaneously with forms of high literature in the Middle Ages, development took place in those low folkloric and semifolkloric forms that tended toward satire and parody. These forms tended to become cycles; parodic and satiric epics emerge. In the Middle Ages, this literature of the dregs of society features three prominent types, enormously significant for the later development of the European novel. These figures are the *rogue*, the *clown* and the *fool*. Of course, they are not in any sense new figures; both classical antiquity and the ancient Orient were familiar with them. If one were to drop a historical sounding-lead into these artistic images, it would not touch bottom in any of them—they are that deep. The cultic significance of the ancient masks corresponding to these figures is not far to seek, even in the full light of historical day: but the images themselves go back even further, into the depths of a folklore that pre-exists class structures. But here, as elsewhere in our study, the problem of genesis will not concern us. For our purposes, what is important is only those particular functions assumed by these masks in the literature of late medieval times, which will later influence the development of the European novel so crucially.

The rogue, the clown and the fool create around themselves their own special little world, their own chronotope. In the chronotopes and eras we have so far discussed, none of these figures occupied an essential place, with the possible partial exception of the everyday-adventure chronotope. These figures carry with them into literature first a vital connection with the theatrical trappings of the public square, with the mask of the public spectacle; they are connected with that highly specific, extremely important area of the square where the common people congregate; second—and this is of course a related phenomenon—the very being of these figures does not have a direct, but rather a metaphorical, significance. Their very appearance, everything they do and say, cannot be understood in a direct and unmediated way but must be grasped metaphorically. Sometimes their significance can be reversed—but one cannot take them literally, because they are not what they seem. Third and last, and this again follows from what has come before, their existence is a reflection of some other's mode of being—and even then, not a direct reflection. They are life's maskers; their being coincides with their role, and outside this role they simply do not exist.

Essential to these three figures is a distinctive feature that is as well a privilege—the right to be "other" in this world, the right not to make common cause with any single one of the existing categories that life makes available; none of these categories quite suits them, they see the underside and the falseness of every situation. Therefore, they can exploit any position they choose, but only as a mask. The rogue still has some ties that bind him to real life; the clown and the fool, however, are "not of this world," and therefore possess their own special rights and privileges. These figures are laughed at by others, and *themselves* as well. Their laughter bears the stamp of the public square where the folk gather. They re-establish the public nature of the human figure: the entire being of characters such as these is, after all, utterly on the surface; everything is brought out on to the square, so to speak; their entire function consists in externalizing things (true enough, it is not their own being they externalize, but a reflected, alien being—however, that is all they have). This creates that distinctive means for externalizing a human being, via parodic laughter.

Where these figures remain real-life people, they are fully understandable, and we take them so much for granted that they do not seem to create any problems at all. But from real life they move into literary fiction, taking with them all of the aforementioned attributes. Here, in novel texts, they themselves undergo a series of transformations, and they transform certain critical aspects of the novel as well.

In this essay we can only scratch the surface of this very complex issue—only insofar as is necessary for our subsequent analysis of several forms of the novel, in particular Rabelais (and to a certain extent Goethe).

The transforming influence of these images we are analyzing branched out in two directions. First of all, they influenced the positioning of the author himself within the novel (and of his image, if he himself is somehow embedded in the novel), as well as the author's point of view.

Indeed, compared with epic, drama and lyric, the position of the author of a novel vis-à-vis the life portrayed in the work is in general highly complex and problematical. The general problem of personal authorship (a particular problem that has arisen only recently, since "autographed" literature is a mere drop in an ocean of anonymous folk literature) is here complicated by the need to have some substantive, "uninvented" mask that would have the capacity both to fix the position of the author vis-à-vis the life he portrays (*how* and *from what angle* he, a participant in the novel, can see and expose all this private life) and to fix the author's position vis-à-vis his readers, his public (for whom he is the vehicle for an "exposé" of life—as a judge, an investigator, a "chief of protocol," a politician, a preacher, a fool, etc.). Of course such questions as these exist whenever personal authorship is an issue, and they can never be resolved by assigning the author to the category of "professional man of letters." By contrast with other literary genres (the epic, the lyric, the drama), however, questions of personal authorship in the novel are posed on a philosophical, cultural or sociopolitical plane. In other genres (the drama, the lyric and their variants) the most contiguous possible position of the author, the point of view necessary to the shaping of the material, is dictated by the genre itself: such a maximal proximity of the creator's position to the material is immanent in the very genre. Within the genre of the novel, there is no such immanent position for the author. You may publish your own real-life diary and call it a novel; under the same label you may publish a packet of business documents, personal letters (a novel in letters), a manuscript by "nobody-knows-who, written for nobody-knows-who and who-found-it-and-where nobody knows." For the novel the issue of authorship is not therefore just one issue among others, as it is for the other genres: it is a formal and generic concern as well. We have already touched upon this question in connection with forms for spying and eavesdropping on private life.

The novelist stands in need of some essential formal and generic mask that could serve to define the position from which he views life, as well as the position from which he makes that life public.

And it is precisely here, of course, that the masks of the clown and the fool (transformed in various ways) come to the aid of the novelist. These masks are not invented: they are rooted deep in the folk. They are linked with the folk through the fool's time-honored privilege not to participate in life, and by the time-honored bluntness of the fool's language; they are linked as well with the chronotope of the public square and with the trappings of the theater. All of this is of the highest importance for the novel. At last a form was found to portray the mode of existence of a man who is in life, but not of it, life's perpetual spy and reflector; at last specific forms had been found to reflect private life and make it public. (We might add here that the making-public of specifically nonpublic spheres of life—for example, the sexual sphere—is one of the more ancient functions of the fool. Cf. Goethe's description of carnival.)

The indirect, metaphorical significance of the entire human image, its thoroughly allegorical nature is of the utmost importance. For this aspect is, of course, related to metamorphosis. The clown and the fool represent a metamorphosis of tsar and god—but the transformed figures are located in the nether world, in death (cf. in Roman Saturnalia and in Christ's passion the analogous feature of the metamorphosis of god or ruler into slave, criminal or fool). Under such conditions man is in a state of allegory. The *allegorical state* has enormous form-generating significance for the novel.

All this acquires special importance when we consider that one of the most basic tasks for the novel will become the laying-bare of any sort of conventionality, the exposure of all that is vulgar and falsely stereotyped in human relationships.

The vulgar conventionality that pervades human life manifests itself first and foremost as a feudal structure, with something like a feudal ideology downplaying the relevance of spatial and temporal categories. Hypocrisy and falsehood saturate all human relationships. The healthy "natural" functions of human nature are fulfilled, so to speak, only in ways that are contraband and savage, because the reigning ideology will not sanction them. This introduces falsehood and duplicity into all human life. All ideological forms, that is, institutions, become hypocritical and false, while real life, denied any ideological directives, becomes crude and bestial.

In *fabliaux*[y] and *Schwänke*,[z] in farces, in parodic and satiric cycles, a battle is launched against this feudal backdrop, vulgar convention and the falsehood that has come to saturate all human relationships. Opposed to convention and functioning as a force for exposing it, we have the level-headed, cheery and clever wit of the rogue (in the form of a villain, a petty townsman-apprentice, a young itinerant cleric, a tramp belonging to no class), the parodied taunts of the clown and the simpleminded incomprehension of the fool. Opposed to ponderous and gloomy deception we have the rogue's cheerful deceit; opposed to greedy falsehood and hypocrisy we have the fool's unselfish simplicity and his healthy failure to understand; opposed to everything that is conventional and false, we have the clown—a synthetic form for the (parodied) exposure of others.

The novel continues this struggle against conventionality, but along lines that have a deeper significance and are more complexly organized. The primary level, the level where the author

---

y. *Fabliaux*, of which almost 150 are still extant, are short satiric tales in octosyllabic verse dating for the most part from the twelfth to fourteenth centuries.

z. *Schwänke*, satiric verses chiefly associated with folk tradition.

makes his transformation, utilizes the images of the clown and the fool (that is, a naiveté expressed as the inability to understand stupid conventions). In the struggle against conventions, and against the inadequacy of all available life-slots to fit an authentic human being, these masks take on an extraordinary significance. They grant the right *not* to understand, the right to confuse, to tease, to hyperbolize life; the right to parody others while talking, the right to not be taken literally, not "to be oneself"; the right to live a life in the chronotope of the entr'acte, the chronotope of theatrical space, the right to act life as a comedy and to treat others as actors, the right to rip off masks, the right to rage at others with a primeval (almost cultic) rage—and finally, the right to betray to the public a personal life, down to its most private and prurient little secrets.

The next stage in the transformation of the rogue, clown and fool occurs when they are introduced into the content of the novel as major protagonists (either in direct or transformed guise).

Quite often the two levels on which these images function come together into one—all the more so because the major protagonist is almost always the bearer of the authorial point of view.

In one form or another, to one degree or another, all the aspects we have analyzed appear in the "picaresque novel," in *Don Quixote*, in Quevedo,[aa] Rabelais, in German humanistic satire (Erasmus, Brandt,[bb] Murner,[cc] Moscherosch,[dd] Wicram),[ee] in Grimmelshausen, Sorel (*Le Berger extravagant*[ff] and to a certain extent in *Francion*),[gg] in Scarron, Lesage, Marivaux; later, during the En-

---

aa. Reference here is to *El Buscon* (written in 1608, but not published until 1626), one of the most heartlessly cruel books ever written.

bb. Sebastian Brandt (1458?–1521), author of the *Narrenschiff* (1494).

cc. Thomas Murner (1475–1537), German satirist, author of *Die Narrenbeschwörung* (1512); but his masterpiece is *Von dem grossen Lutherischen Narren* (1533).

dd. Reference here is to Johann Michael Moscherosch (1601–1669), German satirist whose *Gesichte Philanders von Sittenwald* (1641–1643), modeled on Quevedo's *Sueños*, gives a graphic picture of the ravages of the Thirty Years War.

ee. Jörg Wickram (1520–1562), author of probably the best collection of *Schwänke*, *Das Rollwagenbüchlin* (1555).

ff. Charles Sorel's *Le Berger extravagant* (1627).

gg. *Francion* (cf. footnote n).

lightenment, in Voltaire (especially successfully in *Le Docteur Akakios*),[hh] in Fielding (*Joseph Andrews, Jonathan Wild*, somewhat in *Tom Jones*), occasionally in Smollett and, after his own special fashion, in Swift.

It is characteristic that *internal man*—pure "natural" subjectivity—could be laid bare only with the help of the clown and the fool, since an adequate, direct (that is, from the point of view of practical life, not allegorical) means for expressing his life was not available. We get the figure of the *crank* [*čudak*], who has played a most important role in the history of the novel: in Sterne, Goldsmith, Hippel, Jean Paul, Dickens and others. A personalized eccentricity, "Shandyism" (Sterne's own term), becomes an important means for exposing the "internal man" and his "free and self-sufficient subjectivity"—means that are analogous to the "Pantagruelism" that had served in the Renaissance to reveal a coherent external man.

The device of "not understanding"—deliberate on the part of the author, simpleminded and naive on the part of the protagonists—always takes on great organizing potential when an exposure of vulgar conventionality is involved. Conventions thus exposed—in everyday life, mores, politics, art and so on—are usually portrayed from the point of view of a man who neither participates in nor understands them. The device of "not understanding" was widely employed in the eighteenth century to expose "feudal unreasonableness" (there are well-known examples in Voltaire; I mention also Montesquieu's *Lettres persanes*, which gave rise to a whole genre of analogous exotic letters portraying French social structure from the point of view of a foreigner who does not understand it; Swift, in his *Gulliver's Travels*, makes use of this device in a great variety of ways). Tolstoy employs it very widely: for example, the description of the Battle of Borodino from the point of view of an uncomprehending Pierre (the influence of Stendhal is felt here), the depiction of an Election of the Nobility or a session of the Moscow Duma from the point of view of an uncomprehending Levin, the portrayal of a theatrical performance, a court, the famous description of the mass (in *Resurrection*) and so forth.

---

hh. Voltaire's *Diatribe du docteur Akakia* (1752) is a satirical attack on the president of the Berlin Academy, Maupertuis. It was consigned to the flames by Frederick II.

The picaresque novel by and large works within the chronotope of the everyday-adventure novel—by means of a road that winds through one's native territory. And the positioning of the rogue, as we have said, is analogous to the position of Lucius the Ass. What is new here is the sharply intensified exposure of vulgar conventions and, in fact, the exposure of the entire existing social structure (especially in *Guzman Alfarache* and in *Gil Blas*).[10]

Characteristic for *Don Quixote* is the parodied hybridization of the "alien, miraculous world" chronotope of chivalric romances, with the "high road winding through one's native land" chronotope that is typical of the picaresque novel.

Cervantes' novel has enormous significance in the long history of literature's assimilation of historical time—a novel whose significance is not, of course, exhausted merely by this hybrid of two already familiar chronotopes—and all the more so because the very process of hybridization radically changes their character; both of them take on metaphoric significance and enter into completely new relations with the real world. In this essay, however, we cannot undertake an analysis of Cervantes' novel.

In the history of realism, all forms of the novel linked to a transformation of the rogue, the clown or the fool have enormous significance, but to the present day this significance has not been grasped in its essence. A profounder study of these forms would require first of all a genetic analysis of the meaning and functions of worldwide images of the rogue, clown and fool—from the deep recesses of pre-class folklore up to the Renaissance. We must take into account the enormous (in fact, incomparable) role they have played in folk consciousness; we must study the differentiation of these images, both national and local (there were, no doubt, as many local fools as there were local saints), and the particular role they play in the national and local self-consciousness of the folk. Furthermore, the problem of transforming these images, while at the same time appropriating them for literature in general (nondramatic literature), and especially for the novel, presents particular difficulty. It is a fact not usually fully appreciated that at this point in literary history, literature's sundered tie with the public square is re-established, by means both special and specific. Here, moreover, we encounter new forms for making public all unofficial and forbidden spheres of human life, in par-

---

10. There is, of course, a huge common store of motifs.

ticular the sphere of the sexual and of vital body functions (copulation, food, wine), as well as a decoding of all the symbols that had covered up these processes (common everyday symbols, ritualistic ones and symbols pertaining to the state religion). Finally, there is real difficulty with the problem of *prosaic allegorization,* if you will, the problem of the prosaic metaphor (which of course has nothing in common with the poetic metaphor) that is introduced into literature by the rogue, clown and fool, and for which there is not even an adequate term ("parody," "joke," "humor," "irony," "grotesque," "whimsy," etc., are but narrowly restrictive labels for the heterogeneity and subtlety of the idea). Indeed, what matters here is the allegoricized being of the whole man, up to and including his world view, something that in no way coincides with his playing the role of actor (although there is a point of intersection). Such words as "clownishness," "crookedness," "*jurodstvo*" [holy-foolness], "eccentricity" take on a specific and narrow, experiential meaning. Thus the great practitioners of this prosaic allegorization created their own terms for the concept (taken from the names of their heroes): "Pantagruelism," "Shandyism." Together with this allegorical quality, a special complexity and multi-layeredness entered the novel; "intervalic" chronotopes appeared, such as, for example, the chronotope of the theater. We have an especially lucid example of this new element in the novel (one of many) in Thackeray's *Vanity Fair.* At the heart of *Tristram Shandy* lies the intervalic chronotope of the puppet theater, in disguised form. Sterneanism is the style of a wooden puppet directed and commented upon by the author himself. (Such is the hidden chronotope in Gogol's "Nose" and "Petruška.")

In the Renaissance, the above-mentioned forms of the novel violated that other-worldly vertical axis along which the categories of a spatial and temporal world had been distributed and had given value to its living content. Novels of this kind paved the way for a restoration of the spatial and temporal material wholeness of the world on a new, more profound and more complex level of development. They paved the way for the novel's appropriation of that world, a world in which simultaneously America was being discovered, a sea route to India was being opened up, new fields in natural science and mathematics were being established. And the way was prepared for an utterly new way of seeing and of portraying time in the novel.

In our analysis of Rabelais' *Gargantua and Pantagruel* we hope to provide concrete examples of all the basic suppositions in this section.

VII. The Rabelaisian Chronotope

In our analysis of Rabelais' novel, as in all our previous analyses, we shall avoid dealing with any specialized questions of genesis; we will touch upon them only when absolutely necessary. We will examine the novel as a unified whole, permeated with a single ideology and a single artistic method. It should be mentioned that all our basic analytical positions are derived from the first four books, since the fifth book too sharply departs in its artistic method from the unity of the whole.

One must note, first of all, the extraordinary *spatial and temporal expanses* that leap at us from the pages of Rabelais' novel. But the issue here is not merely that the action of the novel is not yet concentrated in the spaces of rooms where private family life goes on but rather unfolds under the open sky, in movement around the earth, in military campaigns and journeys, taking in various countries. All this we observe in the Greek romance as well, and for that matter also in the chivalric romance; we also see it in the bourgeois adventure novel of travel in the nineteenth and twentieth century. What is at issue here is that special connection between a man and all his actions, between every event of his life and the spatial-temporal world. This special relationship we will designate as the adequacy, the direct proportionality, of degrees of quality ("value") to spatial and temporal quantities (dimension). This does not mean, of course, that in Rabelais' world pearls and precious stones are worse than cobblestones because they are of incommensurately smaller size. But it does mean that if pearls and precious stones are good, they should be as big as possible, and as big as possible in every situation. Every year seven ships, loaded down with gold, pearls and precious stones, are sent to the Abbey of Thélème. In the Abbey itself there are 9,332 bathrooms (one for each room) and each mirror has a frame of pure gold, inset with pearls (book 1, ch. 55). This means that everything of value, everything that is valorized positively, must achieve its full potential in temporal and spatial terms; it must spread out as far and as wide as possible, and it is necessary that everything of significant value be provided with the power to expand spatially and temporally; likewise, everything evaluated negatively is small, pitiable, feeble and must be destroyed—and is helpless to resist this destruction. There is no mutual hostility, no contradiction between spatial and temporal measurements, and value of any kind—food, drink, holy truth, "The Good," beauty, they are directly proportional to one another. Therefore, everything that is good grows: it grows in all respects and in all directions, it cannot help growing because growth is inherent in its very nature. The bad, on the contrary, does not grow but rather degenerates, thins out and perishes; but in this process its real-life diminution is compensated for by a false idealization in the other world. Since it is a function of actual spatial and temporal growth, the category of growth is one of the most basic categories in the Rabelaisian world.

When we speak of direct proportionality, we do not mean to suggest that there was a time when this quality was separated from its spatial and temporal expression in Rabelais' world, only later to be unified with it. On the contrary, these two were from the very start connected in an indissoluble unity of images in that world. But these images were deliberately counterposed to the disproportionality inherent in the feudal and religious world view, where values are opposed to a spatial-temporal reality, treating it as vain, transitory, sinful, a feudal world where the great is symbolized by the small, the powerful by the meek and powerless, the eternal by the moment.

This direct proportionality is responsible for that extraordinary faith in earthly space and time, that passion for spatial and temporal distances and expanses that is so typical of Rabelais, as well as of other great Renaissance figures (Shakespeare, Camoëns, Cervantes).

But this passion for spatial and temporal equivalence in Rabelais is far from naive—as it was in the ancient epic and in folklore. As we have already suggested, equivalence is specifically contrasted with medieval verticality, and this polemical opposition receives a special emphasis. Rabelais' task is to purge the spatial and temporal world of those remnants of a transcendent world view still present in it, to clean away symbolic and hierarchical interpretations still clinging to this vertical world, to purge it of the contagion of "antiphysis" that had infected it. In Rabelais this polemical task is fused with a more affirmative one: the re-creation of a spatially and temporally adequate world able to provide a new chronotope for a new, whole and harmonious man, and for new forms of human communication.

This fusion of the polemical and the affirmative tasks—the tasks of purging and restoring the authentic world and the authentic man—is what determines the distinctive features of Rabelais' artistic method, the idiosyncrasies of his fantastic realism. The essence of this method consists, first of all, in the destruction of all ordinary ties, of all the *habitual matrices* [*sosedstva*] of things and ideas, and the creation of unexpected matrices, unexpected connections, including the most surprising logical links ("allogisms") and linguistic connections (Rabelais' specific etymology, morphology and syntax).

Amid the good things of this here-and-now world are also to be found false connections that distort the authentic nature of things, false associations established and reinforced by tradition and sanctioned by religious and official ideology. Objects and ideas are united by false hierarchical relationships, inimical to their nature; they are sundered and separated from one another by various other-worldly and idealistic strata that do not permit these objects to touch each other in their living corporeality. These false links are reinforced by scholastic thought, by a false theological and legalistic casuistry and ultimately by language itself—shot through with centuries and millennia of error—false links between (on the one hand) good material words, and (on the other) authentically human ideas. It is necessary to destroy and rebuild the entire false picture of the world, to sunder the false hierarchical links between objects and ideas, to abolish the divisive ideational strata. It is necessary to liberate all these objects and permit them to enter into the free unions that are organic to them, no matter how monstrous these unions might seem from the point of view of ordinary, traditional associations. These objects must be permitted to touch each other in all their living corporeality, and in the manifold diversity of the values they bear. It is necessary to devise new matrices between objects and ideas that will answer to their real nature, to once again line up and join together those things that had been falsely disunified and distanced from one another—as well as to disunite those things that had been falsely brought into proximity. On the basis of this new matrix of objects, a new picture of the world necessarily opens up—a world permeated with an internal and authentic necessity. Thus, in Rabelais the destruction of the old picture of the world and the positive construction of a new picture are indissolubly interwoven with each other.

In prosecuting the more positive side of his task, Rabelais relies upon folklore and antiquity—where the contiguity of objects more exactly corresponded to their various natures and where imposed conventionality and other-worldly idealism were quite unknown. In prosecuting his negative task, the foremost device is Rabelaisian laughter—directly linked to the medieval genres of the clown, rogue and fool, whose roots go deep back into pre-class folklore. But Rabelaisian laughter not only destroys traditional connections and abolishes idealized strata; it also brings out the crude, unmediated connections between things that people otherwise seek to keep separate, in pharisaical error.

The disunification of what had traditionally been linked, and the bringing-together of that which had traditionally been kept distant and disunified, is achieved in Rabelais via the construction of series [*rjady*] of the most varied types, which are at times parallel to each other and at times intersect each other. With the help of these series, Rabelais can both put together and take apart. The construction of *series* is a specific characteristic of Rabelais' artistic method. All these widely varied series can be reduced to the following basic groups: (1) series of the human body, in its anatomical and physiological aspects; (2) human clothing series; (3) food series; (4) drink and drunkenness series; (5) sexual series (copulation); (6) death series; (7) defecation series. Each of these seven series possesses its own specific logic, and each series has its own dominants. All these series intersect one another; by constructing and intersecting them, Rabelais is able to put together or take apart anything he finds necessary. Almost all the themes in Rabelais' broad and thematically rich novel are brought about via these series.

We offer a series of examples. Throughout the entire novel Rabelais presents the human body, all its parts and members, all its organs and functions, in their anatomical, physiological and *Naturphilosophie* aspects alone. This idiosyncratic artistic presentation of the human body is a very important element in the Rabelaisian novel. It was important to demonstrate the whole remarkable complexity and depth of the human body and its life, to uncover a new meaning, a new place for human corporeality in the real spatial-temporal world. In the process of accommodating this concrete human corporeality, the entire remaining world also takes on new meaning and concrete reality, a new materiality; it enters into a contact with human beings that is no longer symbolic but material. Here the human body becomes a concrete measuring rod for the world, the measurer of the world's weight and of its value for the individual. And here we have the first attempt of any consequence to structure the entire picture of the world around the human conceived as a body—which is to say, in a zone of physical contact with such a body (although this zone is, in Rabelais, infinitely wide).

This new picture of the world is polemically opposed to the medieval world, in whose ideology the human body is perceived solely under the sign of decay and strife, where in real-life practice, there reigned a crude and dirty physical licentiousness. The reigning ideology served neither to enlighten nor to make sense out of the life of the body, rather it rejected such life; therefore, denied both words and sense, the life of the body could only be licentious, crude, dirty and self-destructive. Between the word and the body there was an immeasurable abyss.

For this reason Rabelais opposes human corporeality (and the surrounding world that is in a direct zone of contact with the body) not only to medieval, ascetic other-worldly ideology, but to the licentiousness and coarseness of medieval practice as well. He wants to return both a language and a meaning to the body, return to it the idealized quality it had in ancient times, and simultaneously return a reality, a materiality, to language and to meaning.

The human body is portrayed by Rabelais in a variety of different aspects, various first of all in its anatomical and physiological aspect. Then follows the clownish and cynical, then the fantastic, grotesque allegorization (the human being as a microcosm). And finally there is its peculiarly folkloric aspect. These aspects interpenetrate each other and are only rarely present unalloyed. But anatomical and physiological precision and attention to detail are sure to be there wherever the human body is present. Thus, Gargantua's birth: it is portrayed with a clownish cynicism, with precise anatomical and physiological details—Gargantua's mother, who had eaten too much tripe, suffers a prolapsus of the rectum resulting in severe diarrhea (the defecation series) and then the birth itself:[ii] "Thanks to this unfortunate accident there took place a weakening of the uterus; the child leapt

---

ii. All citations from Rabelais are from: *Gargantua and Pantagruel*, tr. J. M. Cohen (Baltimore: Penguin, 1955).

up through the Fallopian tubes to a hollow vein and, scrambling across the diaphragm to the upper arm where this vein divides in two, he took the left fork and crawled out through the left ear" (book 1, ch. 6).[11] Here, grotesque fantasy is combined with the precision of anatomical and physiological analysis.

In all his descriptions of battles and beatings, we get, alongside grotesque exaggeration, precise anatomical descriptions of the injuries, wounds and deaths inflicted on the human body.

Thus, in his description of Friar John beating up the enemy who had broken into the monastery vineyard, Rabelais gives us a detailed series of human members and organs (book 1, ch. 27):

He beat the brains out of some, broke the arms and legs of others, disjointed the neckbones, demolished the spines, split the noses, punched out the eyes, smashed the jaws, knocked the death down throats, broke the legs, dislocated the shoulder-blades, hips, cracked the elbow-bones in yet others. If one of them tried to hide himself in the thick vines, he would bruise him up-and-down his spine and break the base of his back, as if he were a dog. If one of them tried to save himself by flight, he knocked the man's head into pieces along the 'lambdoidal' suture.

Here is the same Friar John killing a guard:

. . . and with one blow he sliced the man's head in two, cutting through the skull over the templebone, thus separating from the back of his head both parietal bones and a great part of the frontal bone together with the sagittal suture. With the same blow he sliced through both membranes of the brain thus exposing the ventricles, and the posterior part of the brain was left hanging over the shoulders (just like a doctor's cap, black outside and red within). And then the guard tumbled to the ground dead.

Yet another analogous example: in Panurge's grotesque story of his being roasted on the spit in Turkey and how he saved himself, we notice the same anatomical detail and precision (book 2, ch. 14):

Having run in, he [the master of the house—M.B.] seized the spit on which I was trussed up and struck my tormentor with it on the spot, from which blow he died, for lack of treatment; he ran him through with the spit, a little above and to the right of the navel, and pierced the third lobe of his liver, and the diaphragm as well. Having passed through the pericardium the spit came out through the upper shoulder, between the vertebrae and the left shoulder-blade.

11. [In the Russian original] *Gargantua and Pantagruel* is cited in V. A. Pjast's [Russian] translation.

In Panurge's grotesque tale, the human body series (on its anatomical plane) is crossed with the food-and-kitchen series (Panurge being roasted like meat on a spit, having first been basted with fat) and the death series (the distinctive features of that series appear below).

None of these anatomical analyses appear as static descriptions; they are drawn into the living dynamics of action—battles, fistfights and so on. The anatomical structure of the human body is revealed in action, and it becomes, as it were, a character in the novel in its own right. But it is not the individual body, trapped in an irreversible life sequence, that becomes a character—rather it is the impersonal body, the body of the human race as a whole, being born, living, dying the most varied deaths, being born again, an impersonal body that is manifested in its structure, and in all the processes of its life.

With the same degree of precision and visual clarity Rabelais describes the external actions and movements of the human body—for example, in his description of Gymnaste's acrobatics on horseback (book 1, ch. 35). The expressive possibilities of human body-movement and gesture are illustrated with extraordinary clarity and detail in the mute debate (by means of gestures) between the Englishman Thaumaste and Panurge (here this expressiveness has no precise denotative meaning; it is important precisely because it is self-sufficient; book 2, ch. 19). An analogous example can be found in Panurge's conversation on marriage with the deafmute Goatsnose (book 3, ch. 20).

This grotesque use of the fantastic to describe the human body and all its processes is well illustrated in the portrayal of Pantagruel's illness, whose cure involves lowering into his stomach workers with spades, peasants with pick-shovels and seven men with baskets to clean the filth out of his stomach (book 2, ch. 33). The same is true of the "author's" journey into Pantagruel's mouth (book 2, ch. 32).

In order to describe the human body in its grotesque and fantastic aspect, a mass of the most varied objects and phenomena are drawn into the body series. In this new context they are immersed in an atmosphere of the body and of the life of the body; they enter into a new and unexpected matrix with body organs and processes; in this body series, they are brought down to earth and made more material. We have seen evidence of all this in the two examples offered above.

To purge his stomach, Pantagruel swallows like pills some great copper balls, "like those on Virgil's monument in Rome." Locked up inside these pills are workers with equipment and baskets for the cleaning-out of the stomach. After the purging is over Pantagruel vomits, and the balls spring out. When the workers are released from their pills, Rabelais recalls how the Greeks exited from the Trojan Horse. One of these pills can be seen in Orléans, on the steeple of the Church of the Holy Cross (book 2, ch. 33).

An even wider circle of objects and phenomena enter the grotesque anatomical series of the author's journey inside Pantagruel's mouth. It turns out that there is a whole new world inside the mouth: high mountains (teeth), meadows, forests, fortified towns. There is a plague in one of the towns, the result of foul vapors rising from Pantagruel's stomach. There are over twenty-five populated kingdoms in the mouth; inhabitants tell each other apart by their hailing from the "hither" or "yon" side of the teeth, as in the human world we refer to the "hither" and "yon" side of mountains and so forth. The description of the world disclosed inside Pantagruel's mouth takes up almost two pages. The folkloric basis of this entire grotesque image is patently obvious (cf. analogous images in Lucian).

If the geographical and economic world was drawn into the body series in the episode in Pantagruel's mouth, then the ordinary everyday agricultural world is drawn into the body series in the episode with the giant Slitnose [Brengnarille] (book 4, ch. 17):

The terrifying giant Slitnose had swallowed all the saucepans, cauldrons, pots, pans and even stoves and ovens on the island, owing to the lack of windmills which were his usual fare. As a result shortly before dawn— the hour of his digestion—he fell seriously ill with an upset stomach, caused (as the doctors said) by the fact that the digestive powers of his stomach, naturally accustomed to absorbing windmills, could not fully process stoves and braziers; pots and pans were digested well enough, as witnessed by the sediment found in four barrels of urine that he had filled twice that morning.

Slitnose avails himself of a health-resort cure on the "Island of the Winds." Here he swallows windmills. He tries out—on the advice of local specialists on stomach ailments—spicing the windmills with roosters and chickens. They sing in his belly and fly about, which brings on the colic and cramps. Moreover, the foxes of the island leap down his throat in pursuit of the birds. At that point he must take a wheat-and-millet enema to purge his stomach. The chickens make a dash for the grain, and the foxes rush after them. He puts more pills into his mouth, this time compounded of racing- and hunting-dogs (book 4, ch. 44).

What is characteristic here is the unique, purely Rabelaisian logic by which the series is constructed. The process of digestion, curative machinations, everyday household objects, phenomena of nature, farm life and the hunt are here united in one dynamic, living, grotesque image. A new and unexpected matrix of objects and phenomena is created. It should be obvious that at the heart of grotesque Rabelaisian logic lies the logic of realistic folklore fantasy.

In this minor episode with Slitnose, the body series—as is usual with Rabelais—intersects with the defecation series, the food series and the death series (about which we will be more precise below).

Even more grotesque and monstrously aberrant is the parodied anatomical description of King Lent [Caremprenant], which occupies three chapters in the fourth book (30, 31, 32).

King Lent is a "faster," a grotesque personification of the Catholic fast and *askesis*—in general, a personification of the bias against natural processes characteristic of medieval ideology. The description of Lent ends with Pantagruel's familiar discourse on Antiphysis. All offspring of Antiphysis—Chaos and Disharmony—are drawn as parodies on the human body (book 4, ch. 32):

The heads of these newborn ones were spherical and round on all sides, like a ball, and not flattened slightly on either side as is the case with humans. Their ears were high up on their heads and huge, like asses' ears; their eyes bugged out, eyelashless, fastened to little bones and as hard as crabs' eyes; their feet were round as a ball, their arms were attached backwards to their shoulders. As they walked they continually turned cartwheels, walking on their heads with their feet in the air.

Further on, Rabelais lists a series of other offspring of Antiphysis (ibid.):

Since that time she has brought forth into the world holy hypocrites, bigots and pope-mongers, followed by maniacal nobodies, Calvinist imposters from Geneva, furious Puy-Herbaults, dissemblers, cannibals and in general every sort of belly-stuffing monk, as well as other unnatural and misshapen monsters, brought forth to spite Nature.

Such a series manifests all the ideological monsters of a transcendent world view, brought together in a single all-encompassing series of *bodily* deformities and perversions.

An excellent example of the penchant for making grotesque analogies is found in Panurge's discourse on borrowers and lenders in chapters 3 and 4 of the third book. We are offered, by analogy with the mutual interaction between borrowers and lenders, the description of the harmonious structure of the human body as microcosm:

The intention of the builder of this microcosm is that it should provide shelter for the soul—which he had placed there as a guest—and that it should support life. Life consists of blood: blood is the locus for the soul; therefore, there is only one task in this world, and that is continuously to forge blood. At this forge their hierarchy is such that one is always borrowing from another, one puts another in debt. The material and metals suitable for transmutation into blood are provided by Nature: it is bread and wine. All forms of nourishment are contained in these two. . . . To find, to prepare, to cook this nourishment, hands work, feet move and transport the whole mechanism, eyes act as guides. . . . The tongue tastes, the teeth chew, the stomach receives, digests and evacuates [this food]. The nutritive portion goes to the liver, which again transmutes it and turns it into blood. . . . Then the blood is transported for further refinement to another workshop—to the heart itself, which by its diastolic and systolic movements refines and enflames it, so that it is perfected in the right ventricle and sent through the veins to all members. Each organ—feet, hands, eyes and all the rest—draws the blood to itself and each in its own way takes nourishment from it. Thus they become debtors who were previously creditors.

In this one grotesque series—the analogy with debtors and creditors—Rabelais offers a picture of the harmony of the universe and the harmony of human society.

All these grotesque, parodied and clownish series of the human body on the one hand serve to expose the body's structure and its life and on the other hand drag into the body-matrix a heterogeneous world of things, phenomena and ideas that were, in the medieval picture of the world, infinitely far from the body, and included in completely different series of words and objects. Whatever direct contact these objects and phenomena had with the body was brought about, first and foremost, via a *verbal matrix*, their verbal compacting into a single context, a single phrase, a single compound word. On occasion Rabelais does not shy away from even completely nonsensical compound words, if only they will serve to place in series (to "matricize") these words and concepts that human speech—based as it was on fixed structure, a fixed world view, a fixed system of values—had never as yet used in a single context, a single genre, a single style, a single sentence, with a single intonation. Rabelais is not afraid of a logic along the lines of "the melon is in the garden, but my uncle is in Kiev." He makes frequent use of the peculiar logic of sorcerers, as this was understood in the medieval formulas for blaspheming God and Christ, and the formulas for calling up unclean spirits. He makes wide use of the special logic of profanity (of which more below). This unbridled phantasmagoria has a special significance: it permits him to create verbal series of objects that are in themselves reasonable, but become monstrous when linked together (for example, the episode with Slitnose, the Swallower of Windmills).

But at the same time it must not be thought that Rabelais is preoccupied with form alone. All these word-linkages, even those that seem the most absurd in terms of the objects they name, are aimed primarily at destroying the established hierarchy of values, at bringing down the high and raising up the low, at destroying every nook and cranny of the habitual picture of the world. But simultaneously he is accomplishing a more positive task, one that gives all these word-linkages and grotesque images a definite direction: to "embody" the world, to materialize it, to tie everything in to spatial and temporal series, to measure everything on the scale of the human body, to construct—on that space where the destroyed picture of the world had been—a new picture. Even the most monstrous and unexpected word-matrices are saturated with the unifying force of these ideological impulses of Rabelais. But there is, as we will see below, still another and even more profound and idiosyncratic meaning hiding behind Rabelais' grotesque images and series.

Alongside this grotesque anatomical-physiological use of corporeality for "embodying" the whole world, Rabelais—a humanist physician and pedagogue—was concerned with direct propaganda on behalf of the culture of the body and its harmonious development. Thus, Rabelais opposes to the original scholastic upbringing of Gargantua—one that ignored the body—the subsequent humanist upbringing under Ponocrates, where enormous attention is paid to anatomical and physiological studies, hygiene and various types of sports. To the medieval body—coarse, hawking, farting, yawning, spitting, hiccupping, noisily nose-blowing, endlessly chewing and drinking—there is contrasted the elegant, cultured body of the humanist, harmoniously developed through sports (book 1, ch. 21, 23 and 24). The Abbey of Thélème also devotes enormous attention to body culture (book 1, ch. 52, 57). We will have reason to return to this harmonious, affirmative pole of Rabelais' world view, to this harmonious world with its harmonious human being.

The next series is that of eating and drinking-drunkenness. This series plays an enormous role in the Rabelaisian novel. Almost all the themes of the novel come about through it; hardly an episode could manage without it. The most varied objects and phenomena of the world are brought into direct contact with food and drink—including the most lofty and spiritual things. The "Author's Prologue" begins right off with a nod to drunkards, to whom the author dedicates his writings. In the same prologue he insists that he worked on this book only during periods of eating and drinking: "Indeed, this is the proper time for writing of such lofty matters and profound sciences, as Homer, who was the paragon of all philologists, very well knew, and Ennius, the father of Latin poets, and Horace testifies to it as well, although a certain imbecile declared that his verses smack rather of wine than of oil."

The author's prologue to the third book is even more striking in this respect. Here the barrel of the cynic Diogenes is inscribed into the drink series in order that it may become a wine cask. Here the motif of "drunken creativity" is repeated, and in addition to Homer and Ennius, writers who composed while drunk, we also have Aeschylus, Plutarch and Cato.

The very names of Rabelais' major protagonists derive etymologically from the drink series: Grandgousier (Gargantua's father) is "Great Gulp." Gargantua is born into the world with a terrible cry on his lips: "Drink! Drink! Drink!" "How healthy you are!" (*Que grand tu as!*) says Grandgousier, referring to his son's throat. This first word, spoken to the father, causes the child to be called Gargantua (book 1, ch. 7). Rabelais likewise etymologically interprets the name "Pantagruel" as "he who is always thirsty."

Even the birth of the major protagonists takes place under the sign of eating and drunkenness. Gargantua is born on a day of great feasting and drinking arranged by his father—thus it is that his mother overeats on tripe. The newborn infant is immediately "wined." Pantagruel's birth, on the other hand, is preceded by a great drought and consequently by a great thirst—affecting people, animals, the earth itself. The picture of this drought is given in Biblical style and saturated with concrete reminders of antiquity and the Bible. This lofty plane is interrupted by the physiological series with its grotesque explanation for the salinity of sea water: "The earth was so heated that it burst into a great sweat, which caused it to sweat out the whole sea which for that reason is salty, for all sweat is salt. You will admit this to be true if you taste your own sweat, or the sweat of pox-patients when they are made to sweat—it is all the same to me" (book 2, ch. 2).

The salt motif, as well as the drought motif, prepares the way for, and intensifies, the fundamental motif of thirst under whose aegis Pantagruel is born—the "King of the Thirsty." In the year, the day, the hour of his birth, everything in the world is thirsty.

The motif of salt is introduced in a new way at the very moment of Pantagruel's birth. Before the infant himself appears, out of his mother's womb "leap 68 muleteers, each pulling by the collar a mule heavily laden with salt; after which there follows nine dromedaries loaded down with bales of ham and smoked ox-tongues, seven camels loaded with salted eels, followed by 25 cartloads of leeks, garlics and green onions." After this series of salty thirst-provoking hors d'oeuvres, Pantagruel himself appears in the world.

Thus, Rabelais constructs the grotesque series: drought, heat, sweat (when it is hot people sweat), salt (sweat is salty), salty hors d'oeuvres, thirst, drink, drunkenness. Dragged into this series along the way: the sweat of pox-patients, holy water (whose use is regulated by the church during the drought), the Milky Way, the sources of the Nile and a whole series of Biblical and classical references (mention is made of the parable of Lazarus, Homer, Phoebus, Phaeton, Juno, Hercules, Seneca). All this occurs in the space of a page and a half, describing Pantagruel's birth. Rabelais here creates a characteristic new and monstrous matrix of objects and phenomena—elements that within quite ordinary contexts are completely incompatible.

Gargantua's genealogy is found among the symbols of drunkenness: it is uncovered in a crypt, amid nine wine flasks under a goblet on which was inscribed "Hic bibitur" (book 1, ch. 1). Let us now turn our attention to the matrix of words and things that links the crypt and the drinking of wine.

Almost all the truly important episodes in the novel are introduced into the eating and drinking series. The war between
Grandgousier's kingdom and the kingdom of Picrochole, which
takes up most of the first book, is caused by scones and grapes,
foods that are in addition viewed as a remedy for constipation and
thus intersect with the highly detailed defecation series (cf. ch.
25). Friar John's celebrated battle with Picrochole's warriors is
over the monastery vineyards, which satisfy the monastery's
need for wine (not so much for the Eucharist as for the drunkenness of the monks). Pantagruel's famous journey that fills the
whole fourth book (as well as the fifth) is a search for "the oracle
of the sacred bottle." All the ships that set sail are decorated with
symbols of drunkenness in the form of heraldic devices: a bottle,
a goblet, a pitcher (amphora), a wooden jug, a glass, a cup, a vase, a
wine basket, a wine barrel (Rabelais describes each ship's device
in detail).

The eating and drinking series are, like the body series, highly
detailed and hyperbolized in Rabelais. In every instance we are
given the most detailed enumerations of the most varied ap-
petizers and main dishes, along with a precise account of their exaggerated quantities. Thus, for example, the following list occurs
during a description of the supper in Grandgousier's castle following the battle (book 1, ch. 37):

> Supper was served: first 16 oxen were roasted, then 3 heifers, 32 calves,
> 63 suckling kids, 95 sheep, 300 suckling pigs in a marvelous sauce, 220
> partridges, 700 woodcock, 400 capons from Lundun and Cornouaille and
> 1700 juicy varieties from other breeds, 600 pullets and as many pigeons,
> 600 guinea-fowls, 1400 hares, 303 bustards and 1700 capon chicks. Game
> they could not get in such quantity: there were only 11 wild boars sent by
> the abbot of Turpenay, and 18 fallow deer, a gift from the Lord of Garnd-
> mont, together with 140 pheasants from the Lord of Essars, and some
> dozens of wild pigeons, water-hens, teal, bitterns, curlews, plovers,
> heath-cock, briganders, sea-ducks, lapwings, sheldrakes, both large and
> dwarf, and also creasted herons, storks, bustards and flamingoes with
> red plumage, landrails and turkey-hens, together with various sorts of
> dumplings.

In the description of Gaster's Island (the Maw), there is a particularly detailed enumeration of the most varied dishes and ap-
petizers: two whole chapters (59 and 60 in book 4) are devoted to
this list.

As we have already stated, the most varied objects, phenomena and ideas are drawn into the eating and drinking series—items completely foreign to that series from the reigning point of view (in its ideological and literary practice, as well as in spoken language), items also foreign to the customary way of ordering things. The means of incorporation are the same as in the body series. We offer several examples.

The struggle of Catholicism with Protestantism, and particularly with Calvinism, is portrayed as a struggle between King Lent and the Sausages that inhabit Savage Island. The episode with the Sausages takes up eight chapters in the fourth book (35–42). The sausage series is a highly detailed one, developed through a grotesque obsession with sequence. Starting with the shape of a sausage, Rabelais proves, relying on various authorities, that the serpent that bit Eve was a sausage, that the ancient giants who had stormed Mount Olympus and who had tried to pile Mount Pelion on Ossa were half sausage. Melusine was also half sausage, as was Erichthonius, the inventor of the hearse and the cart (so that he might hide his sausage legs). In preparation for this battle with the Sausages, Friar John concludes a treaty with the cooks. A huge sow is armed to the teeth like the Trojan Horse. The sow is described in a parodied-epic Homeric style, and it takes several pages to list the names of all the warrior-cooks who entered the sow. The battle takes place, and at the critical moment Friar John

opens the doors of his sow and burst out with his stout soldiers. Some of them were dragging iron spits, others frying-pans, dripping-pans, blades, racks, kettles, pots, pokers, tongs, cooking-pots, mortars and pestles—all in battle array like so many firemen, shouting and howling in a deafening roar: "Nebuzar-adan! Nebuzar-adan! Nebuzar-adan!" And with such shouts and uproar they struck out at the Paté and the Wieners.

The Sausages are defeated: there appears over the field of battle the flying "Hog of Minerva" who throws down a barrel of mustard—this is the "Holy Grail" of the Sausages, it heals their wounds and even resurrects their dead.

The intersection of the food series with the death series is of particular interest. In chapter 46 of the fourth book we find a lengthy discourse by the devil on the relative tastiness of various human souls. The souls of slanderers, petty clerks and lawyers are only good when freshly salted. Scholars' souls are good for breakfast, lawyers' souls for dinner, chambermaids' for supper. From vine-dressers' souls one gets a colic in the stomach.

Elsewhere we are told how the devil breakfasts on a fricassee made from the soul of a sergeant, and how he falls seriously ill with an upset stomach. Into the same series are introduced the fires of the Inquisition, which separate men from their faith and thus guarantee devils a steady supply of tasty souls.

A further example of the intersection of the eating series with the death series is found in the Lucianic episode of Epistemon's visit to the Kingdom of the Dead in chapter 30 of the second book. The resurrected Epistemon "promptly begins to speak, saying that he has seen devils, that he has held intimate conversation with Lucifer, and has feasted well both in Hell and in the Elysian Fields. . . ." The eating series is extended throughout the entire episode: in the world beyond the grave, Demosthenes is a vine-dresser, Aeneas a miller; Scipio Africanus trades in yeast, Hannibal in eggs. Epictetus, under a spreading tree and surrounded by numerous maidens, dances and feasts at every opportunity. Pope Julius hawks pasties. Xerxes hawks mustard; since he asks too much for it, François Villon pisses in his mustard tub, "as mustard-makers do in Paris" (an intersection here with the defecation series). Pantagruel interrupts Epistemon's tale of the nether world with words that both resolve the theme of death and the world beyond the grave and serve as a summons to eating and drinking: "Well, now . . . it's time for some feasting and drinking. I beg you, my lads, because it's good drinking season all this month!" (book 2, ch. 30).

Frequently Rabelais will tightly intertwine his eating and drinking series with religious concepts and symbols—the prayers of monks, monasteries, papal decrees and so forth. The young Gargantua, after stuffing himself at dinner (this is during that time when he is still under the tutelage of the scholastics) "only with difficulty managed to mouth a piece of a prayer." On the "Isle of the Papimaniacs" Pantagruel and his fellow travelers are invited to a "dry Mass," that is, a mass without church singing; but Panurge prefers one "moistened with a little good Anjou wine." On this same island they are fed a dinner where every dish, be it kid, capon or hog—which is very plentiful in Papimania—pigeon, rabbit, hare, turkey, and so on and so forth—all were stuffed with "bottomless subtleties." This "stuffing" gives Epistemon a most severe case of diarrhea (book 4, ch. 51 [misprint in Russian original, where it is given as ch. 1, tr.]). Two special chapters are devoted to the theme of "the monks in the kitchen":

chapter 15 of the third book, "Explanation of the Monastic Cabala in the Matter of Salt Beef," and chapter 11 of the fourth book, "Why Monks Love to Be in Kitchens." Here is a highly typical excerpt from the first of these chapters (book 3, ch. 15):

"You like vegetable soup, but I prefer mine with bay leaf, with perhaps the addition of a slice of ploughman salted til the ninth hour." "I understand you," replied Friar John. "You drew that metaphor from the stockpot of the cloister. You call an ox that ploughman who is ploughing, or has ploughed. To salt for nine hours means to cook to a turn. By a certain cabalistic institution of the ancients, unwritten but passed from hand to hand, our good spiritual fathers, having gotten up for matins, would in my time go through certain important preliminaries before entering the Church. They spat in the spitteries, vomited in the vomitoria, dreamed in the dreameries, pissed in the pisseries. And all so that they might bring nothing unclean to the Divine service. Having done all this, they moved devotedly in to the Holy Chapel—for that in their jargon was the name they gave to the convent kitchen—and they devotedly saw to it that from that moment on the beef was on the fire, for the breakfast of our holy friars, brethren in our Lord. Often they lit the fire under the pot themselves. And since the matins lasted nine hours, they had to get up earlier, and consequently as the hours increased so did their appetite and thirst—much more so than if the matins had contained only one or three hours [lessons]. The earlier they arose, thus spake the Cabala, the earlier the beef was on the fire; the longer it was on, the better it stewed, the better it stewed the tenderer it became, the less it wore down the teeth, the more it delighted the palate, the less it weighed on the stomach, and the better it nourished the good monks. And this was the sole purpose and prime aim of the founders of the monastery, who took into consideration the fact that one does not eat to live but rather one lives to eat, there being no other reason to live on this earth."

This excerpt is very typical of Rabelais' artistic methods. First and foremost, we see here a realistically drawn picture of everyday monastic life. But at the same time this genre-painting is given as the decoding of an expression peculiar to monastic (monk's) jargon: "a slice of ploughman, salted til the ninth hour." Hidden behind the allegory in this expression is a tight matrix of meat (the "ploughman") and the mass (the nine hours are the parts read out at the morning service). The number of texts to be read (nine hours) conduces to the best stewing of the meat and to the best appetite. This holy mass-cum-eating series intersects with the defecation series (which would include spitting, vomiting, pissing) and with the bodily physiological series (the role of the teeth, the palate and the stomach). Monastic masses and prayers serve merely to fill up the time necessary for the proper cooking of food and for the whetting of the appetite.[12] From this follows the generalizing conclusion: monks eat not to live, but live to eat. Using the principles for constructing series and images in Rabelais, we will pause in what follows for a more detailed treatment of the material already provided by the five leading series.

As a general principle we are not concerning ourselves with questions of genesis, with questions of sources or influences. But in this instance we will tentatively put forward a general observation. The introduction of religious concepts and symbols into the eating, drunkenness, defecation and sexual-acts series in Rabelais is not, of course, anything new. We are familiar with the most diverse kinds of parody-formulas used by sorcerers in the literature of the late Middle Ages—parodied Gospels, parodied liturgies (the All-Drunkards' Mass of the thirteenth century), parodied holy days and rituals. Such an intersection·of series is typical for the poetry of the Vaganti (Latin poetry) and even for their special argot. And we encounter it, of course, in the poetry of Villon (who is connected with the Vaganti). Along with this parodic-witchcraft literature, black-magic formulas of a type used by sorcerers are of special significance, and they were both widespread and widely known in the late Middle Ages and Renaissance (and without doubt were well known to Rabelais), and, finally, we have the "formulas" for obscene profanity, whose ancient cultic importance has not yet been extinguished; this obscene profanity was widespread in "unofficial" everyday speech and gives rise to the stylistic and ideological idiosyncracies of "unofficial" everyday speech (most especially in the lower social classes). Witchcraft-magical formulas (including obscenity) and everyday billingsgate are themselves related to each other, being in fact two branches of the same tree, whose roots go deep into pre-class folklore—but of course they are branches that have profoundly distorted the original noble nature of the tree.

Besides this medieval tradition, we should also mention a more ancient tradition, and in particular Lucian—who substantially altered the method of rendering the everyday, physiological detail

12. Rabelais cites the monastic proverb: "de missa ad mensam" [from the mass to the meal].

of erotic and quotidian aspects embedded in myths (cf., for example, the copulation of Aphrodite with Ares, Athena's birth from Zeus' forehead and so on). And finally we must mention Aristophanes, who influenced Rabelais (especially in matters of style).

We will return later to the question of Rabelais' reworking of this tradition, as well as to the question of that deeper folkloric tradition that formed the basis for his artistic world. At this point we touch on these questions only provisionally.

Let us return to the eating and drinking series. As with the body series, we have in these, along with grotesque exaggeration, Rabelais' basically affirmative view of the significance, the culture, of eating and drinking. Rabelais by no means advocates crude gluttony and drunkenness. But he does affirm the lofty importance of eating and drinking in human life, and strives to justify them ideologically, to make them respectable, to erect a culture for them. The transcendental ascetic world view had deprived them of any affirmative value, had taken them as nothing more than a sad necessity of the sinful flesh; such a world view knew only one formula for making such processes respectable, and that was the fast—a negative form, hostile to their nature, dictated not by love but by enmity (cf. the figure of "King Lent," the faster, as the typical offspring of "Antiphysis"). But insofar as they were ideologically negative and unstructurable, sanctioned by neither word nor thought, eating and drinking could only take the form of the crudest gluttony and drunkenness. As a consequence of this inevitable falseness inherent in the ascetic world view, gluttony and drunkenness flourished precisely in the monasteries. A monk in Rabelais is first and foremost a glutton and a drunkard (cf. especially chapter 34 concluding book 2). We have already pointed out that whole chapters are devoted to this special affinity between monks and kitchens. The grotesque and fantastic image of gluttony is illustrated by the episode of Pantagruel's visit, along with his fellow travelers, to the island of Gaster. Five chapters are devoted to this episode (57–62) in the fourth book. Here, using material from ancient times—particularly from the poet Persius—the entire philosophy of Gaster (the Maw) is worked out. It was precisely a maw, and not fire, that was the first great teacher of all the arts (ch. 57). The maw is credited with the invention of agriculture, of military arts, transportation, sea travel and so forth (ch. 56–57). The doctrine of famine as the moving force for economic and cultural development is partially a parody, and partially a truth (as is the case with the majority of Rabelais' analogously grotesque images).

The culture of eating and drinking is contrasted with crude gluttony throughout the account of Gargantua's upbringing (in book 1). The theme of culture and moderation in food is discussed in connection with spiritual productivity in chapter 13 of the third book. Rabelais conceives this culture not only in its medical and hygienic aspect (as a function of "the healthy life"), but also from the point of view of the gourmet, the purely culinary. In somewhat parodied form, Friar John's sermon on "humanism in the kitchen" expresses the culinary preference of Rabelais himself (book 4, ch. 10):

By almighty God, *da jurandi*, why don't we remove ourselves into some grand holy kitchen, and there consider the turning of the spits, the music of the hissing chunks of meat, the placing of the bacon fat, the temperature of the soups, the preparation of the dessert, and the order of the wine service. "Beati immaculati in via." That's how it goes in the breviary.

Interest in the culinary details of preparing food and drink in no way contradicts, of course, the Rabelaisian ideal of a whole and harmoniously developed physical and spiritual human being.

Pantagruelian feasts occupy a very special place in the Rabelaisian novel. Pantagruelism means the ability to be cheerful, wise and kind. Therefore, the ability to feast cheerfully and wisely is the very essence of Pantagruelism. But the feasts of the Pantagruelists are in no way feasts of idlers and gluttons, men who are perpetually at table. One may devote to the feast only the evening leisure hours at the completion of the working day. Dinner (in the middle of the working day) should be short and, so to speak, merely utilitarian. Rabelais defends on principle the transfer of the eating-and-drinking center of gravity to the evening supper. And so it was decreed in the pedagogical system of the humanist Ponocrates (book 1, ch. 23):

Gargantua's dinner, note, was moderate and simple—because they ate only to still the gnawings of the stomach; but supper was copious and lengthy, for at that time Gargantua ate as much as he needed to nourish himself and replenish his energies. This is the proper diet prescribed by the art of good sound medicine.

There is that special discourse on supper, put into Panurge's mouth, that we already cited from chapter 15 of the third book:

When I've well and truly breakfasted and my stomach has been cleaned out and well-pumped, in a pinch and in case of necessity I'll do without dinner. But to miss my supper! A pox on that! Why, that's an error, a violation of nature! Nature created man that he may exercise his strengths, that we may work, that each man may occupy himself with his affairs, and to help us do this more conveniently she provides us with a candle, that is, with the gay and joyful light of the sun. But in the evening she begins to withdraw this light from us, as if to say silently: "You, my children, have been good. That's enough work! Night is coming: you must cease from your labors and fortify yourself with good bread, good wine, good meat, and you must enjoy yourselves a bit, then lie down and sleep, so as to rise up in the morning just as fresh and ready to work."

At these Pantagruelian "evenings"—while eating the bread, the wine and the various meats, or directly afterwards—Pantagruelian conversations get going, conversations that are wise but filled as well with laughter and banter. In what follows we will have more to say on the special significance of these "evenings," the new Rabelaisian variant on the Platonic "Feast" [*Symposium*].

In such a way the eating and drinking series, through their grotesque development, perform the task of destroying archaic and false matrices between objects and phenomena, and create new matrices, fleshed-out ones, that materialize the world. At its positive pole this series ends in nothing less than ideological enlightenment, the culture of eating and drinking, which is an essential feature of the new human image, a man who is harmonious and whole.

Let us pass on to the defecation series. This series occupies a large place in the novel. The Antiphysis infection required a strong dose of the Physis antivenin. In general, the defecation series creates the most unexpected matrices of objects, phenomena and ideas, which are destructive of hierarchy and materialize the picture of the world and of life.

We will take as an example of such unexpected matrices the theme of "arse-wiping." The infant Pantagruel delivers a speech on the various means he had investigated for wiping himself, and on the best method he had found. In the grotesque series of items he lists for arse-wiping we find: a lady's velvet muffler, a neckerchief, silk earflaps, a page's hat, a March cat (who scratched his behind with his claws), his mother's gloves scented with benzoin, sage, fennel, marjoram, cabbage leaves, greens, lettuce, spinach (the eating series), roses, nettles, a blanket, curtains, napkins, hay, straw, wool, a cushion, slippers, a game-bag, a basket, a hat. The very best arse-wipe turned out to be a baby goose with soft down: "one feels a marvelous pleasure from the softness of the down, and from the warmth of the goose itself, and this spreads throughout the bum-gut and the rest of the intestines reaching all the way to the heart and the brain." Later, relying on "the opinion of the Master Duns Scotus," Gargantua claims that the heavenly bliss experienced by the heroes and demigods in the Elysian Fields consists precisely in their wiping their arses with baby geese.

In the conversation "in praise of the Decretals" that takes place during a dinner on the Isle of the Papimaniacs, even papal decrees are entered into the defecation series. Friar John once used them for an arse-wipe, from which he got hemorrhoidal tumors. Panurge suffered a severe case of constipation after reading the Decretals (book 4, ch. 52).

An intersection of the body series with the series of eating-drinking and with the defecation series occurs in the episode with the six pilgrims. Gargantua swallows six pilgrims with his salad, and washes them down with a healthy gulp of white wine. At first the pilgrims hide behind the teeth, and then they are all but carried away into the abyss of Gargantua's stomach. With the help of their staffs they manage to hang on to the surface of the teeth. At this point they accidentally touch a sore tooth, and Gargantua spews them out of his mouth. And while the pilgrims are making their escape Gargantua begins to urinate; his urine cuts across the road, and they are forced to make their way across this great current of urine. When they are finally out of danger, one of the pilgrims exclaims that all these tribulations had been foretold in the Psalms of David: "When the people rose up against us it was as if we were to be swallowed alive"—"that's when we were eaten in the salad, with salt," he said. "And since a great wrath fell upon us, as if water had swallowed us up"—"that was when he made that huge swallow. . . ." "Perhaps our soul crosses an insuperable current of water. . . ."—"that's when we crossed the great torrent of his urine, by which he cut off our path of escape" (book 1, ch. 38).

Thus, even the Psalms of David are tightly interwoven with the processes of eating, drinking and urinating.

There is a characteristic episode concerning the "Isle of the Winds," whose inhabitants nourish themselves on wind alone. The theme of "wind" and the entire complex of lofty motifs associated with it in literature and poetry—the wafting of zephyrs, the wind in sea storms, breathing and sighing, the soul as a breath, the spirit and so on are here, via the intermediary expression "to pass wind," pulled into the eating series, the defecation series and the quotidian series (cf. "air," "breath," "wind," which functions as a standard and as the internal form of words, images and motifs from a loftier plane—life, the soul, the spirit, love, death, etc.) (book 4, ch. 42 and 44):

On this island there is no spitting, no urinating, but people pass wind and gas in great abundance. . . . The most widespread disease is inflation of the stomach and colic. As a cure they apply carminatives in great quantities, and use cupping-glasses for aerating the stomach. They all die from swollen stomachs, as if from dropsy; the men passing wind, the women gas. So it is that their souls depart by the back passage.

Here the defecation series intersects with the death series.

Within the defecation series Rabelais constructs a series of "local myths." A local myth explains the genesis of a geographical space. Each locality must be explained, beginning with its place-name and ending up with the fine details of its topographical relief, its soil, plant life and so forth—all emerging from the human event that occurred there and that gave to the place its name and its physiognomy. A locality is the trace of an event, a trace of what had shaped it. Such is the logic of all local myths and legends that attempt, through history, to make sense out of space. And Rabelais also creates, on the plane of parody, such local myths.

Rabelais explains the place-name "Paris" in the following way. When Gargantua enters the city, a crowd of people gather round him and "for the fun of it" ("par ris") "he unbuttoned his magnificent codpiece and then and there drenched them so copiously that 260,418 persons were drowned, not counting women and children. . . . Hence it was that the city was ever afterwards call Paris" (book 1, ch. 17 [misprint in Russian original, where the chapter is given as 42, tr.]).

The explanation given for the source of the hot baths in France and Italy is that Pantagruel's urine, during his illness, was so steaming hot that it has not to this day cooled off (book 2 [cannot be as given in Russian original ch. 17, tr.]).

The stream that flows by Saint Victor was created by dogs' urine (this episode is related in ch. 22 of book 2).

The examples we have cited are sufficient to characterize the functions of the defecation series in the Rabelaisian novel. Let us pass on to the sexual-act series (and to the series of sexual indecencies in general).

The sexual series occupies an enormous place in the novel. It appears in a wide variety of forms: from sheer obscenity to subtly coded ambiguity, from the bawdy joke and anecdote to medical and naturalistic discourses on sexual potency, male semen, sexual reproductive processes, marriage and the significance of the origin of the genders.

Openly indecent expressions and jokes are sprinkled throughout the whole of Rabelais' novel. They are especially frequent in the mouth of Friar John and Panurge, but the other heroes are not strangers to them either. When, during the Pantagruelists' journey, they come upon some frozen words and among them discover a cluster of indecent words, Pantagruel refuses to store in the hold several of these frozen indecencies: "He said it was folly to stock up on those things which one is never short of, and which are always at hand—as are indecent words among the good and jovial Pantagruelists" (book 4, ch. 56).

This principle of word use adhered to by the "good and jovial Pantagruelists" is sustained by Rabelais throughout the entire novel. No matter what themes are discussed, indecencies always find a place for themselves in the verbal fabric that is being woven, drawn in by means of the most remarkable object-associations, as well as by purely verbal ties and analogies.

There is in the novel no small number of short, indecent novellas built on jokes, which are often borrowed from folkloric sources. Such, for instance, is the anecdote about the lion and the old lady, related in chapter 15 of the second book, and the story of "How the Devil Was Deceived by the Old Woman of Popefigland" (book 4, ch. 47). The basis for this story is the ancient folkloric analogy between the female organ and an open wound.

Along the lines of a "local myth" we have the celebrated story "about the reason why in France there are such short leagues," where space is measured by the frequency of occurrence of the sexual act. King Pharamond chose from Paris one hundred splendid young fellows and just as many fine young Picardy maidens. He gave one girl to each youth and ordered them to set out in couples, in all directions; on each spot where the youths made love to their girls he ordered them to set up a stone, and that should be a league. The dispatched couples made love well and often at the beginning, while they were still in France, thus the French leagues are so short. But later on they grew weary, their sexual energy exhausted; they were satisfied with one measly little bout a day; this is what makes the leagues in Brittany, in Landes and in Germany so long (book 2, ch. 23).

A further example could be found in the introduction of world-wide geographical space into the indecency series. Panurge says: "There was a time when Jupiter copulated with fully one-third the world—with animals, humans, rivers and mountains—that is, with Europa" (book 3, ch. 12).

Panurge's bold and grotesque discourse on the best means to build walls around Paris is of a somewhat different character. He says (book 2, ch. 15):

"I see that in this city women are cheaper than stone; therefore, let us build walls out of female organs. And moreover let us lay out those organs with full architectural symmetry; we'll place the big ones in the first rows; next, rising like two slopes, the middle-sized ones, and finally the little ones. Then we will fill them up—as in the great tower of Bourges—with those firmed-up swords which dwell in monastic codpieces. What devil would be able to overthrow walls like that!"

A different logic governs the discussion of the sexual organs of the Roman pope. The papimaniacs consider the kissing of the feet an insufficient expression of respect toward the pope (book 4, ch. 47):

"We want to show more. More respect!" they reply. "It's all decided. We will kiss his bare bum and other parts as well. For he has them, the holy father has! So it is spoken in our great Decretals. Otherwise he wouldn't be the pope. In fact our subtle Decreteline philosophy tells us that this is a necessary consequence—he is a pope, therefore he has these organs. If there ceased to be such organs in the world, the world would have no pope.

We consider the examples cited here fully sufficient to characterize the various means by which Rabelais introduces and develops the series of "sexual indecencies" (for our purposes we do not require, of course, an exhaustive analysis of these means).

In the organization of all the material of the novel, one theme—entered into the indecency series—is of crucial significance: namely, the theme of "horns." Panurge wants to marry but he decides against it, afraid of being "horned." Almost half of the book (beginning with ch. 7) is devoted to Panurge's discourse on marriage: he consults with his friends, makes prophecies on the basis of Virgil, reads dreams, holds conversations with the Panzaust Sibyl, consults first a deafmute, then the dying poet Raminogrobis, then Herr Trippa [Agrippa Nettesgeimski], then the Theologian Hippothadeus, the Physician Rondibilis, the Philosopher Wordspinner, the Fool of Triboulet. The theme of horns and the fidelity of wives figures in to all these episodes, conversations and discourses—a theme that in its turn draws in to the story, via a thematic or a verbal similarity, the most varied themes and motifs from the sexual series; for example, the discussion of male potency and of the perpetual arousability of women in the speeches of the Physician Rondibilis, or the survey of ancient mythology in connection with the bestowing of horns and the fidelity of women (ch. 31 and 12 of the third book).

The fourth book of the novel is organized as a journey of the Pantagruelists to the "oracle of the Sacred Bottle," which was to put to rest, once and for all, Panurge's doubts about marriage and horns (although it is true that the "theme of horns" in itself is almost completely absent from the fourth book).

The sexual series functions, as do all the abovementioned series, to destroy the established hierarchy of values via the creation of new matrices of words, objects and phenomena. He restructures the picture of the world, materializes it and fleshes it out. The traditional image of the human being in literature is also re-structured in a radical way; moreover, it is re-structured in a way that benefits the "unofficial" and extraverbal areas of his life. The whole man is brought out on the surface and into the light, by means of the word, in all the events of his life. But throughout all this the human being is not deheroicized or debased at all, nor does he in any sense become a man of "low life." We might say rather that in Rabelais there is a heroization of all the functions of the life of the body, of eating, drinking, defecating and sexual activity. The very hyperbolization of these acts contributes to their heroization; they lose their commonplace quality, their everyday and naturalistic coloration. We will in what follows return again to this question of Rabelais' "naturalism."

The sexual series has its positive pole as well. The coarse debauchery of medieval man was but the reverse side of the ascetic ideal that had denigrated sexuality. Its harmonious integration is illustrated in Rabelais by the Abbey of Thélème.

The four series selected by us do not exhaust all the "materializing" series of the novel. We have chosen only the dominant series, those that give the work its basic tone. One might also isolate a clothing series, which is worked out by Rabelais most meticulously. Special attention is paid here to the codpiece (that part of the clothing that covers the male sexual organ), which connects this series with the sexual series. And one might also isolate a series of objects from everyday life, or of household objects or a zoological series. All these series, gravitating toward the human being as "body," carry out the same functions: a disunification of what had been traditionally linked and a bringing together of what had been hierarchically disunified and distant, serving to bring about, therefore, the materialization of the world.

Having dealt with these "materializing" series, let us pass on to the final series, which has a different function in the novel: the series of death.

At first glance it might seem that Rabelais' novel does not have anything like a death series. The problem of individual death and the intensity this problem usually has are presented as something absolutely foreign to Rabelais' healthy, whole and virile world. And this impression is absolutely correct. But in that hierarchical picture of the world that Rabelais destroyed, death had occupied a commanding place. Death robbed life on earth of its value, considering it perishable and transitory; death deprived life of any independent value, turning it into a mere service mechanism working toward the future eternal fate of the soul beyond the grave. Death was not perceived as an inevitable aspect of life itself, beyond which life triumphed again and continued (life, taken in either its essential collective or historical aspect), but was perceived rather as a limiting phenomenon, one lying on the fixed boundary between that perishable temporary world and eternal life, like a door opening out on another, transcendental, world. Death was, therefore, conceived not as part of an all-encompassing temporal sequence but rather as something on the boundary of time, not in a life series but at the edge of that series. Rabelais, in destroying the old hierarchical picture of the world and in putting a new one in its place, was obliged to re-evaluate death as well, to put it in its own place in the real world and, most importantly, to portray it as an unavoidable aspect of life itself, to portray it in the all-encompassing temporal series of life that always marches forward and does not collide with death along the way, nor disappear into the abyss of the world beyond, but remains entirely *here*, in this time and space, under this sun; and Rabelais must portray, finally, a death that—even in this world—is not an *absolute* end for anyone, or any thing. This means he must portray the material aspect of death within the triumphant life series that always encompasses it (without, of course, any poetic pathos, which is deeply alien to Rabelais)—while at the same time portraying it as something that occurs "just in passing," without ever overemphasizing its importance.

The death series—with a few exceptions—appears in Rabelais on a grotesque and clownish plane; it intersects with the eating and drinking series, with the defecation series, with the anatomical series. On the same plane there are disquisitions on the question of a world beyond the grave.

We are already familiar with examples of death in the grotesque anatomical series. A detailed anatomical analysis of a fatal blow is given; the physiological inevitability of death is demonstrated. In this instance death is presented as a naked anatomical and physiological fact, in all its clarity and precision. All the descriptions of death in battle are of this type. Here, death is seen as if it were part of the impersonal anatomical-physiological series of the human body, and always in dynamic conflict. The general tone is grotesque, sometimes highlighting one or another of the comic aspects of death.

Thus, we have, for example, the description of Tripet's death (book 1, ch. 35):

Turning around quickly, he [Gymnaste—M.B.] threw himself on Tripet, and gave a flying thrust with the sharp of his sword, and, as the captain covered the upper part of his body, sliced him through the stomach, the colon, and half the liver with one blow, so that he fell to the ground, and falling emptied out more than four potfuls of soup, and mingled with the soup, his soul.

Here the anatomical-physiological image of death is introduced into a dynamic picture of the battle between two human bodies, and the image that results is a death in direct relationship with food: "he emptied out his soul which had been mingled with his soup."

We have cited above a sufficient number of examples of the anatomical image of death in battle (the massacre of the enemy in the monastic vineyard, the murder of the guard, etc.). All these images are analogous, and all present death as an anatomical-physiological fact in an impersonal series constituted by the living and struggling human body. Here death does not interfere with the uninterrupted series comprising the struggling human life; rather, it appears as merely one aspect of this life; it does not violate the logic of this life, and is made out of the same stuff as life itself.

In the defecation series, death has a different, grotesquely clownish character, one involving no anatomical-physiological analysis. Thus, Gargantua drowns in his urine "260,418 persons . . . not counting women and children." Here this "mass destruction" is presented not only as something directly grotesque, but also as a parody on dry accounts of natural disasters, suppressed uprisings, religious wars (from the point of view of these official accounts, human life isn't worth a cent). The description of the enemy drowned in the urine of Gargantua's mare is downright grotesque. The image here is very detailed. Gargantua's companions must make their way across a stream made of urine, across the piled-up corpses of drowned men. Everyone gets across successfully (book 1, ch. 36),

with the exception of Eudemon, whose horse had plunged its right leg knee-deep into the belly of a blubbery fat good-for-nothing who had drowned on his back, and the horse could not pull its leg out and, therefore, stayed stuck there until Gargantua shoved the rest of the scoundrel's giblets into the water with his staff, and then the horse pulled out her leg and (by what miracle of veterinary science!) was cured of a tumor on that leg, through contact with that fat oaf's guts.

What is characteristic here is not only the image of death-in-urine, or the tone and style of the description of the corpse ("belly," "guts," "giblets," "blubbery fat good-for-nothing," "scoundrel," "fat oaf"), but also the healing of the leg through contact with the innards of a corpse. Analogous cases are very widespread in folklore; they are based on one of the general folkloric assumptions concerning the generative power of death and of the fresh corpse (a wound is a womb) and the idea of healing the death of one by the death of another. Here we have the folkloric nexus of death with new life—albeit extraordinarily weakened, of course, to the point of a grotesque image: the healing of a horse's leg through contact with the innards of a blubbery corpse. But the peculiar folkloric logic of this image is clear.

We will mention another example, the intersection of the death series with the defecation series. When the inhabitants of the "Isle of the Winds" die, their souls pass out of their bodies along with their wind (in the case of the males) and with gas (in the case of the females) through the "rear passage."[13]

In all these examples of the grotesque (clownish) portrayal of death, the image of death itself takes on humorous aspects: *death is inseparable from laughter* (while, however, not being associated with it in a series of objects). And in the majority of cases Rabelais portrays death with an inclination to laugh about it; he portrays *cheerful deaths*.

We get a comic portrayal of death in the episode of "Panurge's Herd." Desiring to avenge himself on the merchant who had directed him to a ship full of sheep, Panurge buys the bellwether and tosses it into the sea; all the remaining sheep rush into the sea after the bellwether; the merchant and his herdsmen throw themselves after the sheep in an attempt to hold them back, and they are themselves impelled into the sea (book 4, ch. 8):

Panurge stood beside the galley with an oar in his hand, not to help the herdsmen but to prevent them from somehow clambering aboard and thus escaping their death, and all the while preached to them eloquently . . . with rhetorical flourishes about the miseries of this world and the blessings of the next, affirming that those who had passed on to that place were happier than those who lived on in this vale of tears. . . .

The comic element in this death situation is provided by Panurge's accompanying sermon. The entire situation is a wicked parody on the conception of life and death as it was perceived by the medieval transcendental world view. In another instance, Rabelais tells the story of monks who, instead of giving immediate aid to a drowning man, first felt compelled to advise him about his eternal soul and to confess him, during which time he sank to the bottom.

In keeping with this spirit of violation-by-parody of medieval assumptions about the soul and the world beyond the grave, we are offered the cheerful image of Epistemon's temporary visit to the Kingdom of the Dead (we have already touched on this episode above). Here would belong as well the grotesque discourses

13. In another place Pantagruel generates little men out of his winds, and little women out of his gas (book 2, ch. 27). The heart in these mannikins is close to their rear passage, and therefore they are hot-tempered.

on the gustatory qualities and gastronomic value of the souls of the newly dead, about which we have already spoken.

We must keep in mind the cheerful representation of death in the eating series, in the story of Panurge and his misadventures in Turkey. Here we are given the externalized comic situating of death, which is at the same time in direct relation with food (roasting on the spit and impaling on the spit). The entire episode of the half-roasted Panurge's miraculous salvation ends with an encomium to the roast meat on a spit.

Death and laughter, death and food, death and drink are frequently brought together in Rabelais. Everywhere the setting for death is a cheerful one. In chapter 17 of the fourth book we get a whole series of surprising and, more often than not, comic deaths. Here the story is told of the death of Anacreon, who suffocated on a grape seed (Anacreon—wine—grape seed—death). The praetor Fabius died from a goat's-hair that had fallen into a glass of milk. One man died from holding back the gas in his stomach, which he was embarrassed to release in the presence of the Emperor Claudius and so forth.

If in the above instances it was the external situation that made death laughable, then the death of the duke of Clarence (the brother of Edward IV) was a cheerful death even for the dying man himself; sentenced to death, he himself was offered the choice of his means of execution: "And he chose death by drowning in a barrel of malmsey!" (book 4, ch. 33). Here a cheerful death is directly associated with wine.

The "cheerfully dying man" as a type is illustrated by Rabelais in the figure of the poet Raminagrobis. When Panurge and his traveling companions visited the dying poet, he was already in his death agony, but "he was cheerful in his looks, his face was bright and his eyes clear" (book 3, ch. 21).

In all these instances of a cheerful death there is laughter in the tone, in the style and in the form of portraying death. But laughter also enters the death series in a direct verbal- and object-association with death: in two places in his book, Rabelais lists a series of deaths from *laughing*. In chapter 20 of the first book, Rabelais mentions Crassus, who died laughing at the sight of an ass swallowing a red thistle, and Philemon, who also died laughing at the sight of an ass, this one gobbling down figs. In chapter 17 of the fourth book, Rabelais mentions the artist Zeuxis, who died laughing as he looked at the portrait of an old woman he had just finished painting.

Finally, death is presented in close relationship with the birth of new life and—simultaneously—with laughter.

When Pantagruel is born he is so huge and heavy that he could not appear in this world without suffocating his mother (book 2, ch. 2). The mother of the newborn Pantagruel dies, and his father Gargantua finds himself in a difficult situation: he does not know whether to weep or to laugh. "The doubt which so troubled his reason was due to not knowing whether he should weep of grief on account of his wife, or laugh with delight at the sight of his son." He was not able to resolve his doubt and as a result both wept and laughed. Remembering his wife, "Gargantua bellowed like a cow. And then he suddenly began to laugh like a calf, remembering Pantagruel" (book 2, ch. 3).

The nature of Rabelaisian laughter is revealed in its full vividness in the death series, at the points of intersection of this series with the eating, drinking and sexual series and in its direct association of death with the birth of new life. Here are revealed the authentic sources and traditions of this laughter; the application of this laughter to the whole wide world of sociohistorical life ("the epic of laughter"), to an epoch, or more precisely to the boundary line between two epochs, exposing its perspectives and its subsequent historical generative force.

The "cheerful death" of Rabelais not only coincides with a high value placed on life and with a responsibility to fight to the end for this life—but it is in itself an expression of this high evaluation, an expression of the life force that eternally triumphs over any death. In the Rabelaisian image of the cheerful death there is not, of course, anything decadent; there is no striving toward death, no romanticizing death. In Rabelais, the death theme itself, as we have already said, is in no way foregrounded, in no way emphasized. Of enormous importance in the working-out of this theme is the sober and clear anatomical and physiological aspect of death. And laughter in Rabelais is certainly not set in opposition to the horror of death: this horror is missing entirely, and consequently there can be no sharp contrast.

We find this tight matrix of death with laughter, with food, with drink, with sexual indecencies in other representative figures of the Renaissance as well: in Boccaccio (in the framing story itself, and in the material of the separate stories), in Pulci (the description of deaths and of paradise during the Battle of Roncevalles); in Margutte (a prototype for Panurge, who dies of laughter) and in Shakespeare (in the Falstaff scenes, the cheerful grave-diggers in *Hamlet*, the cheerful drunk porter in *Macbeth*). The similarity among these scenes can be explained by the unity of the epoch and by the shared nature of sources and traditions; the differences are in the breadth and fullness with which these matrices are developed.

In the subsequent history of literary development, these matrices continue to live with great vigor, in Romanticism and then in Symbolism (we are passing over the intervening stages); but in those contexts their character is utterly different. The wholeness of a triumphant life, a whole that embraces death, and laughter, and food and sexual activity, is lost. Life and death are perceived solely within the limits of the sealed-off individual life (where life is unrepeatable, and death an irremediable end), and, therefore, within the limits of life taken in its internal and subjective aspect. Thus, in the artistic imagery of the Romantics and the Symbolists, these matrices are transformed into sharp, static contrasts and oxymorons that are either not resolved at all (since there is no all-encompassing, larger real "whole") or resolved on the plane of mysticism. It suffices to mention those phenomena that are externally more or less similar to the Rabelaisian matrices. There is a short story by Edgar Allan Poe set in the Renaissance called "The Cask of Amontillado." The hero kills his rival during a *carnival*, the man is drunk and dressed in a *clown's* costume with *little bells* on it. The hero persuades his rival to go with him into his wine cellar (the catacombs) in order to determine the authenticity of a cask of Amontillado that he had bought; here, in the cellar, the hero walls his rival up alive in a niche, and the last thing he *hears is laughter and the tinkling of the clown's bells.*

This entire short story is structured on sharp and completely static contrasts: the gay and brightly lit carnival/the gloomy catacombs; the merry clown's costume of the rival/the terrible death awaiting him; the cask of Amontillado and the gay ringing of the clown's bells/the horror at *impending death* felt by the man being immured alive; the terrifying and treacherous murder/the calm, matter-of-fact and dry tone of the protagonist-narrator. At the heart of the story lies a very ancient and time-honored complex (matrix): death—the fool's mask (laughter—wine—the gaiety of the carnival [*carra navalis Bacchus*])—the grave (the catacombs). But the golden key to this complex has been lost: there is no all-encompassing whole of triumphant life, there remain only the denuded, sterile and, therefore, oppressive contrasts. Of course, behind these contrasts there is felt a dark dim forgotten kinship, a long series of reminders of artistic images in world literature in which these very elements were fused together—but this remains a dim sensation, and these reminders affect only the narrowly aesthetic impression that one gets from the story as a whole.

At the heart of the familiar story "The Masque of the Red Death" there lies a Boccaccian matrix: the *plague* (death, the grave)—a *holiday* (gaiety, laughter, wine, eroticism). But here this matrix also turns out to be a naked contrast creating a tragic, in no sense Boccaccian atmosphere. In Boccaccio the all-embracing whole of life (not, of course, a narrowly biological life), life triumphant and moving ever forward, reduces the force of the contrasts. In Poe these contrasts are static and the dominant of the entire image is, therefore, oriented toward death. We see the same thing in the story "King Pest" (drunken soldiers feasting in a plague-infested quarter of a port city), although here the wine and drunken revelry of the healthy body in the *plot* [*sjuzhet*] (but *only* in the plot) insures a victory over the plague and over the phantoms of death.

We are again reminded of the Rabelaisian motifs in the father of Symbolism and "Decadence," Baudelaire. In his poem "Le Mort joyeux" (cf. the concluding gesture to the worms: "Voyez venir à vous un mort libre et joyeux") and in the poem "Le Voyage" (a summoning of death, the "vieux capitaine" in the final stanzas), and finally in the cycle "La Mort" we notice the same indications of decline of the complex (an association that was never very full) and the same orientation of the dominant toward death (the influence of Villonism and "the school of nightmares and horrors."[14] Here death, as is always the case with the Romantics and the Symbolists, ceases to be an aspect of life itself and becomes again a phenomenon on the border between my life here-and-now and a potential other kind of life. The whole problematic is concentrated within the limits of the *individual* and *sealed-off* progression of a single life.

14. Cf. analogous instances in Novalis (the eroticizing of the whole complex, especially in the poem on the Eucharist), in Hugo (*Notre Dame de Paris*); the Rabelaisian tone in Rimbaud, Laforgue.

But let us get back to Rabelais. In his work the death series has an affirmative pole as well, where the theme of death is discussed with almost no trace of the grotesque. We have in mind those chapters devoted to the death of heroes and of the Great Pan, and the celebrated missive of the old Gargantua to his son.

In the chapters on the death of heroes and the Great Pan (book 4, ch. 26, 27 and 28), Rabelais, relying on ancient material, reports with almost no trace of the grotesque the special situation surrounding the death of heroes, whose life and death was not without meaning to mankind. The death of high-born and heroic men is often accompanied by special natural phenomena that reflect the historical dislocation: storms rage, comets, falling stars appear in the sky (ch. 27):

> The heavens tacitly tell us, by means of the airborne ethereal signs of the comets: "Mortal men, if you wish to learn from the dying something concerning public prosperity or profit—call upon the dying as speedily as possible and obtain an answer from them. If you let this moment pass, your regrets will be in vain!"

And in another place (ch. 26):

> While a torch or candle is alive and burning it shines on all those near it, it lights up its surroundings, offers its help and its brilliance to all and does no harm nor displeasure to anyone—but the moment it is extinguished it poisons the air with its smoke and vapor, and offends and displeases everyone near it; it is the same with such noble and famous souls. As long as they inhabit their bodies, their presence brings peace, pleasure, profit and honor. But at the hour of their decease, the isles and the mainland are habitually disturbed by mighty commotions: shuddering and darkness, thunder and hail; the earth trembles and quakes, storms and hurricanes start up over the seas, complaints and distress rise up among the people, religions change, kingdoms fall, states are overthrown.

From the examples cited above it is clear that in Rabelais the deaths of heroes occur in an utterly different tone and style: in place of a grotesque fantastic we have a heroizing fantastic, partly in the spirit of a popular epic, which in its basics provides for a tone and style corresponding to ancient sources (in his retelling, Rabelais adheres to these rather closely). All this bears witness to Rabelais' high evaluation of historical heroism. It is characteristic that those phenomena with which nature and the historical world react to the death of heroes—although they "contradict all the rules of nature"—are by themselves completely natural (storms, comets, earthquakes, revolutions) and they occur in the same external world that was the scene for the life and activity of the heroes. This resonance is epically heroicized; nature also participates in it. Even in this instance Rabelais represents death not in the progression of the individual life (sealed-off and sufficient unto itself), but rather death in the historical world, as a phenomenon of sociohistorical life.

The death of Great Pan is told (or more precisely retold, from Plutarch) in such tones. In his retelling Pantagruel transfers events connected with this death to the death of "the great savior of the faithful," but at the same time includes in his image purely pantheistic content (ch. 28).

The aim of all three chapters is to demonstrate historical heroes as a major and irradicable trace in a single, real world—the world of nature and history. These chapters do not conclude in the manner we have learned to expect from Rabelais. After the conclusion of Pantagruel's speech, a great silence falls.

A little later we noticed how tears fell from his eyes, big ones, like the eggs of ostriches.
Strike me dead, O Lord, if I have uttered one word of untruth.

The grotesque overtones are here combined with a seriousness that is extremely rare for Rabelais (concerning Rabelais' seriousness we shall have something to say later).

Gargantua's letter to Pantagruel, which occupies chapter 8 of the second book, is important not only for the death series but also for the entire affirming (neither grotesque nor critical) pole of Rabelais' novel. In this regard it is similar to the episode on the Abbey of Thélème. In what follows we will, therefore, return to it (as well as to the Abbey of Thélème). Here we shall touch only on those parts that are relevant to the motif of death.

We see developed here the theme of the continuation of the race, of generations and of history. Despite the admixture of canonical Catholic tendencies, inevitable under the conditions of the time, a doctrine nevertheless emerges that contradicts these— the doctrine of the biological and historical immortality of man (the biological and historical do not of course contradict each other), the immortality of the seed, the name and the act.

Among the gifts, graces and prerogatives with which the Creator, God Almighty, endowed and embellished human nature in the beginning, one seems to me to be especially wonderful; that is, the one by which we can, in this mortal state, acquire a kind of immortality and, in the course of this transitory earthly life, perpetuate our name and seed. This we accomplish through descendents sprung from us in lawful marriage.

Thus begins Gargantua's missive.

Thanks to this propagation of seed, there lives on in the children what had perished in the parents, and in the grandchildren what had perished in the children. . . . Not without just and equitable cause, therefore, do I offer thanks to God, my Preserver, for permitting me to see my decrepitude and old age blossom afresh in your youth; and when, at the will of Him who rules and measures all things, my soul shall quit this mortal habitation—not all of me will die, but I shall only pass from one place to another, since in you and by you I shall remain in visible form here in this world of the living, visiting in society with men of honor and with my good friends, as I have been accustomed to do.

In spite of the worshipful turns of phrase characterizing almost all the opening and closing paragraphs of the letter, the letter itself develops the idea of a different kind of immortality, one that is earthly, relative, deliberately and comprehensively opposed to the Christian doctrine of the immortality of souls. In no way does Rabelais posit the possibility of a static immortality of some aged soul that has emerged from the decrepit body in some transcendental realm where it is denied any further earthly growth or development. Gargantua wants to see himself, his old age and decrepitude blossom forth again in the fresh youth of his son, grandson and great-grandson; what for him is precious is his own visible earthly image, whose features are preserved in his descendents. In the person of his descendents he wishes to remain "in the world of the living," it is in his descendents that he wishes to circulate among good friends. What matters here is precisely the possibility of immortalizing the earthly on the earth, and the preservation of all the earthy values of life—a fine physical appearance, blooming youth, good friends and, most important of all, a continuation of physical growth, of development and of the further perfection of the individual. Least of all does he posit an immortality that one might achieve at any particular point of development.

We must emphasize one more feature: for Gargantua (Rabelais), it is not at all important to immortalize one's own "I," one's self as a biological specimen, one's own selfhood, whatever values may attach to it: what matters to him is the "immortalizing" (or more precisely, the further growth) of his best desires and strivings:

And thus if the qualities of my soul did not abide in you as does my bodily form, men would not consider you the guardian and treasure-house of the immortality of our name, in which case my pleasure would be much reduced. For I would see that my lesser part had persisted, that is, my flesh, while the better part, which is the soul, by which our name continues to be blessed among men, that part would have degenerated and become, as it were, bastardized.

Rabelais connects the growth of generations with the growth of culture, and with the growth of the historical development of mankind as well. The son will continue the father, the grandson the son—and on a higher level of cultural development. Gargantua makes reference to a great revolution that had occurred during his lifetime: "In my age dignity and enlightenment were restored to the sciences, and such a change has taken place that I should scarcely be accepted in the first grade of the lowest school—I, who in my ripe years was reputed (not without some justification) to be the most learned man of the age." And somewhat further: "I find that nowadays robbers, hangmen, freebooters and grooms are better educated than the doctors and preachers were in my time."

This kind of growth—where the most learned man of one epoch does not qualify for the first grade of the lowest school in the following (contiguous) epoch—is welcomed by Gargantua; he does not envy his descendents, who will be better than he merely because they were born later than he. In the person of his descendents, in the person of other men (of the human race, his race) he will participate in this growth. Death begins nothing decisive, and ends nothing decisive, in the collective and historical world of human life.

As we will see, the same constellation of problems arises in particularly acute form in the eighteenth century in Germany. The problem of a personal individual perfection and "becoming" of a man, of the perfection (and growth) of the human race, of earthly immortality, of the education [vospitanie] of the human race, of rejuvenating culture through the youth of a new generation—all these problems will arise in conjunction with each other. They inevitably lead to a more profound conceptualization of the problem of historical time. Three basic attempts at a resolution of these problems (which are interdependent) emerged:

Lessing's (*Erziehung des Menschengeschlechts*),[jj] Herder's (*Auch eine Philosophie der Geschichte zur Bildung der Menschheit*)[kk] and finally Goethe's distinctive variant (particularly in *Wilhelm Meister*).

All the series selected by us above serve in Rabelais to destroy the old picture of the world that had been formed in a dying epoch, and to create a new picture, at whose center we have the whole man, both body and soul. In the process of destroying the traditional matrices of objects, phenomena, ideas and words, Rabelais puts together new and more authentic matrices and links that correspond to "nature," and that link up all aspects of the world by means of the most marvelous grotesque and fantastic images and combinations of images. In this complex and contradictory (*productively* contradictory) flow of images, Rabelais brings about a restoration of the most ancient object-associations; this flow enters one of the most fundamental channels of literary thematics. Along this channel flows a full-bodied stream of images, motifs, plots, fed by the springs of pre-class folklore. The direct association of eating, drinking, death, copulation, laughter (the clown) and birth in one image, in one motif and in one plot is the *exterior* index of this current of literary thematics. The elements themselves that make up the whole image, motif or plot—as well as the artistic and ideological functions of the entire matrix taken as a whole at various stages of development— both change drastically. Beneath this matrix, which serves as the exterior index, there is hidden a specific form for experiencing time and a specific relationship between time and the spatial world, that is, there is hidden a specific chronotope.

Rabelais' task is to gather together on a new material base a world that, due to the dissolution of the medieval world view, is disintegrating. The medieval wholeness and roundedness of the world (as it was still alive in Dante's synthesizing work) had been destroyed. There was destroyed as well the medieval conception of history—the Creation of the World, the Fall from Grace, the

---

jj. *Die Erziehung des Menschengeschlechts* (1780) is Lessing's (1729–1781) last work. It is only 100 paragraphs long. It is a testimonial to Lessing's belief in mankind's endless progress.

kk. Herder (1744–1803), *Auch eine Philosophie der Geschichte zur Bildung der Menschheit* (1774), an attack on an overweening rationality in the study of history, specifically opposing ideas of the French Enlightenment.

First Expulsion, Redemption, the Second Exile, the Final Judgment—concepts in which real time is devalued and dissolved in extratemporal categories. In this world view, time is a force that only destroys and annihilates; it creates nothing. It was necessary to find a new form of time and a new relationship of time to space, to earthly space ("The frames of the old *orbis terrarum* had been broken; only now, precisely now, was the earth opened up. . . .").[15] A new chronotope was needed that would permit one to link real life (history) to the real earth. It was necessary to oppose to eschatology a creative and generative time, a time measured by creative acts, by growth and not by destruction. The fundamentals of this "creating" time were present in the images and motifs of folklore.

VIII. The Folkloric Bases of the Rabelaisian Chronotope

The basic forms of this productive and generative time can be traced back to a pre-class, agricultural stage in the development of human society. The preceding stages were poorly suited to the development of a differential feeling for time, and for its reflection in ceremonies and in linguistic images. A powerfully and sharply differentiated feeling for time could arise only on a collective, work-oriented agricultural base. Here was first constituted that feeling for time that had at its heart a taking-apart and putting-together of social everyday time, the time of holidays and ceremonies connected with the agricultural labor cycle, with the seasons of the year, the periods of the day, the stages in the growth of plants and cattle. And here we get, in the oldest motifs and plots, a reflection of such a time consolidated in language for the first time, a reflection of the temporal relationships of growth to the *temporal contiguity* of phenomena having widely differing characteristics (associations based on the unity of time).

What, then, are the distinctive features of this form of time?

This time is collective, that is, it is differentiated and measured only by the events of *collective* life; everything that exists in this time exists solely for the collective. The progression of events in an individual life has not yet been isolated (the interior time of an

---

15. K. Marx and F. Engels, *Works* [*Sočinenija*, vol. 20, p. 346, in Russian, no publication data given].

individual life does not yet exist, the *individuum* lives completely on the surface, within a collective whole). Both labor and the consuming of things are collective.

This is the time of labor. Everyday life and consumption are isolated from the labor and production process. Time is measured by labor events (the phases of agricultural labor and their subcategories). This sense of time works itself out in a collective battle of labor against nature. The practice of collective labor gives birth to this new sense of time, and the ends of this practice serve to differentiate and reshape this sense of time.

This is the time of *productive growth*. It is a time of growth, blossoming, fruit-bearing, ripening, fruitful increase, issue. The passage of time does not destroy or diminish but rather multiplies and increases the quantity of valuable things; where there was but one seed sown, many stalks of grain appear; the new issue always eclipses the passing away of individual specimens. And these single items that perish are neither individualized nor isolated; they are lost in the whole growing and multiplying mass of new lives. Perishing and death are perceived as a *sowing*, after which follows increase and harvest, multiplying that which had been sown. The passage of time marks not only a quantitative but also a qualitative growth—a movement toward flowering and ripening. Insofar as individuality is not isolated, such things as old age, decay and death can be nothing more than aspects subordinated to growth and increase, the necessary ingredients of generative growth. Their negative side, their purely destructive and finalizing nature comes out only on the purely individual plane. Generative time is a pregnant time, a fruit-bearing time, a birthing time and a time that conceives again.

This is a time maximally tensed toward the future. It is a time when collective labor concerns itself for the future: men sow for the future, gather in the harvest for the future, mate and copulate for the sake of the future. All labor processes are aimed forward. Consumption (that process most tending toward stasis, toward the present) is not separated from productive labor, it is not opposed to labor as the self-contained, isolated pleasure that comes from consuming the product. Generally speaking there is as yet no precise differentiation of time into a present, a past and a future (which presumes an *essential individuality* as a point of departure). This time is characterized by a general striving ahead (in the labor act, in movement, in action).

This time is *profoundly spatial and concrete*. It is not separated from the earth or from nature. It, as well as the entire life of the human being, is all on the surface. The agricultural life of men and the life of nature (of the earth) are measured by one and the same scale, by the same events; they have the same intervals, inseparable from each other, present as one (indivisible) act of labor and consciousness. Human life and nature are perceived in the same categories. The seasons of the year, ages, nights and days (and their subcategories), copulation (marriage), pregnancy, ripening, old age and death: all these categorical images serve equally well to plot the course of an individual life and the life of nature (in its agricultural aspect). All these images are profoundly chronotopic. Time here is sunk deeply in the earth, implanted in it and ripening in it. Time in its course binds together the earth and the laboring hand of man; man creates this course, perceives it, smells it (the changing odors of growth and ripening), sees it. Such time is fleshed-out, irreversible (within the limits of the cycle), realistic.

Such a time is *unified* in an unmediated way. However, this imminent unity becomes apparent only in the light of later perceptions of time in literature (and in ideology in general), when the time of personal, everyday family occasions had already been individualized and separated out from the time of the collective historical life of the social whole, at a time when there emerged one scale for measuring the events of a *personal* life and another for measuring the events of *history* (these were experienced on various levels). Although *in the abstract* time remained unified, when it was appropriated for the making of plots it bifurcated. There were not many personal plots to choose from, and these could not be transferred into the life of the social whole (the state, the nation); the plots (occasions) of history became something specifically separate from the plots of personal life (love, marriage); they intersected only at certain specific points (war, the marriage of a king, crime), and took off from these points in a multitude of different directions (as in the double plot of historical novels: on the one hand historical events, and on the other the life of the historical personage as a private individual). The motifs created in the unified time of pre-class folklore were for the most part incorporated into the pool of plots available for personal life—of course only after undergoing thorough reinterpretation and re-grouping, re-placement. But even so, they still preserved their real, albeit extremely fragmented, appearance. These motifs could be incorporated into historical plots only partially, and even then only in a completely sublimated, symbolic form. In the era of developing capitalism, the life of society and the state becomes abstract and almost plotless.

Only against the background of this later bifurcation of time and plotting can we see the measuring of the imminent unity of folkloric time. Individual life-sequences have not yet been made distinct, the private sphere does not exist, there are no private lives. Life is one, and it is all thoroughly "historicized" (to use a later category); food, drink, copulation, birth and death are not aspects of a personal life but are a common affair; they are "historicized," they are indissolubly linked with communal labor, with the battle against nature, with war: as such they find expression and are represented in the same categorical images.

This time attracts everything into its orbit; it will not permit any unmoving or static setting. All objects—the sun, the stars, the earth, the sea and so forth—are present to man not as objects of individual perception ("poetic perception") nor as objects of casual daydreaming, but exclusively as part of the collective process of labor and the battle against nature. Only in such activities does man encounter these objects, and only through the prism of these activities can he perceive and come to know them. (Such consciousness is more realistic, objective and profound than would be possible in unrestricted poetic perception.) All objects are thus attracted into life's orbit; they become living participants in the events of life. They take part in the plot and are not contrasted with its actions as a mere "background" for them. In later and already literary stages in the development of images and plots, there is a decline of material available for narrative events as well as for their setting: the natural landscape, the unchanging armature of the sociopolitical structure, the ethical hierarchy and so forth—it makes no difference whether this setting is perceived as always unmoving and unchanging, or unchanging only as regards the given narrative movement. In later literary development the power of time and consequently of narratability is always restricted.

All the peculiarities that we have pointed out so far may be said to be positive features in folkloric time. But a final feature of this time (on which we will now pause), its *cyclicity*, is a negative feature, one that limits the force and ideological productivity of this

time. The mark of cyclicity, and consequently of cyclical re-
petitiveness, is imprinted on all events occurring in this type of
time. Time's forward impulse is limited by the cycle. For this reason even growth does not achieve an authentic "becoming."

Such are the basic distinctive features of that experience of
time that was formed in the pre-class agricultural stage in the development of human society.

Our characterization of folkloric time has been presented, of
course, against the background of our contemporary perception of
time. We do not posit such a perception as a fact of primitive
man's consciousness; rather, we are attempting to adduce it on
the basis of objective material, since that time—which we glean
from sufficiently ancient motifs—is what determines the unity of
these motifs and plots, as well as determining the logic by which
these images unfold in folklore. It also renders possible and comprehensible that matrix of objects and phenomena with which we
began and to which we will again return. It determines, as well,
the particular logic of cultic rituals and holidays. People lived and
worked with such a sense of time, but it could not, of course, be
something recognized and isolated in abstract consciousness.

It is easy to see that the matrix of objects and phenomena in the
folkloric time outlined by us above must have its own very special character, sharply different from the character of later matrices in literature and, in general, in the ideological cognitive
processes of class society. Under conditions that did not admit
the isolating of individual life-sequences and that took for granted
the immanent unity of time, it is inevitable that such phenomena
as copulation and death (the seeding of the earth, conception), the
grave and the fertile female mons, food and drink (the fruits of the
earth) together with death and copulation and so forth turn up in
the growth-and-fertility category, in direct contiguity with each
other. Into this same sequence are woven, as participants, the
phases of the life of the sun (the alternation of day and night, the
seasons of the year), together with the earth, with growth and fertility. All these phenomena are lumped together into a single
event, each phenomenon signifying different sides of one and the
same whole—the whole growth, of fertility, of life conceived under the sign of growth and fertility. We repeat: the life of nature
and the life of a man are fused together in this complex: the sun is
part of the earth, as a kind of consumer good, it is eaten and
drunk. The events of human life are just as grand as the events of

nature's life (the same words, the same tones are used for both, and in no sense metaphorically). In this context all members of the matrix (all elements of the complex) are *equally valid*. Food and drink are just as significant in this series as death, childbirth and the phases in the life of the sun. The single great event that is life (both human and natural) emerges in its multiple sides and aspects, and they are all equally indispensable and significant within it.

We stress again: the matrix under discussion was experienced by primitive man not as a function of his abstract thought-processes or consciousness, but as an aspect of life itself—in a collective laboring with nature, in the collective consuming of the fruits of his labor and in the collective task of fostering the growth and renewal of the social whole.

It would be absolutely incorrect to suppose that any one of these members of the matrix was privileged over the whole, and it would be particularly wrong to ascribe such a primacy to the sexual element. The sexual element as such has not yet been separated out, and aspects involving it (human copulation) were perceived in absolutely the same way as were other members of the matrix. All of these were merely different sides of one and the same unified event, and all sides shared an identity with one another.

We have taken the matrix in its maximal simplicity, in its crudest, most basic outlines. A huge quantity of ever newer components was continually being incorporated into it, which complicated the motifs and made possible a remarkable multiplicity of narrative combinations. The furthest reaches of the available world were incorporated into this complex, and the world was re-perceived in it and through it (in actual practice).

Insofar as stratification of the communal whole into social classes occurs, the complex undergoes fundamental changes; the motifs and narratives that correspond to those strata are subject to a reinterpretation. A gradual differentiation of ideological spheres sets in. Cultic activity separates itself from undifferentiated production; the sphere of consumption is made more distinct and to a significant extent compartmentalized [*individualizuetsja*]. Members of the complex experience internal decline and transformation. Such elements of the matrix as food, drink, the sexual act, death, abandon the matrix and enter *everyday life*, which is already in the process of being compartmentalized.

From another point of view they enter into ritual, acquiring in this new context a magic significance (which is in general highly specific as regards its cultic or ritualistic meaning). Ritual and everyday life are tightly interwoven with each other, but there is already an interior boundary between them; bread in a ritual is already no longer the actual ordinary bread that one eats every day. This boundary becomes ever sharper and more precise. Ideological reflection (the word, the symbolization) acquires the force of magic. The isolated object becomes a substitute for the whole: this is the source of the substitutive function of the victim (fruit offered in sacrifice functions as a substitute for the entire harvest, an animal is a substitute for the entire herd or for the fruits of the harvest and so on).

At this stage, when the means of production, ritual and everyday life are being differentiated (gradually becoming separate from each other), there come into being such phenomena as *ritualistic violations* [*skvernoslovie*] and, later, *ritualistic laughter, ritualistic parody* and *clownishness*. This is the same growth-fertility complex at new stages of social development and consequently in new redactions. The elements of the matrix (which had in its ancient form encompassed a great deal) are, as before, tightly bound up with each other, but they are interpreted in a ritualistic and magical way, and differentiated on the one hand from communal production, and on the other hand from individual everyday life (although the two sides are interwoven with each other). At this stage (or more precisely, near the end of this stage) the ancient matrix can be seen in great detail in the Roman Saturnalia, where all these occur: the slave and the clown become substitutes for the ruler and God in death, various forms of ritualistic parody make their appearance, and "the passions" are mixed with laughter and gaiety. There are analogous phenomena: the violation of wedding taboos and ridicule of the bridegroom; Roman soldiers' ritualistic ridicule of the commandant-*triumphator* as he enters Rome (the logic is one of the substitute-victim: one wards off real disgrace by a fictive disgrace, which was later interpreted as warding off "Fate's envy"). In all these phenomena, laughter (in its various expressions) is present in permanent conjunction with death, with sexuality and also with food and drink. We find this same conjunction of laughter with cultic food and drink, with sexual indecencies and with death in the very structure of Aristophanes' comedies (cf. also the same complex, on a thematic level, in Euripides' *Alcestes*). In these latter manifestations, the chosen ancient matrix already functions on the purely literary plane.

As class society develops further and as ideological spheres are increasingly differentiated, the internal disintegration (bifurcation) of each element of the matrix becomes more and more intense: food, drink, the sexual act in their real aspect enter personal everyday life, they become predominantly a *personal* and *everyday* affair, they acquire a specific narrowly quotidian coloration, they become the petty and humdrum "coarse" realities of life. On the other hand, all these members are to an extreme degree sublimated in the religious cult, and partially in the high genres of literature and other ideologies. The sexual act is often sublimated and encoded to such an extent that it becomes unrecognizable as such. Such functions take on an abstractly symbolic character; even the connecting links between elements of the complex become abstract and symbolic. It is as if they reject any contact at all with crude, everyday reality.

The gross realities of the ancient pre-class complex—which had all been equally valid—are dissociated from each other, and undergo an internal bifurcation and sharp hierarchical reinterpretation. In ideologies and in literature, the elements of the matrix are scattered throughout various planes, high and low, and throughout various genres, styles, tones. They no longer come together in a single context; they do not line up with one another since the all-embracing whole has been lost. All that has already been severed and disunified in life itself is now reflected in ideology. An element of the complex such as sexuality (the sexual act, sexual organs, and defecation as something connected with the sexual organs) in its realistic and straightforward aspect is almost completely driven out of the official genres and out of official discourse of the ruling social groups. In its sublimated form, *love*, the sexual element of the complex enters the higher genres and there enters into new matrices, establishes new connections. In its everyday civic/secular aspect—marriage, a family, childbirth—the sexual sphere finds a place for itself in the middle genres and there also enters into new and permanent matrices. The sphere of food and drink carries on a semi-official existence and, in a real-life, everyday, unarticulated form, lives on in the middle and low genres as a secondary and quotidian detail of personal life. Death, perceived in the individual's life-sequence, also separates out into its various components and lives a special life in the high genres (literary and other ideologies), and still another life in the middle genres (semi-quotidian and quotidian). It enters into diverse new matrices; its link with laughter, with the sexual act, with parody and so forth is completely severed. All elements of the complex, in their new matrices, lose that link with communal labor. Corresponding tones and stylistic formulations pertaining to the diverse components of these various elements in the complex become differentiated. To the extent that any links between these elements and the phenomena of nature are preserved, such links take on a metaphorical character in the majority of instances.

We are offering here, to be sure, an extremely crude and summary characterization of the fate of various elements of the ancient complex in societies where there is already a hierarchy of classes. What interests us is the *form of time*, only insofar as it is the basis for possible narratives (and narrative matrices) in subsequent life. The folkloric form of time we have characterized above undergoes essential changes. We will pause here on some of these changes.

We must keep in mind the fact that all members of the ancient matrix lose the real pan-contiguity that they had known in the unified time of collective human life. Of course, in abstract thought and in concrete systems of chronology (whatever they might be) time always preserves its abstract unity. But within the limits of this abstract calendaric unity, the concrete time of a human life is broken down. Out of the common time of collective life emerge separate individual life-sequences, individual fates. In the beginning they are not yet sharply distinguished from the life of the collective whole, they stand out from it merely as might an ill-defined bas-relief. Society itself falls apart into class and intraclass groups; individual life-sequences are directly linked with these and together both individual life and subgroups are opposed to the whole. Thus in the early stages of slaveholding society and in feudal society, individual life-sequences are still rather tightly interwoven with the common life of the most immediate social group. But nevertheless they are separate, even here. The course of individual lives, of groups, and of the sociopolitical whole do not fuse together, they are dispersed, there are gaps; they are measured by different scales of value; each of these series has its own logic of development, its own narratives, each makes use of and reinterprets the ancient motifs in its own way. Within the boundaries of individual life-series, an *interior aspect* makes itself apparent. The process of separating out and detaching individual life-sequences from the whole reaches its highest point when financial relations develop in slaveholding society, and under capitalism. Here the individual sequence takes on its specific private character and what is held in common becomes maximally abstract.

The ancient motifs that had passed into the individual life-narratives here undergo a specific kind of degeneration. Food, drink, copulation and so forth lose their ancient "pathos" (their link, their unity with the laboring life of the social whole); they become a petty private matter; they seem to exhaust all their significance within the boundaries of individual life. As a result of this severance from the producing life of the whole and from the collective struggle with nature, their *real* links with the life of nature are weakened—if not severed altogether. These elements— isolated, impoverished, trivialized—in order to retain their significance in narrative must undergo one or another form of sublimation, a metaphorical broadening of their significance (at the expense of links that had been previously actual, i.e., not metaphorical); their metaphorical enrichment is purchased at the expense of any dim traces of the past that might still remain. Finally, in order to acquire this broader significance the *interior aspect* of life must be downplayed. Such, for example, is the motif of wine in Anacreontic poetry (in the very broadest sense), the motif of food in the ancient "gastronomical poems" (in spite of its practical, sometimes directly culinary intention, food is present here not only in its aesthetic-gastronomical aspect but also in sublimated form, albeit with reference to hints of antiquity and with some metaphorical expansion). Then the central and basic motif in the narrative of individual life-sequences became *love*, that is, the *sublimated* form of the sexual act and of fertility. This motif provides a vast number of possible directions for sublimation to take, possibilities for metaphorical expansion in diverse directions (for which language serves as the most readily available medium), possibilities for enrichment at the expense of any remaining survivals of the past. Finally, love provides possibilities for the working out of sublimative tendencies in an internal, subjective-psychological form. But the motif of love occupies its central place thanks to the authentic, real-life role it plays in individual life-sequences: that is, thanks to its link with marriage, the family, childbirth and, finally, with those intrinsic ties that bind through love (marriage, childbirth), a given individual sequence is bound up with the sequences of other individual lives, those of contemporaries as well as those who follow (children, grandchildren) and with the most immediate social group (through the family and marriage). In the literature of different epochs and social groups, in different genres and styles, various aspects of love—both real and sublimated—are employed, and in a variety of ways.

The motif of death undergoes a profound transformation in the temporally sealed-off sequence of an individual life. Here this motif takes on the meaning of an ultimate end. And the more sealed-off the individual life-sequence becomes, the more it is severed from the life of the social whole, the loftier and more ultimate becomes its significance. The link between death and fertility is severed (the sowing, the maternal mons, the sun), as well as its link with the birth of new life, with ritual laughter, with parody and the clown. Some of these links taken from the ancient matrices are retained and even strengthened under cover of the motif of death (death—►the reaper—►the harvest—►sunset—► night—►the grave—►the cradle, etc.), but they bear a *metaphorical* or *mystical-religious* character. (On this metaphorical plane lie the following matrices: death—►a wedding—►the bridegroom—►the nuptial bed—►the bed of death—►death—►birth and so forth.) But on both the plane of metaphor and that of religion and the mystical, in the individual life-sequence as well as in its interior aspect, the motif of death comes to bear the sole meaning of "morituri" [a fated end] (it assumes the function of "consolation," "reconciliation," "rationalization"). It does so not as a surface phenomenon, that is, not in the collective laboring life of the social whole (where the link of death with the earth, the sun, with birth of new life, with the cradle and so forth was *authentic* and *real*). In the individual sealed-off consciousness, which applies all categories to itself alone, death is only an end, and as such is deprived of any real and productive associations. Death and birth of new life are parceled out into different sealed-off individual life-sequences: death ends one life and birth begins a completely other life. Individualized deaths do not overlap with the birth of new lives, they are not swallowed up by triumphant growth, for these deaths have been taken out of that whole in which such growth occurs.

Parallel to these individual life-sequences—above them, but *outside* of them—there is a time-sequence that is *historical*, serving as the channel for the life of the nation, the state, mankind. Whatever its general ideological and literary assumptions, whatever its concrete forms for perceiving historical time and the events that occur within it, this time-sequence is not fused with the individual life-sequences. The historical time-sequence is measured by different standards of value, other kinds of events take place in it, it has no interior aspect, no point of view for perceiving it from the inside out. No matter how its influence on individual life is conceived and represented, its events are in any case different from the events of individual life, and its narratives are different as well. For the student of the novel, the question of this relationship becomes crucial with regard to the historical novel. For a long time the central and almost sole theme of purely historical narrative was the theme of war. This fundamentally historical theme—which has other motifs attached to it, such as conquest, political crimes and the deposing of pretenders, dynastic revolutions, the fall of kingdoms, the founding of new kingdoms, courts, executions and so forth—is interwoven with personal-life narratives of historical figures (with the central motif of love), but the two themes do not fuse. The major task of the modern historical novel has been to overcome this duality: attempts have been made to find an historical aspect of private life, and also to represent history in its "domestic light."

When the immanent unity of time disintegrated, when individual life-sequences were separated out, lives in which the gross realities of communal life had become merely petty private matters; when collective labor and the struggle with nature had ceased to be the only arena for man's encounter with nature and the world—then nature itself ceased to be a living participant in the events of life. Then nature became, by and large, a "setting for action," its backdrop; it was turned into landscape, it was fragmented into metaphors and comparisons serving to sublimate individual and private affairs and adventures not connected in any real or intrinsic way with nature itself.

But in the treasure-house of language and in certain kinds of folklore this immanent unity of time is preserved, insofar as language and folklore continue to insist on a relation to the world and its phenomena based on collective labor. It is in these that the real basis of the ancient matrix is preserved, the authentic logic of a primitive enchaining of images and motifs.

But even in literature, when it is most open to the deepest and most fundamental influences of folklore, we encounter more authentic, ideologically more profound traces of the ancient matrices and even attempts to revive them on the basis of the unity characteristic of folkloric time. We may distinguish several basic forms in which such an attempt has been made in literature.

We will not pause here on the complicated question of classical epic. We note only that the epic, based as it is on the immanent unity of folkloric time, achieves a penetration of historical time that is in its own way unique and profound, but nevertheless localized and limited. Individual life-sequences are present in the epic as mere bas-reliefs on the all-embracing, powerful foundation of collective life. *Individuums* are representatives of the social whole, events of their lives coincide with the events of the life of the social whole, and the significance of such events (on the individual as well as on the social plane) is identical. Internal form fuses with external: man is all on the surface. There are no petty private matters, no common everyday life: all the details of life—food, drink, objects of everyday domestic use—are comparable to the major events of life; it is all equally important and significant. There is no landscape, no immobile dead background; everything acts, everything takes part in the unified life of the whole. Lastly, metaphors, comparisons and in general tropes in the style of Homer have not yet utterly lost their unmediated meaning, they do not yet serve the purposes of sublimation. Thus an image selected for comparison is worth just as much as the other member of the comparison, it has its own independently viable significance and reality; thus a comparison becomes almost a dual episode, a digression (cf. the expansive comparisons in Homer). Here folkloric time still lives under communal conditions, close to those conditions that had given it birth. Its functions here are still unmediated; folkloric time is not yet defined against the backdrop of another and fallen time.

But epic time itself, in its entirety, is an "absolute past," a time of founding fathers and heroes, separated by an unbridgeable gap from the real time of the *present day* (the present day of the creators, the performers and the audience of epic songs).

The elements of the ancient complex assume a different character in Aristophanes. In this context they determine the formal basis, the very foundation of the comedy. The ritual of food, drink, ritual (cultic) indecency, ritual parody and laughter as an approach to death and new life—one can easily sense here the basis of the comedy: cultic acts reinterpreted on the literary plane.

In the comedy of Aristophanes, all the phenomena of everyday life and of private life are completely transformed on this basis: they lose their private-everyday character, they become significant in human terms in all their comic aspect; their dimensions are fantastically exaggerated; we get a peculiar heroics of the comic, or, more precisely, a *comic myth*. A huge sociopolitical common pool of symbols has its images organically linked with comically everyday private features. But these features, clustered together on one symbolic base that is lit up by cultic laughter, tend to lose their limited, personal ordinariness [*bytovizm*]. On the level of individual artistic achievement we have, in Aristophanes' image, the evolution of an ancient sacral mask in a vivid shorthand (a sort of "philogeny recapitulating ontogeny"), from its primitive purely cultic significance to the private everyday type of commedia dell'arte (with its own Pantalone and Dottore). In Aristophanes we can still clearly see the cultic foundation of the comic image, and we can see how everyday nuances have been layered over it, still sufficiently transparent for the foundation to shine through them and transfigure them. Such an image easily links up with a highly specific political and philosophical actuality (having a world view of its own), but it does not thereby become something transitory and topical. While the fantastic is denied such a transformation of the ordinary, at the same time the fantastic cannot completely obscure the deep problematic and the wealth of ideas in the images.

It could be said that individualized and typically everyday features in Aristophanes—whose living wholeness has been annihilated by laughter—are laid down on top of the image of death (which is the root meaning of the cultic comic mask), but these features do not completely obscure that significance. For this cheerful death is always surrounded by food, drink, sexual indecencies and symbols of conception and fertility.

For this reason Aristophanes' influence on the further development of comedy—which, by and large, increasingly involved itself with everyday events—was insignificant and superficial. Nevertheless one may detect a significant kinship between Aristophanes and the medieval parodic farce (in a line of descent from pre-class folklore). The comic and clownish scenes in Elizabethan tragedy reveal a profound kinship (along the same lines), and this is especially true in Shakespeare (the nature of laughter, its association with death and with a tragic atmosphere, cultic indecencies, food and drink).

The direct influence of Aristophanes on the works of Rabelais is evidence of a deep internal kinship (again via pre-class folklore). Here we find, on a different level of development, the same type of laughter, the same grotesque sense of the fantastic, the same reworking of everything that is private and everyday, the same "heroics of the comic and the absurd," the same type of sexual indecencies, the same matrices of food and drink.

Lucian represents an entirely different type of relationship to the folkloric complex, although Lucian as well exercised crucial influence on Rabelais. It is precisely the private-everyday sphere, where one finds food, drink, sexual relations, that is invoked by Lucian in all its specificity as low and private everyday life. He needs this sphere as a seaminess to undercut the lofty planes (spheres) of ideology, which have become rigid and false. In myths one finds both "erotic" and "everyday" elements, but they were recognized as such only in subsequent eras of life and consciousness—after private life had already separated out, when the erotic sphere had been isolated, when these spheres had acquired distinct nuances of the low and the unofficial. In the myths themselves these aspects were significant and each as valid as the other. But the myths died, for the conditions that had given them birth (that had created them) had died. They continued to exist, however, in moribund form, in the lifeless and stilted genres of "high" ideology. It was necessary to strike a blow at the myths and their gods, so that they might "die comically." It is in the works of Lucian that precisely this ultimate, comic death of the gods is accomplished. Lucian takes those aspects of myth that by his time have come to correspond to the latest stage in the development of the private-everyday and erotic sphere and by working them up in great detail and in a deliberately low and "physiological" spirit he brings the gods down into the sphere of the erotic and of ludicrous, philistine everyday life. Elements of the ancient complex are thus deliberately utilized by Lucian in the reduced form they had assumed by his time—a form that they had attained during the decline of ancient society, a decline influenced by the growing power of financial relations in an atmosphere almost diametrically opposed to that in which the myths had arisen. The ridiculous inadequacy of the old myths to the every-day reality of Lucian's present had become patently clear. But this very reality—accepted by Lucian only because he could not avoid it—was not thereby seen as a value in itself (which would have been a Cervantesque solution of the antithesis between ideal and real).

The influence of Lucian on Rabelais makes itself felt not only in the reworking of individual episodes (for example, Epistemon's visit to the Kingdom of the Dead) but also in the methodical de-struction-by-parody of the lofty spheres of ideology. This is ac-complished through the technique of introducing material life-series—although these material series are employed not in their private-everyday philistine aspect (that is, as Lucian uses them) but are given their full human significance, which can occur only under conditions of folkloric time (that is, more in the manner of Aristophanes).

The *Satyricon* of Petronius presents peculiar difficulties. In the novel itself, food, drink, sexual indecencies, death and laughter lie by and large on the everyday plane, but this common everyday life itself (basically the life of the déclassé dregs of the empire) is saturated with folkloric survivals and traces of the past, espe-cially in those parts of the novel dominated by pure adventure: amid all the rank debauchery and crudity, amid all the cynicism one can still catch a whiff of those rituals of fertility now in the process of decay, the sacral roots of cynicism toward marriage, the parodic clown's mask of the dead and sacral fornication at fu-nerals and funeral banquets. In the celebrated inserted story "The Widow of Ephesus" we find all the fundamental elements of the ancient complex united into one splendid and economical real-life narrative: the husband's grave in the vault, the inconsolable young widow who is determined to die of grief and hunger by his grave, the young and cheerful legionnaire who guards the near-by crosses with their crucified thieves, the young widow's gloomy and ascetic stubbornness and longing for death that is broken by the infatuated young legionnaire, food and drink (meat, bread and wine) on the husband's grave, their copulation on the same place, in the vault by the tomb (the conception of new life in direct asso-ciation with death, "at the door of the grave"), the thief's corpse that is stolen from the cross during the couple's lovemaking, the death threatening the legionnaire as atonement for love. All this plus the crucifixion (at the wife's request) of her husband's corpse

in place of the stolen corpse of the thief; the penultimate note—
"It's better that a dead man should be crucified than that a living
man should perish" (the widow's words)—and the final comic as-
tonishment of the passers-by at a dead man's corpse crawling by
itself up on a cross (that is, at the finale, laughter). Such are the
motifs of this story, united in a completely real-life *narrative*, one
whose component parts are all necessary (that is, a narrative with
no slack).

Here we have without any omissions all the basic links in the
classical series: the tomb→youth→food and drink→death→
copulation→the conceiving of new life→laughter. At its simplest, the narrative is an uninterrupted series of victories of life
over death. Life triumphs over death four times: the joys of life
(food, drink, youth, love) triumph over the widow's gloomy de-
spair and longing for death; food and drink as the renewal of life
near the corpse of a dead man; the conceiving of new life near the
tomb (copulation); and saving the legionnaire from death by cru-
cifying a corpse. Introduced into this series is the additional, and
classical, motif of theft; the disappearance of the corpse (the absence of a corpse being equal to an absence of death, in a this-
worldly suggestion of resurrection). The motif of resurrection is
present in its most straightforward expression, that is, the resurrection of the widow from her helpless grief and from the grave-
like gloom of death into new life and love; in the comic aspect of
laughter, there is as well a sham resurrection of a dead man.

We should emphasize the extraordinary concision and therefore compactness of this whole series of motifs. The elements of
the ancient complex are present in one unmediated and tightly
packed matrix; pressed up against one another so that they almost cover each other up—they are not separated by any side-
plots or detours in the narrative, nor by any lengthy discourses,
nor by lyrical digressions, nor by any metaphorical sublimations
that might destroy the unity of the drily realistic surface of the
story.

The distinctive way in which Petronius artistically interprets
the ancient complex will become crystal clear if we recall that
those same elements of the complex, with the same details but in
a sublimated and mystical form, figured in the cults of Hellenis-
tic-oriental mysteries that were current in Petronius' time, especially in the Christian cult (wine and bread on the altar-tomb as
the mystical body of Him Who Was Crucified, Who died and Who

was resurrected; the sacrament of new life and resurrection through food and drink). In the cultic redaction all elements of the complex appear not in a real but in a sublimated form, and are linked with one another not via a real-life narrative, but through mystic-symbolic links and interrelationships, and the triumph of life over death (resurrection) is accomplished not on a real and earthly plane but on a mystical one. What is more, there is a complete absence of laughter, and copulation has been sublimated almost beyond recognition.

In Petronius, these same elements of the complex are brought together by means of an actual event in the life and everyday experience of a Roman province; not only is there no trace of mysticism here, but even simple symbolic features are missing, not a single element is exploited as a metaphor. Everything occurs on the level of real life: it is completely credible that a widow should be aroused through food and drink to new life in the presence of the legionnaire's strong young body; it is completely credible that new life should triumph over death in the act of conception; the sham resurrection of the dead man who climbed up on the cross comes about in a completely credible way and so forth. There are no sublimating processes of any kind in all of this.

But the narrative itself takes on a profound significance thanks precisely to those gross realities of human life that are seized upon by the narrative and set into motion. We see reflected here an enormous event portrayed on a small scale, an event that is enormous by virtue of the elements brought into the narrative, which are linked to an origin lying far beyond the boundaries of that small scrap of real life in which they are reflected. The realistic image is structured here as a special type, one that could arise only on a folkloric base. It is difficult to find an adequate terminology for it. We are compelled to speak of something like a *realistic emblematic*. The total makeup of the image itself remains thoroughly realistic, but concentrated and compacted in it are so many essential and major aspects of life that its meaning far outstrips all spatial, temporal and sociohistorical limits—outstrips them without, however, severing itself from the concrete sociohistorical base from which it sprang.

Petronius' reworking of the folkloric complex exerted an enormous influence on corresponding phenomena during the Renaissance, especially "The Widow of Ephesus," which we have just analyzed. We should note, however, that these analogous phenomena in Renaissance literature are not explained so much by the direct influence of Petronius as by their kinship with general folkloric sources. But the direct influence is nevertheless great. We know that Petronius' story is retold in one of the short stories in Boccaccio's *Decameron*. But the framing story as well, the entire *Decameron* as a whole, also represents a reworking of the folkloric complex in a way that is akin to Petronius. Here there is no symbolism, no sublimation—but no trace of naturalism either. The triumph of life over death, all the joys of life—food, drink, copulation—in direct association with death, at the door of the tomb, the nature of laughter that simultaneously ushers out the old and greets the new era, resurrection out of the gloom of medieval asceticism into a new life through the sacrament of food, drink and sexual life, a sacrament to life's *body*—the *Decameron* gives birth to all this, in Petronian style. Here we have the same outstripping of sociohistorical limits without, however, a breaking-away from them, the same realistic emblematic (on a folkloric base).

As we conclude our analysis of the folkloric bases of the Rabelaisian chronotope we should mention that Rabelais' closest and most direct source was the popular culture of laughter in the Middle Ages and the Renaissance—an analysis of which I have provided in another book.

IX. The Idyllic Chronotope in the Novel

We now move on to another type, one very important in the history of the novel. We have in mind here the idyllic model for restoring the ancient complex and for restoring folkloric time.

Many different kinds of idylls have existed in literature from most ancient times to the present. We may distinguish the following pure types: the love idyll (whose basic form is the pastoral); the idyll with a focus on agricultural labor; the idyll dealing with craft-work; and the family idyll. In addition to these pure types, mixed types are extremely widespread, in which one or another aspect predominates (love, labor or family).

In addition to the abovementioned typological distinctions, there also exist differences of another sort; differences that exist between different types as well as between differing variants of the same type. Of such a sort are the distinctions in character and degree in the metaphorical treatment of individual motifs (for example, natural phenomena) as they are incorporated into the totality of the idyll, that is, differences in the extent to which purely realistic or metaphorical links predominate, differences in the degree to which purely narrative aspects are highlighted, in the degree and nature of the sublimation and so forth.

No matter how these types of idylls, and variations within types, may differ from one another, they all have—and this is its relevance to the problem we are pursuing—several features in common, all determined by their general relationship to the immanent unity of folkloric time. This finds expression predominantly in the special relationship that time has to space in the idyll: an organic fastening-down, a grafting of life and its events to a place, to a familiar territory with all its nooks and crannies, its familiar mountains, valleys, fields, rivers and forests, and one's own home. Idyllic life and its events are inseparable from this concrete, spatial corner of the world where the fathers and grandfathers lived and where one's children and their children will live. This little spatial world is limited and sufficient unto itself, not linked in any intrinsic way with other places, with the rest of the world. But in this little spatially limited world a sequence of generations is localized that is potentially without limit. The unity of the life of generations (in general, the life of men) in an idyll is in most instances primarily defined by the *unity of place*, by the age-old rooting of the life of generations to a single place, from which this life, in all its events, is inseparable. This unity of place in the life of generations weakens and renders less distinct all the temporal boundaries between individual lives and between various phases of one and the same life. The unity of place brings together and even fuses the cradle and the grave (the same little corner, the same earth), and brings together as well childhood and old age (the same grove, stream, the same lime trees, the same house), the life of the various generations who had also lived in that same place, under the same conditions, and who had seen the same things. This blurring of all the temporal boundaries made possible by a unity of place also contributes in an essential way to the creation of the cyclic rhythmicalness of time so characteristic of the idyll.

Also distinctive for the idyll is the fact that it is severely limited to only a few of life's basic realities. Love, birth, death, marriage, labor, food and drink, stages of growth—these are the basic realities of idyllic life. They are brought into close proximity in the crowded little world of the idyll, there are no sharp contrasts among them, and they are all equally valid (in any case that is their tendency). Strictly speaking, the idyll does not know the trivial details of everyday life. Anything that has the appearance of common everyday life, when compared with the central unrepeatable events of biography and history, here begins to look precisely like the most important things in life. But all these basic life-realities are present in the idyll not in their naked realistic aspect (as in Petronius) but in a softened and to a certain extent sublimated form. Thus sexuality is almost always incorporated into the idyll only in sublimated form.

There is finally a third distinctive feature of the idyll, closely linked with the first: the conjoining of human life with the life of nature, the unity of their rhythm, the common language used to describe phenomena of nature and the events of human life. Of course in the idyll, this common language has become in large part purely metaphorical and only to an insignificant degree (most of all in the agricultural idyll) retains anything of the actual about it.

In the love idyll, all the aforementioned aspects are present in their weakest expression. The utterly conventional simplicity of life in the bosom of nature is opposed to social conventions, complexity and the disjunctions of everyday private life; life here is abstracted into a love that is completely sublimated. Beneath the conventional, metaphorical, stylized aspects of such a love one can still dimly perceive the immanent unity of time and the ancient matrices. For this reason the love idyll was able to serve as the foundation for various types of novels, and could enter as a component into other novels (for example, those of Rousseau). But the love idyll has proved especially fruitful in the history of the novel not in its pure form, but in conjunction with the family idyll (*Werther*) and with the agricultural idyll (provincial novels).

One rarely encounters the family idyll in its pure form, but in conjunction with the agricultural idyll it is of enormous significance. This form comes closest to achieving folkloric time; here the ancient matrices are revealed most fully and with the greatest possible actuality. This is explained by the fact that this form of the idyll uses as its model not the conventional pastoral life (which, after all, exists nowhere in such a form) but rather draws upon the real life of the agricultural laborer under conditions of feudal or post-feudal society—although this life is to one degree or another idealized and sublimated (the degree of this idealization varies widely). The *labor* aspect of this idyll is of special importance (present already in Virgil's *Georgics*); it is the agricultural-labor element that creates a *real* link and common bond between the phenomena of nature and the events of human life (as distinct from the *metaphorical* link in the love idyll). Moreover—and this is especially important—agricultural labor transforms all the events of everyday life, stripping them of that private petty character obtaining when man is nothing but consumer; what happens rather is that they are turned into essential life *events*. Thus people consume the produce of their own labor; the produce is figurally linked with the productive process, in it— in this produce—the sun, the earth and the rain are actually present (not merely in some system of metaphorical links). Wine is likewise immersed in the process of its cultivation and production, and drinking it is inseparable from the holidays that are in turn linked to agricultural cycles. Food and drink in the idyll partake of a nature that is social or, more often, family; all *generations* and *age-groups* come together around the table. For the idyll, the association of *food* and *children* is characteristic (even in *Werther* we have the idyllic picture of Lotte feeding the children); this matrix is shot through with the beginnings of growth and the renewing of life. In the idyll, children often function as a sublimation of the sexual act and of conception; they frequently figure in connection with growth, the renewal of life, death (children and an old man, children playing around the grave, etc.). The significance and role of the image of children in idylls of this type is very great. Children first entered the novel from precisely this setting, still permeated with the atmosphere of the idyll.

As an illustration of our comments on the use of food in idylls, we might point to Hebel's familiar idyll "Das Haber-Musz,"[11] translated by Zhukovsky ("Ovsjanij kisel'")—although its didacticism somewhat weakens the force of the ancient matrices (in particular, the association of children and food).

I repeat: the elements of the ancient matrices most often appear in the idyll in sublimated form; one or another element is partially or entirely omitted; or, common everyday life is not always thoroughly transformed—especially in the realistic idylls of

---

11. Johann Peter Hebel (1760–1826), German dialect poet. Reference here is to his poem "Das Haber-Musz," from the *Allemanische Gedichte*.

recent times (nineteenth century). It is sufficient to recall an idyll such as Gogol's "Old-World Landowners," where the aspect of labor is altogether absent, although the other elements of the matrix are relatively well represented (several in highly sublimated form)—old age, love, food, death; food occupies here a very large place and is present on the plane of everyday habit (since there is no mention of labor).

The form of the idyll assumed great significance in the eighteenth century, when the problem of time in literature was posed with particular intensity, a period when precisely a new feeling for time was beginning to awake. One is struck by the wealth and variety of types of idylls in the eighteenth century (especially in the German cantons of Switzerland and in Germany itself). A special form of elegy also developed, an elegy of the meditative type with a strong idyllic component (based on ancient tradition); various graveyard meditations incorporating the matrices of the grave, love, new life, spring, children, old age and so forth. As an example we have the "Elegy Written in a Country Churchyard" by Gray (and Zhukovsky's translations), an elegy with very strong idyllic overtones. The Romantics who continued this tradition subjected the abovementioned elegiac matrices (primarily those of love and death) to a severe reinterpretation (as in Novalis).

The problem of time is elevated to the level of philosophy in several eighteenth-century idylls. The real organic time of idyllic life is opposed to the frivolous, fragmented time of city life or even to historical time (Hebel's "Das unverhofftes Wiedersehen,"[mm] and Zhukovsky's translation "Neožidannoe svidanie").[nn]

The significance of the idyll in the development of the novel is, as we have already said, enormous. Its importance as an underlying image has not been understood and appreciated up to this day, and in consequence all perspectives on the history of the novel have been distorted. Here we can only superficially touch on this enormous question.

The influence of the idyll on the development of the novel of modern times has proceded in five basic directions: (1) the influ-

---

mm. "Das unverhofftes Wiedersehen," from *Das Schatzkästlein des Rheinischen Hausfreundes.*

nn. Bakhtin gives not only the German original but the Russian version as well because Zhukovsky (1787–1852) was a translator of such genius that his reworkings constitute new texts with value in their own right.

ence of the idyll, idyllic time and idyllic matrices on the provincial novel; (2) the destruction of the idyll, as in the *Bildungsroman* of Goethe and in novels of the Sternean type (Hippel, Jean Paul); (3) its influence on the Sentimental novel of the Rousseauan type; (4) its influence on the family novel and the novel of generations; and, finally, (5) its influence on novels belonging to certain other categories (such as novels featuring "a man of the people").

In the provincial novel we witness directly the progress of a family-labor, agricultural or craft-work idyll moving into the major form of the novel. The basic significance of provinciality [*oblastničestvo*] in literature—the uninterrupted, age-old link between the life of generations and a strictly delimited locale—replicates the purely idyllic relationship of time to space, the idyllic unity of the place as locus for the entire life process. In the provincial novel the life process itself is broadened and made more detailed (which is necessary under conditions of the novel), and the ideological aspect—language, belief systems, ethics, mores—begins to assume a greater prominence, yet this aspect of life is nevertheless shown as inextricably bound up with a strictly delimited locale. In the provincial novel, as in the idyll, all temporal boundaries are blurred and the rhythm of human life is in harmony with the rhythm of nature. At the heart of this idyllic resolution of the problem of time in the novel (it is, in the final analysis, a folkloric core), common everyday life is transformed in the provincial novel: the events of everyday life takes on an importance and acquire thematic significance. All the folkloric matrices typical of the idyll and encountered by us in the provincial novel are built around this core. Here as in the idyll, stages of growth and the cyclical repetition of the life process are of crucial importance. The provincial novel has the same heroes as does the idyll—peasants, craftsmen, rural clergy, rural schoolteachers.

While those individual motifs available to the provincial novel were profoundly reworked (especially in such representative writers as Jeremias Gotthelf,[oo] Immermann,[pp] and Gottfried Keller),[qq]

---

oo. Jeremias Gotthelf (pen name of Albert Bitzius, 1797–1854), didactic regional novelist.

pp. Karl Immermann (1796–1839), a novelist who introduced a good deal of actual social detail into traditional German forms such as the *Bildungsroman* (*Die Epigonen* [1836]).

qq. Gottfried Keller (1819–1890), great Swiss humorist, especially dear to Bakhtin not only for his *Grüne Heinrich* (1854, rev. 1876), but for the cycle *Die Leute von Seldwyla* (1856).

this type of novel nevertheless exhibits the most limited novelistic use of folkloric time. Here there is no broad or deep realistic emblematic; meaning does not exceed the sociohistorical limitations inherent in the images. Cyclicity makes itself felt with particular force, therefore the beginnings of growth and the perpetual renewal of life are weakened, separated from the progressive forces of history and even opposed to them; thus growth, in this context, makes life a senseless running-in-place at one historical point, at one level of historical development.

There is a considerably more incisive reworking of idyllic time and idyllic matrices in Rousseau, and in subsequent texts influenced by him. This reworking proceeds in two directions: first, the basic elements of the ancient complex—nature, love, the family and childbearing, death—are isolated and undergo sublimation at a higher philosophical level, where they are treated more or less as forms of the great, eternal, wise force of earthly life. Second, these elements provide material for constituting an isolated individual consciousness, and from the point of view of such a consciousness these elements act as forces that can heal, purify and reassure it, forces that solicit its surrender, its submission, requiring that it fuse with them.

Thus it is that folkloric time and the ancient matrices are perceived here as stages in the development of society and consciousness from a point of view that was contemporary to Rousseau and others working in his spirit, a point of view in which such time and such matrices had become the lost ideal of human life. It was necessary once again to make contact with that lost ideal, but this time at a new stage of development. What precisely should be retained from this more recent stage of development is decided by different authors in a variety of ways (even Rousseau himself had no single point of view on this), but in any case the interior aspect of life is retained, and, in the majority of cases, individuality is preserved as well (although it is transformed).

The outward appearance of the elements of the complex is greatly altered as a result of their philosophical sublimation. Love becomes an elemental, mysterious and—more often than not—fatal force for those who love, and all this is interiorized. It comes to us associated with nature and death. Together with this new vision of love, the more familiar and purely idyllic aspect of love is retained, the one that is associated with the family, with children, with food (thus we have in Rousseau the love between

Saint-Preux and Julie on the one hand, and the love and family life of Julie and Wolmar on the other). The aspect of nature changes as well, depending upon the matrix in which it occurs: either combined with tempestuous love, or with labor.

Narrative undergoes corresponding changes. In the idyll, as a rule, there were no heroes alien to the idyllic world. In the provincial novel, in contrast, one occasionally finds a hero who has broken away from the wholeness of his locale, who has set off for the city and either perishes there or returns, like a prodigal son, to the bosom of his family. In novels of the Rousseauan type, the major protagonists are the author's contemporaries, people who had already succeeded in isolating individual life-sequences, people with an interior perspective. They heal themselves through contact with nature and the life of simple people, learning from them the wisdom to deal with life and death; or they go outside the boundaries of culture altogether, in an attempt to utterly immerse themselves in the wholeness of the primitive collective (as René does in Chateaubriand, and Olenin in Tolstoy).

This line of development, which began with Rousseau, proved to be highly progressive. It succeeded in avoiding the limitations of provincial forms. In it there is no doomed attempt to preserve the dying remnants of little patriarchal (provincial) worlds (which had been, moreover, highly idealized)—on the contrary, the Rousseauan line of development, by sublimating in philosophical terms the ancient sense of the whole, makes of it an ideal for the future and sees in it above all the basis, a norm, for criticizing the current state of society. In the majority of cases this critique is two-pronged: it is directed against feudal hierarchy, against inequality and absolutism, against the false arbitrariness of society (conventionality); but it is directed as well against the anarchy of greed and against the isolated, egoistic bourgeois *individuum*.

In the family novel and the novel of generations, the idyllic element undergoes a radical reworking and as a result perceptibly pales. Of folkloric time and the ancient matrices only those elements remain that can be reinterpreted and that can survive on the soil of the bourgeois family and family-as-genealogy. Nevertheless the connection between the family novel and the idyll is manifested in a whole series of significant aspects, and that connection is precisely what determines the basic—family—nucleus of this type of novel.

The family of the family novel is, of course, no longer the family of the idyll. It has been torn out of its narrow feudal locale, out of its unchanging natural surroundings—the native mountains, fields, rivers, forest—that had nourished it in the idyll. At best the idyllic unity of place is limited to the ancestral family *town* house, to the immovable part (the real estate) of capitalist property. But this unity of place in the family novel is by no means a necessity. What is more, there is a break-off in the course of a character's life from a well-defined and limited spatial locale, a period of wandering in the life of the heroes, before they acquire family and material possessions. Such then are the distinctive features of the classic family novel. What is important here is precisely the stable family and material goods belonging to the heroes, how they overcome the element of chance (random meetings with random people, random situations and occurrences) in which they had initially found themselves, how they create fundamental, that is, *family* connections with people, how they limit their world to a well-defined place and a well-defined narrow circle of relatives, that is, to the family circle. It often happens that in the beginning the hero is homeless, without relatives, without means of support; he wanders through an alien world among alien people; random misfortunes and successes happen to him; he encounters random people who turn out to be—for unknown reasons at this early point in the novel—his enemies or his benefactors (all this is later decoded along family or kinship lines). The novel's movement takes the main hero (or heroes) out of the great but alien world of random occurrence into the small but secure and stable little world of the family, where nothing is foreign, or accidental or incomprehensible, where authentically human relationships are re-established, where the ancient matrices are re-established on a family base: love, marriage, childbearing, a peaceful old age for the in-laws, shared meals around the family table. This narrow and reduced idyllic little world is the red thread running throughout the novel, as well as its resolving chord. Such is the schema for the classic family novel, which opened with Fielding's *Tom Jones* (with certain adjustments, the same schema underlies Smollett's *Peregrine Pickle*). But there is another schema as well (whose foundations were laid by Richardson): an alien force intrudes into the cozy little world of the family, threatening it with destruction. Dickens' variations on the first classic scheme (Fielding and Smollett) make his novels the highest achievement of the European family novel.

Idyllic elements are scattered sporadically throughout the family novel. A constant struggle is waged here between depersonalized alienation in relations between people and human relationships built either on a patriarchal or an abstractly humanist foundation. Scattered throughout the great, cold, alien world there are warm little corners of human feeling and kindness.

The idyllic aspect is the decisive one in the novel of generations (Thackeray, Freytag,[rr] Galsworthy, Thomas Mann). But more often than not, the dominant theme in such novels is the destruction of the idyll, and of the idyllic-type family or patriarchal relationships.

The destruction of the idyll (understood in its widest sense) becomes one of the fundamental themes of literature toward the end of the eighteenth century and in the first half of the nineteenth. The destruction of the craft-work idyll is carried over even into the second half of the nineteenth century (Kretzer's *Meister Timpe*).[ss] In Russian literature, of course, the chronological boundaries of this movement are shifted to the second half of the nineteenth century.

The destruction of the idyll may be treated, of course, in a multitude of ways. The differences are determined by differing conceptions and evaluations of the idyllic world rapidly approaching its end, as well as differing evaluations of the forces that are destroying it—that is, the new capitalist world.

The main classic line of development of this theme—that taken by Goethe, Goldsmith, Jean Paul—does not perceive the destroyed idyllic world as a naked fact of the fleeting feudal world, with all the historical limitations that implies—but rather treats the theme with a considerable degree of philosophical sublimation (à la Rousseau): the deep *humanity* of idyllic man himself and the humanity of his human relationships are foregrounded, as is the *wholeness* of idyllic life, its organic link with nature, with special emphasis on the unmechanized nature of idyllic labor; and finally, there is a highlighting of *idyllic objects*

---

rr. Gustav Freytag (1816–1895), *Die Ahnen* (1873–1881), in six long volumes, which tells the story of a German family from the fourth to the nineteenth century.

ss. Max Kretzer (1854–1941), *Meister Timpe* (1888), one of thirty novels by this author, which describes the passing of the independent artisan and rise of the factory worker in nineteenth-century Germany.

as objects not severed from the labor that produced them, objects indissolubly linked with this labor in the experience of everyday idyllic life. At the same time, the narrowness and isolation of the little idyllic world is emphasized.

Opposed to this little world, a world fated to perish, there is a great but abstract world, where people are out of contact with each other, egoistically sealed-off from each other, greedily practical; where labor is differentiated and mechanized, where objects are alienated from the labor that produced them. It is necessary to constitute this great world on a new basis, to render it familiar, to humanize it. It is necessary to find a new relationship to nature, not to the little nature of one's own corner of the world but to the big nature of the great world, to all the phenomena of the solar system, to the wealth excavated from the earth's core, to a variety of geographical locations and continents. In place of the limited idyllic collective, a new collective must be established capable of embracing all humanity. In crude outline this became the problem posed by Goethe's work (with special forcefulness in *Faust*, part 2, and in *Wanderjahre*) and by other representative writers in this vein. A man must educate or re-educate himself for life in a world that is, from his point of view, enormous and foreign; he must make it his own, domesticate it. In Hegel's definition, the novel must educate man for life in bourgeois society. This educative process is connected with a severing of all previous ties with the idyllic, that is, it has to do with man's *expatriation*. Here the process of a man's re-education is interwoven with the process of society's breakdown and reconstruction, that is, with historical process.

The same problem is posed somewhat differently in *Bildungsromane* of a different line of development, represented this time by Stendhal, Balzac, Flaubert (and in Russia, Goncharov). Here the issue is primarily one of overturning and demolishing the world view and psychology of the idyll, which proved increasingly inadequate to the new capitalist world. In most such cases there is no philosophical sublimation of the idyll. We get a picture of the breakdown of provincial idealism under forces emanating from the capitalist center. We see the breakdown, the heroes' provincial romanticism, which is in no way idealized; the capitalist world is also not idealized, its inhumanity is laid bare, the destruction within it of all ethical systems (which had been formed at earlier stages of development), the disintegration of all previous human relationships (under the influence of money), love, the family, friendship, the deforming of the scholar's and the artist's creative work and so forth—all of these are emphasized. The positive hero of the idyllic world becomes ridiculous, pitiful and unnecessary; he either perishes or is re-educated and becomes an egoistic predator.

Goncharov's novels occupy a peculiar place, associating themselves by and large with the Stendhal-Flaubert line of development (especially *A Common Story*). The theme is developed with exemplary clarity and precision in *Oblomov*. The idyll of Oblomovka and later the idyll in the Vyborg Quarter of Petersburg (along with the idyllic death of Oblomov) are portrayed completely realistically. At the same time we are shown the extraordinary humanity of the idyllic man, Oblomov, with his "dovelike purity." In the idyll itself (especially in the Vyborg Quarter) all the fundamental idyllic matrices come to light—the cult of food and drink, children, the sexual act, death and so forth (a realistic emblematic). What is emphasized is Oblomov's desire for stasis, for an unchanging environment, his fear of moving to a new house, his relationship to time.

The Rabelaisian-idyllic line of development, represented by Sterne, Hippel and Jean Paul, deserves special attention. After all we have said, it should not appear strange to find this coupling of the idyllic (even sentimentally idyllic) aspect with the Rabelaisian element (in Sterne and in those influenced by him). There is an obvious kinship that can be traced back to folklore, although these two schools represent different branches of the folkloric complex's literary development.

The most recent influence of the idyll on the novel has been limited to a fragmentary penetration of isolated elements of the idyllic complex. A "man of the people" in the novel is very often of idyllic descent. Of just such a sort is the servant in Walter Scott (Savelich in Pushkin), in Dickens, in the French novel (from Maupassant's *Une Vie* to Françoise in Proust)—all those figures from the Auvergne and Brittany, bearers of the wisdom of the common folk and of their idyllic locale. A "man of the people" appears in the novel as the one who holds the correct attitude toward life and death, an attitude lost by the ruling classes (Platon Karataev in Tolstoy). More often than not, his teaching is concerned precisely with dying well (Tolstoy's "Three Deaths"). Often connected with this figure is a particular way of treating food, drink, love, childbirth. He is, after all, the representative of eternal productive labor. There is an emphasis on the healthy failure of such a man to understand accepted falsehoods and conventions (which then exposes these for what they are).

Such are the basic directions in which the idyllic complex has influenced the modern novel. With this we will close our brief survey of folkloric time and the ancient matrices in artistic literature. This survey provides an indispensable background for the correct understanding of the peculiarities of the Rabelaisian world (and of other items as well, which we will not deal with here).

* * *

In the world of Rabelais, more decisively significant than any other way of reworking the ancient complex we have considered (with the exception of the Aristophanic and Lucianic types) is *laughter*.

Of all aspects of the ancient complex, only laughter never underwent sublimation of any sort—neither religious, mystical nor philosophical. It never took on an official character, and even in literature the comic genres were the most free, the least regimented.

After the decline of the ancient world, Europe did not know a single cult, a single ritual, a single state or civil ceremony, a single official genre or style serving either the church or the state (hymn, prayer, sacral formulas, declarations, manifestos, etc.) where laughter was sanctioned (in tone, style or language)—even in its most watered-down forms of humor and irony.

Europe knew neither the mysticism nor the magic of laughter; laughter was never infected, even slightly, by the "red tape" of moribund officialdom. Therefore, laughter could not be deformed or falsified as could every other form of seriousness, in particular the pathetic. Laughter remained outside official falsifications, which were coated with a layer of pathetic seriousness. Therefore all high and serious genres, all high forms of language and style, all mere set phrases and all linguistic norms were drenched in conventionality, hypocrisy and falsification. Laughter alone remained uninfected by lies.

We have in mind here laughter not as a biological or psychophysiological act, but rather laughter conceived as an objectivized, sociohistorical cultural phenomenon, which is most often present in verbal expression. For it is in the word that laughter manifests itself most variously (although this has yet to be sufficiently studied in a historically systematic, categorical manner). Alongside the poetic use of a word "not in its primary sense" [*ne v sobstvennom značenii*], that is, alongside tropes, there exists in addition a multiplicity of forms for the various indirect linguistic expression of laughter: irony, parody, humor, the joke, various types of the comic and so forth (as yet no systematic classification of these exists). There is no aspect of language that cannot be used in a figurative sense [*v nesobstvennom značenii*]. In all these approaches, the *point of view* contained within the word is subject to a reinterpretation, as is the modality of language and the very *relationship of language to the object* and *to the speaker*. A relocation of the levels of language occurs—the making contiguous of what is normally not associated and the distancing of what normally is, a destruction of the familiar and the creation of new matrices, a destruction of linguistic norms for language and thought. In addition we get here a constant exceeding of the limits fixed in relationships internal to language. And what is more, there is a continual passing beyond the boundaries of the given, sealed-off verbal whole (one cannot understand parody without reference to the parodied material, that is, without exceeding the boundaries of the given context). All these above features for expressing laughter in the word contribute to that special force and capability to strip, as it were, the object of the false verbal and ideological husk that encloses it. Rabelais takes this capability of language as far as it will go.

The extraordinary force of laughter in Rabelais, its radicalism, is explained predominantly by its deep-rooted folkloric base, by its link with the elements of the ancient complex—with death, the birth of new life, fertility and growth. This is real world-embracing laughter, one that can play with all the things of this world—from the most insignificant to the greatest, from distant things to those close at hand. This connection on the one hand with fundamental realities of life, and on the other with the most radical destruction of all false verbal and ideological shells that had distorted and kept separate these realities, is what so sharply distinguishes Rabelaisian laughter from the laughter of other practitioners of the grotesque, humor, satire and irony. Subsequently we see in Swift, Sterne, Voltaire and Dickens a relative softening of Rabelaisian laughter, a weakening of its ties with folklore (although they are still strong in Sterne, even more so in Gogol) and a rupture with the gross realities of life.

Here we must again take up the question of Rabelais' specific sources, of the enormous importance extraliterary sources had for him. Rabelais' first and foremost source was the unofficial side of speech, with its rich store of curses both simple and complex, with its various indecencies, the enormous weight carried by words and expressions connected with hard drinking. To this very day, the unofficial (male) side of speech reflects a Rabelaisian degree of indecency in it, of words concerning drunkenness and defecation and so forth, but all this is by now clichéd and no longer creative. In this unofficial side of speech used by the dregs of city and country (but primarily the city), Rabelais divined specific points of view on the world, a specific selection of realities, a specific system of language that differed sharply from the official side. He perceived in this speech a complete absence of any sublimation, as well a special system of matrices opposed to the official sides of speech, and to literature. Rabelais broadly incorporated into his novel this "crude frankness of folk passions," this "license that is granted statements on the public square" (Pushkin).[tt]

The unofficial side of language already had within it ready-to-hand, before Rabelais, lexical as well as other minor folkloric genres—either as whole units or in a scattered and fragmented form, such as current jokes, short stories, proverbs, puns, sayings, catchwords, erotic riddles, ditties and so forth. Contained within each of these forms is a point of view peculiar to it, its own selection of realities (themes), its own distribution of these realities and finally its own relationship to language.

In a later period we get written works of semi-official literature: stories about clowns and fools, farces, *fabliaux*, *facéties*,[uu] novellas (which result from a further reworking of such material), chapbooks, fairy tales and so forth. And even later we have the specifically literary sources that Rabelais uses, above all those from classical antiquity.[16]

---

16. As we mentioned above, we have analyzed Rabelais' source in detail in a special monograph on Rabelais.

---

tt. Citations are from Pushkin's 1830 essay on *Marfa Posadnitsa*. See editor's footnote s, where the relevant paragraph is given in full.

uu. Anonymous farces—frequently very crude—of the late Middle Ages and early Renaissance.

Whatever these various sources for Rabelais, they were all reworked from a single perspective, tailored to the unifying influence of a completely new artistic and ideological project. Thus all traditional aspects in Rabelais' novel take on new meaning and bear new functions.

This is especially true of the compositional and generic structure of the novel. The first two books are structured according to a traditional scheme: the hero's birth and the miraculous circumstances surrounding it; then the hero's childhood; then his years of study; then his military exploits and conquests. And the fourth book is structured along the lines of a traditional novel of travel. The third book, however, has a different order, the special scheme of the (ancient) quest for counsel and true wisdom: visiting oracles, wise men, philosophical schools and so on. This schema of "visitations" (to notables, various representatives of social groups, etc.) subsequently became very widespread in the literature of more recent times (*Dead Souls, Resurrection*).

But these traditional schemes of ancient literature are reinterpreted in Rabelais, since the material is treated as if it were subject to folkloric time. In the first two books of the novel, biographical time is dissolved in the apersonal time of indiscriminate growth: the growth and development of the human body, of the sciences and the arts, of a new world view, of a new world alongside the one that is old, dying, disintegrating. Growth is not tied down here to a specific *individuum* as his own growth; it exceeds the boundaries of any individual personality. Everything in the world is in the process of growth, all its objects and phenomena, the whole world grows.

Therefore the evolution and completion of a man as an individual is not distinguished in Rabelais from historical growth and cultural progress. The basic aspects, states or phases of growth and development are understood here in a folkloric sense, not as part of the sealed-off sequence of an individual life but as part of the all-embracing common life of the whole human race. We should emphasize the fact that in Rabelais life has absolutely no *individual* aspect. A human being is completely external. The known limits to a man's possible exteriority are achieved. For indeed, there is not a single instance in the entire expanse of Rabelais' huge novel where we are shown what a character is thinking, what he is experiencing, his internal dialogue. In this sense there is in Rabelais' novel no world of interiority. All that a man is finds expression in actions and in dialogue. There is nothing that cannot adequately be made public (outwardly expressed). On the contrary, all that a man is acquires its full significance only in external expression: only externally does it become associated with authentic life experience and authentic, real time. Thus this time is a unity, no internal categories segment it; there are no individualized, internal beginnings or dead ends; its moments follow sequentially one after the other in one world that everyone shares in common and that is the same for all. Thus growth subsumes the limitations of any individual and becomes historical growth. Therefore the task of assuming a complete personality is conceived in Rabelais as the growth of a new man combined with the growth of a new historical era, in a world that knows a new history but that is also connected with the death of the old man and the old world.

Thus the ancient matrices are re-established here on a new and loftier base. They are freed from all that had disunited and distorted them in the old world. They are freed from all otherworldly explanations, sublimations, interdicts. These new realities are purged through laughter, taken out of the high contexts that had disunited them, distorted their nature, and are brought into the real context (the real plane) of a freely developing human life. These realities are present in a world of freely realized human possibilities. There is nothing to limit this potential. This is the most fundamental distinguishing feature of Rabelais' work. All historical limits are, as it were, destroyed and swept away by laughter. The field remains open to human nature, to a free unfolding of all the possibilities inherent in man. In this respect Rabelais' world is diametrically opposed to the limited locale of the tiny idyllic world. Rabelais develops the authentic expanses of the folkloric world on a new base. Nothing fetters Rabelais' imagination, nothing within the given boundaries of the spatial and temporal world can confine him or restrict the authentic potentialities of man's nature. All limitations are bequeathed to the dying world, now in the process of being laughed out of existence. All representatives of the old world—monks, religious fanatics, feudal lords and royal courtiers, kings (Picrochole, Anarch), judges, pedants and others—are treated as absurd and doomed. They are completely limited beings, their potential is utterly exhausted by their pitiful reality. Opposed to them we have Gargantua, Pantagruel, Ponocrates, Epistemon and, in part, Friar John and Panurge (who succeed in overcoming their limitations). There are the models for unlimited human potential.

The major heroes, Gargantua and Pantagruel, are certainly not kings in the same restricted sense that the feudal kings Picrochole and Anarch are kings; but not only is there a fleshing-out of the humanist-king ideal as opposed to the feudal king (although that aspect is, to be sure, present)—at their core these images are modeled on the kings of folklore. What Hegel had to say about the Homeric epic would apply with equal force here: such men were selected as heroes of a work "not because of any sense of superiority, but because of their absolute freedom of will and the creativity they demonstrate in establishing their kingdoms." Such heroes become kings so that they may experience the greatest possible potential and full freedom to realize themselves and their nature as human beings. Such kings as Picrochole represent the real-life kings of a dying sociohistorical world—kings who are as limited and pathetic as the sociohistorical reality that is theirs. There is no freedom to be found in them, no further potential.

Thus Gargantua and Pantagruel are fundamentally folkloric kings and giants-*bogatyri*. For this reason they are, above all else, *men*, who can freely realize all the possibilities and demands made on a man without recourse to ethical or religious consolation for our limitations as mortal men, for our weakness and need. This determines the distinctiveness of Rabelais' version of the *great man*. The great man in Rabelais is profoundly democratic. In no sense is he opposed to the mass, as something out of the ordinary, as a man of another species. On the contrary, he is made of the same generally human stuff as are all other men. He eats, drinks, defecates, passes wind—but he does all this on a grand scale. Nothing in him is incomprehensible or alien to general human nature, to the mass of men. Goethe's words about great men fully apply to him: "The greatest men are merely those with the greatest scope, they partake of the same virtues and shortcomings as the majority, only writ large." The great man in Rabelais is ordinary man raised to a higher power. Such greatness diminishes no one, for everyone sees in such a man a glorification of his own human nature.

Thus does the heroism of Rabelais' great man differ categorically from all other heroisms, which oppose the hero to the mass of other men as something out of the ordinary due to his lineage, his nature, the extraordinary demands and the exalted value he reads into life and the world (he is different therefore from the heroic man of the knightly and Baroque novel, from heroism of the Romantic and Byronic sort and from the Nietzschean *Übermensch*). But he also differs categorically from that glorification of the "little man" that occurs as compensation for his real-life limitations and the weakness of his ethical standards and purity (such are the heroes and heroines of Sentimentalism). The great man in Rabelais, rooted in folklore as he is, is great not in his differences vis-à-vis other men but in his humanity; he is great in the fullness of his development and in his realization of all human potentialities. As such, he is great in the space and time of the actual world, where interior is not opposed to exterior (as we know, he is completely on the surface in the positive sense).

The figure of Panurge is also constructed on a folkloric basis, but here in its clownish variant. The folk clown is present in this figure with more vigor and substance than in parallel instances in the picaresque novel and short story.

But Rabelais is already adding to the folkloric base of his major heroes various features essential to his idea of a monarch and a humanist, embellishing them with certain realistic historical gestures. Nevertheless through all these features the folkloric base remains visible and is responsible for the profound realistic emblematic constituted by these figures.

The free growth of all human capabilities is of course not understood by Rabelais on the narrowly biological level. The spatial-temporal world of Rabelais was the newly opened cosmos of the Renaissance. It was first of all a geographically precise cultural and historical world. Later it was the whole universe illuminated by astronomy. Man can and must conquer this entire spatial and temporal world. The images for this technological conquest of the universe are also folkloric at their core. The miraculous plant "Pantagruelion" is the "magic grass" [*razryv-trava*] frequently encountered in world folklore.

In his novel Rabelais unfolds before us, as it were, the completely unrestricted, universal chronotope of human life. And this was fully in accord with the approaching era of great geographical and astronomical discoveries.

X. Concluding Remarks

A literary work's artistic unity in relationship to an actual reality is defined by its chronotope. Therefore the chronotope in a work always contains within it an evaluating aspect that can be isolated from the whole artistic chronotope only in abstract analysis. In literature and art itself, temporal and spatial determinations are inseparable from one another, and always colored by emotions and values. Abstract thought can, of course, think time and space as separate entities and conceive them as things apart from the emotions and values that attach to them. But *living* artistic perception (which also of course involves thought, but not abstract thought) makes no such divisions and permits no such segmentation. It seizes on the chronotope in all its wholeness and fullness. Art and literature are shot through with *chronotopic values* of varying degree and scope. Each motif, each separate aspect of artistic work bears value.

In these chapters we have analyzed only the major chronotopes that endure as types and that determine the most important generic variations on the novel in the early stages of its development. As we draw our essay to a close we will simply list, and merely touch upon, certain other chronotopic values having different degree and scope.

In the first chapter we mentioned the chronotope of encounter; in such a chronotope the temporal element predominates, and it is marked by a higher degree of intensity in emotions and values. The chronotope of the *road* associated with encounter is characterized by a broader scope, but by a somewhat lesser degree of emotional and evaluative intensity. Encounters in a novel usually take place "on the road." The road is a particularly good place for random encounters. On the road ("the high road"), the spatial and temporal paths of the most varied people—representatives of all social classes, estates, religions, nationalities, ages—intersect at one spatial and temporal point. People who are normally kept separate by social and spatial distance can accidentally meet; any contrast may crop up, the most various fates may collide and interweave with one another. On the road the spatial and temporal series defining human fates and lives combine with one another in distinctive ways, even as they become more complex and more concrete by the collapse of *social distances*. The chronotope of the road is both a point of new departures and a place for events to find their denouement. Time, as it were, fuses together with space and flows in it (forming the road); this is the source of the rich metaphorical expansion on the image of the road as a course: "the course of a life," "to set out on a new course," "the course of history" and so on; varied and multi-leveled are the ways in which road is turned into a metaphor, but its fundamental pivot is the flow of time.

The road is especially (but not exclusively) appropriate for portraying events governed by chance. This explains the important narrative role of the road in the history of the novel. A road passes through the ancient everyday novel of wandering, through Petronius' *Satyricon* and Apuleius' *Golden Ass*. Heroes of medieval chivalric romances set out on the road, and it often happens that all the events of a novel either take place on the road or are concentrated along the road (distributed on both sides of it).

And in such a novel as Wolfram von Eschenbach's *Parzival*, the hero's real-life course or path to Montsalvat passes imperceptibly into a metaphor of the road, life's course, the course of the soul that now approaches God, now moves away from Him (depending on the mistakes and failings of the hero and on the events that he encounters in the course of his real life). The road is what determined the plots of the Spanish picaresque novel of the sixteenth century (*Lazarillo* and *Guzman de Alfarache*). On the boundary line between the sixteenth and seventeenth centuries, Don Quixote sets out on the road in order that he might encounter all of Spain on that road—from galley-slaves to dukes. By this time the road had been profoundly, intensely etched by the flow of historical time, by the traces and signs of time's passage, by markers of the era. In the seventeenth century, Simplicissimus sets out on a road rutted by the events of the Thirty Years War. This road stretches onward, always maintaining its significance as major artery, through such critical works in the history of the novel as Sorel's *Francion* and Lesage's *Gil Blas*. The importance of the road is retained (although weakened) in Defoe's (picaresque) novels, and in Fielding. The road and encounters on the road remain important in both Wilhelm Meister's *Lehrejahre* and *Wanderjahre* (although here their ideological sense is substantially changed, since the concepts of "chance" and "fate" have been radically reinterpreted). Novalis' Heinrich von Ofterdingen and other heroes of the Romantic novel set out on a road that is half-real, half-metaphorical. Finally, the road and encounters on it are important in the historical novel. Zagoskin's *Yury Miloslavsky*,^{vv} for example, is structured around the road and road encounters. Grinev's meeting Pugachev on the road in a snowstorm determines the plot in *The Captain's Daughter*. We recall as well the role of the road in Gogol's *Dead Souls* and Nekrasov's "Who Lives Well in Russia."

Without touching here upon the question of the changing functions of the "road" and "encounter" in the history of the novel, we will mention but one crucial feature of the "road" common to all the various types of novels we have covered: the road is always one that passes through *familiar territory*, and not through some exotic *alien world* (Gil Blas' "Spain" is artificial, and Simplicissimus' temporary stay in France is also artificial, since the foreignness of this foreign country is illusory, there is not a trace of the exotic); it is the *sociohistorical heterogeneity* of one's own country that is revealed and depicted (and for this reason, if one may speak at all about the exotic here, then it can only be the "social exotic"—"slums," "dregs," the world of thieves). This function of the "road" was exploited outside the novel as well, in such nonnarrative genres as journalistic accounts of travel in the eighteenth century (the classic example is Radishchev's *Journey from Petersburg to Moscow*), and in the journalistic travel notes of the first half of the nineteenth century (for example, Heine's). The peculiarity of the "road" serves to distinguish these novels from that other line of development present in the novel of travel, represented by such novelistic types as the ancient novel of wandering, the Greek Sophist novel (to whose analysis we have devoted the first part of this essay) and the Baroque novel of the seventeenth century. In these novels, a function analogous to the road is played by an "alien world" separated from one's own native land by sea and distance.

Toward the end of the seventeenth century in England, a new territory for novelistic events is constituted and reinforced in the so-called "Gothic" or "black" novel—the *castle* (first used in this meaning by Horace Walpole in *The Castle of Otranto*, and later in Radcliffe, Monk Lewis and others). The castle is saturated

---

vv. *Yury Miloslavsky* (1829) is a historical novel about the Polish occupation of Moscow in 1612. Its author, M. N. Zagoskin (1789–1852), while far from being in the same class as his idol Walter Scott, did help to create a vogue for historical romance.

through and through with a time that is historical in the narrow sense of the word, that is, the time of the historical past. The castle is the place where the lords of the feudal era lived (and consequently also the place of historical figures of the past); the traces of centuries and generations are arranged in it in visible form as various parts of its architecture, in furnishings, weapons, the ancestral portrait gallery, the family archives and in the particular human relationships involving dynastic primacy and the transfer of hereditary rights. And finally legends and traditions animate every corner of the castle and its environs through their constant reminders of past events. It is this quality that gives rise to the specific kind of narrative inherent in castles and that is then worked out in Gothic novels.

The historicity of castle time has permitted it to play a rather important role in the development of the historical novel. The castle had its origins in the distant past; its orientation is toward the past. Admittedly the traces of time in the castle do bear a somewhat antiquated, museum-like character. Walter Scott succeeded in overcoming the danger of excessive antiquarianism by relying heavily on the legend of the castle, on the link between the castle and its historically conceived, comprehensible setting. The organic cohesion of spatial and temporal aspects and categories in the castle (and its environs), the historical intensity of this chronotope, is what had determined its productivity as a source for images at different stages in the development of the historical novel.

In the novels of Stendhal and Balzac a fundamentally new space appears in which novelistic events may unfold—the space of parlors and salons (in the broad sense of the word). Of course this is not the first appearance of such space, but only in these texts does it achieve its full significance as the place where the major spatial and temporal sequences of the novel intersect. From a narrative and compositional point of view, this is the place where encounters occur (no longer emphasizing their specifically random nature as did meetings "on the road" or "in an alien world"). In salons and parlors the webs of intrigue are spun, denouements occur and finally—this is where *dialogues* happen, something that acquires extraordinary importance in the novel, revealing the character, "ideas" and "passions" of the heroes.

The narrative and compositional importance of this is easy to understand. In the parlors and salons of the Restoration and July

Monarchy is found the barometer of political and business life; political, business, social, literary reputations are made and destroyed, careers are begun and wrecked, here are decided the fates of high politics and high finance as well as the success or failure of a proposed bill, a book, a play, a minister, a courtesan-singer; here in their full array (that is, brought together in one place at one time) are all the gradations of the new social hierarchy; and here, finally, there unfold forms that are concrete and visible, the supreme power of life's new king—money.

Most important in all this is the weaving of historical and socio-public events together with the personal and even deeply private side of life, with the secrets of the boudoir; the interweaving of petty, private intrigues with political and financial intrigues, the interpenetration of state with boudoir secrets, of historical sequences with the everyday and biographical sequences. Here the graphically visible markers of historical time as well as of biographical and everyday time are concentrated and condensed; at the same time they are intertwined with each other in the tightest possible fashion, fused into unitary markers of the epoch. The epoch becomes not only graphically visible [space], but narratively visible [time].

For the great realist writers, Stendhal and Balzac, parlors and salons are not, of course, the only places of intersection of temporal and spatial sequences. They constitute only one such place. Balzac's ability to "*see*" time in space was extraordinary. We need mention only Balzac's marvelous depiction of houses as materialized history and his description of streets, cities, rural landscapes at the level where they are being worked upon by time and history.

We will merely touch upon one more example of the intersection of spatial and temporal sequences. In Flaubert's *Madame Bovary* the *provincial town* serves as the locus of action. The petty-bourgeois provincial town with its stagnant life is a very widespread setting for nineteenth-century novels (both before and after Flaubert). Such towns occur in several different variants, including a very important one, the idyllic (in the works of the provincialists). We will deal with the Flaubertian category alone (which was not, of course, created by Flaubert). Such towns are the locus for cyclical everyday time. Here there are no events, only "doings" that constantly repeat themselves. Time here has no advancing historical movement; it moves rather in narrow circles: the circle of the day, of the week, of the month, of a person's entire life. A day is just a day, a year is just a year—a life is just a life. Day in, day out the same round of activities are repeated, the same topics of conversation, the same words and so forth. In this type of time people eat, drink, sleep, have wives, mistresses (casual affairs), involve themselves in petty intrigues, sit in their shops or offices, play cards, gossip. This is commonplace, philistine cyclical everyday time. It is familiar to us in many variants in Gogol, Turgenev, Gleb Uspensky, Saltykov-Shchedrin, Chekhov. The markers of this time are simple, crude, material, fused with the everyday details of specific locales, with the quaint little houses and rooms of the town, with the sleepy streets, the dust and flies, the club, the billiards and so on and on. Time here is without event and therefore almost seems to stand still. Here there are no "meetings," no "partings." It is a viscous and sticky time that drags itself slowly through space. And therefore it cannot serve as the primary time of the novel. Novelists use it as an ancillary time, one that may be interwoven with other noncyclical temporal sequences or used merely to intersperse such sequences; it often serves as a contrasting background for temporal sequences that are more charged with energy and event.

We will mention one more chronotope, highly charged with emotion and value, the chronotope of *threshold*; it can be combined with the motif of encounter, but its most fundamental instance is as the chronotope of *crisis* and *break* in a life. The word "threshold" itself already has a metaphorical meaning in everyday usage (together with its literal meaning), and is connected with the breaking point of a life, the moment of crisis, the decision that changes a life (or the indecisiveness that fails to change a life, the fear to step over the threshold). In literature, the chronotope of the threshold is always metaphorical and symbolic, sometimes openly but more often implicitly. In Dostoevsky, for example, the threshold and related chronotopes—those of the staircase, the front hall and corridor, as well as the chronotopes of the street and square that extend those spaces into the open air— are the main places of action in his works, places where crisis events occur, the falls, resurrections, renewals, epiphanies, decisions that determine the whole life of a man. In this chronotope, time is essentially instantaneous; it is as if it has no duration and falls out of the normal course of biographical time. In Dostoevsky these moments of decision become part of the great all-embracing chronotopes of *mystery-* and carnival-time. These times relate to one another in Dostoevsky in a highly distinctive way; they are interwoven with one another much as they had been intermingled for centuries on the public squares of the Middle Ages and the Renaissance (and in essence as they had been intermingled on the ancient squares of Greece and Rome, although in somewhat different forms). It is as if Dostoevsky's landscape is animated and illuminated by the ancient public square's spirit of carnival and mystery: in the streets (outside) and in his mass scenes, especially the parlor scenes (inside).[17] This does not, of course, exhaust the range of chronotopes in Dostoevsky; they are complex and multi-faceted, as are the traditions that they infuse with new life.

In Tolstoy as distinct from Dostoevsky the fundamental chronotope is biographical time, which flows smoothly in the spaces— the interior spaces—of townhouses and estates of the nobility. In Tolstoy there are, of course, also crises, falls, spiritual renewals and resurrections, but they are not instantaneous and are not cast out of the course of biographical time; in fact, they are welded firmly to it. For example, Ivan Ilyich's crisis and dawning awareness drags on for the whole duration of the final phase of his illness, and comes to a close only at the very end of his life. Pierre Bezukhov's spiritual renewal is also a lengthy and gradual one, fully biographical. Less lengthy but still not instantaneous is the renewal and repentance of Nikita ("The Power of Darkness"). We find in Tolstoy only one exception: Brekhunov's radical spiritual rebirth at the last moment of his life ("Master and Man"), something that is in no way prepared for, completely unexpected. Tolstoy did not value the moment, he did not strive to fill it with something fundamental and decisive: one rarely encounters the word "suddenly" in his works, and it never ushers in a significant event. In contrast to Dostoevsky, Tolstoy loves duration, the stretching-out of time. After biographical time and space, Tolstoy

17. Cultural and literary traditions (including the most ancient) are preserved and continue to live not in the individual subjective memory of a single individual and not in some kind of collective "psyche," but rather in the objective forms that culture itself assumes (including the forms of language and spoken speech), and in this sense they are inter-subjective and inter-individual (and consequently social); from there they enter literary works, sometimes almost completely bypassing the subjective individual memory of their creators.

attached most significance to the chronotope of nature, the family-idyllic chronotope and even the chronotope of the labor idyll (in his descriptions of peasant labor).

* * *

What is the significance of all these chronotopes? What is most obvious is their meaning for *narrative*. They are the organizing centers for the fundamental narrative events of the novel. The chronotope is the place where the knots of narrative are tied and untied. It can be said without qualification that to them belongs the meaning that shapes narrative.

We cannot help but be strongly impressed by the *representational* importance of the chronotope. Time becomes, in effect, palpable and visible; the chronotope makes narrative events concrete, makes them take on flesh, causes blood to flow in their veins. An event can be communicated, it becomes information, one can give precise data on the place and time of its occurrence. But the event does not become a figure [*obraz*]. It is precisely the chronotope that provides the ground essential for the showing-forth, the representability of events. And this is so thanks precisely to the special increase in density and concreteness of time markers—the time of human life, of historical time—that occurs within well-delineated spatial areas. It is this that makes it possible to structure a representation of events in the chronotope (around the chronotope). It serves as the primary point from which "scenes" in a novel unfold, while at the same time other "binding" events, located far from the chronotope, appear as mere dry information and communicated facts (in Stendhal, for instance, informing and communicating carry great weight; representation is concentrated and condensed in a few scenes and these scenes cast a light that makes even the "informing" parts of the novel seem more concrete—cf., for example, the structure of *Armance*). Thus the chronotope, functioning as the primary means for materializing time in space, emerges as a center for concretizing representation, as a force giving body to the entire novel. All the novel's abstract elements—philosophical and social generalizations, ideas, analyses of cause and effect—gravitate toward the chronotope and through it take on flesh and blood, permitting the imaging power of art to do its work. Such is the representational significance of the chronotope.

The chronotopes we have discussed provide the basis for distinguishing generic types; they lie at the heart of specific varieties of the novel genre, formed and developed over the course of many centuries (although it is true that some of the functions of the chronotope of the road, for example, change in the process of this development). But any and every literary image is chronotopic. Language, as a treasure-house of images, is fundamentally chronotopic. Also chronotopic is the internal form of a word, that is, the mediating marker with whose help the root meanings of spatial categories are carried over into temporal relationships (in the broadest sense). This is not the place to deal with this more specialized problem. We refer the reader to the appropriate chapter in Cassirer's work (*The Philosophy of Symbolic Forms*), where his analysis of the ways time is reflected in language (the assimilation of time by language) provides a rich fund of factual material.

It was Lessing in the *Laocoön* who first made clearly apparent the principle of chronotopicity in the literary image. He established the temporal character of the literary image. Those things that are static in space cannot be statically described, but must rather be incorporated into the temporal sequence of represented events and into the story's own representational field. Thus, in Lessing's familiar example, the beauty of Helen is not so much described by Homer as it is demonstrated in the reactions of the Trojan elders; these come to light simultaneously in the sequence comprised by the activities and deeds of the elders. Beauty is drawn in to a chain of represented events and yet at the same time is not the subject of static description, but rather the subject of a dynamic story.

Despite the fundamental and seminal way he posed the problem of time in literature, Lessing nevertheless posed this problem primarily on the formal and technical plane (not, of course, in the formalistic sense). The problem of assimilating real time, that is, the problem of assimilating historical reality into the poetic image, was not posed by him, although the question is touched upon in his work.

The distinctiveness of those generically typical plot-generating chronotopes discussed by us above becomes clear against the background of this general (formal and material) chronotopicity of the poetic images conceived as an image of temporal art, one that represents spatially perceptible phenomena in their movement and development. Such are the specific novel-epic chronotopes that serve for the assimilation of actual temporal (including historical) reality, that permit the essential aspects of this reality to be reflected and incorporated into the artistic space of the novel.

* * *

We have been speaking so far only of the major chronotopes, those that are most fundamental and wide-ranging. But each such chronotope can include within it an unlimited number of minor chronotopes; in fact, as we have already said, any motif may have a special chronotope of its own.

Within the limits of a single work and within the total literary output of a single author we may notice a number of different chronotopes and complex interactions among them, specific to the given work or author; it is common moreover for one of these chronotopes to envelope or dominate the others (such, primarily, are those we have analyzed in this essay). Chronotopes are mutually inclusive, they co-exist, they may be interwoven with, replace or oppose one another, contradict one another or find themselves in ever more complex interrelationships. The relationships themselves that exist *among* chronotopes cannot enter into any of the relationships contained *within* chronotopes. The general characteristic of these interactions is that they are *dialogical* (in the broadest use of the word). But this dialogue cannot enter into the world represented in the work, nor into any of the chronotopes represented in it; it is outside the world represented, although not outside the work as a whole. It (this dialogue) enters the world of the author, of the performer, and the world of the listeners and readers. And all these worlds are chronotopic as well.

How are the chronotopes of the author and the listener or reader presented to us? First and foremost, we experience them in the external material being of the work and in its purely external composition. But this material of the work is not dead, it is speaking, signifying (it involves signs); we not only see and perceive it but in it we can always hear voices (even while reading silently to ourselves). We are presented with a text occupying a certain specific place in space; that is, it is localized; our creation of it, our acquaintance with it occurs through time. The text as such never appears as a dead thing; beginning with any text—and sometimes passing through a lengthy series of mediating links—we always arrive, in the final analysis, at the human voice, which is to say we come up against the human being. But the text is always imprisoned in dead material of some sort: in the early stages of literature's development, that is, in inscriptions (on stone, brick, leather, papyrus, paper); later on, the inscribing could take the form of a book (scrolls or codices). But inscriptions and books in any form already lie on the boundary line between culture and a dead nature; if we approach these items as carriers of the text, then they enter into the realm of culture and (in our example) into the realm of literature. In the completely real-life time-space where the work resonates, where we find the inscription or the book, we find as well a real person—one who originates spoken speech as well as the inscription and the book—and real people who are hearing and reading the text. Of course these real people, the authors and the listeners or readers, may be (and often are) located in differing time-spaces, sometimes separated from each other by centuries and by great spatial distances, but nevertheless they are all located in a real, unitary and as yet incomplete historical world set off by a sharp and categorical boundary from the *represented* world in the text. Therefore we may call this world the world that *creates* the text, for all its aspects—the reality reflected in the text, the authors creating the text, the performers of the text (if they exist) and finally the listeners or readers who recreate and in so doing renew the text—participate equally in the creation of the represented world in the text. Out of the actual chronotopes of our world (which serve as the source of representation) emerge the reflected and *created* chronotopes of the world represented in the work (in the text).

As we have already said, there is a sharp and categorical boundary line between the actual world as source of representation and the world represented in the work. We must never forget this, we must never confuse—as has been done up to now and as is still often done—the *represented* world with the world outside the text (naive realism); nor must we confuse the author-creator of a work with the author as a human being (naive biographism); nor confuse the listener or reader of multiple and varied periods, recreating and renewing the text, with the passive listener or reader of one's own time (which leads to dogmatism in interpretation and evaluation). All such confusions are methodologically impermissible. But it is also impermissible to take this categorical boundary line as something absolute and impermeable (which leads to an oversimplified, dogmatic splitting of hairs). However forcefully the real and the represented world resist fusion, however immutable the presence of that categorical boundary line between them, they are nevertheless indissolubly tied up with each other and find themselves in continual mutual interaction; uninterrupted exchange goes on between them, similar to the uninterrupted exchange of matter between living organisms and the environment that surrounds them. As long as the organism lives, it resists a fusion with the environment, but if it is torn out of its environment, it dies. The work and the world represented in it enter the real world and enrich it, and the real world enters the work and its world as part of the process of its creation, as well as part of its subsequent life, in a continual renewing of the work through the creative perception of listeners and readers. Of course this process of exchange is itself chronotopic: it occurs first and foremost in the historically developing social world, but without ever losing contact with changing historical space. We might even speak of a special *creative* chronotope inside which this exchange between work and life occurs, and which constitutes the distinctive life of the work.

*   *   *

We must pause briefly on the author, who is the creator of the work, and the distinctive form of his activity.

We find the author *outside* the work as a human being living his own biographical life. But we also meet him as the creator of the work itself, although he is located outside the chronotopes represented in his work, he is as it were tangential to them. We meet him (that is, we sense his activity) most of all in the composition of the work: it is he who segments the work into parts (songs, chapters and so on) that assume, of course, a kind of external expression—without however directly reflecting the represented chronotopes. This segmentation might be different in different genres, since in some of them the segmentation has been preserved as a matter of tradition; such divisions were determined by the actual conditions under which works in these genres were performed and heard in the early stages of their prewritten (oral) existence. Thus we can with relative clarity sense in the segmentation of ancient epic songs the chronotope of the singer and his audience, or the chronotope of storytelling in traditional tales. But even in the segmentation of a modern literary work we sense the chronotope of the represented world as well as the chronotope of the readers and creators of the work. That is, we get a mutual interaction between the world represented in the work and the world outside the work. This interaction is pinpointed very precisely in certain elementary features of composition: every work has a *beginning* and an *end*, the event represented in it likewise has a beginning and an end, but these beginnings and ends lie in different worlds, in different chronotopes that can never fuse with each other or be identical to each other but that are, at the same time, interrelated and indissolubly tied up with each other. We might put it as follows: before us are two events—the event that is narrated in the work and the event of narration itself (we ourselves participate in the latter, as listeners or readers); these events take place in different times (which are marked by different durations as well) and in different places, but at the same time these two events are indissolubly united in a single but complex event that we might call the work in the totality of all its events, including the external material givenness of the work, and its text, and the world represented in the text, and the author-creator and the listener or reader; thus we perceive the fullness of the work in all its wholeness and indivisibility, but at the same time we understand the diversity of the elements that constitute it.

The author-creator moves freely in his own time: he can begin his story at the end, in the middle, or at any moment of the events represented without violating the objective course of time in the event he describes. Here we get a sharp distinction between representing and represented time.

But a more general question arises: from what temporal and spatial point of view does the author look upon the events that he describes?

In the first place, he does his observing from his own unresolved and still evolving contemporaneity, in all its complexity and fullness, insofar as he himself is located as it were tangentially to the reality he describes. That contemporaneity from which the author observes includes, first and foremost, the realm of literature—and not only contemporary literature in the strict sense of the word, but also the literature of the past that continues to live and renew itself in the present. The realm of literature and more broadly of culture (from which literature cannot be separated) constitutes the indispensable context of a literary work and of the author's position within it, outside of which it is impossible to understand either the work or the author's intentions reflected in it.[18] The author's relationship to the various phenomena of literature and culture has a dialogical character, which is analogous to the interrelationships between chronotopes within the literary work (of which we spoke above). But these dialogical relationships enter into a special *semantic* sphere that is purely chronotopic—this, however, exceeds the bounds of our present survey.

As we have already said, the author-creator, finding himself outside the chronotopes of the world he represents in his work, is nevertheless not simply outside but as it were tangential to these chronotopes. He represents the world either from the point of view of the hero participating in the represented event, or from the point of view of a narrator, or from that of an assumed author or—finally—without utilizing any intermediary at all he can deliver the story directly from himself as the author pure and simple (in direct authorial discourse). But even in the last instance he can represent the temporal-spatial world and its events only *as if* he had seen and observed them himself, only *as if* he were an omnipresent witness to them. Even had he created an autobiography or a confession of the most astonishing truthfulness, all the same he, as its creator, remains outside the world he has represented in his work. If I relate (or write about) an event that has just happened to me, then I as the *teller* (or writer) of this event am already outside the time and space in which the event occurred. It is just as impossible to forge an identity between myself, my own "I," and that "I" that is the subject of my stories as it is to lift myself up by my own hair. The represented world, however realistic and truthful, can never be chronotopically identical with the real world it represents, where the author and creator of the literary work is to be found. That is why the term "image of the author" seems to me so inadequate: everything that becomes an image in the literary work, and consequently enters its chronotopes, is a created thing and not a force that itself creates. The "image of the author"—if we are to understand by that the author-creator— is a contradiction in terms; every image ·is a created, and not a creating, thing. It goes without saying that the listener or reader

18. We will not deal here with other areas of the social and personal experience of the author-creator.

may create for himself an image of the author (and usually does; that is, in some way he pictures the author to himself); this enables him to make use of autobiographical and biographical material, to study the appropriate era in which the author lived and worked as well as other material about him. But in so doing he (the listener or reader) is merely creating an artistic and historical image of the author that may be, to a greater or lesser extent, truthful and profound—that is, this image is subject to all those criteria that usually apply in these types of images. And this image of the author cannot, of course, itself enter into the fabric of images that makes up the literary work. However if this image is deep and truthful, it can help the listener or reader more correctly and profoundly to understand the work of the given author.

In the present work we will not consider the complex problem of the listener-reader, his chronotopic situation and his role in *renewing* the work or art (his role in the process of the work's life); we will point out merely that every literary work *faces outward away from itself*, toward the listener-reader, and to a certain extent thus anticipates possible reactions to itself.

* * *

In conclusion we should touch upon one more important problem, that of the boundaries of chronotopic analysis. Science, art and literature also involve *semantic* elements that are not subject to temporal and spatial determinations. Of such a sort, for instance, are all mathematical concepts: we make use of them for measuring spatial and temporal phenomena but they themselves have no intrinsic spatial and temporal determinations; they are the object of our abstract cognition. They are an abstract and conceptual figuration indispensable for the formalization and strict scientific study of many concrete phenomena. But meanings exist not only in abstract cognition, they exist in artistic thought as well. These artistic meanings are likewise not subject to temporal and spatial determinations. We somehow manage however to endow all phenomena with meaning, that is, we incorporate them not only into the sphere of spatial and temporal existence but also into a semantic sphere. This process of assigning meaning also involves some assigning of value. But questions concerning the form that existence assumes in this sphere, and the nature and form of the evaluations that give sense to existence, are purely philosophical (although not, of course, metaphysical) and we will not engage them here. For us the following is important: whatever these meanings turn out to be, in order to enter our experience (which is social experience) they must take on the *form of a sign* that is audible and visible for us (a hieroglyph, a mathematical formula, a verbal or linguistic expression, a sketch, etc.). Without such temporal-spatial expression, even abstract thought is impossible. Consequently, every entry into the sphere of meanings is accomplished only through the gates of the chronotope.

* * *

As we stated in the beginning of our essay, the study of temporal and spatial relationships in literary works has only recently begun, and it has been temporal relationships by and large that have been studied—and these in isolation from the spatial relationships indissolubly tied up with them. Whether the approach taken in this present work will prove fundamental and productive, only the further development of literary research can determine.

1937–1938[19]

19. The "Concluding Remarks" were written in 1973.

DISCOURSE IN THE NOVEL

The principal idea of this essay is that the study of verbal art can and must overcome the divorce between an abstract "formal" approach and an equally abstract "ideological" approach. Form and content in discourse are one, once we understand that verbal discourse is a social phenomenon—social throughout its entire range and in each and every of its factors, from the sound image to the furthest reaches of abstract meaning.

It is this idea that has motivated our emphasis on "the stylistics of genre." The separation of style and language from the question of genre has been largely responsible for a situation in which only individual and period-bound overtones of a style are the privileged subjects of study, while its basic social tone is ignored. The great historical destinies of genres are overshadowed by the petty vicissitudes of stylistic modifications, which in their turn are linked with individual artists and artistic movements. For this reason, stylistics has been deprived of an authentic philosophical and sociological approach to its problems; it has become bogged down in stylistic trivia; it is not able to sense behind the individual and period-bound shifts the great and anonymous destinies of artistic discourse itself. More often than not, stylistics defines itself as a stylistics of "private craftsmanship" and ignores the social life of discourse outside the artist's study, discourse in the open spaces of public squares, streets, cities and villages, of social groups, generations and epochs. Stylistics is concerned not with living discourse but with a histological specimen made from it, with abstract linguistic discourse in the service of an artist's individual creative powers. But these individual and tendentious overtones of style, cut off from the fundamentally social modes in which discourse lives, inevitably come across as flat and abstract in such a formulation and cannot therefore be studied in organic unity with a work's semantic components.

Modern Stylistics & the Novel

Before the twentieth century, problems associated with a stylistics of the novel had not been precisely formulated—such a formulation could only have resulted from a recognition of the stylistic uniqueness of novelistic (artistic-prose) discourse.

For a long time treatment of the novel was limited to little more than abstract ideological examination and publicistic commentary. Concrete questions of stylistics were either not treated at all or treated in passing and in an arbitrary way: the discourse of artistic prose was either understood as being poetic in the narrow sense, and had the categories of traditional stylistics (based on the study of tropes) uncritically applied to it, or else such questions were limited to empty, evaluative terms for the characterization of language, such as "expressiveness," "imagery," "force," "clarity" and so on—without providing these concepts with any stylistic significance, however vague and tentative.

Toward the end of the last century, as a counterweight to this abstract ideological way of viewing things, interest began to grow in the concrete problems of artistic craftsmanship in prose, in the problems of novel and short-story technique. However, in questions of stylistics the situation did not change in the slightest; attention was concentrated almost exclusively on problems of composition (in the broad sense of the word). But, as before, the peculiarities of the stylistic life of discourse in the novel (and in the short story as well) lacked an approach that was both principled and at the same time concrete (one is impossible without the other); the same arbitrary judgmental observations about language—in the spirit of traditional stylistics—continued to reign supreme, and they totally overlooked the authentic nature of artistic prose.

There is a highly characteristic and widespread point of view that sees novelistic discourse as an extra-artistic medium, a discourse that is not worked into any special or unique style. After failure to find in novelistic discourse a purely poetic formulation ("poetic" in the narrow sense) as was expected, prose discourse is denied any artistic value at all; it is the same as practical speech for everyday life, or speech for scientific purposes, an artistically neutral means of communication.[1]

1. As recently as the 1920s, V. M. Žirmunskij [important fellow-traveler of the Formalists, ed.] was writing: "When lyrical poetry appears to be authen-

Such a point of view frees one from the necessity of undertaking stylistic analyses of the novel; it in fact gets rid of the very problem of a stylistics of the novel, permitting one to limit oneself to purely thematic analyses of it.

It was, however, precisely in the 1920s that this situation changed: the novelistic prose word began to win a place for itself in stylistics. On the one hand there appeared a series of concrete stylistic analyses of novelistic prose; on the other hand, systematic attempts were made to recognize and define the stylistic uniqueness of artistic prose as distinct from poetry.

But it was precisely these concrete analyses and these attempts at a principled approach that made patently obvious the fact that all the categories of traditional stylistics—in fact the very concept of a *poetic* artistic discourse, which lies at the heart of such categories—were not applicable to novelistic discourse. Novelistic discourse proved to be the acid test for this whole way of conceiving style, exposing the narrowness of this type of thinking and its inadequacy in all areas of discourse's artistic life.

All attempts at concrete stylistic analysis of novelistic prose either strayed into linguistic descriptions of the language of a given novelist or else limited themselves to those separate, isolated stylistic elements of the novel that were includable (or gave the appearance of being includable) in the traditional categories of stylistics. In both instances the stylistic whole of the novel and of novelistic discourse eluded the investigator.

The novel as a whole is a phenomenon multiform in style and variform in speech and voice. In it the investigator is confronted with several heterogeneous stylistic unities, often located on different linguistic levels and subject to different stylistic controls.

---

tically a work of *verbal art*, due to its choice and combination of words (on semantic as well as sound levels) all of which are completely subordinated to the aesthetic project, Tolstoy's novel, by contrast, which is free in its verbal composition, does not use words as an artistically significant element of interaction but as a neutral medium or as a system of significations subordinated (as happens in practical speech) to the communicative function, directing our attention to thematic aspects quite abstracted from purely verbal considerations. We cannot call such a *literary work* a work of *verbal art* or, in any case, not in the sense that the term is used for lyrical poetry" ["On the Problem of the Formal Method," in an anthology of his articles, *Problems of a Theory of Literature* (Leningrad, 1928, p. 173); Russian edition: "K voprosu o 'formal'nom metode'," in *Voprosy teorii literatury*, (L., 1928)].

We list below the basic types of compositional-stylistic unities into which the novelistic whole usually breaks down:

(1) Direct authorial literary-artistic narration (in all its diverse variants);

(2) Stylization of the various forms of oral everyday narration (*skaz*);

(3) Stylization of the various forms of semiliterary (written) everyday narration (the letter, the diary, etc.);

(4) Various forms of literary but extra-artistic authorial speech (moral, philosophical or scientific statements, oratory, ethnographic descriptions, memoranda and so forth);

(5) The stylistically individualized speech of characters.

These heterogeneous stylistic unities, upon entering the novel, combine to form a structured artistic system, and are subordinated to the higher stylistic unity of the work as a whole, a unity that cannot be identified with any single one of the unities subordinated to it.

The stylistic uniqueness of the novel as a genre consists precisely in the combination of these subordinated, yet still relatively autonomous, unities (even at times comprised of different languages) into the higher unity of the work as a whole: the style of a novel is to be found in the combination of its styles; the language of a novel is the system of its "languages." Each separate element of a novel's language is determined first of all by one such subordinated stylistic unity into which it enters directly— be it the stylistically individualized speech of a character, the down-to-earth voice of a narrator in *skaz*, a letter or whatever. The linguistic and stylistic profile of a given element (lexical, semantic, syntactic) is shaped by that subordinated unity to which it is most immediately proximate. At the same time this element, together with its most immediate unity, figures into the style of the whole, itself supports the accent of the whole and participates in the process whereby the unified meaning of the whole is structured and revealed.

The novel can be defined as a diversity of social speech types (sometimes even diversity of languages) and a diversity of individual voices, artistically organized. The internal stratification of any single national language into social dialects, characteristic group behavior, professional jargons, generic languages, languages of generations and age groups, tendentious languages, languages of the authorities, of various circles and of passing fashions, languages that serve the specific sociopolitical purposes of the day, even of the hour (each day has its own slogan, its own vocabulary, its own emphases)—this internal stratification present in every language at any given moment of its historical existence is the indispensable prerequisite for the novel as a genre. The novel orchestrates all its themes, the totality of the world of objects and ideas depicted and expressed in it, by means of the social diversity of speech types [*raznorečie*] and by the differing individual voices that flourish under such conditions. Authorial speech, the speeches of narrators, inserted genres, the speech of characters are merely those fundamental compositional unities with whose help heteroglossia [*raznorečie*] can enter the novel; each of them permits a multiplicity of social voices and a wide variety of their links and interrelationships (always more or less dialogized). These distinctive links and interrelationships between utterances and languages, this movement of the theme through different languages and speech types, its dispersion into the rivulets and droplets of social heteroglossia, its dialogization—this is the basic distinguishing feature of the stylistics of the novel.

Such a combining of languages and styles into a higher unity is unknown to traditional stylistics; it has no method for approaching the distinctive social dialogue among languages that is present in the novel. Thus stylistic analysis is not oriented toward the novel as a whole, but only toward one or another of its subordinated stylistic unities. The traditional scholar bypasses the basic distinctive feature of the novel as a genre; he substitutes for it another object of study, and instead of novelistic style he actually analyzes something completely different. He transposes a symphonic (orchestrated) theme on to the piano keyboard.

We notice two such types of substitutions: in the first type, an analysis of novelistic style is replaced by a description of the language of a given novelist (or at best of the "languages" of a given novel); in the second type, one of the subordinated styles is isolated and analyzed as if it were the style of the whole.

In the first type, style is cut off from considerations of genre, and from the work as such, and regarded as a phenomenon of language itself: the unity of style in a given work is transformed either into the unity of an individual language ("individual dialect"), or into the unity of an individual speech (*parole*). It is precisely the individuality of the speaking subject that is recognized to be that style-generating factor transforming a phenomenon of language and linguistics into a stylistic unity.

We have no need to follow where such an analysis of novelistic style leads, whether to a disclosing of the novelist's individual dialect (that is, his vocabulary, his syntax) or to a disclosing of the distinctive features of the work taken as a "complete speech act," an "utterance." Equally in both cases, style is understood in the spirit of Saussure: as an individualization of the general language (in the sense of a system of general language norms). Stylistics is transformed either into a curious kind of linguistics treating individual languages, or into a linguistics of the utterance.

In accordance with the point of view selected, the unity of a style thus presupposes on the one hand a unity of language (in the sense of a system of general normative forms) and on the other hand the unity of an individual person realizing himself in this language.

Both these conditions are in fact obligatory in the majority of verse-based poetic genres, but even in these genres they far from exhaust or define the style of the work. The most precise and complete description of the individual language and speech of a poet—even if this description does choose to treat the expressiveness of language and speech elements—does not add up to a stylistic analysis of the work, inasmuch as these elements relate to a system of language or to a system of speech, that is, to various linguistic unities and not to the system of the artistic work, which is governed by a completely different system of rules than those that govern the linguistic systems of language and of speech.

But—we repeat—in the majority of poetic genres, the unity of the language system and the unity (and uniqueness) of the poet's individuality as reflected in his language and speech, which is directly realized in this unity, are indispensable prerequisites of poetic style. The novel, however, not only does not require these conditions but (as we have said) even makes of the internal stratification of language, of its social heteroglossia and the variety of individual voices in it, the prerequisite for authentic novelistic prose.

Thus the substitution of the individualized language of the novelist (to the extent that one can recover this language from the "speech" and "language" systems of the novel) for the style of the novel itself is doubly imprecise: it distorts the very essence of a stylistics of the novel. Such substitution inevitably leads to the selection from the novel of only those elements that can be fitted within the frame of a single language system and that express, directly and without mediation, an authorial individuality in language. The whole of the novel and the specific tasks involved in constructing this whole out of heteroglot, multi-voiced, multi-styled and often multi-languaged elements remain outside the boundaries of such a study.

Such is the first type of substitution for the proper object of study in the stylistic analysis of the novel. We will not delve further into the diverse variations of this type, which are determined by the different ways in which such concepts as "the speech whole," "the system of language," "the individuality of the author's language and speech" are understood, and by a difference in the very way in which the relationship between style and language is conceived (and also the relationship between stylistics and linguistics). In all possible variants on this type of analysis, which acknowledge only one single language and a single authorial individuality expressing itself directly in that language, the stylistic nature of the novel slips hopelessly away from the investigator.

The second type of substitution is characterized not by an orientation toward the language of the author, but rather toward the style of the novel itself—although style thus understood is narrowed down to mean the style of merely one out of the several subordinated unities (which are relatively autonomous) within the novel.

In the majority of cases the style of the novel is subsumed under the concept of "epic style," and the appropriate categories of traditional stylistics are applied to it. In such circumstances only those elements of epic representation (those occurring predominantly in direct authorial speech) are isolated from the novel for consideration. The profound difference between novelistic and purely epic modes of expression is ignored. Differences between the novel and the epic are usually perceived on the level of composition and thematics alone.

In other instances, different aspects of novelistic style are selected out as most characteristic of one or another concrete literary work. Thus the narrational aspect can be considered from the point of view not of its objective descriptive mode, but of its subjective expression mode (expressiveness). One might select elements of vernacular extraliterary narration (*skaz*) or those aspects that provide the information necessary to further the plot (as one might do, for example, in analyzing an adventure novel).[2] And it is possible, finally, to select those purely dramatic elements of the novel that lower the narrational aspect to the level of a commentary on the dialogues of the novel's characters. But the system of languages in drama is organized on completely different principles, and therefore its languages sound utterly different than do the languages of the novel. In drama there is no all-encompassing language that addresses itself dialogically to separate languages, there is no second all-encompassing plotless (nondramatic) dialogue outside that of the (nondramatic) plot.

All these types of analysis are inadequate to the style not only of the novelistic whole but even of that element isolated as fundamental for a given novel—inasmuch as that element, removed from its interaction with others, changes its stylistic meaning and ceases to be that which it in fact had been in the novel.

The current state of questions posed by a stylistics of the novel reveals, fully and clearly, that all the categories and methods of traditional stylistics remain incapable of dealing effectively with the artistic uniqueness of discourse in the novel, or with the specific life that discourse leads in the novel. "Poetic language," "individuality of language," "image," "symbol," "epic style" and other general categories worked out and applied by stylistics, as well as the entire set of concrete stylistic devices subsumed by these categories (no matter how differently understood by individual critics), are all equally oriented toward the single-languaged and single-styled genres, toward the poetic genres in the narrow sense of the word. Their connection with this exclusive orientation explains a number of the particular features and limitations of traditional stylistic categories. All these categories, and the very philosophical conception of poetic discourse in which they are grounded, are too narrow and cramped, and cannot accommodate the artistic prose of novelistic discourse.

---

2. Artistic prose style has been studied in Russia by the Formalists largely on these two last levels, that is, either *skaz* (Eichenbaum) or plot-informational aspects (Shklovsky) were studied as most characteristic of literary prose.

Thus stylistics and the philosophy of discourse indeed confront a dilemma: either to acknowledge the novel (and consequently all artistic prose tending in that direction) an unartistic or quasi-artistic genre, or to radically reconsider that conception of poetic discourse in which traditional stylistics is grounded and which determines all its categories.

This dilemma, however, is by no means universally recognized. Most scholars are not inclined to undertake a radical revision of the fundamental philosophical conception of poetic discourse. Many do not even see or recognize the philosophical roots of the stylistics (and linguistics) in which they work, and shy away from any fundamental philosophical issues. They utterly fail to see behind their isolated and fragmented stylistic observations and linguistic descriptions any theoretical problems posed by novelistic discourse. Others—more principled—make a case for consistent individualism in their understanding of language and style. First and foremost they seek in the stylistic phenomenon a direct and unmediated expression of authorial individuality, and such an understanding of the problem is least likely of all to encourage a reconsideration of basic stylistic categories in the proper direction.

However, there is another solution of our dilemma that does take basic concepts into account: one need only consider oft-neglected rhetoric, which for centuries has included artistic prose in its purview. Once we have restored rhetoric to all its ancient rights, we may adhere to the old concept of poetic discourse, relegating to "rhetorical forms" everything in novelistic prose that does not fit the Procrustean bed of traditional stylistic categories.[3]

Gustav Shpet,[a] in his time, proposed such a solution to the dilemma, with all due rigorousness and consistency. He utterly ex-

---

3. Such a solution to the problem was especially tempting to adherents of the formal method in poetics: in fact, the re-establishment of rhetoric, with all its rights, greatly strengthens the Formalist position. Formalist rhetoric is a necessary addition to Formalist poetics. Our Formalists were being completely consistent when they spoke of the necessity of reviving rhetoric alongside poetics (on this, see B. M. Eichenbaum, *Literature*, [*Literatura*; Leningrad, 1927], pp. 147–148).

---

a. Gustav Shpet (1879–1937), outstanding representative of the neo-Kantian and (especially) Husserlian traditions in Russia; as professor at the University of Moscow for many years he influenced many (among others, the young Roman Jakobson).

cluded artistic prose and its ultimate realization—the novel—from the realm of poetry, and assigned it to the category of purely rhetorical forms.[4]

Here is what Shpet says about the novel: "The recognition that contemporary forms of moral propaganda—i.e., the *novel*—do not spring from *poetic creativity* but are purely rhetorical compositions, is an admission, and a conception, that apparently cannot arise without immediately confronting a formidable obstacle in the form of the universal recognition, despite everything, that the novel *does* have a certain aesthetic value."[5]

Shpet utterly denies the novel any aesthetic significance. The novel is an extra-artistic rhetorical genre, "the contemporary form of moral propaganda"; artistic discourse is exclusively poetic discourse (in the sense we have indicated above).

Viktor Vinogradov[b] adopted an analogous point of view in his book *On Artistic Prose*, assigning the problem of artistic prose to rhetoric. While agreeing with Shpet's basic philosophical definitions of the "poetic" and the "rhetorical," Vinogradov was, however, not so paradoxically consistent: he considered the novel a syncretic, mixed form ("a hybrid formation") and admitted that it contained, along with rhetorical elements, some purely poetic ones.[6]

The point of view that completely excludes novelistic prose, as a rhetorical formation, from the realm of poetry—a point of view that is basically false—does nevertheless have a certain indisputable merit. There resides in it an acknowledgment in principle and in substance of the inadequacy of all contemporary stylistics, along with its philosophical and linguistic base, when it comes to defining the specific distinctive features of novelistic prose. And what is more, the very reliance on rhetorical forms has a great heuristic significance. Once rhetorical discourse is

4. Originally in his *Aesthetic Fragments* [*Estetičeskie fragmenty*]; in a more complete aspect in the book *The Inner Form of the Word* [*Vnutrennjaja forma slova*] (M., 1927).
5. *Vnutrennjaja forma slova*, p. 215.
6. V. V. Vinogradov, *On Artistic Prose* [*O xudožestvennom proze*], Moscow-Leningrad, 1930, pp. 75–106.

b. Viktor Vinogradov (1895–1969), outstanding linguistic and student of style in literature, a friendly critic of the Formalists, and an important theorist in his own right (especially his work on *skaz* technique).

brought into the study with all its living diversity, it cannot fail to have a deeply revolutionizing influence on linguistics and on the philosophy of language. It is precisely those aspects of any discourse (the internally dialogic quality of discourse, and the phenomena related to it), not yet sufficiently taken into account and fathomed in all the enormous weight they carry in the life of language, that are revealed with great external precision in rhetorical forms, provided a correct and unprejudiced approach to those forms is used. Such is the general methodological and heuristic significance of rhetorical forms for linguistics and for the philosophy of language.

The special significance of rhetorical forms for understanding the novel is equally great. The novel, and artistic prose in general, has the closest genetic, family relationship to rhetorical forms. And throughout the entire development of the novel, its intimate interaction (both peaceful and hostile) with living rhetorical genres (journalistic, moral, philosophical and others) has never ceased; this interaction was perhaps no less intense than was the novel's interaction with the artistic genres (epic, dramatic, lyric). But in this uninterrupted interrelationship, novelistic discourse preserved its own qualitative uniqueness and was never reducible to rhetorical discourse.

The novel is an artistic genre. Novelistic discourse is poetic discourse, but one that does not fit within the frame provided by the concept of poetic discourse as it now exists. This concept has certain underlying presuppositions that limit it. The very concept—in the course of its historical formulation from Aristotle to the present day—has been oriented toward the specific "official" genres and connected with specific historical tendencies in verbal ideological life. Thus a whole series of phenomena remained beyond its conceptual horizon.

Philosophy of language, linguistics and stylistics [i.e., such as they have come down to us] have all postulated a simple and unmediated relation of speaker to his unitary and singular "own" language, and have postulated as well a simple realization of this language in the monologic utterance of the individual. Such disciplines actually know only two poles in the life of language, between which are located all the linguistic and stylistic phenomena they know: on the one hand, the system of a *unitary language*, and on the other the *individual* speaking in this language.

Various schools of thought in the philosophy of language, in linguistics and in stylistics have, in different periods (and always in close connection with the diverse concrete poetic and ideological styles of a given epoch), introduced into such concepts as "system of language," "monologic utterance," "the speaking *individuum*," various differing nuances of meaning, but their basic content remains unchanged. This basic content is conditioned by the specific sociohistorical destinies of European languages and by the destinies of ideological discourse, and by those particular historical tasks that ideological discourse has fulfilled in specific social spheres and at specific stages in its own historical development.

These tasks and destinies of discourse conditioned specific verbal-ideological movements, as well as various specific genres of ideological discourse, and ultimately the specific philosophical concept of discourse itself—in particular, the concept of poetic discourse, which had been at the heart of all concepts of style.

The strength and at the same time the limitations of such basic stylistic categories become apparent when such categories are seen as conditioned by specific historical destinies and by the task that an ideological discourse assumes. These categories arose from and were shaped by the historically *aktuell* forces at work in the verbal-ideological evolution of specific social groups; they comprised the theoretical expression of actualizing forces that were in the process of creating a life for language.

These forces are *the forces that serve to unify and centralize the verbal-ideological world.*

Unitary language constitutes the theoretical expression of the historical processes of linguistic unification and centralization, an expression of the centripetal forces of language. A unitary language is not something given [*dan*] but is always in essence posited [*zadan*]—and at every moment of its linguistic life it is opposed to the realities of heteroglossia. But at the same time it makes its real presence felt as a force for overcoming this heteroglossia, imposing specific limits to it, guaranteeing a certain maximum of mutual understanding and crystalizing into a real, although still relative, unity—the unity of the reigning conversational (everyday) and literary language, "correct language."

A common unitary language is a system of linguistic norms. But these norms do not constitute an abstract imperative; they are rather the generative forces of linguistic life, forces that struggle to overcome the heteroglossia of language, forces that unite and centralize verbal-ideological thought, creating within a heteroglot national language the firm, stable linguistic nucleus of an officially recognized literary language, or else defending an already formed language from the pressure of growing heteroglossia. What we have in mind here is not an abstract linguistic minimum of a common language, in the sense of a system of elementary forms (linguistic symbols) guaranteeing a *minimum* level of comprehension in practical communication. We are taking language not as a system of abstract grammatical categories, but rather language conceived as ideologically saturated, language as a world view, even as a concrete opinion, insuring a *maximum* of mutual understanding in all spheres of ideological life. Thus a unitary language gives expression to forces working toward concrete verbal and ideological unification and centralization, which develop in vital connection with the processes of sociopolitical and cultural centralization.

Aristotelian poetics, the poetics of Augustine, the poetics of the medieval church, of "the one language of truth," the Cartesian poetics of neoclassicism, the abstract grammatical universalism of Leibniz (the idea of a "universal grammar"), Humboldt's insistence on the concrete—all these, whatever their differences in nuance, give expression to the same centripetal forces in sociolinguistic and ideological life; they serve one and the same project of centralizing and unifying the European languages. The victory of one reigning language (dialect) over the others, the supplanting of languages, their enslavement, the process of illuminating them with the True Word, the incorporation of barbarians and lower social strata into a unitary language of culture and truth, the canonization of ideological systems, philology with its methods of studying and teaching dead languages, languages that were by that very fact "unities," Indo-European linguistics with its focus of attention, directed away from language plurality to a single proto-language—all this determined the content and power of the category of "unitary language" in linguistic and stylistic thought, and determined its creative, style-shaping role in the majority of the poetic genres that coalesced in the channel formed by those same centripetal forces of verbal-ideological life.

But the centripetal forces of the life of language, embodied in a "unitary language," operate in the midst of heteroglossia. At any given moment of its evolution, language is stratified not only into linguistic dialects in the strict sense of the word (according to formal linguistic markers, especially phonetic), but also—and for us this is the essential point—into languages that are socio-ideological: languages of social groups, "professional" and "generic" languages, languages of generations and so forth. From this point of view, literary language itself is only one of these heteroglot languages—and in its turn is also stratified into languages (generic, period-bound and others). And this stratification and heteroglossia, once realized, is not only a static invariant of linguistic life, but also what insures its dynamics: stratification and heteroglossia widen and deepen as long as language is alive and developing. Alongside the centripetal forces, the centrifugal forces of language carry on their uninterrupted work; alongside verbal-ideological centralization and unification, the uninterrupted processes of decentralization and disunification go forward.

Every concrete utterance of a speaking subject serves as a point where centrifugal as well as centripetal forces are brought to bear. The processes of centralization and decentralization, of unification and disunification, intersect in the utterance; the utterance not only answers the requirements of its own language as an individualized embodiment of a speech act, but it answers the requirements of heteroglossia as well; it is in fact an active participant in such speech diversity. And this active participation of every utterance in living heteroglossia determines the linguistic profile and style of the utterance to no less a degree than its inclusion in any normative-centralizing system of a unitary language.

Every utterance participates in the "unitary language" (in its centripetal forces and tendencies) and at the same time partakes of social and historical heteroglossia (the centrifugal, stratifying forces).

Such is the fleeting language of a day, of an epoch, a social group, a genre, a school and so forth. It is possible to give a concrete and detailed analysis of any utterance, once having exposed it as a contradiction-ridden, tension-filled unity of two embattled tendencies in the life of language.

The authentic environment of an utterance, the environment in which it lives and takes shape, is dialogized heteroglossia, anonymous and social as language, but simultaneously concrete, filled with specific content and accented as an individual utterance.

At the time when major divisions of the poetic genres were developing under the influence of the unifying, centralizing, centripetal forces of verbal-ideological life, the novel—and those artistic-prose genres that gravitate toward it—was being historically shaped by the current of decentralizing, centrifugal forces. At the time when poetry was accomplishing the task of cultural, national and political centralization of the verbal-ideological world in the higher official socio-ideological levels, on the lower levels, on the stages of local fairs and at buffoon spectacles, the heteroglossia of the clown sounded forth, ridiculing all "languages" and dialects; there developed the literature of the *fabliaux* and *Schwänke* of street songs, folksayings, anecdotes, where there was no language-center at all, where there was to be found a lively play with the "languages" of poets, scholars, monks, knights and others, where all "languages" were masks and where no language could claim to be an authentic, incontestable face.

Heteroglossia, as organized in these low genres, was not merely heteroglossia vis-à-vis the accepted literary language (in all its various generic expressions), that is, vis-à-vis the linguistic center of the verbal-ideological life of the nation and the epoch, but was a heteroglossia consciously opposed to this literary language. It was parodic, and aimed sharply and polemically against the official languages of its given time. It was heteroglossia that had been dialogized.

Linguistics, stylistics and the philosophy of language that were born and shaped by the current of centralizing tendencies in the life of language have ignored this dialogized heteroglossia, in which is embodied the centrifugal forces in the life of language. For this very reason they could make no provision for the dialogic nature of language, which was a struggle among socio-linguistic points of view, not an intra-language struggle between individual wills or logical contradictions. Moreover, even intra-language dialogue (dramatic, rhetorical, cognitive or merely casual) has hardly been studied linguistically or stylistically up to the present day. One might even say outright that the dialogic aspect of discourse and all the phenomena connected with it have remained to the present moment beyond the ken of linguistics.

Stylistics has been likewise completely deaf to dialogue. A literary work has been conceived by stylistics as if it were a hermetic and self-sufficient whole, one whose elements constitute a closed system presuming nothing beyond themselves, no other utterances. The system comprising an artistic work was thought to be analogous with the system of a language, a system that could not stand in a dialogic interrelationship with other languages. From the point of view of stylistics, the artistic work as a whole—whatever that whole might be—is a self-sufficient and closed authorial monologue, one that presumes only passive listeners beyond its own boundaries. Should we imagine the work as a rejoinder in a given dialogue, whose style is determined by its interrelationship with other rejoinders in the same dialogue (in the totality of the conversation)—then traditional stylistics does not offer an adequate means for approaching such a dialogized style. The sharpest and externally most marked manifestations of this stylistic category—the polemical style, the parodic, the ironic—are usually classified as rhetorical and not as poetic phenomena. Stylistics locks every stylistic phenomenon into the monologic context of a given self-sufficient and hermetic utterance, imprisoning it, as it were, in the dungeon of a single context; it is not able to exchange messages with other utterances; it is not able to realize its own stylistic implications in a relationship with them; it is obliged to exhaust itself in its own single hermetic context.

Linguistics, stylistics and the philosophy of language—as forces in the service of the great centralizing tendencies of European verbal-ideological life—have sought first and foremost for *unity* in diversity. This exclusive "orientation toward unity" in the present and past life of languages has concentrated the attention of philosophical and linguistic thought on the firmest, most stable, least changeable and most mono-semic aspects of discourse—on the *phonetic* aspects first of all—that are furthest removed from the changing socio-semantic spheres of discourse. Real ideologically saturated "language consciousness," one that participates in actual heteroglossia and multi-languagedness, has remained outside its field of vision. It is precisely this orientation toward unity that has compelled scholars to ignore all the verbal genres (quotidian, rhetorical, artistic-prose) that were the carriers of the decentralizing tendencies in the life of language, or that were in any case too fundamentally implicated in heteroglossia. The expression of this hetero- as well as polyglot consciousness in the specific forms and phenomena of verbal life remained utterly without determinative influence on linguistics and stylistic thought.

Therefore proper theoretical recognition and illumination could not be found for the specific feel for language and discourse that one gets in stylizations, in *skaz*, in parodies and in various forms of verbal masquerade, "not talking straight," and in the more complex artistic forms for the organization of contradiction, forms that orchestrate their themes by means of languages—in all characteristic and profound models of novelistic prose, in Grimmelshausen, Cervantes, Rabelais, Fielding, Smollett, Sterne and others.

The problem of stylistics for the novel inevitably leads to the necessity of engaging a series of fundamental questions concerning the philosophy of discourse, questions connected with those aspects in the life of discourse that have had no light cast on them by linguistic and stylistic thought—that is, we must deal with the life and behavior of discourse in a contradictory and multi-languaged world.

Discourse in Poetry and Discourse in the Novel

For the philosophy of language, for linguistics and for stylistics structured on their base, a whole series of phenomena have therefore remained almost entirely beyond the realm of consideration: these include the specific phenomena that are present in discourse and that are determined by its dialogic orientation, first, amid others' utterances inside a *single* language (the primordial dialogism of discourse), amid other "social languages" within a single *national* language and finally amid different national languages within the same *culture*, that is, the same socio-ideological conceptual horizon.[7]

In recent decades, it is true, these phenomena have begun to attract the attention of scholars in language and stylistics, but their fundamental and wide-ranging significance in all spheres of the life of discourse is still far from acknowledged.

The dialogic orientation of a word among other words (of all kinds and degrees of otherness) creates new and significant artistic potential in discourse, creates the potential for a distinctive art of prose, which has found its fullest and deepest expression in the novel.

7. Linguistics acknowledges only a mechanical reciprocal influencing and intermixing of languages, (that is, one that is unconscious and determined by social conditions) which is reflected in abstract linguistic elements (phonetic and morphological).

We will focus our attention here on various forms and degrees of dialogic orientation in discourse, and on the special potential for a distinctive prose-art.

As treated by traditional stylistic thought, the word acknowledges only itself (that is, only its own context), its own object, its own direct expression and its own unitary and singular language. It acknowledges another word, one lying outside its own context, only as the neutral word of language, as the word of no one in particular, as simply the potential for speech. The direct word, as traditional stylistics understands it, encounters in its orientation toward the object only the resistance of the object itself (the impossibility of its being exhausted by a word, the impossibility of saying it all), but it does not encounter in its path toward the object the fundamental and richly varied opposition of another's word. No one hinders this word, no one argues with it.

But no living word relates to its object in a *singular* way: between the word and its object, between the word and the speaking subject, there exists an elastic environment of other, alien words about the same object, the same theme, and this is an environment that it is often difficult to penetrate. It is precisely in the process of living interaction with this specific environment that the word may be individualized and given stylistic shape.

Indeed, any concrete discourse (utterance) finds the object at which it was directed already as it were overlain with qualifications, open to dispute, charged with value, already enveloped in an obscuring mist—or, on the contrary, by the "light" of alien words that have already been spoken about it. It is entangled, shot through with shared thoughts, points of view, alien value judgments and accents. The word, directed toward its object, enters a dialogically agitated and tension-filled environment of alien words, value judgments and accents, weaves in and out of complex interrelationships, merges with some, recoils from others, intersects with yet a third group: and all this may crucially shape discourse, may leave a trace in all its semantic layers, may complicate its expression and influence its entire stylistic profile.

The living utterance, having taken meaning and shape at a particular historical moment in a socially specific environment, cannot fail to brush up against thousands of living dialogic threads, woven by socio-ideological consciousness around the given object of an utterance; it cannot fail to become an active participant in social dialogue. After all, the utterance arises out of this dialogue as a continuation of it and as a rejoinder to it—it does not approach the object from the sidelines.

The way in which the word conceptualizes its object is a complex act—all objects, open to dispute and overlain as they are with qualifications, are from one side highlighted while from the other side dimmed by heteroglot social opinion, by an alien word about them.[8] And into this complex play of light and shadow the word enters—it becomes saturated with this play, and must determine within it the boundaries of its own semantic and stylistic contours. The way in which the word conceives its object is complicated by a dialogic interaction within the object between various aspects of its socio-verbal intelligibility. And an artistic representation, an "image" of the object, may be penetrated by this dialogic play of verbal intentions that meet and are interwoven in it; such an image need not stifle these forces, but on the contrary may activate and organize them. If we imagine the *intention* of such a word, that is, its *directionality toward the object,* in the form of a ray of light, then the living and unrepeatable play of colors and light on the facets of the image that it constructs can be explained as the spectral dispersion of the ray-word, not within the object itself (as would be the case in the play of an image-as-trope, in poetic speech taken in the narrow sense, in an "autotelic word"), but rather as its spectral dispersion in an atmosphere filled with the alien words, value judgments and accents through which the ray passes on its way toward the object; the social atmosphere of the word, the atmosphere that surrounds the object, makes the facets of the image sparkle.

The word, breaking through to its own meaning and its own expression across an environment full of alien words and variously evaluating accents, harmonizing with some of the elements in this environment and striking a dissonance with others, is able, in this dialogized process, to shape its own stylistic profile and tone.

Such is the *image in artistic prose* and the image of *novelistic*

8. Highly significant in this respect is the struggle that must be undertaken in such movements as Rousseauism, Naturalism, Impressionism, Acmeism, Dadaism, Surrealism and analogous schools with the "qualified" nature of the object (a struggle occasioned by the idea of a return to primordial consciousness, to original consciousness, to the object itself in itself, to pure perception and so forth).

prose in particular. In the atmosphere of the novel, the direct and unmediated intention of a word presents itself as something impermissably naive, something in fact impossible, for naiveté itself, under authentic novelistic conditions, takes on the nature of an internal polemic and is consequently dialogized (in, for example, the work of the Sentimentalists, in Chateaubriand and in Tolstoy). Such a dialogized image can occur in all the poetic genres as well, even in the lyric (to be sure, without setting the tone).[9] But such an image can fully unfold, achieve full complexity and depth and at the same time artistic closure, only under the conditions present in the genre of the novel.

In the poetic image narrowly conceived (in the image-as-trope), all activity—the dynamics of the image-as-word—is completely exhausted by the play between the word (with all its aspects) and the object (in all its aspects). The word plunges into the inexhaustible wealth and contradictory multiplicity of the object itself, with its "virginal," still "unuttered" nature; therefore it presumes nothing beyond the borders of its own context (except, of course, what can be found in the treasure-house of language itself). The word forgets that its object has its own history of contradictory acts of verbal recognition, as well as that heteroglossia that is always present in such acts of recognition.

For the writer of artistic prose, on the contrary, the object reveals first of all precisely the socially heteroglot multiplicity of its names, definitions and value judgments. Instead of the virginal fullness and inexhaustibility of the object itself, the prose writer confronts a multitude of routes, roads and paths that have been laid down in the object by social consciousness. Along with the internal contradictions inside the object itself, the prose writer witnesses as well the unfolding of social heteroglossia *surrounding* the object, the Tower-of-Babel mixing of languages that goes on around any object; the dialectics of the object are interwoven with the social dialogue surrounding it. For the prose writer, the object is a focal point for heteroglot voices among which his own voice must also sound; these voices create the background necessary for his own voice, outside of which his artistic prose nuances cannot be perceived, and without which they "do not sound."

The prose artist elevates the social heteroglossia surrounding objects into an image that has finished contours, an image com-

9. The Horatian lyric, Villon, Heine, Laforgue, Annenskij and others—despite the fact that these are extremely varied instances.

pletely shot through with dialogized overtones; he creates artistically calculated nuances on all the fundamental voices and tones of this heteroglossia. But as we have already said, every extra-artistic prose discourse—in any of its forms, quotidian, rhetorical, scholarly—cannot fail to be oriented toward the "already uttered," the "already known," the "common opinion" and so forth. The dialogic orientation of discourse is a phenomenon that is, of course, a property of *any* discourse. It is the natural orientation of any living discourse. On all its various routes toward the object, in all its directions, the word encounters an alien word and cannot help encountering it in a living, tension-filled interaction. Only the mythical Adam, who approached a virginal and as yet verbally unqualified world with the first word, could really have escaped from start to finish this dialogic inter-orientation with the alien word that occurs in the object. Concrete historical human discourse does not have this privilege: it can deviate from such inter-orientation only on a conditional basis and only to a certain degree.

It is all the more remarkable that linguistics and the philosophy of discourse have been primarily oriented precisely toward this artificial, preconditioned status of the word, a word excised from dialogue and taken for the norm (although the primacy of dialogue over monologue is frequently proclaimed). Dialogue is studied merely as a compositional form in the structuring of speech, but the internal dialogism of the word (which occurs in a monologic utterance as well as in a rejoinder), the dialogism that penetrates its entire structure, all its semantic and expressive layers, is almost entirely ignored. But it is precisely this internal dialogism of the word, which does not assume any external compositional forms of dialogue, that cannot be isolated as an independent act, separate from the word's ability to form a concept [koncipirovanie] of its object—it is precisely this internal dialogism that has such enormous power to shape style. The internal dialogism of the word finds expression in a series of peculiar features in semantics, syntax and stylistics that have remained up to the present time completely unstudied by linguistics and stylistics (nor, what is more, have the peculiar semantic features of ordinary dialogue been studied).

The word is born in a dialogue as a living rejoinder within it; the word is shaped in dialogic interaction with an alien word that is already in the object. A word forms a concept of its own object in a dialogic way.

But this does not exhaust the internal dialogism of the word. It encounters an alien word not only in the object itself: every word is directed toward an *answer* and cannot escape the profound influence of the answering word that it anticipates.

The word in living conversation is directly, blatantly, oriented toward a future answer-word: it provokes an answer, anticipates it and structures itself in the answer's direction. Forming itself in an atmosphere of the already spoken, the word is at the same time determined by that which has not yet been said but which is needed and in fact anticipated by the answering word. Such is the situation in any living dialogue.

All rhetorical forms, monologic in their compositional structure, are oriented toward the listener and his answer. This orientation toward the listener is usually considered the basic constitutive feature of rhetorical discourse.[10] It is highly significant for rhetoric that this relationship toward the concrete listener, taking him into account, is a relationship that enters into the very internal construction of rhetorical discourse. This orientation toward an answer is open, blatant and concrete.

This open orientation toward the listener and his answer in everyday dialogue and in rhetorical forms has attracted the attention of linguists. But even where this has been the case, linguists have by and large gotten no further than the compositional forms by which the listener is taken into account; they have not sought influence springing from more profound meaning and style. They have taken into consideration only those aspects of style determined by demands for comprehensibility and clarity—that is, precisely those aspects that are deprived of any internal dialogism, that take the listener for a person who passively understands but not for one who actively answers and reacts.

The listener and his response are regularly taken into account when it comes to everyday dialogue and rhetoric, but every other sort of discourse as well is oriented toward an understanding that is "responsive"—although this orientation is not particularized in an independent act and is not compositionally marked. Responsive understanding is a fundamental force, one that participates in the formulation of discourse, and it is moreover an *active*

10. Cf. V. Vinogradov's book *On Artistic Prose*, the chapter "Rhetoric and Poetics," pp. 75ff., where definitions taken from the older rhetorics are introduced.

understanding, one that discourse senses as resistance or support enriching the discourse.

Linguistics and the philosophy of language acknowledge only a passive understanding of discourse, and moreover this takes place by and large on the level of common language, that is, it is an understanding of an utterance's *neutral signification* and not its *actual meaning*.

The linguistic significance of a given utterance is understood against the background of language, while its actual meaning is understood against the background of other concrete utterances on the same theme, a background made up of contradictory opinions, points of view and value judgments—that is, precisely that background that, as we see, complicates the path of any word toward its object. Only now this contradictory environment of alien words is present to the speaker not in the object, but rather in the consciousness of the listener, as his apperceptive background, pregnant with responses and objections. And every utterance is oriented toward this apperceptive background of understanding, which is not a linguistic background but rather one composed of specific objects and emotional expressions. There occurs a new encounter between the utterance and an alien word, which makes itself felt as a new and unique influence on its style.

A passive understanding of linguistic meaning is no understanding at all, it is only the abstract aspect of meaning. But even a more concrete *passive* understanding of the meaning of the utterance, an understanding of the speaker's intention insofar as that understanding remains purely passive, purely receptive, contributes nothing new to the word under consideration, only mirroring it, seeking, at its most ambitious, merely the full reproduction of that which is already given in the word—even such an understanding never goes beyond the boundaries of the word's context and in no way enriches the word. Therefore, insofar as the speaker operates with such a passive understanding, nothing new can be introduced into his discourse; there can be no new aspects in his discourse relating to concrete objects and emotional expressions. Indeed the purely negative demands, such as could only emerge from a passive understanding (for instance, a need for greater clarity, more persuasiveness, more vividness and so forth), leave the speaker in his own personal context, within his own boundaries; such negative demands are completely immanent in the speaker's own discourse and do not go beyond his semantic or expressive self-sufficiency.

In the actual life of speech, every concrete act of understanding is active: it assimilates the word to be understood into its own conceptual system filled with specific objects and emotional expressions, and is indissolubly merged with the response, with a motivated agreement or disagreement. To some extent, primacy belongs to the response, as the activating principle: it creates the ground for understanding, it prepares the ground for an active and engaged understanding. Understanding comes to fruition only in the response. Understanding and response are dialectically merged and mutually condition each other; one is impossible without the other.

Thus an active understanding, one that assimilates the word under consideration into a new conceptual system, that of the one striving to understand, establishes a series of complex interrelationships, consonances and dissonances with the word and enriches it with new elements. It is precisely such an understanding that the speaker counts on. Therefore his orientation toward the listener is an orientation toward a specific conceptual horizon, toward the specific world of the listener; it introduces totally new elements into his discourse; it is in this way, after all, that various different points of view, conceptual horizons, systems for providing expressive accents, various social "languages" come to interact with one another. The speaker strives to get a reading on his own word, and on his own conceptual system that determines this word, within the alien conceptual system of the understanding receiver; he enters into dialogical relationships with certain aspects of this system. The speaker breaks through the alien conceptual horizon of the listener, constructs his own utterance on alien territory, against his, the listener's, apperceptive background.

This new form of internal dialogism of the word is different from that form determined by an encounter with an alien word within the object itself: here it is not the object that serves as the arena for the encounter, but rather the subjective belief system of the listener. Thus this dialogism bears a more subjective, psychological and (frequently) random character, sometimes crassly accommodating, sometimes provocatively polemical. Very often, especially in the rhetorical forms, this orientation toward the listener and the related internal dialogism of the word may simply overshadow the object: the strong point of any concrete listener becomes a self-sufficient focus of attention, and one that interferes with the word's creative work on its referent.

Although they differ in their essentials and give rise to varying stylistic effects in discourse, the dialogic relationship toward an alien word within the object and the relationship toward an alien word in the anticipated answer of the listener can, nevertheless, be very tightly interwoven with each other, becoming almost indistinguishable during stylistic analysis.

Thus, discourse in Tolstoy is characterized by a sharp internal dialogism, and this discourse is moreover dialogized in the belief system of the reader—whose peculiar semantic and expressive characteristics Tolstoy acutely senses—as well as in the object. These two lines of dialogization (having in most cases polemical overtones) are tightly interwoven in his style: even in the most "lyrical" expressions and the most "epic" descriptions, Tolstoy's discourse harmonizes and disharmonizes (more often disharmonizes) with various aspects of the heteroglot socio-verbal consciousness ensnaring the object, while at the same time polemically invading the reader's belief and evaluative system, striving to stun and destroy the apperceptive background of the reader's active understanding. In this respect Tolstoy is an heir of the eighteenth century, especially of Rousseau. This propagandizing impulse sometimes leads to a narrowing-down of heteroglot social consciousness (against which Tolstoy polemicizes) to the consciousness of his immediate contemporary, a contemporary of the day and not of the epoch; what follows from this is a radical concretization of dialogization (almost always undertaken in the service of a polemic). For this reason Tolstoy's dialogization, no matter how acutely we sense it in the expressive profile of his style, sometimes requires special historical or literary commentary: we are not sure with *what* precisely a given tone is in harmony or disharmony, for this dissonance or consonance has entered into the positive project of creating a style.[11] It is true that such extreme concreteness (which approaches at time the feuilleton) is present only in those secondary aspects, the overtones of internal dialogization in Tolstoy's discourse.

In those examples of the internal dialogization of discourse that we have chosen (the internal, as contrasted with the external, compositionally marked, dialogue) the relationship to the alien word, to an alien utterance enters into the positing of the

11. Cf. B. M. Eichenbaum's book *Lev Tolstoj*, book 1 (Leningrad, 1928), which contains much relevant material; for example, an explication of the topical context of "Family Happiness."

style. Style organically contains within itself indices that reach outside itself, a correspondence of its own elements and the elements of an alien context. The internal politics of style (how the elements are put together) is determined by its external politics (its relationship to alien discourse). Discourse lives, as it were, on the boundary between its own context and another, alien, context.

In any actual dialogue the rejoinder also leads such a double life: it is structured and conceptualized in the context of the dialogue as a whole, which consists of its own utterances ("own" from the point of view of the speaker) and of alien utterances (those of the partner). One cannot excise the rejoinder from this combined context made up of one's own words and the words of another without losing its sense and tone. It is an organic part of a heteroglot unity.

The phenomenon of internal dialogization, as we have said, is present to a greater or lesser extent in all realms of the life of the word. But if in extra-artistic prose (everyday, rhetorical, scholarly) dialogization usually stands apart, crystallizes into a special kind of act of its own and runs its course in ordinary dialogue or in other, compositionally clearly marked forms for mixing and polemicizing with the discourse of another—then in *artistic* prose, and especially in the novel, this dialogization penetrates from within the very way in which the word conceives its object and its means for expressing itself, reformulating the semantics and syntactical structure of discourse. Here dialogic inter-orientation becomes, as it were, an event of discourse itself, animating from within and dramatizing discourse in all its aspects.

In the majority of poetic genres (poetic in the narrow sense), as we have said, the internal dialogization of discourse is not put to artistic use, it does not enter into the work's "aesthetic object," and is artificially extinguished in poetic discourse. In the novel, however, this internal dialogization becomes one of the most fundamental aspects of prose style and undergoes a specific artistic elaboration.

But internal dialogization can become such a crucial force for creating form only where individual differences and contradictions are enriched by social heteroglossia, where dialogic reverberations do not sound in the semantic heights of discourse (as happens in the rhetorical genres) but penetrate the deep strata of discourse, dialogize language itself and the world view a particular language has (the internal form of discourse)—where the dialogue of voices arises directly out of a social dialogue of "languages," where an alien utterance begins to sound like a socially alien language, where the orientation of the word among alien utterances changes into an orientation of a word among socially alien languages within the boundaries of one and the same national language.

In genres that are poetic in the narrow sense, the natural dialogization of the word is not put to artistic use, the word is sufficient unto itself and does not presume alien utterances beyond its own boundaries. Poetic style is by convention suspended from any mutual interaction with alien discourse, any allusion to alien discourse.

Any way whatever of alluding to alien languages, to the possibility of another vocabulary, another semantics, other syntactic forms and so forth, to the possibility of other linguistic points of view, is equally foreign to poetic style. It follows that any sense of the boundedness, the historicity, the social determination and specificity of one's own language is alien to poetic style, and therefore a critical qualified relationship to one's own language (as merely one of many languages in a heteroglot world) is foreign to poetic style—as is a related phenomenon, the incomplete commitment of oneself, of one's full meaning, to a given language.

Of course this relationship and the relationship to his own language (in greater or lesser degree) could never be foreign to a historically existent poet, as a human being surrounded by living hetero- and polyglossia; but this relationship could not find a place in the *poetic style* of his work without destroying that style, without transposing it into a prosaic key and in the process turning the poet into a writer of prose.

In poetic genres, artistic consciousness—understood as a unity of all the author's semantic and expressive intentions—fully realizes itself within its own language; in them alone is such consciousness fully immanent, expressing itself in it directly and without mediation, without conditions and without distance. The language of the poet is *his* language, he is utterly immersed in it, inseparable from it, he makes use of each form, each word, each expression according to its unmediated power to assign meaning (as it were, "without quotation marks"), that is, as a pure and direct expression of his own intention. No matter what "agonies of the word" the poet endured in the process of creation, in the finished work language is an obedient organ, fully adequate to the author's intention.

The language in a poetic work realizes itself as something about which there can be no doubt, something that cannot be disputed, something all-encompassing. Everything that the poet sees, understands and thinks, he does through the eyes of a given language, in its inner forms, and there is nothing that might require, for its expression, the help of any other or alien language. The language of the poetic genre is a unitary and singular Ptolemaic world outside of which nothing else exists and nothing else is needed. The concept of many worlds of language, all equal in their ability to conceptualize and to be expressive, is organically denied to poetic style.

The world of poetry, no matter how many contradictions and insoluble conflicts the poet develops within it, is always illumined by one unitary and indisputable discourse. Contradictions, conflicts and doubts remain in the object, in thoughts, in living experiences—in short, in the subject matter—but they do not enter into the language itself. In poetry, even discourse about doubts must be cast in a discourse that cannot be doubted.

To take responsibility for the language of the work as a whole at all of its points as *its* language, to assume a full solidarity with each of the work's aspects, tones, nuances—such is the fundamental prerequisite for poetic style; style so conceived is fully adequate to a single language and a single linguistic consciousness. The poet is not able to oppose his own poetic consciousness, his own intentions to the language that he uses, for he is completely within it and therefore cannot turn it into an object to be perceived, reflected upon or related to. Language is present to him only from inside, in the work it does to effect its intention, and not from outside, in its objective specificity and boundedness. Within the limits of poetic style, direct unconditional intentionality, language at its full weight and the objective display of language (as a socially and historically limited linguistic reality) are all simultaneous, but incompatible. The unity and singularity of language are the indispensable prerequisites for a realization of the direct (but not objectively typifying) intentional individuality of poetic style and of its monologic steadfastness.

This does not mean, of course, that heteroglossia or even a foreign language is completely shut out of a poetic work. To be sure, such possibilities are limited: a certain latitude for heteroglossia exists only in the "low" poetic genres—in the satiric and comic genres and others. Nevertheless, heteroglossia (other socio-ideological languages) can be introduced into purely poetic genres, primarily in the speeches of characters. But in such a context it is objective. It appears, in essence, as a *thing*, it does not lie on the *same* plane with the real language of the work: it is the depicted gesture of one of the characters and does not appear as an aspect of the word doing the depicting. Elements of heteroglossia enter here not in the capacity of another language carrying its own particular points of view, about which one can say things not expressible in one's own language, but rather in the capacity of a depicted thing. Even when speaking of alien things, the poet speaks in his own language. To shed light on an alien world, he never resorts to an alien language, even though it might in fact be more adequate to that world. Whereas the writer of prose, by contrast—as we shall see—attempts to talk about even his *own* world in an alien language (for example, in the nonliterary language of the teller of tales, or the representative of a specific socio-ideological group); he often measures his own world by alien linguistic standards.

As a consequence of the prerequisites mentioned above, the language of poetic genres, when they approach their stylistic limit,[12] often becomes authoritarian, dogmatic and conservative, sealing itself off from the influence of extraliterary social dialects. Therefore such ideas as a special "poetic language," a "language of the gods," a "priestly language of poetry" and so forth could flourish on poetic soil. It is noteworthy that the poet, should he not accept the given literary language, will sooner resort to the artificial creation of a new language specifically for poetry than he will to the exploitation of actual available social dialects. Social languages are filled with specific objects, typical, socially localized and limited, while the artificially created language of poetry must be a directly intentional language, unitary and singular. Thus, when Russian prose writers at the beginning of the twen-

---

12. It goes without saying that we continually advance as typical the extreme to which poetic genres aspire; in concrete examples of poetic works it is possible to find features fundamental to prose, and numerous hybrids of various generic types exist. These are especially widespread in periods of shift in literary poetic languages.

tieth century began to show a profound interest in dialects and *skaz*, the Symbolists (Bal'mont, V. Ivanov) and later the Futurists dreamed of creating a special "language of poetry," and even made experiments directed toward creating such a language (those of V. Khlebnikov).

The idea of a special unitary and singular language of poetry is a typical utopian philosopheme of poetic discourse: it is grounded in the actual conditions and demands of poetic style, which is always a style adequately serviced by one directly intentional language from whose point of view other languages (conversational, business and prose languages, among others) are perceived as objects that are in no way its equal.[13] The idea of a "poetic language" is yet another expression of that same Ptolemaic conception of the linguistic and stylistic world.

Language—like the living concrete environment in which the consciousness of the verbal artist lives—is never unitary. It is unitary only as an abstract grammatical system of normative forms, taken in isolation from the concrete, ideological conceptualizations that fill it, and in isolation from the uninterrupted process of historical becoming that is a characteristic of all living language. Actual social life and historical becoming create within an abstractly unitary national language a multitude of concrete worlds, a multitude of bounded verbal-ideological and social belief systems; within these various systems (identical in the abstract) are elements of language filled with various semantic and axiological content and each with its own different sound.

Literary language—both spoken and written—although it is unitary not only in its shared, abstract, linguistic markers but also in its forms for conceptualizing these abstract markers, is itself stratified and heteroglot in its aspect as an expressive system, that is, in the forms that carry its meanings.

This stratification is accomplished first of all by the specific organisms called *genres*. Certain features of language (lexicological, semantic, syntactic) will knit together with the intentional aim, and with the overall accentual system inherent in one or another genre: oratorical, publicistic, newspaper and journalistic genres, the genres of low literature (penny dreadfuls, for instance) or, fi-

---

13. Such was the point of view taken by Latin toward national languages in the Middle Ages.

nally, the various genres of high literature. Certain features of language take on the specific flavor of a given genre: they knit together with specific points of view, specific approaches, forms of thinking, nuances and accents characteristic of the given genre.

In addition, there is interwoven with this generic stratification of language a *professional* stratification of language, in the broad sense of the term "professional": the language of the lawyer, the doctor, the businessman, the politician, the public education teacher and so forth, and these sometimes coincide with, and sometimes depart from, the stratification into genres. It goes without saying that these languages differ from each other not only in their vocabularies; they involve specific forms for manifesting intentions, forms for making conceptualization and evaluation concrete. And even the very language of the writer (the poet or novelist) can be taken as a professional jargon on a par with professional jargons.

What is important to us here is the intentional dimensions, that is, the denotative and expressive dimension of the "shared" language's stratification. It is in fact not the neutral linguistic components of language being stratified and differentiated, but rather a situation in which the intentional possibilities of language are being expropriated: these possibilities are realized in specific directions, filled with specific content, they are made concrete, particular, and are permeated with concrete value judgments; they knit together with specific objects and with the belief systems of certain genres of expression and points of view peculiar to particular professions. Within these points of view, that is, for the speakers of the language themselves, these generic languages and professional jargons are directly intentional—they denote and express directly and fully, and are capable of expressing themselves without mediation; but outside, that is, for those not participating in the given purview, these languages may be treated as objects, as typifactions, as local color. For such outsiders, the intentions permeating these languages become *things*, limited in their meaning and expression; they attract to, or excise from, such language a particular word—making it difficult for the word to be utilized in a directly intentional way, without any qualifications.

But the situation is far from exhausted by the generic and professional stratification of the common literary language. Although at its very core literary language is frequently socially homogeneous, as the oral and written language of a dominant social group, there is nevertheless always present, even here, a certain degree of social differentiation, a social stratification, that in other eras can become extremely acute. Social stratification may here and there coincide with generic and professional stratification, but in essence it is, of course, a thing completely autonomous and peculiar to itself.

Social stratification is also and primarily determined by differences between the forms used to convey meaning and between the expressive planes of various belief systems—that is, stratification expresses itself in typical differences in ways used to conceptualize and accentuate elements of language, and stratification may not violate the abstractly linguistic dialectological unity of the shared literary language.

What is more, all socially significant world views have the capacity to exploit the intentional possibilities of language through the medium of their specific concrete instancing. Various tendencies (artistic and otherwise), circles, journals, particular newspapers, even particular significant artistic works and individual persons are all capable of stratifying language, in proportion to their social significance; they are capable of attracting its words and forms into their orbit by means of their own characteristic intentions and accents, and in so doing to a certain extent alienating these words and forms from other tendencies, parties, artistic works and persons.

Every socially significant verbal performance has the ability— sometimes for a long period of time, and for a wide circle of persons—to infect with its own intention certain aspects of language that had been affected by its semantic and expressive impulse, imposing on them specific semantic nuances and specific axiological overtones; thus, it can create slogan-words, curse-words, praise-words and so forth.

In any given historical moment of verbal-ideological life, each generation at each social level has its own language; moreover, every age group has as a matter of fact its own language, its own vocabulary, its own particular accentual system that, in their turn, vary depending on social level, academic institution (the language of the cadet, the high school student, the trade school student are all different languages) and other stratifying factors. All this is brought about by socially typifying languages, no matter how narrow the social circle in which they are spoken. It is even possible to have a family jargon define the societal limits of a language, as, for instance, the jargon of the Irtenevs in Tolstoy, with its special vocabulary and unique accentual system.

And finally, at any given moment, languages of various epochs and periods of socio-ideological life cohabit with one another. Even languages of the day exist: one could say that today's and yesterday's socio-ideological and political "day" do not, in a certain sense, share the same language; every day represents another socio-ideological semantic "state of affairs," another vocabulary, another accentual system, with its own slogans, its own ways of assigning blame and praise. Poetry depersonalizes "days" in language, while prose, as we shall see, often deliberately intensifies difference between them, gives them embodied representation and dialogically opposes them to one another in unresolvable dialogues.

Thus at any given moment of its historical existence, language is heteroglot from top to bottom: it represents the co-existence of socio-ideological contradictions between the present and the past, between differing epochs of the past, between different socio-ideological groups in the present, between tendencies, schools, circles and so forth, all given a bodily form. These "languages" of heteroglossia intersect each other in a variety of ways, forming new socially typifying "languages."

Each of these "languages" of heteroglossia requires a methodology very different from the others; each is grounded in a completely different principle for marking differences and for establishing units (for some this principle is functional, in others it is the principle of theme and content, in yet others it is, properly speaking, a socio-dialectological principle). Therefore languages do not *exclude* each other, but rather intersect with each other in many different ways (the Ukrainian language, the language of the epic poem, of early Symbolism, of the student, of a particular generation of children, of the run-of-the-mill intellectual, of the Nietzschean and so on). It might even seem that the very word "language" loses all meaning in this process—for apparently there is no single plane on which all these "languages" might be juxtaposed to one another.

In actual fact, however, there does exist a common plane that methodologically justifies our juxtaposing them: all languages of heteroglossia, whatever the principle underlying them and making each unique, are specific points of view on the world, forms for conceptualizing the world in words, specific world views, each characterized by its own objects, meanings and values. As such they all may be juxtaposed to one another, mutually supplement one another, contradict one another and be interrelated dialogically. As such they encounter one another and co-exist in the consciousness of real people—first and foremost, in the creative consciousness of people who write novels. As such, these languages live a real life, they struggle and evolve in an environment of social heteroglossia. Therefore they are all able to enter into the unitary plane of the novel, which can unite in itself parodic stylizations of generic languages, various forms of stylizations and illustrations of professional and period-bound languages, the languages of particular generations, of social dialects and others (as occurs, for example, in the English comic novel). They may all be drawn in by the novelist for the orchestration of his themes and for the refracted (indirect) expression of his intentions and values.

This is why we constantly put forward the referential and expressive—that is, intentional—factors as the force that stratifies and differentiates the common literary language, and not the linguistic markers (lexical coloration, semantic overtones, etc.) of generic languages, professional jargons and so forth—markers that are, so to speak, the sclerotic deposits of an intentional process, signs left behind on the path of the real living project of an intention, of the particular way it imparts meaning to general linguistic norms. These external markers, linguistically observable and fixable, cannot in themselves be understood or studied without understanding the specific conceptualization they have been given by an intention.

Discourse lives, as it were, beyond itself, in a living impulse [*napravlennost'*] toward the object; if we detach ourselves completely from this impulse all we have left is the naked corpse of the word, from which we can learn nothing at all about the social situation or the fate of a given word in life. *To study the word as such, ignoring the impulse that reaches out beyond it, is just as senseless as to study psychological experience outside the context of that real life toward which it was directed and by which it is determined.*

By stressing the intentional dimension of stratification in literary language, we are able, as has been said, to locate in a single series such methodologically heterogeneous phenomena as professional and social dialects, world views and individual artistic works, for in their intentional dimension one finds that common plane on which they can all be juxtaposed, and juxtaposed dialogically. The whole matter consists in the fact that there may be, between "languages," highly specific dialogic relations; no matter how these languages are conceived, they may all be taken as particular points of view on the world. However varied the social forces doing the work of stratification—a profession, a genre, a particular tendency, an individual personality—the work itself everywhere comes down to the (relatively) protracted and socially meaningful (collective) saturation of language with specific (and consequently limiting) intentions and accents. The longer this stratifying saturation goes on, the broader the social circle encompassed by it and consequently the more substantial the social force bringing about such a stratification of language, then the more sharply focused and stable will be those traces, the linguistic changes in the language markers (linguistic symbols), that are left behind in language as a result of this social force's activity—from stable (and consequently social) semantic nuances to authentic dialectological markers (phonetic, morphological and others), which permit us to speak of particular social dialects.

As a result of the work done by all these stratifying forces in language, there are no "neutral" words and forms—words and forms that can belong to "no one"; language has been completely taken over, shot through with intentions and accents. For any individual consciousness living in it, language is not an abstract system of normative forms but rather a concrete heteroglot conception of the world. All words have the "taste" of a profession, a genre, a tendency, a party, a particular work, a particular person, a generation, an age group, the day and hour. Each word tastes of the context and contexts in which it has lived its socially charged life; all words and forms are populated by intentions. Contextual overtones (generic, tendentious, individualistic) are inevitable in the word.

As a living, socio-ideological concrete thing, as heteroglot opinion, language, for the individual consciousness, lies on the borderline between oneself and the other. The word in language is half someone else's. It becomes "one's own" only when the speaker populates it with his own intention, his own accent, when he appropriates the word, adapting it to his own semantic and expressive intention. Prior to this moment of appropriation, the word does not exist in a neutral and impersonal language (it is not, after all, out of a dictionary that the speaker gets his words!), but rather it exists in other people's mouths, in other people's contexts, serving other people's intentions: it is from there that one must take the word, and make it one's own. And not all words for just anyone submit equally easily to this appropriation, to this seizure and transformation into private property: many words stubbornly resist, others remain alien, sound foreign in the mouth of the one who appropriated them and who now speaks them; they cannot be assimilated into his context and fall out of it; it is as if they put themselves in quotation marks against the will of the speaker. Language is not a neutral medium that passes freely and easily into the private property of the speaker's intentions; it is populated—overpopulated—with the intentions of others. Expropriating it, forcing it to submit to one's own intentions and accents, is a difficult and complicated process.

We have so far proceeded on the assumption of the abstract-linguistic (dialectological) unity of literary language. But even a literary language is anything but a closed dialect. Within the scope of literary language itself there is already a more or less sharply defined boundary between everyday-conversational language and written language. Distinctions between genres frequently coincide with dialectological distinctions (for example, the high—Church Slavonic—and the low—conversational—genres of the eighteenth century); finally, certain dialects may be legitimized in literature and thus to a certain extent be appropriated by literary language.

As they enter literature and are appropriated to literary language, dialects in this new context lose, of course, the quality of closed socio-linguistic systems; they are deformed and in fact cease to be that which they had been simply as dialects. On the other hand, these dialects, on entering the literary language and preserving within it their own dialectological elasticity, their other-languagedness, have the effect of deforming the literary language; it, too, ceases to be that which it had been, a closed socio-linguistic system. Literary language is a highly distinctive phenomenon, as is the linguistic consciousness of the educated person who is its agent; within it, intentional diversity of speech [*raznorečivost'*] (which is present in every living dialect as a closed system) is transformed into diversity of language [*raznojazyčie*]; what results is not a single language but a dialogue of languages.

The national literary language of a people with a highly developed art of prose, especially if it is novelistic prose with a rich and tension-filled verbal-ideological history, is in fact an organized microcosm that reflects the macrocosm not only of national heteroglossia, but of European heteroglossia as well. The unity of a literary language is not a unity of a single, closed language system, but is rather a highly specific unity of several "languages" that have established contact and mutual recognition with each other (merely one of which is poetic language in the narrow sense). Precisely this constitutes the peculiar nature of the methodological problem in literary language.

Concrete socio-ideological language consciousness, as it becomes creative—that is, as it becomes active as literature—discovers itself already surrounded by heteroglossia and not at all a single, unitary language, inviolable and indisputable. The actively literary linguistic consciousness at all times and everywhere (that is, in all epochs of literature historically available to us) comes upon "languages," and not language. Consciousness finds itself inevitably facing the necessity of *having to choose a language*. With each literary-verbal performance, consciousness must actively orient itself amidst heteroglossia, it must move in and occupy a position for itself within it, it chooses, in other words, a "language." Only by remaining in a closed environment, one without writing or thought, completely off the maps of socio-ideological becoming, could a man fail to sense this activity of selecting a language and rest assured in the inviolability of his own language, the conviction that his language is predetermined.

Even such a man, however, deals not in fact with a single language, but with languages—except that the place occupied by each of these languages is fixed and indisputable, the movement from one to the other is predetermined and not a thought process; it is as if these languages were in different chambers. They do not collide with each other in his consciousness, there is no attempt to coordinate them, to look at one of these languages through the eyes of another language.

Thus an illiterate peasant, miles away from any urban center, naively immersed in an unmoving and for him unshakable everyday world, nevertheless lived in several language systems: he prayed to God in one language (Church Slavonic), sang songs in another, spoke to his family in a third and, when he began to dictate petitions to the local authorities through a scribe, he tried speaking yet a fourth language (the official-literate language, "paper" language). All these are *different languages*, even from the point of view of abstract socio-dialectological markers. But these languages were not dialogically coordinated in the linguistic consciousness of the peasant; he passed from one to the other without thinking, automatically: each was indisputably in its own place, and the place of each was indisputable. He was not yet able to regard one language (and the verbal world corresponding to it) through the eyes of another language (that is, the language of everyday life and the everyday world with the language of prayer or song, or vice versa).[14]

As soon as a critical interanimation of languages began to occur in the consciousness of our peasant, as soon as it became clear that these were not only various different languages but even internally variegated languages, that the ideological systems and approaches to the world that were indissolubly connected with these languages contradicted each other and in no way could live in peace and quiet with one another—then the inviolability and predetermined quality of these languages came to an end, and the necessity of actively choosing one's orientation among them began.

The language and world of prayer, the language and world of song, the language and world of labor and everyday life, the specific language and world of local authorities, the new language and world of the workers freshly immigrated to the city—all these languages and worlds sooner or later emerged from a state of peaceful and moribund equilibrium and revealed the speech diversity in each.

Of course the actively literary linguistic consciousness comes upon an even more varied and profound heteroglossia within literary language itself, as well as outside it. Any fundamental study of the stylistic life of the word must begin with this basic fact. The nature of the heteroglossia encountered and the means by which one orients oneself in it determine the concrete stylistic life that the word will lead.

The poet is a poet insofar as he accepts the idea of a unitary and singular language and a unitary, monologically sealed-off utterance. These ideas are immanent in the poetic genres with which

14. We are of course deliberately simplifying: the real-life peasant could and did do this to a certain extent.

he works. In a condition of actual contradiction, these are what determine the means of orientation open to the poet. The poet must assume a complete single-personed hegemony over his own language, he must assume equal responsibility for each one of its aspects and subordinate them to his own, and only his own, intentions. Each word must express the poet's *meaning* directly and without mediation; there must be no distance between the poet and his word. The meaning must emerge from language as a single intentional whole: none of its stratification, its speech diversity, to say nothing of its language diversity, may be reflected in any fundamental way in his poetic work.

To achieve this, the poet strips the word of others' intentions, he uses only such words and forms (and only in such a way) that they lose their link with concrete intentional levels of language and their connection with specific contexts. Behind the words of a poetic work one should not sense any typical or reified images of genres (except for the given poetic genre), nor professions, tendencies, directions (except the direction chosen by the poet himself), nor world views (except for the unitary and singular world view of the poet himself), nor typical and individual images of speaking persons, their speech mannerisms or typical intonations. *Everything that enters the work must immerse itself in Lethe, and forget its previous life in any other contexts: language may remember only its life in poetic contexts (in such contexts, however, even concrete reminiscences are possible).*

Of course there always exists a limited sphere of more or less concrete contexts, and a connection with them must be deliberately evidenced in poetic discourse. But these contexts are purely semantic and, so to speak, accented in the abstract; in their linguistic dimension they are impersonal or at least no particularly concrete linguistic specificity is sensed behind them, no particular manner of speech and so forth, no socially typical linguistic face (the possible personality of the narrator) need peek out from behind them. Everywhere there is only one face—the linguistic face of the author, answering for every word as if it were his own. No matter how multiple and varied these semantic and accentual threads, associations, pointers, hints, correlations that emerge from every poetic word, one language, one conceptual horizon, is sufficient to them all; there is no need of heteroglot social contexts. What is more, the very movement of the poetic symbol (for example, the unfolding of a metaphor) presumes precisely this unity of language, an unmediated correspondence with its object. Social diversity of speech, were it to arise in the work and stratify its language, would make impossible both the normal development and the activity of symbols within it.

The very rhythm of poetic genres does not promote any appreciable degree of stratification. *Rhythm, by creating an unmediated involvement between every aspect of the accentual system of the whole* (via the most immediate rhythmic unities), destroys in embryo those social worlds of speech and of persons that are potentially embedded in the word: in any case, rhythm puts definite limits on them, does not let them unfold or materialize. Rhythm serves to strengthen and concentrate even further the unity and hermetic quality of the surface of poetic style, and of the unitary language that this style posits.

As a result of this work—stripping all aspects of language of the intentions and accents of other people, destroying all traces of social heteroglossia and diversity of language—a tension-filled unity of language is achieved in the poetic work. This unity may be naive, and present only in those extremely rare epochs of poetry, when poetry had not yet exceeded the limits of a closed, unitary, undifferentiated social circle whose language and ideology were not yet stratified. More often than not, we experience a profound and conscious tension through which the unitary poetic language of a work rises from the heteroglot and language-diverse chaos of the literary language contemporary to it.

This is how the poet proceeds. The novelist working in prose (and almost any prose writer) takes a completely different path. He welcomes the heteroglossia and language diversity of the literary and extraliterary language into his own work not only not weakening them but even intensifying them (for he interacts with their particular self-consciousness). It is in fact out of this stratification of language, its speech diversity and even language diversity, that he constructs his style, while at the same time he maintains the unity of his own creative personality and the unity (although it is, to be sure, unity of another order) of his own style.

The prose writer does not purge words of intentions and tones that are alien to him, he does not destroy the seeds of social heteroglossia embedded in words, he does not eliminate those language characterizations and speech mannerisms (potential narrator-personalities) glimmering behind the words and forms, each at a different distance from the ultimate semantic nucleus of his work, that is, the center of his own personal intentions.

The language of the prose writer deploys itself according to degrees of greater or lesser proximity to the author and to his ultimate semantic instantiation: certain aspects of language directly and unmediatedly express (as in poetry) the semantic and expressive intentions of the author, others refract these intentions; the writer of prose does not meld completely with any of these words, but rather accents each of them in a particular way—humorously, ironically, parodically and so forth;[15] yet another group may stand even further from the author's ultimate semantic instantiation, still more thoroughly refracting his intentions; and there are, finally, those words that are completely denied any authorial intentions: the author does not express *himself* in them (as the author of the word)—rather, he *exhibits* them as a unique speech-thing, they function for him as something completely reified. Therefore the stratification of language—generic, professional, social in the narrow sense, that of particular world views, particular tendencies, particular individuals, the social speech diversity and language-diversity (dialects) of language—upon entering the novel establishs its own special order within it, and becomes a unique artistic system, which orchestrates the intentional theme of the author.

Thus a prose writer can distance himself from the language of his own work, while at the same time distancing himself, in varying degrees, from the different layers and aspects of the work. He can make use of language without wholly giving himself up to it, he may treat it as semi-alien or completely alien to himself, while compelling language ultimately to serve all his own intentions. The author does not speak in a given language (from which he distances himself to a greater or lesser degree), but he speaks, as it were, *through* language, a language that has somehow more or less materialized, become objectivized, that he merely ventriloquates.

The prose writer as a novelist does not strip away the intentions of others from the heteroglot language of his works, he does not violate those socio-ideological cultural horizons (big and little worlds) that open up behind heteroglot languages—rather, he welcomes them into his work. The prose writer makes use of

15. That is to say, the words are not his if we understand them as direct words, but they are his as things that are being transmitted ironically, exhibited and so forth, that is, as words that are understood from the distances appropriate to humor, irony, parody, etc.

words that are already populated with the social intentions of others and compels them to serve his own new intentions, to serve a second master. Therefore the intentions of the prose writer are refracted, and refracted *at different angles*, depending on the degree to which the refracted, heteroglot languages he deals with are socio-ideologically alien, already embodied and already objectivized.

The orientation of the word amid the utterances and languages of others, and all the specific phenomena connected with this orientation, takes on *artistic* significance in novel style. Diversity of voices and heteroglossia enter the novel and organize themselves within it into a structured artistic system. This constitutes the distinguishing feature of the novel as a genre.

Any stylistics capable of dealing with the distinctiveness of the novel as a genre must be a *sociological stylistics*. The internal social dialogism of novelistic discourse requires the concrete social context of discourse to be exposed, to be revealed as the force that determines its entire stylistic structure, its "form" and its "content," determining it not from without, but from within; for indeed, social dialogue reverberates in all aspects of discourse, in those relating to "content" as well as the "formal" aspects themselves.

The development of the novel is a function of the deepening of dialogic essence, its increased scope and greater precision. Fewer and fewer neutral, hard elements ("rock bottom truths") remain that are not drawn into dialogue. Dialogue moves into the deepest molecular and, ultimately, subatomic levels.

Of course, even the poetic word is social, but poetic forms reflect lengthier social processes, i.e., those tendencies in social life requiring centuries to unfold. The novelistic word, however, registers with extreme subtlety the tiniest shifts and oscillations of the social atmosphere; it does so, moreover, while registering it as a whole, in all of its aspects.

When heteroglossia enters the novel it becomes subject to an artistic reworking. The social and historical voices populating language, all its words and all its forms, which provide language with its particular concrete conceptualizations, are organized in the novel into a structured stylistic system that expresses the differentiated socio-ideological position of the author amid the heteroglossia of his epoch.

Heteroglossia in the Novel

The compositional forms for appropriating and organizing hetero-glossia in the novel, worked out during the long course of the genre's historical development, are extremely heterogeneous in their variety of generic types. Each such compositional form is connected with particular stylistic possibilities, and demands particular forms for the artistic treatment of the heteroglot "languages" introduced into it. We will pause here only on the most basic forms that are typical for the majority of novel types.

The so-called comic novel makes available a form for appropriating and organizing heteroglossia that is both externally very vivid and at the same time historically profound: its classic representatives in England were Fielding, Smollett, Sterne, Dickens, Thackeray and others, and in Germany Hippel and Jean Paul.

In the English comic novel we find a comic-parodic re-processing of almost all the levels of literary language, both conversational and written, that were current at the time. Almost every novel we mentioned above as being a classic representative of this generic type is an encyclopedia of all strata and forms of literary language: depending on the subject being represented, the story-line parodically reproduces first the forms of parliamentary eloquence, then the eloquence of the court, or particular forms of parliamentary protocol, or court protocol, or forms used by reporters in newspaper articles, or the dry business language of the City, or the dealings of speculators, or the pedantic speech of scholars, or the high epic style, or Biblical style, or the style of the hypocritical moral sermon or finally the way one or another concrete and socially determined personality, the subject of the story, happens to speak.

This usually parodic stylization of generic, professional and other strata of language is sometimes interrupted by the direct authorial word (usually as an expression of pathos, of Sentimental or idyllic sensibility), which directly embodies (without any refracting) semantic and axiological intentions of the author. But the primary source of language usage in the comic novel is a highly specific treatment of "common language." This "common language"—usually the average norm of spoken and written language for a given social group—is taken by the author precisely as the *common view*, as the verbal approach to people and things normal for a given sphere of society, as the *going point of view* and the going *value*. To one degree or another, the author distances himself from this common language, he steps back and objectifies it, forcing his own intentions to refract and diffuse themselves through the medium of this common view that has become embodied in language (a view that is always superficial and frequently hypocritical).

The relationship of the author to a language conceived as the common view is not static—it is always found in a state of movement and oscillation that is more or less alive (this sometimes is a rhythmic oscillation): the author exaggerates, now strongly, now weakly, one or another aspect of the "common language," sometimes abruptly exposing its inadequacy to its object and sometimes, on the contrary, becoming one with it, maintaining an almost imperceptible distance, sometimes even directly forcing it to reverberate with his own "truth," which occurs when the author completely merges his own voice with the common view. As a consequence of such a merger, the aspects of common language, which in the given situation had been parodically exaggerated or had been treated as mere things, undergo change. The comic style demands of the author a lively to-and-fro movement in his relation to language, it demands a continual shifting of the distance between author and language, so that first some, then other aspects of language are thrown into relief. If such were not the case, the style would be monotonous or would require a greater individualization of the narrator—would, in any case, require a quite different means for introducing and organizing heteroglossia.

Against this same backdrop of the "common language," of the impersonal, going opinion, one can also isolate in the comic novel those parodic stylizations of generic, professional and other languages we have mentioned, as well as compact masses of direct authorial discourse—pathos-filled, moral-didactic, sentimental-elegiac or idyllic. In the comic novel the direct authorial word is thus realized in direct, unqualified stylizations of poetic genres (idyllic, elegiac, etc.) or stylizations of rhetorical genres (the pathetic, the moral-didactic). Shifts from common language to parodying of generic and other languages and shifts to the direct authorial word may be gradual, or may be on the contrary quite abrupt. Thus does the system of language work in the comic novel.

We will pause for analysis on several examples from Dickens, from his novel *Little Dorrit*.

(1) The conference was held at four or five o'clock in the afternoon, when all the region of Harley Street, Cavendish Square, was resonant of carriage-wheels and double-knocks. It had reached this point when Mr. Merdle came home *from his daily occupation of causing the British name to be more and more respected in all parts of the civilized globe capable of appreciation of wholewide commercial enterprise and gigantic combinations of skill and capital.* For, though nobody knew with the least precision what Mr. Merdle's business was, except that it was to coin money, these were the terms in which everybody defined it on all ceremonious occasions, and which it was the last new polite reading of the parable of the camel and the needle's eye to accept without inquiry. [book 1, ch. 33]

The italicized portion represents a parodic stylization of the language of ceremonial speeches (in parliaments and at banquets). The shift into this style is prepared for by the sentence's construction, which from the very beginning is kept within bounds by a somewhat ceremonious epic tone. Further on—and already in the language of the author (and consequently in a different style)—the parodic meaning of the ceremoniousness of Merdle's labors becomes apparent: such a characterization turns out to be "another's speech," to be taken only in quotation marks ("these were the terms in which everybody defined it on all ceremonious occasions").

Thus the speech of another is introduced into the author's discourse (the story) in *concealed form*, that is, without any of the *formal* markers usually accompanying such speech, whether direct or indirect. But this is not just another's speech in the same "language"—it is another's utterance in a language that is itself "other" to the author as well, in the archaicized language of oratorical genres associated with hypocritical official celebrations.

(2) In a day or two it was announced to all the town, that Edmund Sparkler, Esquire, son-in-law of the eminent Mr. Merdle of worldwide renown, was made one of the Lords of the Circumlocution Office; and proclamation was issued, to all true believers, that this admirable *appointment was to be hailed as a graceful and gracious mark of homage, rendered by the graceful and gracious Decimus, to that commercial interest which must ever in a great commercial country—and all the rest of it, with blast of trumpet.* So, bolstered by this mark of Government homage, the *wonderful* Bank and all the other *wonderful* undertakings went on and went up; and gapers came to Harley Street, Cavendish Square, only to look at the house where the golden wonder lived. [book 2, ch. 12]

Here, in the italicized portion, another's speech in another's (official-ceremonial) language is openly introduced as indirect discourse. But it is surrounded by the hidden, diffused speech of another (in the same official-ceremonial language) that clears the way for the introduction of a form more easily perceived *as* another's speech and that can reverberate more fully as such. The clearing of the way comes with the word "Esquire," characteristic of official speech, added to Sparkler's name; the final confirmation that this is another's speech comes with the epithet "wonderful." This epithet does not of course belong to the author but to that same "general opinion" that had created the commotion around Merdle's inflated enterprises.

(3) It was a dinner to provoke an appetite, though he had not had one. The rarest dishes, sumptuously cooked and sumptuously served; the choicest fruits, the most exquisite wines; marvels of workmanship in gold and silver, china and glass; innumerable things delicious to the senses of taste, smell, and sight, were insinuated into its composition. *O, what a wonderful man this Merdle, what a great man, what a master man, how blessedly and enviably endowed*—in one word, what a rich man! [book 2, ch. 12]

The beginning is a parodic stylization of high epic style. What follows is an enthusiastic glorification of Merdle, a chorus of his admirers in the form of the concealed speech of another (the italicized portion). The whole point here is to expose the real basis for such glorification, which is to unmask the chorus' hypocrisy: "wonderful," "great," "master," "endowed" can all be replaced by the single word "rich." This act of authorial unmasking, which is openly accomplished within the boundaries of a single simple sentence, merges with the unmasking of another's speech. The ceremonial emphasis on glorification is complicated by a second emphasis that is indignant, ironic, and this is the one that ultimately predominates in the final unmasking words of the sentence.

We have before us a typical double-accented, double-styled *hybrid construction.*

What we are calling a hybrid construction is an utterance that belongs, by its grammatical (syntactic) and compositional markers, to a single speaker, but that actually contains mixed within it two utterances, two speech manners, two styles, two "languages," two semantic and axiological belief systems. We repeat, there is no formal—compositional and syntactic—boundary between these utterances, styles, languages, belief systems; the division of voices and languages takes place within the limits of a single syntactic whole, often within the limits of a simple sentence. It frequently happens that even one and the same word will belong simultaneously to two languages, two belief systems that intersect in a hybrid construction—and, consequently, the word has two contradictory meanings, two accents (examples below). As we shall see, hybrid constructions are of enormous significance in novel style.[16]

(4) But Mr. Tite Barnacle was a buttoned-up man, and *consequently* a weighty one. [book 2, ch. 12]

The above sentence is an example of *pseudo-objective motivation*, one of the forms for concealing another's speech—in this example, the speech of "current opinion." If judged by the formal markers above, the logic motivating the sentence seems to belong to the author, i.e., he is formally at one with it; but in actual fact, the motivation lies within the subjective belief system of his characters, or of general opinion.

Pseudo-objective motivation is generally characteristic of novel style,[17] since it is one of the manifold forms for concealing another's speech in hybrid constructions. Subordinate conjunctions and link words ("thus," "because," "for the reason that," "in spite of" and so forth), as well as words used to maintain a logical sequence ("therefore," "consequently," etc.) lose their direct authorial intention, take on the flavor of someone else's language, become refracted or even completely reified.

Such motivation is especially characteristic of comic style, in which someone else's speech is dominant (the speech of concrete persons, or, more often, a collective voice).[18]

(5) As a vast fire will fill the air to a great distance with its roar, so the sacred flame which the mighty Barnacles had fanned caused the air to resound more and more with the name of Merdle. It was deposited on every lip, and carried into every ear. There never was, there never had been, there never again should be, such a man as Mr. Merdle. Nobody,

16. For more detail on hybrid constructions and their significance, see ch. 4 of the present essay.
17. Such a device is unthinkable in the epic.
18. Cf. the grotesque pseudo-objective motivations in Gogol.

as aforesaid, knew what he had done; but *everybody knew him to be the greatest that had appeared.* [book 2, ch. 13]

Here we have an epic, "Homeric" introduction (parodic, of course) into whose frame the crowd's glorification of Merdle has been inserted (concealed speech of another in another's language). We then get direct authorial discourse; however, the author gives an objective tone to this "aside" by suggesting that "everybody knew" (the italicized portion). It is as if even the author himself did not doubt the fact.

(6) That illustrious man and great national ornament, Mr. Merdle, continued his shining course. It began to be widely understood that one who had done society the admirable service *of making so much money out of it,* could not be suffered to remain a commoner. A baronetcy was spoken of with confidence; a peerage was frequently mentioned. [book 2, ch. 24]

We have here the same fictive solidarity with the hypocritically ceremonial general opinion of Merdle. All the epithets referring to Merdle in the first sentences derive from general opinion, that is, they are the concealed speech of another. The second sentence—"it began to be widely understood," etc.—is kept within the bounds of an emphatically objective style, representing not subjective opinion but the admission of an objective and completely indisputable fact. The epithet "who had done society the admirable service" is completely at the level of common opinion, repeating its official glorification, but the subordinate clause attached to that glorification ("of making so much money out of it") are the words of the author himself (as if put in parentheses in the quotation). The main sentence then picks up again at the level of common opinion. We have here a typical hybrid construction, where the subordinate clause is in direct authorial speech and the main clause in someone else's speech. The main and subordinate clauses are constructed in different semantic and axiological conceptual systems.

The whole of this portion of the novel's action, which centers around Merdle and the persons associated with him, is depicted in the language (or more accurately, the languages) of hypocritically ceremonial common opinion about Merdle, and at the same time there is a parodic stylization of that everyday language of banal society gossip, or of the ceremonial language of official pronouncements and banquet speeches, or the high epic style or

Biblical style. This atmosphere around Merdle, the common opinion about him and his enterprises, infects the positive heroes of the novel as well, in particular the sober Pancks, and forces him to invest his entire estate—his own, and Little Dorrit's—in Merdle's hollow enterprises.

(7) Physician had engaged to break the intelligence in Harley Street. Bar could not at once return to his inveiglements of the most enlightened and remarkable jury he had ever seen in that box, with whom, he could tell his learned friend, no shallow sophistry would go down, and no unhappily abused professional tact and skill prevail (this was the way he meant to begin with them); so he said he would go too, and would loiter to and fro near the house while his friend was inside. [Book 2, ch. 25, mistakenly given as ch. 15 in Russian text, tr.]

Here we have a clear example of hybrid construction where within the frame of authorial speech (informative speech)—the beginning of a speech prepared by the lawyer has been inserted, "The Bar could not at once return to his inveiglements . . . of the jury . . . so he said he would go too. . . ." etc.—while this speech is simultaneously a fully developed epithet attached to the subject of the author's speech, that is, "jury." The word "jury" enters into the context of informative authorial speech (in the capacity of a necessary object to the word "inveiglements") as well as into the context of the parodic-stylized speech of the lawyer. The author's word "inveiglement" itself emphasizes the parodic nature of the re-processing of the lawyer's speech, the hypocritical meaning of which consists precisely in the fact that it would be impossible to inveigle such a remarkable jury.

(8) It followed that Mrs. Merdle, as a woman of fashion and good breeding *who had been sacrificed to wiles of a vulgar barbarian* (for Mr. Merdle was found out from the crown of his head to the sole of his foot, the moment he was found out in his pocket), must be actively championed by her order for her order's sake. [book 2, ch. 33]

This is an analogous hybrid construction, in which the definition provided by the general opinion of society—"a sacrifice to the wiles of a vulgar barbarian"—merges with authorial speech, exposing the hypocrisy and greed of common opinion.

So it is throughout Dickens' whole novel. His entire text is, in fact, everywhere dotted with quotation marks that serve to separate out little islands of scattered direct speech and purely authorial speech, washed by heteroglot waves from all sides. But it would have been impossible actually to insert such marks, since, as we have seen, one and the same word often figures both as the speech of the author and as the speech of another—and at the same time.

Another's speech—whether as storytelling, as mimicking, as the display of a thing in light of a particular point of view, as a speech deployed first in compact masses, then loosely scattered, a speech that is in most cases impersonal ("common opinion," professional and generic languages)—is at none of these points clearly separated from authorial speech: the boundaries are deliberately flexible and ambiguous, often passing through a single syntactic whole, often through a simple sentence, and sometimes even dividing up the main parts of a sentence. This varied *play with the boundaries of speech types*, languages and belief systems is one most fundamental aspects of comic style.

Comic style (of the English sort) is based, therefore, on the stratification of common language and on the possibilities available for isolating from these strata, to one degree or another, one's own intentions, without ever completely merging with them. *It is precisely the diversity of speech, and not the unity of a normative shared language, that is the ground of style.* It is true that such speech diversity does not exceed the boundaries of literary language conceived as a linguistic whole (that is, language defined by abstract linguistic markers), does not pass into an authentic heteroglossia and is based on an abstract notion of language as unitary (that is, it does not require knowledge of various dialects or languages). However a mere concern for language is but the abstract side of the concrete and active (i.e., dialogically engaged) understanding of the living heteroglossia that has been introduced into the novel and artistically organized within it.

In Dickens' predecessors, Fielding, Smollett and Sterne, the men who founded the English comic novel, we find the same parodic stylization of various levels and genres of literary language, but the distance between these levels and genres is greater than it is in Dickens and the exaggeration is stronger (especially in Sterne). The parodic and objectivized incorporation into their work of various types of literary language (especially in Sterne) penetrates the deepest levels of literary and ideological thought itself, resulting in a parody of the logical and expressive structure of any ideological discourse as such (scholarly, moral and rhetorical, poetic) that is almost as radical as the parody we find in Rabelais.

Literary parody understood in the narrow sense plays a fundamental role in the way language is structured in Fielding, Smollett and Sterne (the Richardsonian novel is parodied by the first two, and almost all contemporary novel-types are parodied by Sterne). Literary parody serves to distance the author still further from language, to complicate still further his relationship to the literary language of his time, especially in the novel's own territory. The novelistic discourse dominating a given epoch is itself turned into an object and itself becomes a means for refracting new authorial intentions.

Literary parody of dominant novel-types plays a large role in the history of the European novel. One could even say that the most important novelistic models and novel-types arose precisely during this parodic destruction of preceding novelistic worlds. This is true of the work of Cervantes, Mendoza, Grimmelshausen, Rabelais, Lesage and many others.

In Rabelais, whose influence on all novelistic prose (and in particular the comic novel) was very great, a parodic attitude toward almost all forms of ideological discourse—philosophical, moral, scholarly, rhetorical, poetic and in particular the pathos-charged forms of discourse (in Rabelais, pathos almost always is equivalent to lie)—was intensified to the point where it became a parody of the very act of conceptualizing anything in language. We might add that Rabelais taunts the deceptive human word by a parodic destruction of syntactic structures, thereby reducing to absurdity some of the logical and expressively accented aspects of words (for example, predication, explanations and so forth). Turning away from language (by means of language, of course), discrediting any direct or unmediated intentionality and expressive excess (any "weighty" seriousness) that might adhere in ideological discourse, presuming that all language is conventional and false, maliciously inadequate to reality—all this achieves in Rabelais almost the maximum purity possible in prose. But the truth that might oppose such falsity receives almost no direct intentional and verbal expression in Rabelais, it does not receive its *own* word—it reverberates only in the parodic and unmasking accents in which the lie is present. Truth is restored by reducing the lie to an absurdity, but truth itself does not seek words; she is afraid to entangle herself in the word, to soil herself in verbal pathos.

Rabelais' "philosophy of the word"—a philosophy expressed

not as much in direct utterances as in stylistic practice—has had enormous influence on all consequent novel prose and in particular of the great representative forms of the comic novel; with that in mind we bring forward the purely Rabelaisian formulation of Sterne's Yorick, which might serve as an epigraph to the history of the most important stylistic lines of development in the European novel:

> For aught I know there might be some mixture of unlucky wit at the bottom of such Fracas:—For, to speak the truth, Yorick had an invincible dislike and opposition in his nature to gravity;—not to gravity as such;— for where gravity was wanted, he would be the most grave or serious of mortal men for days and weeks together;—but he was an enemy to the affectation of it, and declared open war against it, only as it appeared a cloak for ignorance, or for folly; and then, whenever it fell his way, however sheltered and protected, he seldom gave it much quarter.
>
> Sometimes, in his wild way of talking, he would say, That gravity was an errant scoundrel; and he would add,—of the most dangerous kind too,—because a sly one; and that, he verily believed, more honest, well-meaning people were bubbled out of their goods and money by it in one twelve-month, than by pocket-picking and shop-lifting in seven. In the naked temper which a merry heart discovered, he would say, There was no danger,—but to itself:—whereas the very essence of gravity was design, and consequently deceit;—'twas a taught trick to gain credit of the world for more sense and knowledge than a man was worth; and that, with all its pretensions,—it was no better, but often worse, than what a French wit had long ago defined it,—viz. A mysterious carriage of the body to cover the defects of the mind;—which definition of gravity, Yorick, with great imprudence, would say, deserved to be wrote in letters of gold. [Bakhtin does not locate citation; it is from *Tristram Shandy*, vol. i, ch. ii, tr.]

Close to Rabelais, but in certain respects even exceeding him in the decisive influence he had on all of novelistic prose, is Cervantes. The English comic novel is permeated through and through with the spirit of Cervantes. It is no accident that this same Yorick, on his deathbed, quotes the words of Sancho Panza.

While the attitude toward language and toward its stratification (generic, professional and otherwise) among the German comic writers, in Hippel and especially in Jean Paul, is basically of the Sternean type, it is raised—as it is in Sterne himself—to the level of a purely philosophical problem, the very possibility of literary and ideological speech as such. The philosophical and ideological element in an author's attitude toward his own language forces into the background the play between intention and the concrete, primarily generic and ideological levels of literary language (cf. the reflection of just this in the aesthetic theories of Jean Paul).[19]

Thus the stratification of literary language, its speech diversity, is an indispensable prerequisite for comic style, whose elements are projected onto different linguistic planes while at the same time the intention of the author, refracted as it passes through these planes, does not wholly give itself up to any of them. It is as if the author has no language of his own, but does possess his own style, his own organic and unitary law governing the way he plays with languages and the way his own real semantic and expressive intentions are refracted within them. Of course this play with languages (and frequently the complete absence of a direct discourse of his own) in no sense degrades the general, deep-seated intentionality, the overarching ideological conceptualization of the work as a whole.

In the comic novel, the incorporation of heteroglossia and its stylistic utilization is characterized by two distinctive features:

(1) Incorporated into the novel are a multiplicity of "language" and verbal-ideological belief systems—generic, professional, class-and-interest-group (the language of the nobleman, the farmer, the merchant, the peasant); tendentious, everyday (the languages of rumour, of society chatter, servants' language) and so forth, but these languages are, it is true, kept primarily within the limits of the literary written and conversational language; at the same time these languages are not, in most cases, consolidated into fixed persons (heroes, storytellers) but rather are incorporated in an impersonal form "from the author," alternating (while ignoring precise formal boundaries) with direct authorial discourse.

(2) The incorporated languages and socio-ideological belief systems, while of course utilized to refract the author's intentions, are unmasked and destroyed as something false, hypocritical,

---

19. Intellect as embodied in the forms and the methods of verbal and ideological thought (i.e., the linguistic horizon of normal human intellectual activity) becomes in Jean Paul something infinitely petty and ludicrous when seen in the light of "reason." His humor results from play with intellectual activity and its forms.

greedy, limited, narrowly rationalistic, inadequate to reality. In most cases these languages—already fully formed, officially recognized, reigning languages that are authoritative and reactionary—are (in real life) doomed to death and displacement. Therefore what predominates in the novel are various forms and degrees of *parodic stylization* of incorporated languages, a stylization that, in the most radical, most Rabelaisian[20] representatives of this novel-type (Sterne and Jean Paul), verges on a rejection of any straightforward and unmediated seriousness (true seriousness is the destruction of all false seriousness, not only in its pathos-charged expression but in its Sentimental one as well);[21] that is, it limits itself to a principled criticism of the word as such.

There is a fundamental difference between this comic form for incorporating and organizing heteroglossia in the novel and other forms that are defined by their use of a personified and concretely posited author (written speech) or teller (oral speech).

Play with a posited author is also characteristic of the comic novel (Sterne, Hippel, Jean Paul), a heritage from *Don Quixote*. But in these examples such play is purely a compositional device, which strengthens the general trend toward relativity, objectification and the parodying of literary forms and genres.

The posited author and teller assume a completely different significance where they are incorporated as carriers of a particular verbal-ideological linguistic belief system, with a particular point of view on the world and its events, with particular value judgments and intonations—"particular" both as regards the author, his real direct discourse, and also as regards "normal" literary narrative and language.

This particularity, this distancing of the posited author or teller from the real author and from conventional literary expectations, may occur in differing degrees and may vary in its nature. But in every case a particular belief system belonging to someone else, a particular point of view on the world belonging to someone else, is used by the author because it is highly productive, that is, it is able on the one hand to show the object of representation in a new light (to reveal new sides or dimensions in it) and on the

20. It is of course impossible in the strict sense to include Rabelais himself—either chronologically or in terms of his essential character—among the representatives of comic novelists.

21. Nevertheless sentimentality and "high seriousness" is not completely eliminated (especially in Jean Paul).

other hand to illuminate in a new way the "expected" literary horizon, that horizon against which the particularities of the teller's tale are perceivable.

For example: Belkin was chosen (or better, created) by Pushkin because of his particular "unpoetic" point of view on objects and plots that are traditionally poetic (the highly characteristic and calculated use of the *Romeo and Juliet* plot in "Mistress into Maid" or the romantic "Dances of Death" in "The Coffinmaker"). Belkin, who is on the same level with those narrators-at-third-remove out of whose mouths he has taken his stories, is a "prosaic" man, a man without a drop of poetic pathos. The successful "prosaic" resolutions of the plots and the very means of the story's telling destroy any expectation of traditional poetic effects. The fruitfulness of the prosaic quality in Belkin's point of view consists in just this failure to understand poetic pathos.

Maxim Maximych in *A Hero of Our Time*, Rudy Panko, the narrators of "Nose" and "Overcoat," Dostoevsky's chroniclers, folkloric narrators and storytellers who are themselves characters in Melnikov-Pechersky and Mamin-Sibiryak, the folkloric and down-to-earth storytellers in Leskov, the character-narrators in populist literature and finally the narrators in Symbolist and post-Symbolist prose (in Remizov, Zamyatin and others)—with all their widely differing forms of narration (oral and written), with all their differing narrative languages (literary, professional, social-and-special-interest-group language, everyday, slang, dialects and others)—everywhere, they recommend themselves as specific and limited verbal ideological points of view, belief systems, opposed to the literary expectations and points of view that constitute the background needed to perceive them; but these narrators are productive precisely *because* of this very limitedness and specificity.

The speech of such narrators is always *another's speech* (as regards the real or potential direct discourse of the author) and in *another's language* (i.e., insofar as it is a particular variant of the literary language that clashes with the language of the narrator).

Thus we have in this case "nondirect speaking"—not *in* language but *through* language, through the linguistic medium of another—and consequently through a refraction of authorial intentions.

The author manifests himself and his point of view not only in his effect on the narrator, on his speech and his language (which are to one or another extent objectivized, objects of display) but also in his effect on the subject of the story—as a point of view that differs from the point of view of the narrator. Behind the narrator's story we read a second story, the author's story; he is the one who tells us how the narrator tells stories, and also tells us about the narrator himself. We acutely sense two levels at each moment in the story; one, the level of the narrator, a belief system filled with his objects, meanings and emotional expressions, and the other, the level of the author, who speaks (albeit in a refracted way) by means of this story and through this story. The narrator himself, with *his* own discourse, enters into this authorial belief system along with what is actually being told. We puzzle out the author's emphases that overlie the subject of the story, while we puzzle out the story itself and the figure of the narrator as he is revealed in the process of telling his tale. If one fails to sense this second level, the intentions and accents of the author himself, then one has failed to understand the work.

As we have said above, the narrator's story or the story of the posited author is structured against the background of normal literary language, the expected literary horizon. Every moment of the story has a conscious relationship with this normal language and its belief system, is in fact set against them, and set against them *dialogically*: one point of view opposed to another, one evaluation opposed to another, one accent opposed to another (i.e., they are not contrasted as two abstractly linguistic phenomena). This interaction, this dialogic tension between two languages and two belief systems, permits authorial intentions to be realized in such a way that we can acutely sense their presence at every point in the work. The author is not to be found in the language of the narrator, not in the normal literary language to which the story opposes itself (although a given story may be closer to a given language)—but rather, the author utilizes now one language, now another, in order to avoid giving himself up wholly to either of them; he makes use of this verbal give-and-take, this dialogue of languages at every point in his work, in order that he himself might remain as it were neutral with regard to language, a third party in a quarrel between two people (although he might be a *biased* third party).

All forms involving a narrator or a posited author signify to one degree or another by their presence the author's freedom from a unitary and singular language, a freedom connected with the relativity of literary and language systems; such forms open up the possibility of never having to define oneself in language, the possibility of translating one's own intentions from one linguistic system to another, of fusing "the language of truth" with "the language of the everyday," of saying "I am me" in someone else's language, and in my own language, "I am other."

Such a refracting of authorial intentions takes place in all these forms (the narrator's tale, the tale of a posited author or that of one of the characters); it is therefore possible to have in them, as in the comic novel, a variety of different distances between distinct aspects of the narrator's language and the author's language: the refraction may be at times greater, at times lesser, and in some aspects of language there may be an almost complete fusion of voices.

The next form for incorporating and organizing heteroglossia in the novel—a form that every novel without exception utilizes—is the language used by characters.

The language used by characters in the novel, how they speak, is verbally and semantically autonomous; each character's speech possesses its own belief system, since each is the speech of another in another's language; thus it may also refract authorial intentions and consequently may to a certain degree constitute a second language for the author. Moreover, the character speech almost always influences authorial speech (and sometimes powerfully so), sprinkling it with another's words (that is, the speech of a character perceived as the concealed speech of another) and in this way introducing into it stratification and speech diversity.

Thus even where there is no comic element, no parody, no irony and so forth, where there is no narrator, no posited author or narrating character, speech diversity and language stratification still serve as the basis for style in the novel. Even in those places where the author's voice seems at first glance to be unitary and consistent, direct and unmediatedly intentional, beneath that smooth single-languaged surface we can nevertheless uncover prose's three-dimensionality, its profound speech diversity, which enters the project of style and is its determining factor.

Thus the language and style of Turgenev's novels have the appearance of being single-languaged and pure. Even in Turgenev, however, this unitary language is very far from poetic absolutism. Substantial masses of this language are drawn into the battle between points of view, value judgments and emphases that the characters introduce into it; they are infected by mutually contradictory intentions and stratifications; words, sayings, expressions, definitions and epithets are scattered throughout it, infected with others' intentions with which the author is to some extent at odds, and through which his own personal intentions are refracted. We sense acutely the various distances between the author and various aspects of his language, which smack of the social universes and belief systems of others. We acutely sense in various aspects of his language varying degrees of the presence of the author and of his *most recent semantic instantiation*. In Turgenev, heteroglossia and language stratification serve as the most fundamental factors of style, and orchestrate an authorial truth of their own; the author's linguistic consciousness, his consciousness as a writer of prose, is thereby relativized.

In Turgenev, social heteroglossia enters the novel primarily in the direct speeches of his characters, in dialogues. But this heteroglossia, as we have said, is also diffused throughout the authorial speech that surrounds the characters, creating highly particularized *character zones* [*zony geroev*]. These zones are formed from the fragments of character speech [*polureč'*], from various forms for hidden transmission of someone else's word, from scattered words and sayings belonging to someone else's speech, from those invasions into authorial speech of others' expressive indicators (ellipsis, questions, exclamations). Such a character zone is the field of action for a character's voice, encroaching in one way or another upon the author's voice.

However—we repeat—in Turgenev, the novelistic orchestration of the theme is concentrated in direct dialogues; the characters do not create around themselves their own extensive or densely saturated zones, and in Turgenev fully developed, complex stylistic hybrids are relatively rare.

We pause here on several examples of diffuse heteroglossia in Turgenev.[c]

(1) His name is Nikolai Petrovich Kirsanov. Some ten miles from the coaching-inn stands a respectable little property of his consisting of a couple of hundred serfs—or five thousand acres, as he expresses it now that he has divided up his land and let it to the peasants, and started a "farm." [*Fathers and Sons*, ch. 1]

---

c. Citations from *Fathers and Sons* are from: Ivan Turgenev, *Fathers and Sons*, tr. Rosemary Edmonds (London: Penguin, 1965).

Here the new expressions, characteristic of the era and in the style of the liberals, are put in quotation marks or otherwise "qualified."

(2) He was secretly beginning to feel irritated. Bazarov's complete indifference exasperated his aristocratic nature. *This son of a medico was not only self-assured: he actually returned abrupt and reluctant answers, and there was a churlish, almost insolant note in his voice.* [*Fathers and Sons*, ch. 4]

The third sentence of this paragraph, while being a part of the author's speech if judged by its formal syntactic markers, is at the same time in its choice of expressions ("this son of a medico") and in its emotional and expressive structure the hidden speech of someone else (Pavel Petrovich).

(3) Pavel Petrovich sat down at the table. He was wearing an elegant suit cut in the English fashion, and a gay little fez graced his head. The fez and the carelessly knotted cravat carried a suggestion of the more free life in the country but the stiff collar of his shirt—not white, it is true, but striped *as is correct for morning wear*—stood up as inexorably as ever against his well-shaven chin. [*Fathers and Sons*, ch. 5]

This ironic characterization of Pavel Petrovich's morning attire is consistent with the tone of a gentleman, precisely in the style of Pavel Petrovich. The statement "as is correct for morning wear" is not, of course, a simple authorial statement, but rather the norm of Pavel Petrovich's gentlemanly circle, conveyed ironically. One might with some justice put it in quotation marks. This is an example of a pseudo-objective underpinning.

(4) *Matvei Ilyich's suavity of demeanour was equalled only by his stately manner.* He had a gracious word for everyone—with an added shade of disgust in some cases and deference in others; he was gallant, "un vrai chevalier français," to all the ladies, and was continually bursting into hearty resounding laughter, in which no one else took part, as befits a high official. [*Fathers and Sons*, ch. 14]

Here we have an analogous case of an ironic characterization given from the point of view of the high official himself. Such is the nature of this form of pseudo-objective underpinning: "as befits a high official."

(5) The following morning Nezhdanov betook himself to Sipyagin's town residence, and there, in a magnificent study, filled with furniture of a severe style, *in full harmony with the dignity of a liberal politician and modern gentleman.* . . . [*Virgin Soil*, ch. 4]

This is an analogous pseudo-objective construction.

(6) Semyon Petrovich was in the ministry of the Court, he had the title of a *kammeryunker. He was prevented by his patriotism from joining the diplomatic service,* for which he seemed destined by everything, his education, his knowledge of the world, his popularity with women, and his very appearance. . . . [*Virgin Soil*, ch. 5][d]

The motivation for refusing a diplomatic career is pseudo-objective. The entire characterization is consistent in tone and given from the point of view of Kallomyetsev himself, fused with his direct speech, being—at least judging by its syntactic markers—a subordinate clause attached to authorial speech ("for which he seemed destined by everything . . . mais quitter la Russie!" and so forth).

(7) Kallomyetsev had come to S——— Province on a two months' leave to look after his property, that is to say, "to scare some and squeeze others." *Of course, there's no doing anything without that.* [*Virgin Soil*, ch. 5]

The conclusion of the paragraph is a characteristic example of a pseudo-objective statement. Precisely in order to give it the appearance of an objective authorial judgment, it is not put in quotation marks, as are the preceding words of Kallomyetsev himself; it is incorporated into authorial speech and deliberately placed directly after Kallomyetsev's own words.

(8) But Kallomyetsev deliberately stuck his round eyeglass between his nose and his eyebrow, and stared at the [snit of a] *student who dared not share* his "apprehensions." [*Virgin Soil*, ch. 7]

This is a typical hybrid construction. Not only the subordinate clause but also the direct object ("the [snit of a] student") of the main authorial sentence is rendered in Kallomyetsev's tone. The choice of words ("snit of a student," "dared not share") are determined by Kallomyetsev's irritated intonation, and at the same time, in the context of authorial speech, these words are permeated with the ironic intonation of the author; therefore the construction has two accents (the author's ironic transmission, and a mimicking of the irritation of the character).

---

d. Citations from *Virgin Soil* are from: Ivan Turgenev, *Virgin Soil*, tr. Constance Garnett (New York: Grove Press, n.d.).

Finally, we adduce examples of an intrusion of the emotional aspects of someone else's speech into the syntactic system of authorial speech (ellipsis, questions, exclamations).

(9) Strange was the state of his mind. In the last two days so many new sensations, new faces. . . . For the first time in his life he had come close to a girl, whom, in all probability, he loved; he was present at the beginning of the thing to which, in all probability, all his energies were consecrated. . . . Well? was he rejoicing? No. Was he wavering, afraid, confused? Oh, certainly not. Was he at least, feeling that tension of his whole being, that impulse forward into the front ranks of the battle, to be expected as the struggle grew near? No again. Did he believe, then, in this cause? Did he believe in his own love? "Oh, damned artistic temperament! sceptic!" his lips murmured inaudibly. Why this weariness, this disinclination to speak even, without shrieking and raving? What inner voice did he want to stifle with those ravings? [Virgin Soil, ch. 18]

Here we have, in essence, a form of a character's quasi-direct discourse [nesobstvenno-prjamaja reč']. Judging by its syntactic markers, it is authorial speech, but its entire emotional structure belongs to Nezhdanov. This is his inner speech, but transmitted in a way regulated by the author, *with provocative questions from the author and with ironically debunking reservations* ("in all probability"), although Nezhdanov's emotional overtones are preserved.

Such a form for transmitting inner speech is common in Turgenev (and is generally one of the most widespread forms for transmitting inner speech in the novel). This form introduces order and stylistic symmetry into the disorderly and impetuous flow of a character's internal speech (a disorder and impetuosity would otherwise have to be re-processed into direct speech) and, moreover, through its syntactic (third-person) and basic stylistic markers (lexicological and other), such a form permits another's inner speech to merge, in an organic and structured way, with a context belonging to the author. But at the same time it is precisely this form that permits us to preserve the expressive structure of the character's inner speech, its inability to exhaust itself in words, its flexibility, which would be absolutely impossible within the dry and logical form of indirect discourse [kosvennaja reč']. Precisely these features make this form the most convenient for transmitting the inner speech of characters. It is of course a hybrid form, for the author's voice may be present in varying degrees of activity and may introduce into the transmitted speech a second accent of its own (ironic, irritated and so on).

The same hybridization, mixing of accents and erasing of boundaries between authorial speech and the speech of others is also present in other forms for transmitting characters' speech. With only three templates for speech transcription (direct speech [*prjamaja reč'*], indirect speech [*kosvennaja reč'*] and quasi-direct speech [*nesobstvenno-prjamaja reč'*]) a great diversity is nevertheless made possible in the treatment of character speech—i.e., the way characters overlap and infect each other—the main thing being how the authorial context succeeds in exploiting the various means for replicating frames and re-stratifying them.

The examples we have offered from Turgenev provide a typical picture of the character's role in stratifying the language of the novel and incorporating heteroglossia into it. A character in a novel always has, as we have said, a zone of his own, his own sphere of influence on the authorial context surrounding him, a sphere that extends—and often quite far—beyond the boundaries of the direct discourse allotted to him. The area occupied by an important character's voice must in any event be broader than his direct and "actual" words. This zone surrounding the important characters of the novel is stylistically profoundly idiosyncratic: the most varied hybrid constructions hold sway in it, and it is always, to one degree or another, dialogized; inside this area a dialogue is played out between the author and his characters—not a dramatic dialogue broken up into statement-and-response, but that special type of novelistic dialogue that realizes itself within the boundaries of constructions that externally resemble monologues. The potential for such dialogue is one of the most fundamental privileges of novelistic prose, a privilege available neither to dramatic nor to purely poetic genres.

Character zones are a most interesting object of study for stylistic and linguistic analysis: in them one encounters constructions that cast a completely new light on problems of syntax and stylistics.

Let us pause finally on one of the most basic and fundamental forms for incorporating and organizing heteroglossia in the novel—"incorporated genres."

The novel permits the incorporation of various genres, both artistic (inserted short stories, lyrical songs, poems, dramatic scenes, etc.) and extra-artistic (everyday, rhetorical, scholarly, religious genres and others). In principle, any genre could be included in the construction of the novel, and in fact it is difficult to find any genres that have not at some point been incorporated into a novel by someone. Such incorporated genres usually preserve within the novel their own structural integrity and independence, as well as their own linguistic and stylistic peculiarities.

There exists in addition a special group of genres that play an especially significant role in structuring novels, sometimes by themselves even directly determining the structure of a novel as a whole—thus creating novel-types named after such genres. Examples of such genres would be the confession, the diary, travel notes, biography, the personal letter and several others. All these genres may not only enter the novel as one of its essential structural components, but may also determine the form of the novel as a whole (the novel-confession, the novel-diary, the novel-in-letters, etc.). Each of these genres possesses its own verbal and semantic forms for assimilating various aspects of reality. The novel, indeed, utilizes these genres precisely because of their capacity, as well-worked-out forms, to assimilate reality in words.

So great is the role played by these genres that are incorporated into novels that it might seem as if the novel is denied any primary means for verbally appropriating reality, that it has no approach of its own, and therefore requires the help of other genres to re-process reality; the novel itself has the appearance of being merely a secondary syncretic unification of other seemingly primary verbal genres.

All these genres, as they enter the novel, bring into it their own languages, and therefore stratify the linguistic unity of the novel and further intensify its speech diversity in fresh ways. It often happens that the language of a nonartistic genre (say, the epistolary), when introduced into the novel, takes on a significance that creates a chapter not only in the history of the novel, but in the history of literary language as well.

The languages thus introduced into a novel may be either directly intentional or treated completely as objects, that is, deprived of any authorial intentions—not as a word that has been spoken, but as a word to be displayed, like a thing. But more often than not, these languages do refract, to one degree or another, authorial intentions—although separate aspects of them may in various ways *not* coincide with the semantic operation of the work that immediately precedes their appearance.

Thus poetic genres of verse (the lyrical genres, for example) when introduced into the novel may have the direct intentionality, the full semantic charge, of poetry. Such, for example, are the verses Goethe introduced into *Wilhelm Meister*. In such a way did the Romantics incorporate their own verses into their prose—and, as is well known, the Romantics considered the presence of verses in the novel (verses taken as directly intentional expressions of the author) one of its constitutive features. In other examples, incorporated verses refract authorial intentions; for example, Lensky's poem in *Evgenij Onegin*, "Where, o where have you gone. . . ." Although the verses from *Wilhelm Meister* may be directly attributed to Goethe (which is actually done), then "Where, o where have you gone. . . ." can in no way be attributed to Pushkin, or if so, only as a poem belonging to a special group comprising "parodic stylizations" (where we must also locate Grinev's poem in *The Captain's Daughter*). Finally, poems incorporated into a novel can also be completely objectified, as are, for example, Captain Lebyadkin's verses in Dostoevsky's *The Possessed*.

A similar situation is the novel's incorporation of every possible kind of maxim and aphorism; they too may oscillate between the purely objective (the "word on display") and the directly intentional, that is, the fully conceptualized philosophical dicta of the author himself (unconditional discourse spoken with no qualifications or distancing). Thus we find, in the novels of Jean Paul—which are so rich in aphorisms—a broad scale of gradations between the various aphorisms, from purely objective to directly intentional, with the author's intentions refracted in varying degrees in each case.

In *Evgenij Onegin* aphorisms and maxims are present either on the plane of parody or of irony—that is, authorial intentions in these dicta are to a greater or lesser extent refracted. For example, the maxim

He who has lived and thought can never
Look on mankind without disdain;
He who has felt is haunted ever
By days that will not come again;
No more for him enchantments semblance,
On him the serpent of remembrance
Feeds, and remorse corrodes his heart.[e]

---

e. Citations from *Eugene Onegin* are from the Walter Arndt translation (New York: Dutton, 1963), slightly modified to correspond with Bakhtin's remarks about particulars.

is given us on a lighthearted, parodic plane, although one can still feel throughout a close proximity, almost a fusion with authorial intentions. And yet the lines that immediately follow:

All this is likely to impart
An added charm to conversation

(a conversation of the posited author with Onegin) strengthen the parodic-ironic emphasis, make the maxim more of an inert thing. We sense that the maxim is constructed in a field of activity dominated by Onegin's voice, in his—Onegin's—belief system, with his—Onegin's—emphases.

But this refraction of authorial intentions, in the field that resounds with Onegin's voice, in Onegin's zone—is different than the refraction in, say, Lensky's zone (cf. the almost objective parody on his poems).

This example may also serve to illustrate the influence of a character's language on authorial speech, something discussed by us above: the aphorism in question here is permeated with Onegin's (fashionably Byronic) intentions, therefore the author maintains a certain distance and does not completely merge with him.

The question of incorporating those genres fundamental to the novel's development (the confession, the diary and others) is much more complicated. Such genres also introduce into the novel their own languages, of course, but these languages are primarily significant for making available points of view that are generative in a material sense, since they exist outside literary conventionality and thus have the capacity to broaden the horizon of language available to literature, helping to win for literature new worlds of verbal perception, worlds that had been already sought and partially subdued in other—extraliterary—spheres of linguistic life.

A comic playing with languages, a story "not from the author" (but from a narrator, posited author or character), character speech, character zones and lastly various introductory or framing genres are the basic forms for incorporating and organizing heteroglossia in the novel. All these forms permit languages to be used in ways that are indirect, conditional, distanced. They all signify a relativizing of linguistic consciousness in the perception of language borders—borders created by history and society, and even the most fundamental borders (i.e., those between languages as such)—and permit expression of a feeling for the materiality of language that defines such a relativized consciousness. This relativizing of linguistic consciousness in no way requires a corresponding relativizing in the semantic intentions themselves: even within a prose linguistic consciousness, intentions themselves can be unconditional. But because the idea of a singular language (a sacrosanct, unconditional language) is foreign to prose, prosaic consciousness must orchestrate its *own*—even though unconditional—semantic intentions. Prose consciousness feels cramped when it is confined to only *one* out of a multitude of heteroglot languages, for one linguistic timbre is inadequate to it.

We have touched upon only those major forms typical of the most important variants of the European novel, but in themselves they do not, of course, exhaust all the possible means for incorporating and organizing heteroglossia in the novel. A combination of all these forms in separate given novels, and consequently in various generic types generated by these novels, is also possible. Of such a sort is the classic and purest model of the novel as genre—Cervantes' *Don Quixote*, which realizes in itself, in extraordinary depth and breadth, all the artistic possibilities of heteroglot and internally dialogized novelistic discourse.

Heteroglossia, once incorporated into the novel (whatever the forms for its incorporation), is *another's speech in another's language*, serving to express authorial intentions but in a refracted way. Such speech constitutes a special type of *double-voiced discourse*. It serves two speakers at the same time and expresses simultaneously two different intentions: the direct intention of the character who is speaking, and the refracted intention of the author. In such discourse there are two voices, two meanings and two expressions. And all the while these two voices are dialogically interrelated, they—as it were—know about each other (just as two exchanges in a dialogue know of each other and are structured in this mutual knowledge of each other); it is as if they actually hold a conversation with each other. Double-voiced discourse is always internally dialogized. Examples of this would be comic, ironic or parodic discourse, the refracting discourse of a narrator, refracting discourse in the language of a character and finally the discourse of a whole incorporated genre—all these discourses are double-voiced and internally dialogized. A potential dialogue is embedded in them, one as yet unfolded, a concentrated dialogue of two voices, two world views, two languages.

Double-voiced, internally dialogized discourse is also possible, of course, in a language system that is hermetic, pure and unitary, a system alien to the linguistic relativism of prose consciousness; it follows that such discourse is also possible in the purely poetic genres. But in those systems there is no soil to nourish the development of such discourse in the slightest meaningful or essential way. Double-voiced discourse is very widespread in rhetorical genres, but even there—remaining as it does within the boundaries of a single language system—it is not fertilized by a deep-rooted connection with the forces of historical becoming that serve to stratify language, and therefore rhetorical genres are at best merely a distanced echo of this becoming, narrowed down to an individual polemic.

Such poetic and rhetorical double-voicedness, cut off from any process of linguistic stratification, may be adequately unfolded into an individual dialogue, into individual argument and conversation between two persons, even while the exchanges in the dialogue are immanent to a single unitary language: they may not be in agreement, they may even be opposed, but they are diverse neither in their speech nor in their language. Such double-voicing, remaining within the boundaries of a single hermetic and unitary language system, without any underlying fundamental socio-linguistic orchestration, may be only a stylistically secondary accompaniment to the dialogue and forms of polemic.[22] The internal bifurcation (double-voicing) of discourse, sufficient to a single and unitary language and to a consistently monologic style, can never be a fundamental form of discourse: it is merely a game, a tempest in a teapot.

The double-voicedness one finds in prose is of another sort altogether. There—on the rich soil of novelistic prose—double-voicedness draws its energy, its dialogized ambiguity, not from *individual* dissonances, misunderstandings or contradictions (however tragic, however firmly grounded in individual destinies);[23] in the novel, this double-voicedness sinks its roots deep into a fun-

22. In neoclassicism, this double-voicing becomes crucial only in the low genres, especially in satire.
23. Within the limits of the world of poetry and a unitary language, everything important in such disagreements and contradictions can and must be laid out in a direct and pure dramatic dialogue.

damental, socio-linguistic speech diversity and multi-languaged-ness. True, even in the novel heteroglossia is by and large always personified, incarnated in individual human figures, with dis-agreements and oppositions individualized. But such oppositions of individual wills and minds are submerged in *social* heteroglos-sia, they are reconceptualized through it. Oppositions between individuals are only surface upheavals of the untamed elements in social heteroglossia, surface manifestations of those elements that play *on* such individual oppositions, make them contradic-tory, saturate their consciousness and discourses with a more fun-damental speech diversity.

Therefore the internal dialogism of double-voiced prose dis-course can never be exhausted thematically (just as the meta-phoric energy of language can never be exhausted thematically); it can never be developed into the motivation or subject for a manifest dialogue, such as might fully embody, with no residue, the internally dialogic potential embedded in linguistic hetero-glossia. The internal dialogism of authentic prose discourse, which grows organically out of a stratified and heteroglot lan-guage, cannot fundamentally be dramatized or dramatically re-solved (brought to an authentic end); it cannot ultimately be fitted into the frame of any manifest dialogue, into the frame of a mere conversation between persons; it is not ultimately divisible into verbal exchanges possessing precisely marked boundaries.[24] This double-voicedness in prose is prefigured in language itself (in authentic metaphors, as well as in myth), in language as a so-cial phenomenon that is becoming in history, socially stratified and weathered in this process of becoming.

The relativizing of linguistic consciousness, its crucial par-ticipation in the social multi- and vari-languagedness of evolving languages, the various wanderings of semantic and expressive in-tentions and the trajectory of this consciousness through various languages (languages that are all equally well conceptualized and equally objective), the inevitable necessity for such a conscious-ness to speak indirectly, conditionally, in a refracted way—these are all indispensable prerequisites for an authentic double-voiced prose discourse. This double-voicedness makes its presence felt by the novelist in the living heteroglossia of language, and in the

24. The more consistent and unitary the language, the more acute, dra-matic and "finished" such exchanges generally are.

multi-languagedness surrounding and nourishing his own consciousness; it is not invented in superficial, isolated rhetorical polemics with another person.

If the novelist loses touch with this linguistic ground of prose style, if he is unable to attain the heights of a relativized, Galilean linguistic consciousness, if he is deaf to organic double-voicedness and to the internal dialogization of living and evolving discourse, then he will never comprehend, or even realize, the actual possibilities and tasks of the novel as a genre. He may, of course, create an artistic work that compositionally and thematically will be similar to a novel, will be "made" exactly as a novel is made, but he will not thereby have created a novel. The style will always give him away. We will recognize the naively self-confident or obtusely stubborn unity of a smooth, pure single-voiced language (perhaps accompanied by a primitive, artificial, worked-up double-voicedness). We quickly sense that such an author finds it easy to purge his work of speech diversity: he simply does not listen to the fundamental heteroglossia inherent in actual language; he mistakes social overtones, which create the timbres of words, for irritating noises that it is his task to eliminate. The novel, when torn out of authentic linguistic speech diversity, emerges in most cases as a "closet drama," with detailed, fully developed and "artistically worked out" stage directions (it is, of course, bad drama). In such a novel, divested of its language diversity, authorial language inevitably ends up in the awkward and absurd position of the language of stage directions in plays.[25]

The double-voiced prose word has a double meaning. But the poetic word, in the narrow sense, also has a double, even a multiple, meaning. It is this that basically distinguishes it from the word as concept, or the word as term. The poetic word is a trope, requiring a precise feeling for the two meanings contained in it.

But no matter how one understands the interrelationship of meanings in a poetic symbol (a trope), this interrelationship is never of the dialogic sort; it is impossible under any conditions or at any time to imagine a trope (say, a metaphor) being unfolded

---

25. In his well-known works on the theory and technique of the novel, Spielhagen focuses on precisely such unnovelistic novels, and ignores precisely the kind of potential specific to the novel as a genre. As a theoretician Spielhagen was deaf to heteroglot language and to that which it specifically generates: double-voiced discourse.

into the two exchanges of a dialogue, that is, two meanings parceled out between two separate voices. For this reason the dual meaning (or multiple meaning) of the symbol never brings in its wake dual accents. On the contrary, one voice, a single-accent system, is fully sufficient to express poetic ambiguity. It is possible to interpret the interrelationships of different meanings in a symbol logically (as the relationship of a part or an individual to the whole, as for example a proper noun that has become a symbol, or the relationship of the concrete to the abstract and so on); one may grasp this relationship philosophically and ontologically, as a special kind of representational relationship, or as a relationship between essence and appearance and so forth, or one may shift into the foreground the emotional and evaluative dimension of such relationship—but all these types of relationships between various meanings do not and cannot go beyond the boundaries of the relationship between a word and its object, or the boundaries of various aspects in the object. The entire event is played out between the word and its object; all of the play of the poetic symbol is in that space. A symbol cannot presuppose any fundamental relationship to another's word, to another's voice. The polysemy of the poetic symbol presupposes the unity of a voice with which it is identical, and it presupposes that such a voice is completely alone within its own discourse. As soon as another's voice, another's accent, the possibility of another's point of view breaks through this play of the symbol, the poetic plane is destroyed and the symbol is translated onto the plane of prose.

To understand the difference between ambiguity in poetry and double-voicedness in prose, it is sufficient to take any symbol and give it an ironic accent (in a correspondingly appropriate context, of course), that is, to introduce into it one's own voice, to refract within it one's own fresh intention.[26] In this process the poetic symbol—while remaining, of course, a symbol—is at one and the same time translated onto the plane of prose and becomes a dou-

26. Alexei Alexandrovich Karenin had the habit of avoiding certain words, and expressions connected with them. He made up double-voiced constructions outside any context, exclusively on the intonational plane: "'Well, yes, as you see, your devoted husband, as devoted as in the first year of marriage, is burning with impatience to see you,' he said in his slow high-pitched voice and in the tone in which he almost always addressed her, a tone of derision for anyone who could really talk like that" (*Anna Karenina* [New York: Signet, 1961] part 1, ch. 30; translation by David Magarshack).

ble-voiced word: in the space between the word and its object another's word, another's accent intrudes, a mantle of materiality is
cast over the symbol (an operation of this sort would naturally result in a rather simple and primitive double-voiced structure).

An example of this simplest type of prosification of the poetic
symbol in *Evgenij Onegin* is the stanza on Lensky:

Of love he [Lensky] sang, love's service choosing,
And timid was his simple tune
As ever artless maiden's musing,
As babes aslumber, as the moon. . . .[27]

The poetic symbols of this stanza are organized simultaneously
at two levels: the level of Lensky's lyrics themselves—in the semantic and expressive system of the "Göttigen Geist"—and on
the level of Pushkin's speech, for whom the "Göttigen Geist"
with its language and its poetics is merely an instantiation of the
literary heteroglossia of the epoch, but one that is already becoming typical: a fresh tone, a fresh voice amid the multiple voices of
literary language, literary world views and the life these world
views regulate. Some other voices in this heteroglossia—of literature and of the real life contemporaneous with it—would be
Onegin's Byronic-Chateaubriandesque language, the Richardsonian language and world of the provincial Tatiana, the down-to-
earth rustic language spoken at the Larins' estate, the language
and the world of Tatiana in Petersburg and other languages as
well—including the indirect languages of the author—which undergo change in the course of the work. The whole of this heteroglossia (*Evgenij Onegin* is an encyclopedia of the styles and languages of the epoch) orchestrates the intentions of the author and
is responsible for the authentically novelistic style of this work.

Thus the images in the above-cited stanza, being ambiguous
(metaphorical) poetic symbols serving Lensky's intentions in
Lensky's belief system, become double-voiced prose symbols in
the system of Pushkin's speech. These are, of course, authentic
prose symbols, arising from the heteroglossia inherent in the epoch's evolving literary language, not a superficial, rhetorical parody or irony.

Such is the distinction between true double-voicedness in fic-

---

27. We offer an analysis of this example in the essay "From the Prehistory
of Novelistic Discourse" (cf. pp. 43–45 in the current volume).

tive practice, and the *single-voiced* double or multiple meaning that finds expression in the purely poetic symbol. The ambiguity of double-voiced discourse is internally dialogized, fraught with dialogue, and may in fact even give birth to dialogues comprised of truly separate voices (but such dialogues are not dramatic; they are, rather, interminable prose dialogues). What is more, double-voicedness is never exhausted in these dialogues, it cannot be extracted fully from the discourse—not by a rational, logical counting of the individual parts, nor by drawing distinctions between the various parts of a monologic unit of discourse (as happens in rhetoric), nor by a definite cut-off between the verbal exchanges of a finite dialogue, such as occurs in the theater. Authentic double-voicedness, although it generates novelistic prose dialogues, is not exhausted in these dialogues and remains in the discourse, in language, like a spring of dialogism that never runs dry—for the internal dialogism of discourse is something that inevitably accompanies the social, contradictory historical becoming of language.

If the central problem in poetic theory is the problem of the poetic symbol, then the central problem in prose theory is the problem of the double-voiced, internally dialogized word, in all its diverse types and variants.

For the novelist working in prose, the object is always entangled in someone else's discourse about it, it is already present with qualifications, an object of dispute that is conceptualized and evaluated variously, inseparable from the heteroglot social apperception of it. The novelist speaks of this "already qualified world" in a language that is heteroglot and internally dialogized. Thus both object and language are revealed to the novelist in their historical dimension, in the process of social and heteroglot becoming. For the novelist, there is no world outside his socioheteroglot perception—and there is no language outside the heteroglot intentions that stratify that world. Therefore it is possible to have, even in the novel, that profound but unique unity of a language (or more precisely, of languages) with its own object, with its own world, unity of the sort one finds in poetry. Just as the poetic image seems to have been born out of language itself, to have sprung organically from it, to have been pre-formed in it, so also novelistic images seem to be grafted organically on to their own double-voiced language, pre-formed, as it were, within it, in the innards of the distinctive multi-speechedness organic to that language. In the novel, the "already bespoke quality" [*ogovorennost'*] of the world is woven together with the "already uttered" quality [*peregovorennost'*] of language, into the unitary event of the world's heteroglot becoming, in both social consciousness and language.

Even the poetic word (in the narrow sense) must break through to its object, penetrate the alien word in which the object is entangled; it also encounters heteroglot language and must break through in order to create a unity and a pure intentionality (which is neither given nor ready-made). But the trajectory of the poetic word toward its own object and toward the unity of language is a path along which the poetic word is continually encountering someone else's word, and each takes new bearings from the other; the records of the passage remain in the slag of the creative process, which is then cleared away (as scaffolding is cleared away once construction is finished), so that the finished work may rise as unitary speech, one co-extensive with its object, as if it were speech about an "Edenic" world. This single-voiced purity and unqualified directness that intentions possess in poetic discourse so crafted is purchased at the price of a certain conventionality in poetic language.

If the art of poetry, as a utopian philosophy of genres, gives rise to the conception of a purely poetic, extrahistorical language, a language far removed from the petty rounds of everyday life, a language of the gods—then it must be said that the art of prose is close to a conception of languages as historically concrete and living things. The prose art presumes a deliberate feeling for the historical and social concreteness of living discourse, as well as its relativity, a feeling for its participation in historical becoming and in social struggle; it deals with discourse that is still warm from that struggle and hostility, as yet unresolved and still fraught with hostile intentions and accents; prose art finds discourse in this state and subjects it to the dynamic-unity of its own style.

The Speaking Person in the Novel

We have seen that social heteroglossia, the heteroglot sense of the world and of society orchestrating a novelistic theme, either enters the novel as impersonal stylizations of generic, professional and other social languages—impersonal, but pregnant with the images of speaking persons—or it enters as the fully embodied image of a posited author, of narrators or, finally, as characters.

The novelist does not acknowledge any unitary, singular, naively (or conditionally) indisputable or sacrosanct language. Language is present to the novelist only as something stratified and heteroglot. Therefore, even when heteroglossia remains outside the novel, when the novelist comes forward with his own unitary and fully affirming language (without any distancing, refraction or qualifications) he knows that such language is not self-evident and is not in itself incontestable, that it is uttered in a heteroglot environment, that such a language must be championed, purified, defended, motivated. In a novel even such unitary and direct language is polemical and apologetic, that is, it interrelates dialogically with heteroglossia. It is precisely this that defines the utterly distinctive orientation of discourse in the novel—an orientation that is contested, contestable and contesting—for this discourse cannot forget or ignore, either through naiveté or by design, the heteroglossia that surrounds it.

Thus heteroglossia either enters the novel in person (so to speak) and assumes material form within it in the images of speaking persons, or it determines, as a dialogizing background, the special resonance of novelistic discourse.

From this follows the decisive and distinctive importance of the novel as a genre: the human being in the novel is first, foremost and always a speaking human being; the novel requires speaking persons bringing with them their own unique ideological discourse, their own language.

The fundamental condition, that which makes a novel a novel, that which is responsible for its stylistic uniqueness, is the *speaking person and his discourse*.

To properly understand this statement one must distinguish with great care between three aspects.

(1) The speaking person and his discourse in the novel is an object of *verbal* artistic representation. A speaking person's discourse in the novel is not merely transmitted or reproduced; it is, precisely, *artistically represented* and thus—in contrast to drama—it is represented *by means of* (authorial) *discourse*. But the speaking person and his discourse as the object of discourse are highly specific: one cannot talk about discourse as one talks about other objects of speech—mute things, phenomena, events and so forth; such discourse requires absolutely special formal devices of speech and its own devices for representing words.

(2) Individual character and individual fates—and the individual discourse that is determined by these and only these—are in themselves of no concern for the novel. The distinctive qualities of a character's discourse always strive for a certain social significance, a social breadth; such discourses are always potential languages. Therefore a character's discourse may also be a factor stratifying language, introducing heteroglossia into it.

(3) The speaking person in the novel is always, to one degree or another, an *ideologue*, and his words are always *ideologemes*. A particular language in a novel is always a particular way of viewing the world, one that strives for a social significance. It is precisely as ideologemes that discourse becomes the object of representation in the novel, and it is for the same reason novels are never in danger of becoming a mere aimless verbal play. The novel, being a dialogized representation of an ideologically freighted discourse (in most cases actual and really present) is of all verbal genres the one least susceptible to aestheticism as such, to a purely formalistic playing about with words. Thus when an aesthete undertakes to write a novel, his aestheticism is not revealed in the novel's formal construction, but exclusively in the fact that in the novel there is represented a speaking person who happens to be an ideologue for aestheticism, who exposes convictions that then are subjected in the novel to contest. Of such a sort is Wilde's *Picture of Dorian Gray*, and such are the early works of Thomas Mann, Henri de Régnier,[f] the early Huysmans,[g] the early Barrès[h] and the early André Gide. Thus even an aesthete, working on a novel, becomes in this genre an ideologue who must defend and try out his ideological positions, who must become both a polemicist and an apologist.

The speaking person and his discourse is, as we have said, what makes a novel a novel, the thing responsible for the uniqueness of the genre. But in a novel, of course, the speaking person is not all that is represented, and people themselves need not be represented *only* as speakers. No less than a person in drama or in epic,

---

f. Henri de Régnier (1864–1936). Reference is to such works as *Le Bon plaisir* (1904).

g. Joris Karl Huysmans (1848–1907). Reference is to *À rebours* (1884).

h. Maurice Barrès (1862–1923). Reference here is to the trilogy, *Culte du moi* (consisting of *Sous l'oeil des barbares* [1888], *Un Homme libre* [1889] and *Le Jardin de Bérénice* [1891]).

the person in a novel may *act*—but such action is always high-lighted by ideology, is always harnessed to the character's discourse (even if that discourse is as yet only a potential discourse), is associated with an ideological motif and occupies a definite ideological position. The action and individual act of a character in a novel are essential in order to expose—as well as to test—his ideological position, his discourse. The nineteenth-century novel, it is true, created an important novel-type in which the hero is a man who *only* talks, who is unable to act and is condemned to naked words: to dreams, to ineffective preaching, to school teaching, to fruitless meditation and so forth. Of such a sort, for example, is the Russian novel-type in which an intellectual ideologue is tested (the simplest model is *Rudin*).

Such an inactive hero is only one thematic variant possible for the novelistic hero. Usually a hero acts no less in a novel than he does in an epic. The crucial distinction between him and the epic hero is to be found in the fact that the hero of a novel not only acts but talks, too, and his action has no shared meaning for the community, is not uncontested and takes place not in an uncontested epic world where all meanings are shared. Such action therefore always requires some ideological qualification, there is always some ideological position behind it and it will not be the only one possible; such a position is therefore always open to contest. The ideological position of the epic hero is meaningful for the whole community and for the whole epic world; the hero does not have any *particular* ideology that functions as one ideology among other possible ideologies. It is of course possible for the epic hero to deliver lengthy speeches (just as it is possible for a novelistic hero to be silent), but the epic hero's discourse is not ideologically demarcated (it is marked off only formally, in terms of composition and plot); it merges with the author's discourse. But the author, too, does not demarcate his own ideology, which merges with that of the community—the only ideology possible. In the epic there is one unitary and singular belief system. In the novel there are many such belief systems, with the hero generally acting within his *own* system. For this reason there are no speaking persons in the epic who function as representatives of different languages—in the epic, the speaker is, in essence, solely the author alone, and discourse is a single, unitary authorial discourse.

In the novel a character may also be depicted who thinks and acts (and, of course, talks) in compliance with the author's wishes, a character who acts irreproachably, precisely as he is supposed to act. But such novelistic irreproachability is far from being the kind of naive conflictlessness that characterizes the epic. Even if the ideological position of such a character is not demarcated vis-à-vis that of the author (that is, if it merges with it), it is in any case demarcated vis-à-vis the heteroglossia surrounding it: the irreproachability of the character is contrasted to this heteroglossia in a forensic and polemical way. Examples of such characters are the irreproachable heroes of the Baroque novel and the heroes of Sentimentalism, such as Grandison. The acts of such characters are highlighted ideologically and qualified by means of a forensic and polemical discourse.

The activity of a character in a novel is always ideologically demarcated: he lives and acts in an ideological world of his own (and not in the unitary world of the epic), he has his own perception of the world that is incarnated in his action and in his discourse.

But is it impossible to reveal, through a character's acts and through these acts alone, his ideological position and the ideological world at its heart, without representing his discourse?

It cannot be done, because it is impossible to represent an alien ideological world adequately without first permitting it to sound, without having first revealed the special discourse peculiar to it. After all, a really adequate discourse for portraying a world's unique ideology can only be that world's own discourse, although not that discourse in itself, but only in conjunction with the discourse of an author. A novelist may even choose not to give his character a direct discourse of his own, he may confine himself to the representation of the character's actions alone; in such an authorial representation, however, if it is thorough and adequate, the alien discourse (i.e., the discourse of the character himself) always sounds together with authorial speech (cf. the hybrid constructions analyzed by us in the previous chapter).

As we saw in the preceding chapter, the speaking person in the novel need not necessarily be incarnated in a character. A character is but one of the forms a speaking person might assume (although, true, the one that is most important). Heteroglot languages may also enter the novel in the form of impersonal, parodied stylizations (as in the work of English and German comic novelists), or in the form of (relatively nonparodic) stylizations or in the form of inserted genres, posited authors or *skaz*; finally, even unqualified authorial speech is a language in this sense insofar as it is polemical and forensic, i.e., insofar as it contrasts itself as a distinctive language different from other such languages in the heteroglot world by being to a certain extent focused on itself—that is, insofar as such authorial language not only represents, but is itself represented.

All these languages—even when they are not incarnated in a character—have been made socially and historically concrete and to one degree or another have become reified—only a single and unitary language, one that does not acknowledge other languages alongside itself, can be subject to reification—and therefore the images of speaking persons, clothed in the specifics of a given society at a given point in history, show through behind them. Characteristic for the novel as a genre is not the image of a man in his own right, but a man who is precisely the *image of a language*. But in order that language become an artistic image, it must become speech from speaking lips, conjoined with the image of a speaking person.

If the subject making the novel specifically a novel is defined as a speaking person and his discourse, striving for social significance and a wider general application as one distinctive language in a heteroglot world—then the central problem for a stylistics of the novel may be formulated as the problem of *artistically representing language, the problem of representing the image of a language.*

It must be said that this problem has not yet been posed in terms adequate to its scope or to the basic principles it engages. For this reason the specific features of a stylistics for the novel have eluded investigators. Tentative gestures have however been made: scholarly attention has tended increasingly in its study of prose to focus on such unique phenomena as the stylization of languages, parodies of languages and *skaz*. It is characteristic of all these phenomena that the discourse in them not only represents, but is *itself* represented; social language in them (whether generic, professional or that of a literary trend) becomes the object of a re-processing, reformulation and artistic transformation that is free and oriented toward art: typical aspects of language are selected as characteristic of or symbolically crucial to the language. Departures from the empirical reality of the represented language may under these circumstances be highly significant, not only in the sense of their being biased choices or exaggerations of certain aspects peculiar to the given language, but even in the sense that they are a free creation of new elements—which, while true to the spirit of the given language, are utterly foreign to the actual language's empirical evidence. It is precisely such an elevation of language aspects into symbols of language that is especially characteristic of *skaz* (Leskov, and in particular Remizov). All such phenomena (stylization, parody, *skaz*) are also, as has been shown above, double-voiced and double-languaged phenomena.

Simultaneously, and parallel with this interest in stylization, parody and *skaz*, there developed an acute interest in the problem of transmitting another's speech, and in the problem of syntactic and stylistic forms available for such transmission. This interest developed specifically in Germany, in the philological study of French and German. Its representatives concentrated by and large on the linguistic and stylistic (or even narrowly grammatical) side of the question, but some nevertheless came close (Leo Spitzer) to dealing with the problem of the artistic representation of another's speech—which is the central problem of novelistic prose. All the same, the problem of the *image of a language* was not posed by them with adequate clarity, and in fact the very positing of the problem of means for transmitting another's speech failed to receive the breadth or principled treatment it required.

The transmission and assessment of the speech of others, the discourse of another, is one of the most widespread and fundamental topics of human speech. In all areas of life and ideological activity, our speech is filled to overflowing with other people's words, which are transmitted with highly varied degrees of accuracy and impartiality. The more intensive, differentiated and highly developed the social life of a speaking collective, the greater is the importance attaching, among other possible subjects of talk, to another's word, another's utterance, since another's word will be the subject of passionate communication, an object of interpretation, discussion, evaluation, rebuttal, support, further development and so on.

The theme of the speaking person and his discourse everywhere requires special formal devices of speech. As we have already said, discourse as the subject of discourse is after all a subject *sui generis*, one that poses special tasks for our language in *all* its spheres.

Before, then, taking up the issue of the artistic representation of another's speech conceived as the image of a language, we should say something about the importance in extra-artistic areas of life and ideology of the topic of the speaking person and his discourse. While in the many forms available for transmitting another's speech outside the novel there is no defining concern for the images of a language, such forms are used in the novel for self-enrichment—but not before they are first transformed and subjected within it to the new holistic unity of the novel itself (and, conversely, novels have a powerful influence on the extra-artistic perception and transmission of another's discourse).

The topic of a speaking person has enormous importance in everyday life. In real life we hear speech about speakers and their discourse at every step. We can go so far as to say that in real life people talk most of all about what others talk about—they transmit, recall, weigh and pass judgment on other people's words, opinions, assertions, information; people are upset by others' words, or agree with them, contest them, refer to them and so forth. Were we to eavesdrop on snatches of raw dialogue in the street, in a crowd, in lines, in a foyer and so forth, we would hear how often the words "he says," "people say," "he said . . . " are repeated, and in the conversational hurly-burly of people in a crowd, everything often fuses into one big "he says . . . you say . . . I say. . . ." Reflect how enormous is the weight of "everyone says" and "it is said" in public opinion, public rumor, gossip, slander and so forth. One must also consider the psychological importance in our lives of what others say about us, and the importance, for us, of understanding and interpreting these words of others ("living hermeneutics").

The importance of this motif is in no way diminished in the higher and better-organized areas of everyday communication. Every conversation is full of transmissions and interpretations of other people's words. At every step one meets a "quotation" or a "reference" to something that a particular person said, a reference to "people say" or "everyone says," to the words of the person one is talking with, or to one's own previous words, to a newspaper, an official decree, a document, a book and so forth. The majority of our information and opinions is usually not communicated in direct form as our own, but with reference to some indefinite and general source: "I heard," "It's generally held that . . . ," "It is thought that . . ." and so forth. Take one of the most widespread occurrences in our everyday life, conversations about some official meeting: they are all constructed on the transmission, interpretation and evaluation of various kinds of verbal performance, resolutions, the rejected and accepted corrections that are made to them and so forth. Thus talk goes on about speaking people and their words everywhere—this motif returns again and again; it either accompanies the development of the other topics in everyday life, or directly governs speech as its leading theme.

Further examples of the significance of the topic of the speaking person in everyday life would be superfluous. We need only keep our ears open to the speech sounding everywhere around us to reach such a conclusion: in the everyday speech of any person living in society, no less than half (on the average) of all the words uttered by him will be someone else's words (consciously someone else's), transmitted with varying degrees of precision and impartiality (or more precisely, partiality).

It goes without saying that not all transmitted words belonging to someone else lend themselves, when fixed in writing, to enclosure in quotation marks. That degree of otherness and purity in another's word that in written speech would require quotation marks (as per the intention of the speaker himself, how he himself determines this degree of otherness) is required much less frequently in everyday speech.

Furthermore, syntactic means for formulating the transmitted speech of another are far from exhausted by the grammatical paradigms of direct and indirect discourse: the means for its incorporation, for its formulation and for indicating different degrees of shading are highly varied. This must be kept in mind if we are to make good our claim that of all words uttered in everyday life, no less than half belong to someone else.

The speaking person and his discourse are not, in everyday speech, subjects for artistic representation, but rather they are topics in the engaged transmission of practical information. For this reason everyday speech is not concerned with forms of representation, but only with means of *transmission*. These means, conceived both as a way to formulate verbally and stylistically another's speech and as a way to provide an interpretive frame, a tool for re-conceptualization and re-accenting—from direct verbatim quotation in a verbal transmission to malicious and deliberately parodic distortion of another's word, slander—are highly varied.[28]

28. There are different ways to falsify someone else's words while taking them to their furthest extreme, to reveal their *potential* content. Rhetoric, the art of argument and "heuristics" explore this area somewhat.

The following must be kept in mind: that the speech of another, once enclosed in a context, is—no matter how accurately transmitted—always subject to certain semantic changes. The context embracing another's word is responsible for its dialogizing background, whose influence can be very great. Given the appropriate methods for framing, one may bring about fundamental changes even in another's utterance accurately quoted. Any sly and ill-disposed polemicist knows very well which dialogizing backdrop he should bring to bear on the accurately quoted words of his opponent, in order to distort their sense. By manipulating the effects of context, it is very easy to emphasize the brute materiality of another's words, and to stimulate dialogic reactions associated with such "brute materiality"; thus it is, for instance, very easy to make even the most serious utterance comical. Another's discourse, when introduced into a speech context, enters the speech that frames it not in a mechanical bond but in a chemical union (on the semantic and emotionally expressive level); the degree of dialogized influence, one on the other, can be enormous. For this reason we cannot, when studying the various forms for transmitting another's speech, treat any of these forms in isolation from the means for its contextualized (dialogizing) framing—the one is indissolubly linked with the other. The formulation of another's speech as well as its framing (and the context can begin preparing for the introduction of another's speech far back in the text) both express the unitary act of dialogic interaction with that speech, a relation determining the entire nature of its transmission and all the changes in meaning and accent that take place in it during transmission.

The speaking person and his discourse in everyday speech, we have said, serves as a *subject* for the engaged, practical transmission of information, and not as a *means* of representation. As a matter of fact, all everyday forms for transmitting another's discourse, as well as the changes in discourse connected with these forms—from subtle nuances in meaning and emphasis to gross externalized distortions of the verbal composition—are defined by this practical engagement. But this emphasis on engaged discourse does not exclude certain aspects of representability. In order to assess and divine the real meaning of others' words in everyday life, the following are surely of decisive significance: *who* precisely is speaking, and under *what* concrete circumstances? When we attempt to understand and make assessments in everyday life, we do not separate discourse from the personality speaking it (as we can in the ideological realm), because the personality is so materially present to us. And the entire speaking situation is very important: who is present during it, with what expression or mimicry is it uttered, with what shades of intonation? During everyday verbal transmission of another's words, the entire complex of discourse as well as the personality of the speaker may be expressed and even played with (in the form of anything from an exact replication to a parodic ridiculing and exaggeration of gestures and intonations). This representation is always subordinated to the tasks of practical, engaged transmission and is wholly determined by these tasks. This of course does not involve the artistic image of a speaking person and the artistic image of his discourse, and even less the image of a language. Nevertheless, everyday episodes involving the same person, when they become linked, already entail prose devices for the double-voiced an even double-languaged representation of another's words.

These conversations about speaking persons and others' words in everyday life do not go beyond the boundaries of the superficial aspects of discourse, the weight it carries in a specific situation; the deeper semantic and emotionally expressive levels of discourse do not enter the game. The topic of a speaking person takes on quite another significance in the ordinary ideological workings of our consciousness, in the process of assimilating our consciousness to the ideological world. The ideological becoming of a human being, in this view, is the process of selectively assimilating the words of others.

When verbal disciplines are taught in school, two basic modes are recognized for the appropriation and transmission—simultaneously—of another's words (a text, a rule, a model): "reciting by heart" and "retelling in one's own words." The latter mode poses on a small scale the task implicit in all prose stylistics: retelling a text in one's own words is to a certain extent a double-voiced narration of another's words, for indeed "one's own words" must not completely dilute the quality that makes another's words unique; a retelling in one's own words should have a mixed character, able when necessary to reproduce the style and expressions of the transmitted text. It is this second mode used in schools for transmitting another's discourse, "retelling in one's own words," that includes within it an entire series of forms for the appropriation while transmitting of another's words, depending upon the character of the text being appropriated and the pedagogical environment in which it is understood and evaluated.

The tendency to assimilate others' discourse takes on an even deeper and more basic significance in an individual's ideological becoming, in the most fundamental sense. Another's discourse performs here no longer as information, directions, rules, models and so forth—but strives rather to determine the very bases of our ideological interrelations with the world, the very basis of our behavior; it performs here as *authoritative discourse*, and an *internally persuasive discourse*.

Both the authority of discourse and its internal persuasiveness may be united in a single word—one that is *simultaneously* authoritative and internally persuasive—despite the profound differences between these two categories of alien discourse. But such unity is rarely a given—it happens more frequently that an individual's becoming, an ideological process, is characterized precisely by a sharp gap between these two categories: in one, the authoritative word (religious, political, moral; the word of a father, of adults and of teachers, etc.) that does not know internal persuasiveness, in the other internally persuasive word that is denied all privilege, backed up by no authority at all, and is frequently not even acknowledged in society (not by public opinion, nor by scholarly norms, nor by criticism), not even in the legal code. The struggle and dialogic interrelationship of these categories of ideological discourse are what usually determine the history of an individual ideological consciousness.

The authoritative word demands that we acknowledge it, that we make it our own; it binds us, quite independent of any power it might have to persuade us internally; we encounter it with its authority already fused to it. The authoritative word is located in a distanced zone, organically connected with a past that is felt to be hierarchically higher. It is, so to speak, the word of the fathers. Its authority was already *acknowledged* in the past. It is a *prior* discourse. It is therefore not a question of choosing it from among other possible discourses that are its equal. It is given (it sounds) in lofty spheres, not those of familiar contact. Its language is a special (as it were, hieratic) language. It can be profaned. It is akin to taboo, i.e., a name that must not be taken in vain.

We cannot embark here on a survey of the many and varied types of authoritative discourse (for example, the authority of religious dogma, or of acknowledged scientific truth or of a currently fashionable book), nor can we survey different degrees of authoritativeness. For our purposes only formal features for the transmission and representation of authoritative discourse are important, those common to all types and degrees of such discourse.

The degree to which a word may be conjoined with authority—whether the authority is recognized by us or not—is what determines its specific demarcation and individuation in discourse; it requires a *distance* vis-à-vis itself (this distance may be valorized as positive or as negative, just as our attitude toward it may be sympathetic or hostile). Authoritative discourse may organize around itself great masses of other types of discourses (which interpret it, praise it, apply it in various ways), but the authoritative discourse itself does not merge with these (by means of, say, gradual transitions); it remains sharply demarcated, compact and inert: it demands, so to speak, not only quotation marks but a demarcation even more magisterial, a special script, for instance.[29] It is considerably more difficult to incorporate semantic changes into such a discourse, even with the help of a framing context: its semantic structure is static and dead, for it is fully complete, it has but a single meaning, the letter is fully sufficient to the sense and calcifies it.

It is not a free appropriation and assimilation of the word itself that authoritative discourse seeks to elicit from us; rather, it demands our unconditional allegiance. Therefore authoritative discourse permits no play with the context framing it, no play with its borders, no gradual and flexible transitions, no spontaneously creative stylizing variants on it. It enters our verbal consciousness as a compact and indivisible mass; one must either totally affirm it, or totally reject it. It is indissolubly fused with its authority—with political power, an institution, a person—and it stands and falls together with that authority. One cannot divide it up—agree with one part, accept but not completely another part, reject utterly a third part. Therefore the distance we ourselves observe vis-à-vis this authoritative discourse remains unchanged in all its projections: a playing with distances, with fusion and dis-

29. Often the authoritative word is in fact a word spoken by another in a foreign language (cf. for example the phenomenon of foreign-language religious texts in most cultures).

solution, with approach and retreat, is not here possible.

All these functions determine the uniqueness of authoritative discourse, both as a concrete means for formulating itself during transmission and as its distinctive means for being framed by contexts. The zone of the framing context must likewise be distanced—no familiar contact is possible here either. The one perceiving and understanding this discourse is a distant descendent; there can be no arguing with him.

These factors also determine the potential role of authoritative discourse in prose. Authoritative discourse can not be represented—it is only transmitted. Its inertia, its semantic finiteness and calcification, the degree to which it is hard-edged, a thing in its own right, the impermissibility of any free stylistic development in relation to it—all this renders the artistic representation of authoritative discourse impossible. Its role in the novel is insignificant. It is by its very nature incapable of being double-voiced; it cannot enter into hybrid constructions. If completely deprived of its authority it becomes simply an object, a *relic*, a *thing*. It enters the artistic context as an alien body, there is no space around it to play in , no contradictory emotions—it is not surrounded by an agitated and cacophonous dialogic life, and the context around it dies, words dry up. For this reason images of official-authoritative truth, images of virtue (of any sort: monastic, spiritual, bureaucratic, moral, etc.) have never been successful in the novel. It suffices to mention the hopeless attempts of Gogol and Dostoevsky in this regard. For this reason the authoritative text always remains, in the novel, a dead quotation, something that falls out of the artistic context (for example, the evangelical texts in Tolstoy at the end of *Resurrection*).[30]

Authoritative discourses may embody various contents: authority as such, or the authoritativeness of tradition, of generally acknowledged truths, of the official line and other similar authorities. These discourses may have a variety of zones (determined by the degree to which they are distanced from the zone of contact) with a variety of relations to the presumed listener or interpreter (the apperceptive background presumed by the discourse, the degree of reciprocation between the two and so forth).

30. When analyzing a concrete example of authoritative discourse in a novel, it is necessary to keep in mind the fact that purely authoritative discourse may, in another epoch, be internally persuasive; this is especially true where ethics are concerned.

In the history of literary language, there is a struggle constantly being waged to overcome the official line with its tendency to distance itself from the zone of contact, a struggle against various kinds and degrees of authority. In this process discourse gets drawn into the contact zone, which results in semantic and emotionally expressive (intonational) changes: there is a weakening and degradation of the capacity to generate metaphors, and discourse becomes more reified, more concrete, more filled with everyday elements and so forth. All of this has been studied by psychology, but not from the point of view of its verbal formulation in possible inner monologues of developing human beings, the monologue that lasts a whole life. What confronts us is the complex problem presented by forms capable of expressing such a (dialogized) monologue.

When someone else's ideological discourse is internally persuasive for us and acknowledged by us, entirely different possibilities open up. Such discourse is of decisive significance in the evolution of an individual consciousness: consciousness awakens to independent ideological life precisely in a world of alien discourses surrounding it, and from which it cannot initially separate itself; the process of distinguishing between one's own and another's discourse, between one's own and another's thought, is activated rather late in development. When thought begins to work in an independent, experimenting and discriminating way, what first occurs is a separation between internally persuasive discourse and authoritarian enforced discourse, along with a rejection of those congeries of discourses that do not matter to us, that do not touch us.

Internally persuasive discourse—as opposed to one that is externally authoritative—is, as it is affirmed through assimilation, tightly interwoven with "one's own word."[31] In the everyday rounds of our consciousness, the internally persuasive word is half-ours and half–someone else's. Its creativity and productiveness consist precisely in the fact that such a word awakens new and independent words, that it organizes masses of our words from within, and does not remain in an isolated and static condition. It is not so much interpreted by us as it is further, that is, freely, developed, applied to new material, new conditions; it en-

---

31. One's own discourse is gradually and slowly wrought out of others' words that have been acknowledged and assimilated, and the boundaries between the two are at first scarcely perceptible.

ters into interanimating relationships with new contexts. More than that, it enters into an intense interaction, a *struggle* with other internally persuasive discourses. Our ideological development is just such an intense struggle within us for hegemony among various available verbal and ideological points of view, approaches, directions and values. The semantic structure of an internally persuasive discourse is *not finite*, it is *open*; in each of the new contexts that dialogize it, this discourse is able to reveal ever newer *ways to mean*.

The internally persuasive word is either a contemporary word, born in a zone of contact with unresolved contemporaneity, or else it is a word that has been reclaimed for contemporaneity; such a word relates to its descendents as well as to its contemporaries as if *both* were contemporaries; what is constitutive for it is a special conception of listeners, readers, perceivers. Every discourse presupposes a special conception of the listener, of his apperceptive background and the degree of his responsiveness; it presupposes a specific distance. All this is very important for coming to grips with the historical life of discourse. Ignoring such aspects and nuances leads to a reification of the word (and to a muffling of the dialogism native to it).

All of the above determine the methods for formulating internally persuasive discourse during its transmission, as well as methods for framing it in contexts. Such methods provide maximal interaction between another's word and its context, for the dialogizing influence they have on each other, for the free and creative development of another's word, for a gradation of transitions. They serve to govern the play of boundaries, the distance between that point where the context begins to prepare for the introduction of another's word and the point where the word is actually introduced (its "theme" may sound in the text long before the appearance of the actual word). These methods account for other peculiarities as well, which also express the essence of the internally persuasive word, such as that word's semantic openness to us, its capacity for further creative life in the context of our ideological consciousness, its unfinishedness and the inexhaustibility of our further dialogic interaction with it. We have not yet learned from it all it might tell us; we can take it into new contexts, attach it to new material, put it in a new situation in order to wrest new answers from it, new insights into its meaning, and even wrest from it new words of its *own* (since another's discourse, if productive, gives birth to a new word from us in response).

The means for formulating and framing internally persuasive discourse may be supple and dynamic to such an extent that this discourse may literally be *omnipresent* in the context, imparting to everything its own specific tones and from time to time breaking through to become a completely materialized thing, as another's word fully set off and demarcated (as happens in character zones). Such variants on the theme of another's discourse are widespread in all areas of creative ideological activity, and even in the narrowly scientific disciplines. Of such a sort is any gifted, creative exposition defining alien world views: such an exposition is always a free stylistic variation on another's discourse; it expounds another's thought in the style of that thought even while applying it to new material, to another way of posing the problem; it conducts experiments and gets solutions in the language of another's discourse.

In other less obvious instances we notice analogous phenomena. We have in mind first of all those instances of powerful influence exercised by another's discourse on a given author. When such influences are laid bare, the half-concealed life lived by another's discourse is revealed within the new context of the given author. When such an influence is deep and productive, there is no external imitation, no simple act of reproduction, but rather a further creative development of another's (more precisely, half-other) discourse in a new context and under new conditions.

In all these instances the important thing is not only forms for transmitting another's discourse, but the fact that in such forms there can always be found the embryonic beginnings of what is required for an artistic representation of another's discourse. A few changes in orientation and the internally persuasive word easily becomes an object of representation. For certain kinds of internally persuasive discourse can be fundamentally and organically fused with the image of a speaking person: ethical (discourse fused with the image of, let us say, a preacher), philosophical (discourse fused with the image of a wise man), sociopolitical (discourse fused with an image of a Leader). While creatively stylizing upon and experimenting with another's discourse, we attempt to guess, to imagine, how a person with authority might conduct himself in the given circumstances, the light he would cast on them with his discourse. In such experimental guesswork the image of the speaking person and his discourse become the object of creative, artistic imagination.[32]

This process—experimenting by turning persuasive discourse into speaking persons—becomes especially important in those cases where a struggle against such images has already begun, where someone is striving to liberate himself from the influence of such an image and its discourse by means of objectification, or is striving to expose the limitations of both image and discourse. The importance of struggling with another's discourse, its influence in the history of an individual's coming to ideological consciousness, is enormous. One's own discourse and one's own voice, although born of another or dynamically stimulated by another, will sooner or later begin to liberate themselves from the authority of the other's discourse. This process is made more complex by the fact that a variety of alien voices enter into the struggle for influence within an individual's consciousness (just as they struggle with one another in surrounding social reality). All this creates fertile soil for experimentally objectifying another's discourse. A conversation with an internally persuasive word that one has begun to resist may continue, but it takes on another character: it is questioned, it is put in a new situation in order to expose its weak sides, to get a feel for its boundaries, to experience it physically as an object. For this reason stylizing discourse by attributing it to a person often becomes parodic, although not crudely parodic—since another's word, having been at an earlier stage internally persuasive, mounts a resistance to this process and frequently begins to sound with no parodic overtones at all. Novelistic images, profoundly double-voiced and double-languaged, are born in such a soil, seek to objectivize the struggle with all types of internally persuasive alien discourse that had at one time held sway over the author (of such a type, for instance, is Pushkin's Onegin or Lermontov's Pechorin). At the heart of the *Prüfungsroman* is the same kind of subjective struggle with internally persuasive, alien discourse, and just such a liberation from this discourse by turning it into an object. Another illustration of what we mean here is provided by the *Bildungsroman*, but in such novels the maturation—a selecting, ideological process—is developed as a theme within the novel, whereas in

32. In Plato, Socrates serves as just such an artistic image of the wise man and teacher, an image employed for the purposes of experiment.

the *Prüfungsroman* the subjectivity of the author himself remains outside the work.

The works of Dostoevsky, in such a view, can be seen to occupy an extraordinary and unique place. The acute and intense interaction of another's word is present in his novels in two ways. In the first place in his characters' language there is a profound and unresolved conflict with another's word on the level of lived experience ("another's word about me"), on the level of ethical life (another's judgment, recognition or nonrecognition by another) and finally on the level of ideology (the world views of characters understood as unresolved and unresolvable dialogue). What Dostoevsky's characters *say* constitutes an arena of never-ending struggle with others' words, in all realms of life and creative ideological activity. For this reason these utterances may serve as excellent models of the most varied forms for transmitting and framing another's discourse. In the second place, the works (the novels) in their entirety, taken as utterances of their *author*, are the same never-ending, internally unresolved dialogues among characters (seen as embodied points of view) and between the author himself and his characters; the characters' discourse is never entirely subsumed and remains free and open (as does the discourse of the author himself). In Dostoevsky's novels, the life experience of the characters and their discourse may be resolved as far as plot is concerned, but internally they remain incomplete and unresolved.[33]

The enormous significance of the motif of the speaking person is obvious in the realm of ethical and legal thought and discourse. The speaking person and his discourse is, in these areas, the major topic of thought and speech. All fundamental categories of ethical and legal inquiry and evaluation refer to speaking persons precisely as such: conscience (the "voice of conscience," the "inner word"), repentance (a free admission, a statement of wrongdoing by the person himself), truth and falsehood, being liable and not liable, the right to vote [*pravo golosa*] and so on. An independent, responsible and active discourse is *the* fundamental indica-

---

33. Cf. our book *Problems of Dostoevsky's Art* [*Problemy tvorčestva Dostoevskogo*], Leningrad, 1929 (in its second and third editions, *Problems of Dostoevsky's Poetics* [*Problemy poetiki Dostoevskogo*], Moscow, 1963; Moscow, 1972). This book contains stylistic analyses of characters' utterances, revealing various forms of transmission and contextual framing.

tor of an ethical, legal and political human being. Challenges to this discourse, provocations of it, interpretations and assessments of it, the establishing of boundaries and forms for its activity (civil and political rights), the juxtaposing of various wills and discourses and so on—all these acts carry enormous weight in the realms of ethics and the law. It is enough to point out the role played in narrowly judicial spheres by formulation, analysis and interpretation of testimony, declarations, contracts, various documents and other forms of others' utterances; finally, of course, there is legal hermeneutics.

All this calls for further study. Juridical (and ethical) techniques have been developed for dealing with the discourse of another [after it has been uttered], for establishing authenticity, for determining degrees of veracity and so forth (for example, the process of notarizing and other such techniques). But problems connected with the methods used for formulating such kinds of discourse—compositional, stylistic, semantic and other—have not as yet been properly posed.

The problem of *confession* in cases being investigated for trial (what has made it necessary and what provokes it) has so far been interpreted only at the level of laws, ethics and psychology. Dostoevsky provides a rich body of material for posing this problem at the level of a philosophy of language (of discourse): the problem of a thought, a desire, a motivation that is authentic—as in the case of Ivan Karamazov, for instance—and how these problems are exposed in words; the role of the other in formulating discourse, problems surrounding an inquest and so forth.

The speaking person and his discourse, as subject of thought and speech, is of course treated in the ethical and legal realms only insofar as it contributes to the specific interests of these disciplines. All methods for transmitting, formulating and framing another's discourse are made subordinate to such special interests and orientations. However, even here elements of an artistic representation of another's word are possible, especially in the ethical realm: for example, a representation of the struggle waged by the voice of conscience with other voices that sound in a man, the internal dialogism leading to repentance and so forth. Artistic prose, the novelistic element present in ethical tracts, especially in confessions, may be quite significant—for example, in Epictetus, Marcus Aurelius, Augustine and Petrarch we can detect the embryonic beginnings of the *Prüfungs-* and *Bildungsroman*.

Our motif carries even greater weight in the realm of religious thought and discourse (mythological, mystical and magical). The primary subject of this discourse is a being who speaks: a deity, a demon, a soothsayer, a prophet. Mythological thought does not, in general, acknowledge anything not alive or not responsive. Divining the will of a deity, of a demon (good or bad), interpreting signs of wrath or beneficence, tokens, indications and finally the transmission and interpretation of words directly spoken by a deity (revelation), or by his prophets, saints, soothsayers—all in all, the transmission and interpretation of the divinely inspired (as opposed to the profane) word are acts of religious thought and discourse having the greatest importance. All religious systems, even primitive ones, possess an enormous, highly specialized methodological apparatus (hermeneutics) for transmitting and interpreting various kinds of holy word.

The situation is somewhat different in the case of scientific thought. Here, the significance of discourse as such is comparatively weak. Mathematical and natural sciences do not acknowledge discourse as a subject in its own right. In scientific activity one must, of course, deal with another's discourse—the words of predecessors, the judgments of critics, majority opinion and so forth; one must deal with various forms for transmitting and interpreting another's word—struggle with an authoritative discourse, overcoming influences, polemics, references, quotations and so forth—but all this remains a mere operational necessity and does not affect the subject matter itself of the science, into whose composition the speaker and his discourse do not, of course, enter. The entire methodological apparatus of the mathematical and natural sciences is directed toward mastery over *mute objects, brute things,* that do not reveal themselves in words, that do not *comment on themselves.* Acquiring knowledge here is not connected with receiving and interpreting words or signs from the object itself under consideration.

In the humanities—as distinct from the natural and mathematical sciences—there arises the specific task of establishing, transmitting and interpreting the words of others (for example, the problem of sources in the methodology of the historical disciplines). And of course in the philological disciplines, the speaking person and his discourse is the fundamental object of investigation.

Philology has specific aims and approaches to its subject (the speaker and his discourse) that determine the ways it transmits and represents others' words (for example, discourse as an object of study in the history of language). However, within the limits of the humanities (and even of philology in the narrow sense) there is possible a twofold approach to another's word when it is treated as something we seek to understand.

The word can be perceived purely as an object (something that is, in its essence, a thing). It is perceived as such in the majority of the linguistic disciplines. In such a word-object even meaning becomes a thing: there can be no dialogic approach to such a word of the kind immanent to any deep and actual understanding. Understanding, so conceived, is inevitably abstract: it is completely separated from the living, ideological power of the word to mean—from its truth or falsity, its significance or insignificance, beauty or ugliness. Such a reified word-thing cannot be understood by attempts to penetrate its meaning dialogically: there can be no conversing with such a word.

In philology, however, a dialogic penetration into the word is obligatory (for indeed without it no sort of understanding is possible): dialogizing it opens up fresh aspects in the word (semantic aspects, in the broadest sense), which, since they were revealed by dialogic means, become more immediate to perception. Every step forward in our knowledge of the word is preceded by a "stage of genius"—*a sharpened dialogic relationship to the word*—that in turn uncovers fresh aspects within the word.

Precisely such an approach is needed, more concrete and that does not deflect discourse from its actual power to mean in real ideological life, an approach where objectivity of understanding is linked with dialogic vigor and a deeper penetration into discourse itself. No other approach is in fact possible in the area of poetics, or the history of literature (and in the history of ideologies in general) or to a considerable extent even in the philosophy of discourse: even the driest and flattest positivism in these disciplines cannot treat the word neutrally, as if it were a thing, but is obliged to initiate talk not only about words but in words, in order to penetrate their ideological meanings—which can only be grasped dialogically, and which include evaluation and response. The forms in which a dialogic understanding is transmitted and interpreted may, if the understanding is deep and vigorous, even come to have significant parallels with the double-voiced representations of another's discourse that we find in prose art. It should be noted that the novel always includes in itself the activity of coming to know another's word, a coming to knowledge whose process is represented in the novel.

Finally, a few words about the importance of our theme in the rhetorical genres. The speaker and his discourse is, indisputably, one of the most important subjects of rhetorical speech (and all other themes are inevitably implicated in the topic of discourse). In the rhetoric of the courts, for example, rhetorical discourse accuses or defends the subject of a trial, who is, of course, a speaker, and in so doing relies on his words, interprets them, polemicizes with them, creatively erecting *potential* discourses for the accused or for the defense (just such free creation of likely, but never actually uttered, words, sometimes whole speeches—"as he must have said" or "as he might have said"—was a device very widespread in ancient rhetoric); rhetorical discourse tries to outwit possible retorts to itself, it passes on and compiles the words of witnesses and so forth. In political rhetoric, for example, discourse can support some candidacy, represent the personality of a candidate, present and defend his point of view, his verbal statements, or in other cases protest against some decree, law, order, announcement, occasion—that is, protest against the specific verbal utterances toward which it is dialogically aimed.

Publicistic discourse also deals with the word itself and with the individual as its agent: it criticizes a speech, an article, a point of view; it polemicizes, exposes, ridicules and so forth. When it analyzes an act it uncovers its verbal motifs, the point of view in which it is grounded, it formulates such acts in words, providing them the appropriate emphases—ironic, indignant and so on. This does not mean, of course, that the rhetoric behind the word forgets that there are deeds, acts, a reality outside words. But such rhetoric has always to do with social man, whose most fundamental gestures are made meaningful ideologically through the word, or directly embodied in words.

The importance of another's speech as a subject in rhetoric is so great that the word frequently begins to cover over and substitute itself for reality; when this happens the word itself is diminished and becomes shallow. Rhetoric is often limited to purely verbal victories over the word; when this happens, rhetoric degenerates into a formalistic verbal play. But, we repeat, when discourse is torn from reality, it is fatal for the word itself as well: words grow sickly, lose semantic depth and flexibility, the capac-

ity to expand and renew their meanings in new living contexts—
they essentially die as discourse, for the signifying word lives
beyond itself, that is, it lives by means of directing its purposive-
ness outward. The exclusive concentration on another's discourse as a subject does not, however, in *itself* inevitably indicate
such a rupture between discourse and reality.

Rhetorical genres possess the most varied forms for transmitting another's speech, and for the most part these are intensely
dialogized forms. Rhetoric relies heavily on the vivid re-accentuating of the words it transmits (often to the point of distorting
them completely) that is accomplished by the appropriate framing context. Rhetorical genres provide rich material for studying
a variety of forms for transmitting another's speech, the most varied means for formulating and framing such speech. Using rhetoric, even a representation of a speaker and his discourse of the
sort one finds in prose art is possible—but the rhetorical double-
voicedness of such images is usually not very deep: its roots do
not extend to the dialogical essence of evolving language itself; it
is not structured on authentic heteroglossia but on a mere diversity of voices; in most cases the double-voicedness of rhetoric is
abstract and thus lends itself to formal, purely logical analysis of
the ideas that are parceled out in voices, an analysis that then
exhausts it. For this reason it is proper to speak of a distinctive
rhetorical double-voicedness, or, put another way, to speak of
the double-voiced rhetorical transmission of another's word (although it may involve some artistic aspects), in contrast to the
double-voiced *representation* of another's word in the novel with
its orientation toward the *image of a language*.

Such, then, is the importance of the speaker and his discourse
as a topic in all areas of everyday, as well as verbal-ideological,
life. It might be said, on the basis of our argument so far, that in
the makeup of almost every utterance spoken by a social person—from a brief response in a casual dialogue to major verbal-
ideological works (literary, scholarly and others)—a significant
number of words can be identified that are implicitly or explicitly
admitted as someone else's, and that are transmitted by a variety
of different means. Within the arena of almost every utterance an
intense interaction and struggle between one's own and another's
word is being waged, a process in which they oppose or dialogically interanimate each other. The utterance so conceived is a
considerably more complex and dynamic organism than it ap-

pears when construed simply as a thing that articulates the intention of the person uttering it, which is to see the utterance as a direct, single-voiced vehicle for expression.

That one of the main subjects of human speech is discourse itself has not up to now been sufficiently taken into consideration, nor has its crucial importance been appreciated. There has been no comprehensive philosophical grasp of all the ramifications of this fact. The specific nature of discourse as a topic of speech, one that requires the transmission and re-processing of another's word, has not been understood: one may speak of another's discourse only with the help of that alien discourse itself, although in the process, it is true, the speaker introduces into the other's words his own intentions and highlights the context of those words in his own way. To speak of discourse as one might speak of any other subject, that is, thematically, without any dialogized transmission of it, is possible only when such discourse is utterly reified, a thing; it is possible, for example, to talk about the word in such a way in grammar, where it is precisely the dead, thinglike shell of the word that interests us.

All the highly varied forms worked out for the dialogized transmission of another's word, both in everyday life and in extraartistic ideological communication, are utilized in the novel in two ways. In the first place, all these forms are present and reproduced in the ideologically meaningful as well as the casual utterances of the novel's characters, and they are also present in the inserted genres—in diaries, confessions, journalistic articles and so on. In the second place, all the forms for dialogizing the transmission of another's speech are directly subordinated to the task of artistically representing the speaker and his discourse as the image of a language, in which case the others' words must undergo special artistic reformulation.

What, we may ask, is the basic distinction between forms for transmitting another's word as they exist outside the world of art and the artistic representation of such transmission in the novel?

All extra-artistic forms, even those that closely approach artistic representation—as, for instance, in certain rhetorical doublevoiced genres (parodic stylizations)—are oriented toward the utterance of individual persons. These are practically engaged exchanges of others' isolated utterances, at best serving only to elevate single utterances to a point where they may be perceived as generalized utterances in someone else's manner of speaking, thus utterances that may be taken as socially typical or characteristic. These extra-artistic forms, concentrated as they are on the transmission (even if free and creative) of utterances, do not endeavor to recognize and intensify images lying *behind* the isolated utterances of social language, a language that realizes itself in them but is not exhausted by them, for it is precisely an *image*—and not a positivistic, empirical given of that language. In an authentic novel there can be sensed behind each utterance the elemental force of social languages, with their internal logic and internal necessity. The image in such cases reveals not only the reality of a given language but also, as it were, its potential, its ideal limits and its total meaning conceived as a whole, its truth together with its limitations.

Thus double-voicedness in the novel, as distinct from double-voicedness in rhetorical or other forms, always tends toward a double-*languagedness* as its own outside limit. Therefore novelistic double-voicedness cannot be unfolded into logical contradictions or into purely dramatic contrasts. It is this quality that determines the distinctiveness of novelistic dialogues, which push to the limit the mutual nonunderstanding represented by people *who speak in different languages.*

We must once again emphasize that what is meant here by social language is not the undifferentiated mass [*sovokupnost'*] of linguistic markers determining the way in which a language is dialectologically organized and individuated, but rather the concrete, living, integral mass [*celokupnost'*] made up of all the markers that give that language its social profile, a profile that by defining itself through semantic shifts and lexical choices can be established even within the boundaries of a linguistically unitary language. A social language, then, is a concrete socio-linguistic belief system that defines a distinct identity for itself within the boundaries of a language that is unitary only in the abstract. Such a language system frequently does not admit a strict linguistic definition, but it is pregnant with possibilities for further dialectological individuation: it is a potential dialect, its embryo not yet fully formed. Language in its historical life, in its heteroglot development, is full of such potential dialects: they intersect one another in a multitude of ways; some fail to develop, some die off, but others blossom into authentic languages. We repeat: language is something that is historically real, a process of heteroglot development, a process teeming with future and former languages, with prim but moribund aristocrat-languages, with parvenu-languages and with countless pretenders to the status of language— which are all more or less successful, depending on their degree of social scope and on the ideological area in which they are employed.

The image of such a language in a novel is the image assumed by a set of social beliefs, the image of a social ideologeme that has fused with its own discourse, with its own language. Therefore such an image is very far from being formalistic, and artistic play with such languages far from being formalistic play. In the novel formal markers of languages, manners and styles are symbols for sets of social beliefs. External linguistic features are frequently used as peripheral means to mark socio-linguistic differences, sometimes even in the form of direct authorial commentaries on the characters' language. In *Fathers and Sons*, for example, Turgenev sometimes goes out of his way to emphasize his characters' peculiarities in word usage or pronunciation (which can be, by the way, extremely characteristic from a sociohistorical point of view).

Thus the different ways the word "principle" is pronounced in the novel can serve to mark off different historical and cultural social worlds: the world of noble-landowner culture of the twenties and thirties, raised on French literature but a stranger to the Latin language and to German science, or the world of the *raznočinec* intelligentsia of the fifties, with the tone of a seminarist or doctor raised on Latin and on German science. The hard Latin or German pronunciation of the word "principles" won out in the Russian language. As a further example we might note Kukshina's use of the word *gospodin* [gentleman] for *čelovek* [man], a word choice rooted in the lower and middle genres of literary language.

Such direct, external commentary on the peculiarities of characters' languages is typical for the novel as a genre, but it is not of course through *them* that the image of a language is created in a novel. Such commentary has already itself been turned into an object: in such situations the author's words have dialogized, double-voiced and double-languaged overtones to them (for example, as they interact with the characterological zones discussed in the preceding chapter).

The context surrounding represented speech plays a major role in creating the image of a language. The framing context, like the sculptor's chisel, hews out the rough outlines of someone else's speech, and carves the image of a language out of the raw empirical data of speech life; it concentrates and fuses the internal impulse of the represented language with the exterior objects it names. The words of the author that represent and frame another's speech create a perspective for it; they separate light from shadow, create the situation and conditions necessary for it to sound; finally, they penetrate into the interior of the other's speech, carrying into it their own accents and their own expressions, creating for it a dialogizing background.

Thanks to the ability of a language to represent another language while still retaining the capacity to sound simultaneously both outside it and within it, to talk about it and at the same time to talk in and with it—and thanks to the ability of the language being represented simultaneously to serve as an object of representation while continuing to be able to speak to itself—thanks to all this, the creation of specific novelistic images of languages becomes possible. Therefore, the framing authorial context can least of all treat the language it is representing as a thing, a mute and unresponsive speech object, something that remains outside the authorial context as might any other object of speech.

All devices in the novel for creating the image of a language may be reduced to three basic categories: (1) hybridizations, (2) the dialogized interrelation of languages and (3) pure dialogues.

These three categories of devices can only theoretically be separated in this fashion since in reality they are always inextricably woven together into the unitary artistic fabric of the image.

What is a hybridization? It is a mixture of two social languages within the limits of a single utterance, an encounter, within the arena of an utterance, between two different linguistic consciousnesses, separated from one another by an epoch, by social differentiation or by some other factor.

Such mixing of two languages within the boundaries of a single utterance is, in the novel, an artistic device (or more accurately, a system of devices) that is deliberate. But unintentional, unconscious hybridization is one of the most important modes in the historical life and evolution of all languages. We may even say that language and languages change historically primarily by means of hybridization, by means of a mixing of various "languages" co-existing within the boundaries of a single dialect, a single national language, a single branch, a single group of different branches or different groups of such branches, in the historical as well as paleontological past of languages—but the crucible for this mixing always remains the utterance.[34]

The artistic image of a language must by its very nature be a linguistic hybrid (an intentional hybrid): it is obligatory for two linguistic consciousnesses to be present, the one being represented and the other doing the representing, with each belonging to a different system of language. Indeed, if there is not a second representing consciousness, if there is no second representing language-intention, then what results is not an *image* [*obraz*] of language but merely a *sample* [*obrazec*] of some other person's language, whether authentic or fabricated.

The image of a language conceived as an intentional hybrid is first of all a *conscious* hybrid (as distinct from a historical, organic, obscure language hybrid); an intentional hybrid is precisely the perception of one language by another language, its illumination by another linguistic consciousness. An image of language may be structured only from the point of view of another language, which is taken as the norm.

What is more, an intentional and conscious hybrid is not a mixture of two *impersonal* language consciousnesses (the correlates of two languages) but rather a mixture of two *individualized* language consciousnesses (the correlates of two specific utterances, not merely two languages) and two individual language-intentions as well: the individual, representing authorial consciousness and will, on the one hand, and the individualized linguistic consciousness and will of the character represented, on the other. For indeed, since concrete, isolated utterances are constructed in this represented language, it follows that the represented linguistic consciousness must necessarily be embodied in "authors"[35] of some sort who speak in the given language, who structure utterances in that language and who therefore introduce into the potentialities of language itself their own actualizing language-

34. Such historically unconscious hybrids are similar to double-languaged hybrids but they are, of course, single-voiced. Semi-organic, semi-intentional hybridization is characteristic of a system of literary language.

35. Even though these "authors" may be impersonal, merely types—as in the stylizations of generic languages and of public opinion.

intention. Thus there are always two consciousnesses, two language-intentions, two *voices* and consequently two accents participating in an intentional and conscious artistic hybrid.

While noting the individual element in intentional hybrids, we must once again strongly emphasize the fact that in novelistic artistic hybrids that structure the *image of a language*, the individual element, indispensable as it is for the actualization of language and for its subordination to the artistic whole of the novel (here the destinies of languages are interwoven with the individual destinies of speaking persons), is nevertheless inexorably merged with the socio-linguistic element. In other words, the novelistic hybrid is not only double-voiced and double-accented (as in rhetoric) but is also double-languaged; for in it there are not only (and not even so much) two individual consciousnesses, two voices, two accents, as there are two socio-linguistic consciousnesses, two epochs, that, true, are not here unconsciously mixed (as in an organic hybrid), but that come together and consciously fight it out on the territory of the utterance..

In an intentional novelistic hybrid, moreover, the important activity is not only (in fact not so much) the mixing of linguistic forms—the markers of two languages and styles—as it is the collision between differing points of views on the world that are embedded in these forms. Therefore an intentional artistic hybrid is a *semantic* hybrid; not semantic and logical in the abstract (as in rhetoric), but rather a *semantics that is concrete and social*.

It is of course true that even in historical, organic hybrids it is not only two languages but also two socio-linguistic (thus organic) world views that are mixed with each other; but in such situations, the mixture remains mute and opaque, never making use of conscious contrasts and oppositions. It must be pointed out, however, that while it is true the mixture of linguistic world views in organic hybrids remains mute and opaque, such unconscious hybrids have been at the same time profoundly productive historically: they are pregnant with potential for new world views, with new "internal forms" for perceiving the world in words.

Intentional semantic hybrids are inevitably internally dialogic (as distinct from organic hybrids). Two points of view are not mixed, but set against each other dialogically. The internal, essentially dialogic quality of novelistic hybrids, insofar as it is a dialogue composed of socio-linguistic points of view, cannot of course be unfolded into a distinct, rounded-off dialogue with its own individual semantics: essential to it is a certain elemental, organic energy and openendedness.

Finally, the intentional double-voiced and internally dialogized hybrid possesses a syntactic structure utterly specific to it: in it, within the boundaries of a single utterance, two potential utterances are fused, two responses are, as it were, harnessed in a potential dialogue. It is true that these potential responses can never be fully actualized, can never be fused into finished utterances, but their insufficiently developed forms are nevertheless acutely felt in the syntactic construction of the double-voiced hybrid. What is involved here, of course, is not the kind of mixture of heterogeneous syntactic forms characteristic of language systems (forms that might take place in *organic* hybrids), but rather precisely the fusion of *two* utterances into one. Such a fusion is also possible in single-languaged rhetorical hybrids (in which case it is even more fully articulated syntactically). It is typical for a novelistic hybrid to fuse into a single utterance two utterances that are socially distinct. The syntactic construction of intentional hybrids is fractured into two individualized language-intentions.

Summing up the characteristics of a novelistic hybrid, we can say: as distinct from the opaque mixing of languages in living utterances that are spoken in a historically evolving language (in essence, any *living* utterance in a *living* language is to one or another extent a hybrid), the novelistic hybrid is *an artistically organized system for bringing different languages in contact with one another*, a system having as its goal the illumination of one language by means of another, the carving-out of a living image of another language.

Intentional, artistically oriented hybridization is one of the most fundamental devices for structuring the image of a language. We must note that where hybridization occurs, the language being used to illuminate another language (this is usually accomplished using the contemporary literary language system) is reified to the point where it itself becomes an image of a language. The more broadly and deeply the device of hybridization is employed in a novel—since it occurs not with one but with several languages—the more reified becomes the representing and illuminating language itself, until it finally is transformed into one more of the images of languages the novel contains. Classic examples of this are *Don Quixote*, the English comic novel (Fielding, Smollett, Sterne) and the German Romantic-comic novel (Hippel and Jean Paul). In these cases the very process of writing the novel, as well as the image of the novelist, is usually reified (this was already partially the case in *Don Quixote*, and later more completely in Sterne, Hippel and Jean Paul).

Hybridization, in the strict sense, differs from internally dialogized interillumination of language systems taken as a whole. In the former case there is no direct mixing of two languages within the boundaries of a single utterance—rather, only one language is actually present in the utterance, but it is rendered *in the light of another language*. This second language is not, however, actualized and remains outside the utterance.

The clearest and most characteristic form of an internally dialogized mutual illumination of languages is *stylization*.

Every authentic stylization, as we have already said, is an artistic representation of another's linguistic style, an artistic image of another's language. Two individualized linguistic consciousnesses must be present in it: the one that *represents* (that is, the linguistic consciousness of the stylizer) and the one that is *represented*, which is stylized. Stylization differs from style proper precisely by virtue of its requiring a specific linguistic consciousness (the contemporaneity of the stylizer and his audience), under whose influence a style becomes a stylization, against whose background it acquires new meaning and significance.

This second linguistic consciousness, that of the stylizer and those contemporary with him, uses stylized language as raw material; it is only in a stylized language, one not his own, that the stylizer can speak about the subject directly. But this stylized language is itself exhibited in the light of the language consciousness of a stylizer contemporary with it. Contemporaneous language casts a special light over the stylized language: it highlights some elements, leaves others in the shade, creates a special pattern of accents that has the effect of making its various aspects all aspects of language, creating specific resonances between the stylized language and the linguistic consciousness contemporaneous with it—in short, it creates a free image of another's language, which expresses not only a stylized but also a stylizing language-and art-intention.

Such is the nature of stylization. Another type of mutual illumination, very close to it, is *variation*. In stylization the linguistic consciousness of the stylizer works exclusively with the raw material provided by the language he stylizes: it highlights this stylized language by carrying into it its own interests—in an alien language—but not the alien linguistic *material* comprised of elements in the language contemporaneous with the stylization. Stylization as such must be internally consistent in the highest degree. Should contemporaneous linguistic material (a word, a form, a turn of phrase, etc.) penetrate a stylization, it becomes a flaw in the stylization, its mistake: an anachronism, a modernism.

Such inconsistency may, however, be deliberate and organized: the stylizing language consciousness may not only illuminate the stylized language, but may also itself pick up a word from outside and introduce it as its own thematic and linguistic material into the stylized language. In this case we no longer have stylization, but variation (something that frequently borders on hybridization).

Variation freely incorporates material from alien languages into contemporary topics, joins the stylized world with the world of contemporary consciousness, projects the stylized language into new scenarios, testing it in situations that would have been impossible for it on its own.

In the history of the novel the significance of direct stylization, as well as of variation, is enormous, and is surpassed only by the importance of parody. It was in stylizations that prose first learned how to represent languages artistically—although, in the beginning, it is true, these were languages already fully formed and stylistically shaped (or they were already styles in their own right), they were not the raw and often as yet only potential languages of a living heteroglossia (where languages are still evolving, and do not yet possess a style of their own). The image of a language created by stylization is the least fraught and most artistically rounded-off of such images, one that permits the maximal aestheticism available to novelistic prose. For this reason the great masters of stylization such as Mérimée, France, Henri de Régnier and others represent the principle of aestheticism in the novel (available to the genre only within narrow limits).

The importance of stylization in the epoch during which the basic trends and stylistic lines of novelistic discourse were formed is a special topic in its own right, with which we will deal in the final historical chapter of this essay.

In another type of internally dialogized interillumination of languages, the intentions of the representing discourse are at odds with the intentions of the represented discourse; they fight against them, they depict a real world of objects not by using the represented language as a productive point of view, but rather by using it as an exposé to destroy the represented language. This is the nature of *parodic stylization.*

Such a parodic stylization can, however, create an image of language and a world corresponding to it only on condition that the stylization not function as a gross and superficial destruction of the other's language, as happens in rhetorical parody. In order to be authentic and productive, parody must be precisely a parodic *stylization,* that is, it must re-create the parodied language as an authentic whole, giving it its due as a language possessing its own internal logic and one capable of revealing its own world inextricably bound up with the parodied language.

Between stylization and parody, as between two extremes, are distributed the most varied forms for languages to mutually illuminate each other and for direct hybrids, forms that are themselves determined by the most varied interactions among languages, the most varied wills to language and to speech, that encounter one another within the limits of a single utterance. The struggle going on within discourse, the degree of resistance that the parodied language offers to the parodying language, the degree to which the represented social languages are fully formed entities and the degree to which they are individualized representation and finally the surrounding heteroglossia (which always serves as a dialogizing background and resonator)—all these create a multitude of devices for representing another's language.

The dialogic opposition of pure languages in a novel, when taken together with hybridization, is a powerful means for creating images of languages. The dialogic contrast of *languages* (but not of meanings within the limits of a single language) delineates the boundaries of languages, creates a feeling for these boundaries, compels one to sense physically the plastic forms of different languages.

Dialogue itself, as a compositional form, is in novels inextricably bound up with a dialogue of languages, a dialogue that can be heard in its hybrids and in the dialogizing background of the novel. Therefore dialogue in the novel is dialogue of a special sort. First and foremost (as we have already said) it can never be exhausted in pragmatically motivated dialogues of characters.

Novelistic dialogue is pregnant with an endless multitude of dialogic confrontations, which do not and cannot resolve it, and which, as it were, only locally (as one out of many possible dialogues) illustrate this endless, deep-lying dialogue of languages; novel dialogue is determined by the very socio-ideological evolution of languages and society. A dialogue of languages is a dialogue of social forces perceived not only in their static co-existence, but also as a dialogue of different times, epochs and days, a dialogue that is forever dying, living, being born: co-existence and becoming are here fused into an indissoluble concrete unity that is contradictory, multi-speeched and heterogeneous. It is freighted down with novelistic images; from this dialogue of languages these images take their openendedness, their inability to say anything once and for all or to think anything through to its end, they take from it their lifelike concreteness, their "naturalistic quality"—everything that so sharply distinguishes them from dramatic dialogues.

Pure languages in the novel, in the dialogues and monologues of novelistic characters, are subordinated to the same task of creating images of language.

The plot itself is subordinated to the task of coordinating and exposing languages to each other. The novelistic plot must organize the exposure of social languages and ideologies, the exhibiting and experiencing of such languages: the experience of a discourse, a world view and an ideologically based act, or the exhibiting of the everyday life of social, historical and national worlds or micro-worlds (as is the case with novels concerned primarily with description, everyday life or travel), or of the socio-ideological worlds of epochs (the novel-memoir, or various types of historical novel) or of age groups and generations linked with epochs and socio-ideological worlds (the *Bildungsroman* and *Entwicklungsroman*). In a word, the novelistic plot serves to represent speaking persons and their ideological worlds. What is realized in the novel is the process of coming to know one's own language as it is perceived in someone else's language, coming to know one's own belief system in someone else's system. There takes place within the novel an ideological translation of another's language, and an overcoming of its otherness—an otherness that is only contingent, external, illusory. Characteristic for the historical novel is a positively weighted modernizing, an erasing of temporal boundaries, the recognition of an eternal present in the past. The primary stylistic project of the novel as a genre is to create images of languages.

Every novel, taken as the totality of all the languages and consciousnesses of language embodied in it, is a *hybrid*. But we emphasize once again: it is an intentional and conscious hybrid, one artistically organized, and not an opaque mechanistic mixture of languages (more precisely, a mixture of the brute elements of language). *The artistic image of a language*—such is the aim that novelistic hybridization sets for itself.

For this reason the novelist makes no effort at all to achieve a linguistically (dialectologically) exact and complete reproduction of the empirical data of those alien languages he incorporates into his text—he attempts merely to achieve an artistic consistency among the *images* of these languages.

An artistic hybrid demands enormous effort: it is stylized through and through, thoroughly premeditated, achieved, distanced. This is what distinguishes it from the frivolous, mindless and unsystematic mixing of languages—often bordering on simple illiteracy—characteristic of mediocre prose writers. In such hybrids there is no joining together of consistent language systems, merely a random combination of the brute elements out of which languages are made. This is not orchestration by means of heteroglossia, but in most cases merely a directly authorial language that is impure and incompletely worked out.

The novel not only labors, therefore, under the necessity of knowing literary language in all its depth and subtlety, but it must in addition know all the other languages of heteroglossia. The novel demands a broadening and deepening of the language horizon, a sharpening in our perception of socio-linguistic differentiations.

The Two Stylistic Lines of Development in the European Novel

The novel is the expression of a Galilean perception of language, one that denies the absolutism of a single and unitary language— that is, that refuses to acknowledge its own language as the sole verbal and semantic center of the ideological world. It is a perception that has been made conscious of the vast plenitude of national and, more to the point, social languages—all of which are equally capable of being "languages of truth," but, since such is the case, all of which are equally relative, reified and limited, as they are merely the languages of social groups, professions and other cross-sections of everyday life. The novel begins by presuming a verbal and semantic decentering of the ideological world, a certain linguistic homelessness of literary consciousness, which no longer possesses a sacrosanct and unitary linguistic medium for containing ideological thought; it is a consciousness manifesting itself in the midst of social languages that are surrounded by a single [national] language, and in the midst of [other] national languages that are surrounded by a single culture (Hellenistic, Christian, Protestant), or by a single cultural-political world (the Hellenistic kingdoms, the Roman Empire and so forth).

What is involved here is a very important, in fact a radical revolution in the destinies of human discourse: the fundamental liberation of cultural-semantic and emotional intentions from the hegemony of a single and unitary language, and consequently the simultaneous loss of a feeling for language as myth, that is, as an absolute form of thought. Therefore it is not enough merely to uncover the multiplicity of languages in a cultural world or the speech diversity within a particular national language—we must see through to the heart of this revolution, to all the consequences flowing from it, possible only under very specific sociohistorical conditions.

In order that an artistically profound play with social languages become possible, it is necessary to alter radically the feel for discourse at the level of general literature and language. It is necessary to come to terms with discourse as a reified, "typical" but at the same time intentional phenomenon; we must learn how to become sensitive to the "internal form" (in the Humboldtian sense) of an alien language, and to the "internal form" of one's own language as an alien form; we must learn how to develop a sensitivity toward the brute materiality, the typicality, that is the essential attribute not only of actions, gestures and separate words and expressions, but the basic ingredient as well in points of view, in how the world is seen and felt, ways that are organically part and parcel with the language that expresses them. Such a perception is possible only for a consciousness organically participating in the *universum* of mutually illuminating languages. What is wanted for this to happen is a fundamental intersecting of languages in a single given consciousness, one that participates equally in several languages.

The decentralizing of the verbal-ideological world that finds its expression in the novel begins by presuming fundamentally differentiated social groups, which exist in an intense and vital interaction with other social groups. A sealed-off interest group, caste or class, existing within an internally unitary and unchanging core of its own, cannot serve as socially productive soil for the development of the novel unless it becomes riddled with decay or shifted somehow from its state of internal balance and self-sufficiency. This is the case because a literary and language consciousness operating from the heights of its own uncontestably authoritative unitary language fails to take into account the fact of heteroglossia and multi-languagedness. The heteroglossia that rages beyond the boundaries of such a sealed-off cultural universe, a universe having its own literary language, is capable of sending into the lower genres only purely reified, unintentional speech images, word-things that lack any novelistic-prose potential. It is necessary that heteroglossia wash over a culture's awareness of itself and its language, penetrate to its core, relativize the primary language system underlying its ideology and literature and deprive it of its naive absence of conflict.

But even this will not suffice. Even a community torn by social struggle—if it remains isolated and sealed-off as a national entity—will be insufficient social soil for relativization of literary-language consciousness at the deepest level, for its re-tuning into a new prosaic key. The internal speech diversity of a literary dialect and of its surrounding extraliterary environment, that is, the entire dialectological makeup of a given national language, must have the sense that it is surrounded by an ocean of heteroglossia, heteroglossia that is, moreover, primary and that fully reveals an intentionality, a mythological, religious, sociopolitical, literary system of its own, along with all the other cultural-ideological systems that belong to it. Even were an extranational multi-languagedness not actually to penetrate the system of literary language and the system of prose genres (in the way that the extraliterary dialects of one and the same language do, in fact, penetrate these systems)—nevertheless, such external multi-languagedness strengthens and deepens the internal contradictoriness of literary language itself; it undermines the authority of custom and of whatever traditions still fetter linguistic consciousness; it erodes that system of national myth that is organically fused with language, in effect destroying once and for all a mythic and magical attitude to language and the word. A deeply involved participation in alien cultures and languages (one is impossible without the other) inevitably leads to an awareness of the disassociation between language and intentions, language and thought, language and expression.

By "disassociation" we have in mind here a destruction of any absolute bonding of ideological meaning to language, which is *the* defining factor of mythological and magical thought. An absolute fusion of word with concrete ideological meaning is, without a doubt, one of the most fundamental constitutive features of myth, on the one hand determining the development of mythological images, and on the other determining a special feeling for the forms, meanings and stylistic combinations of language. Mythological thinking in the power of the language containing it—a language generating out of itself a mythological reality that has its own linguistic connections and interrelationships—then substitutes itself for the connections and interrelationships of reality itself (this is the transposition of language categories and dependences into theogonic and cosmogonic categories). But language too is under the power of images of the sort that dominate mythological thinking, and these fetter the free movement of its intentions and thus make it more difficult for language categories to achieve a wider application and greater flexibility, a purer formal structure (this would result from their fusion with materially concrete relationships); they limit the word's potential for greater expressiveness.[36]

The absolute hegemony of myth over language as well the hegemony of language over the perception and conceptualization of reality are of course located in the prehistorical (and therefore necessarily hypothetical) past of language consciousness.[37] But

36. We cannot here engage in depth the problem of the interrelationship of language and myth. In the relevant literature this problem has up to now been treated on the psychological level alone, with an orientation toward folklore, and without linking it to concrete problems in the history of language consciousness (Steinthal, Lazarus, Wundt and others). In Russia Potebnja and Veselovskij demonstrated the fundamental relationship between these two problems.

37. This scientific area is first deemed worthy of scientific inquiry in the "paleontology of meanings" of the Japhetists.

even in those eras where the absolutism of this hegemony has long since been displaced—in the already historical epochs of language consciousness—a mythological feeling for the authority of language and a faith in the unmediated transformation into a seamless unity of the entire sense, the entire expressiveness inherent in that authority, are still powerful enough in all higher ideological genres to exclude the possibility of any *artistic* use of linguistic speech diversity in the major literary forms. The resistance of a unitary, canonic language, of a national myth bolstered by a yet-unshaken unity, is still too strong for heteroglossia to relativize and decenter literary and language consciousness. This verbal-ideological decentering will occur only when a national culture loses its sealed-off and self-sufficient character, when it becomes conscious of itself as only one among *other* cultures and languages. It is this knowledge that will sap the roots of a mythological feeling for language, based as it is on an absolute fusion of ideological meaning with language; there will arise an acute feeling for language boundaries (social, national and semantic), and only then will language reveal its essential *human* character; from behind its words, forms, styles, nationally characteristic and socially typical faces begin to emerge, the images of speaking human beings. This will occur, moreover, at all layers of language without exception, even in the layers of greatest intentionality—the languages of the high ideological genres. Language (or more precisely, languages) will itself become an artistically complete image of a characteristic human way of sensing and seeing the world. Language, no longer conceived as a sacrosanct and solitary embodiment of meaning and truth, becomes merely one of many possible ways to hypothesize meaning.

The situation is analogous in those cases where a single and unitary literary language is at the same time another's language. What inevitably happens is a decay and collapse of the religious, political and ideological authority connected with that language. It is during this process of decay that the decentered language consciousness of prose art ripens, finding its support in the social heteroglossia of national languages that are actually spoken.

This is how those germs of novelistic prose appear in the poly- and heteroglot world of the Hellenistic era, in Imperial Rome and during the disintegration and collapse of the church-directed centralization of discourse and ideology in the Middle Ages. Even in modern times, the flowering of the novel is always connected with a disintegration of stable verbal-ideological systems and with an intensification and intentionalization of speech diversity that are counterpoised to the previously reigning stable systems, an activity that goes on both within the limits of the literary dialect itself and outside it.

The problem of novelistic prose in ancient times is extremely complex. The embryonic beginnings of authentic double-voiced and double-languaged prose did not in ancient times always achieve the status of novel, as a definite compositional and thematic structure. For the most part novelistic prose flourished in other generic formats: in realistic novellas, in satires,[38] in some biographical and autobiographical forms,[39] and in certain purely rhetorical genres (for example, in the diatribe),[40] in historical and, finally, in epistolary genres.[41] In all these forms the germs of novelistic prose can be found, that is, there is an orchestration of meaning by means of heteroglossia. On this double-voiced, authentically prose plane, variants were structured (and have survived) on the theme of "a novel about an ass" (pseudo-Lucian, and Apuleius) as well as Petronius' novel.

---

38. The ironic honorific reference to the self in Horace's satires is well known. A humorous orientation toward one's own "I" in satires always includes elements of parodic stylization of the accepted approaches, others' points of view, the going opinions. The satires of Varro are even closer to a novelistic orchestration of meaning; from the surviving fragments we can form some idea of the character of parodic stylization of scholarly and morally exhortative speech.

39. There are elements of orchestration-by-heteroglossia and the embryonic beginnings of an authentic prose style in the *Apology* of Socrates. In Plato, the figure of Socrates and his speeches are by and large cast in authentic prose. But even more interesting are the forms of late Hellenistic and Christian autobiography, which link the confessional history of a transformation with elements of adventure and the *Sittenroman*, of which information has come down to us (the words themselves have not survived): St. John Chrysostom, Justin Martyr, Cyprian and the so-called Climentine cycle of legends. We find, finally, the same elements in the work of Boethius.

40. Of all the Hellenistic forms, the diatribe contains the largest amount of novelistic-prose potential: it permits, and even requires, a great variety of speech manners, a dramatized and parodic-ironic appropriation of other points of view; it permits a mixing of verse and prose and so forth. On the relationship of rhetorical forms to the novel, see below.

41. It is sufficient to mention the letters of Cicero to Atticus.

Thus did the most important elements of the double-voiced and double-languaged novel coalesce in ancient times, elements that in the Middle Ages had (and in recent times continue to have) a powerful influence on the most important novel-types: the *Prüfungsroman* (that branch containing the confessional type of vita and the adversity-adventure type of novel, up to Dostoevsky and the present day), the *Bildungsroman* and the *Entwicklungsroman* (the autobiographical branch in particular), the everyday satiric novel and others—that is, it influenced precisely those novel-types that incorporate dialogized heteroglossia *directly* into their composition, a heteroglossia of the sort that characterizes the lower genres and everyday speech. But in the ancient world itself these elements, scattered as they were throughout heterogeneous genres, did not come together to form the mighty body of the novel; such elements were isolated, insufficiently complex models for what was to become a particular stylistic line of development in the novel (Apuleius and Petronius).

The so-called "Sophistic novels"[42] belong to a completely different stylistic line of development. Such a novel is characterized by sharp and relentless stylization of all its material, that is, by a purely monologic—abstractly idealized—consistency of style. It is precisely these Sophistic novels, in fact, that express most fully the thematic and compositional nature of the novel as a genre in its ancient form. They had a powerful influence on the development of the higher generic types of the European novel up until the nineteenth century: they also influenced the medieval novel, the fifteenth- and sixteenth-century "novel of gallantry" (*Amadis*, and the pastoral novel in particular), the Baroque novel and, finally, even the novel of the *Lumières* (for example, Voltaire). To a significant extent it was the Sophistic novels that determined theoretical presumptions about the novel as a genre, and about its norms, that were to hold sway until the end of the eighteenth century.[43]

42. Cf. B. Grifcov, *The Theory of the Novel* [*Teorija romana*] (Moscow, 1927), also A. Boldyrev's introductory article to the translation of Achilles Tatius' *Leucippe and Clitophon* (Moscow, 1925); the article casts some light on the question of the Sophistic novel.

43. These ideas found their expression in the first and most authoritative specialized work on the novel, in Huet's book (1670). In its treatment of those special problems that arise in connection with the ancient novel, this book found its successor only with the work of Erwin Rohde—that is, only after 200 years (1876).

The highly abstract and idealizing stylization of Sophistic novels nevertheless permitted a certain degree of variety in stylistic manners, an inevitable consequence of the variety of (relatively) independent structural units and genres that go into such novels and that are found there in such abundance. These might include a story told by another author, or stories told by protagonists and witnesses, descriptions of a country, nature, cities, noteworthy places, works of art (descriptions that seek to be definitive, and even to pass a certain judgment on the material they describe), pronouncements (which also strive to be definitive and exhaustive treatments of their scholarly, philosophical and moral themes), aphorisms, embedded stories, rhetorical speeches related to various rhetorical forms, letters and developed forms of dialogue. It is true that the degree of independence such structural units have in the style of the novel does not in any way correspond to their degree of structural independence or to the degree they are definitive genres in their own right, but—and this is the main thing—all these elements are treated in Sophistic novels as if they were *equally* intentional and *equally* conventional: they all exist on the same verbal and semantic plane, they are all used to express, directly and with equal force, the intentions of the author.

The very conventionality and extreme (abstract) consistency of this stylization is, moreover, of a sort peculiar to itself. It has no single, primary or stable system of ideology behind it—religious, sociopolitical or philosophical. From an ideological point of view the Sophistic novel is absolutely decentered (as in all the rhetoric of the "Second Sophistics"). The very unity of the style is presumed to be self-sufficient from the very start; it is rooted in nothing, nor is it reinforced by the unity of any cultural-ideological world. The unity of this style is a peripheral phenomenon, merely "a matter of words." The very abstractness and extreme isolation of the stylization betrays veritable oceans of the most primal heteroglossia, out of which these works, in all their verbal unity, well up. But such unity wells up without having assimilated the heteroglossia by introducing it into its subject (an activity that authentic poetry also avoids). Unfortunately we do not know to what extent this style was predicated on its reception against the background of that very heteroglossia. The possibility of a dialogic interrelationship between aspects of it and existing languages of heteroglossia can by no means be ruled out. We do not know, for instance, the functions performed here by the countless, highly various references that fill such novels: is it a directly intentional function, such as a poetic reference, or is it something else, perhaps prosaic (that is, such references *may* be double-voiced formulations)? Are pronouncements and maxims always directly intentional, semantically integral? Might they not frequently have an ironic or directly parodic character? In a whole series of cases, the place such statements occupy in the composition forces us to assume as much. Thus, where lengthy and abstract discussions serve a retarding function and interrupt the story at its most intense and tension-filled moment, the very inappropriateness of such an interruption (especially where pedantically proliferating discussions are hooked up with pretexts that are obviously arbitrary) throws a mantle of materiality over everything, forcing us to suspect the presence of parodic stylization.[44]

Except in those cases where it is grossly apparent, the presence of parody is in general very difficult to identify (that is, difficult to identify precisely in literary prose, where it rarely is gross), without knowing the background of alien discourse against which it is projected, that is, without knowing its second context. In world literature there are probably many works whose parodic nature has not even been suspected. In world literature in general there are probably very few words that are uttered unconditionally, purely single-voiced. And yet we look at world literature from a tiny island limited in time and space, from a monotone, single-voiced verbal culture. And, as we shall see in what follows, there do exist such types and variants of double-voiced discourse, whose double-voicedness is very easily exhausted in the process of their perception and that do not totally lose their artistic significance even when re-accented in a direct, single-voiced way (they flow together with the great mass of direct authorial words).

The presence of parodic stylization (and other variants of double-voiced discourse) in the Sophistic novel[45] cannot be doubted but it is difficult to determine the actual weight such discourse carried in them. To a very real extent we have lost forever the

44. Cf. the extreme use that Sterne makes of this device, and the more highly varied oscillations in degree of parody practiced by Jean Paul.

45. Thus Boldyrev, in the above-mentioned article, notes Achilles Tatius' parodic use of the traditional motif of the prophetic dream. Boldyrev, by the way, considers Tatius' novel to be a deviation from the traditional type, tending rather toward a comic novel of manners.

background of heteroglot words and meanings against which these novels sounded and with which they dialogically interacted. Perhaps the abstract, hard-edged stylization in these novels, striking us now as so monotonous and flat, seemed more vivid and more diversified against the background of the heteroglot world contemporaneous with them; or perhaps this stylization entered into double-voiced play with certain aspects of this heteroglot world and initiated dialogic exchanges with them.

The Sophistic novel is the starting point for the European novel's *First* (so we will arbitrarily designate it) *Stylistic Line of development.* In contrast to what we shall call the Second Line—for which, in ancient times, the ground was only prepared in a variety of different genres and which never coalesced into a form that was, in itself, a full-blown novel-type (not even the Apuleian or Petronian novel can be considered a complete type representative of this Second Line)—the First Line found, in the Sophistic novel, a sufficiently full and finished expression. It was an expression that determined (as we have already said) the entire subsequent history of development in that line. Its primary characteristic is the fact that it knows only a single language and a single style (which is more or less rigorously consistent); heteroglossia remains *outside* the novel, although it does nevertheless have its effect on the novel as a dialogizing background in which the language and world of the novel is polemically and forensically implicated.

In the further history of the European novel we will continue to notice the same two fundamental lines of stylistic development. The Second Line, to which belong the greatest representatives of the novel as a genre (its greatest subgenres as well as the greatest individual examples), incorporates heteroglossia *into* a novel's composition, exploiting it to orchestrate its own meaning and frequently resisting altogether any unmediated and pure authorial discourse. The First Line, which most strongly exhibits the influence of the Sophistic novel, leaves heteroglossia outside itself, that is, outside the language of the novel; such language is stylized in a special way, a novelized way. But as we have said, even *its* perception presumes heteroglossia as a background, and even it interacts dialogically with various aspects of this heteroglossia. Consequently, the abstract, idealizing stylization of such a novel is determined not only by its own subject and by the direct expression of a speaking person (as is the case in pure poetic discourse), but also by *another's* word, by heteroglossia. Such stylization involves a sideways glance at others' languages, at other points of view and other conceptual systems, each with its own set of objects and meanings. This is one of the most fundamental distinctions between novelistic stylization and poetic stylization.

Both the First and Second Stylistic Lines of development— each in its own way—divide into a series of specific stylistic variants. Both lines crisscross and are interwoven with each other in a number of different ways; that is, ultimately a unity is forged between the stylization of the material and its heteroglot orchestration.

We will briefly touch on the classical chivalric romance in verse.

The literary-language (and more broadly, the ideological-language) consciousness of these novels' creators and audience was quite complex: on the one hand, this consciousness was highly centralized socially and ideologically, it rested on a socioeconomic class base that was both firm and stable. This consciousness was almost a caste consciousness in the degree to which it was hermetically self-sufficient. But at the same time this highly centralized consciousness lacked a unitary language, one fused organically with its cultural-ideological world of myth, customs, sets of beliefs, traditions, ideological systems. In terms of the cultural language available for its expression, this consciousness was profoundly decentralized and, to a significant degree, international. The decisive factor in this literary-language consciousness was above all the gap between language and its expressive material (on the one hand) and (on the other) the gap between this material and contemporary reality. Such a consciousness lived in a world of alien languages and alien cultures. As these were reworked, assimilated and subjected to the unity of a belief system of a type peculiar to class society and its ideals, and as these were ultimately opposed to the surrounding heteroglot world created by the popular lower strata, the literary-language consciousness of the creators and audience of the chivalric romance in verse coalesced and was born. This consciousness was constantly obliged to deal with an alien discourse and alien world: ancient literature, early Christian legend, Breton-Celtic oral tales (but not the native national epic, which reached its peak in the same era as did the chivalric romance, parallel with it but independent of it and exercising no influence on it)—all of this served to intensify the heterogeneous and polyglot material (Latin plus various national languages) in which the unity of the socioeconomic class consciousness of the chivalric romance was clothed, a unity that was nevertheless strong enough to overcome the alien qualities of the material. Translation, reworking, re-conceptualizing, re-accenting—manifold degrees of mutual inter-orientation with alien discourse, alien intentions—these were the activities shaping the literary consciousness that created the chivalric romance. The individual consciousness of a given creator of chivalric romances need not exploit all stages in this interaction with alien discourses, but it was nevertheless the case that this process was fully worked out in the literary-language consciousness of the era, and determined the creative activity of separate individuals. Material and language were not given as a seamless whole (as they were for the creators of the epic), but were rather fragmented, separated from each other, had to seek each other out.

It is this that defines the uniqueness of style in chivalric romances. There is not a drop of naiveté in it, in language or in speech. Naiveté (if it is to be found at all) is due to the still undifferentiated and rigid unity of the dominant class. This unity permeated all aspects of the alien material, and could reformulate and re-accent them to such a degree that the world of these novels appears to have the unitary quality of epic. The classic chivalric romance in verse actually lies on the boundary between epic and novel, but it clearly tends more toward the novel's pole. The most profound and perfected models of this genre, such as Wolfram von Eschenbach's *Parzival*, are already authentic novels. Eschenbach's *Parzival* can no longer be considered a pure example of the First Line of novelistic development. It is the first German novel to be profoundly and fundamentally double-voiced, capable of coordinating the unconditional quality of its intentions with a subtle and considered observing of distances vis-à-vis language, all of which takes into account language that has been somewhat reified and relativized, removing it ever so slightly from the author's lips by means of a faint smile.[46]

The first prose novels were in an analogous situation with regard to language. The element of translation and reworking is foregrounded in them even more sharply and bluntly. It could

46. *Parzival* is the first "problem" novel and the first *Entwicklungsroman*. This generic variety—as distinct from the purely didactic (rhetorical), primarily single-voiced *Prüfungsroman* (*Cyropaedia, Télémaque, Émile*) is one that requires a double-voiced discourse. The humorous *Prüfungsroman* with a sharp parodic bent is a specific variation on this type.

even be said that *European novel prose is born and shaped in the process of a free (that is, reformulating) translation of others' works*. It is only with French novelistic prose that the aspect of translation, in the strict sense, was not so characteristic in the early stages—for the French, the process of "transposing" epic verses into prose was more fundamental. The birth of novelistic prose in Germany is especially paradigmatic in this regard: it was created by a Germanized French aristocracy in the process of their translation and transposition of *French* prose and poetry. These were the beginnings of novelistic prose in Germany.

The language consciousness characteristic for those who created the prose novel was fully decentered and relativized. It wandered freely among languages in search of material it could make its own, easily detaching any material from any language (that is, from among the languages available) and assimilating it into "its own" language and world. And this "language of its own"—still unstable, still coalescing—offered no resistance to the translator-transposer. The result was a complete rupture between language and its material, the profound indifference of one to the other. The "style" specific to such prose has its origins in this mutual otherness of language and its material.

To speak of style in such cases is not really possible; we can only speak of a form of exposition. For what takes place here is precisely the substitution of sheer exposition for style. Style can be defined as the fundamental and creative [triple] relationship of discourse to its object, to the speaker himself and to another's discourse; style strives organically to assimilate material into language and language into material. Style cannot accommodate anything that is in excess of this exposition, anything given, already shaped, formed in words; style either permeates the object directly and without any mediation, as in poetry, or refracts its own intentions, as in literary prose (even the prose novelist does not *expound* the speech of another, but rather constructs an artistic image of it). Thus the chivalric romance in verse, while it too is defined by a rupture between material and language, is able to overcome this gap and to assimilate material to its language, thereby creating a special variant of authentic novelistic style.[47]

---

47. Translating and assimilating alien material is completed here not in the individual consciousness of the creators of novels: this process, lengthy and multi-staged, is accomplished in the literary-language consciousness of the epoch. Individual consciousness neither begins it nor ends it, but is part of its progress.

Europe's earliest novelistic prose arises and is shaped precisely as expository prose, and for a long time this fact governed its fate.

It is not of course only the elementary fact of a free translation of alien texts, nor the cultural internationalism of its creators, that determines the specific quality of this expository prose. Indeed, both creators *and* audience of chivalric verse romances were sufficiently international in terms of their culture. Of great importance also was the fact that such prose lacked a firm unitary social basis, possessed no calm and assured self-confidence such as would derive from an association with a fixed social stratum.

As is well known, the printing of books played an extremely important role in the history of the chivalric romance, for it served to shift and displace its audience.[48] It served to shift discourse into a *mute* mode of perception, a shift decisive for the novel as a genre. This societal disorientation becomes deeper and more pervasive as the novel continues its development, and the chivalric romance, a product of the fourteenth and fifteenth centuries, begins a period of wandering between social classes, a wandering that ends only when it is absorbed into the "folk literature" of a reading public made up of lower social groups: from this low level it is brought back up into the light of a literarily sophisticated consciousness by the Romantics.

Let us pause briefly on the specific features in this earliest of prose novels. It is a discourse divorced from its material and not permeated by the unity of a social ideology; it is surrounded by speech as well as language diversity, it lacks any support or center. Wandering between social classes, lacking any roots, this discourse was forced to assume a character compounded of specific conventions; this was not however the healthy conventionality of poetic discourse but rather one resulting from the impossibility, under these conditions, of making full artistic use of discourse, or of formulating it in a wide diversity of aspects.

Discourse that is divorced from its material or from a supportive ideological unity organic to it has much in it that is superfluous, unnecessary, not available for authentic artistic conceptualization. It is necessary to neutralize or somehow structure all this excess in the discourse in such a way that it not prove an

---

48. At the end of the fifteenth and beginning of the sixteenth century there emerged printed editions of almost all the courtly romances that had been created up to that time.

obstacle; discourse must be freed from its status as mere raw material. The special conventionality of such a discourse serves just such a purpose: everything that cannot be conceptualized is ordered on the template of convention, smoothed out, straightened, polished, touched up. Everything that cannot be authentically conceptualized in art must find for itself a substitute form in indiscriminately chosen conventions or in mere decorativeness.

Divorced from its material as well as from an ideological unity, how is discourse to deal with all the associations suggested by its sounds [zvukovoj obraz], how is it to deal with its inexhaustible wealth of diverse forms, shadings and nuances, its wealth of syntactic and intonation structures, the inexhaustible multiplicity of meanings it assigns objects and social realities? All such considerations are superfluous in expository discourse, for it cannot under any circumstances be organically fused with its material, intentions cannot penetrate it. Expository discourse is therefore forced to conform to a conventional external structure—the image suggested by the sound seeks no more than an empty euphony, and the syntactic and intonational structure seeks no more than an empty ease of manner, a smooth finish, or it might seek (in the other direction) an equally empty rhetorical complexity, something florid and overblown, an ornamented exterior, a reduction of semantic polysemy to empty single meanings. Expository prose may, of course, even adorn itself with poetic tropes, but in such a context they lose the kinds of meanings they have in poetry.

Thus does expository prose legalize and (as it were) canonize the absolute rupture between language and material, and seek for itself a form that will permit this rupture to be overcome by *style*—no matter how conventional and obvious that style might at first glance seem. This form can avail itself of any material from any source. Language used in this way is a neutral element that appeals precisely because it is dressed up, permitting its surface charms to be emphasized, its merely external meanings, the wit and pathos of the material itself.

The expository prose of chivalric romances continued to develop in this direction until it reached its apogee in *Amadis*,[49] and again in the pastoral novel. In the course of this development,

49. *Amadis*, when it spread from its Spanish homeland, turned into a thoroughly international novel.

however, expository prose was enriched by new and important elements that permitted it to approximate authentic novel style and to determine the First Line of development in the European novel. The full organic unification and interaction of language with its material in the novel does not, it is true, take place here, but rather in the Second Line, in a style that fragments and orchestrates its own intentions—that is, it takes place in the line that was to prove essential and highly productive in the later history of the European novel.

As expository novel prose develops there arises a special category of value, "the literariness of language," or (closer to the spirit of the original understanding of this category) "making language respectable." This is not a category of style in the strict sense of the word, for no specific, normative, artistic requirements of a genre stand behind it; but at the same time it is not a category of language either, which would serve to isolate literary language as a specific socio-dialectological unity. The category of "literariness" and "respectability" lies on the boundary between the requirements and value judgments inhering in *style*, on the one hand, and the constitutive and normative requirements of *language* on the other (that is, on the boundary between considering a given form part of, or not part of, a specific dialect in the former case, and establishing its linguistic correctness in the latter).

The categories of popularity and approachability are pertinent here—accommodations that are made to the apperceptive background so that utterances may be easily dealt with against that background without its being dialogized, without calling forth any sharp dialogic cacophony between context and what is said, in other words, the smoothing and ironing-out of style.

In different national languages and different epochs, the general and, as it were, extra-generic category of the "literary language" is filled with a variety of concrete content; it has differing degrees of importance in the history of literature as well as in the history of literary language. But everywhere and always "literary language" has as its area of activity the conversational language of a literarily educated circle (in the example cited above, the language of "respectable society"), the written language of its everyday and semiliterary genres (letters, diaries, etc.), the language of socio-ideological genres (speeches of any kind, pronouncements, descriptions, printed articles, etc.) and ultimately of the artistic prose genres, in particular the novel. In other words, this category attempts to regulate the area of literary and everyday (in the sense of dialectological) language not already regulated by the strict, previously coalesced genres, with the specific and well-differentiated demands they make on their own languages; the category of a "general literariness" does not of course apply at all in the areas of the lyric, the epic and the tragedy. The concept "general literariness" regulates the area of spoken and written heteroglossia that swirls in from all sides on the fixed and strict poetic genre—genres whose demands spring neither from conversational nor from everyday written language.[50] "General literariness" attempts to introduce order into this heteroglossia, to make a single, particular style canonical for it.

We repeat, the concrete content of this extra-generic literariness of language can be profoundly diverse, with varying degrees of specificity and concreteness; for its support it may rely on a variety of cultural-ideological intentions, it may motivate itself with the most diverse interests and values—and all this in order to preserve the socially sealed-off quality of a privileged community ("the language of respectable society"), or to preserve local interests at the national level—for example, to reinforce the hegemony of the Tuscan dialect in the Italian literary language—or to defend the interests of cultural-political centralization, as occurred for example in France in the seventeenth century. A wide variety of concrete forces may fill this category: its function may be served by an academic grammar, a school, salons, literary tendencies, specific genres and so forth. And this category may seek to extend its borders to the limit of *language* [as opposed to style], that is, to the outer limits defining a language: in such cases it achieves a maximal degree of generality but is deprived of almost all ideological coloration and specificity (in such cases it motivates itself with phrases of the type "such is the spirit of language," "that is very French," etc.). But it may also do the opposite, and seek its *stylistic* [as opposed to linguistic] limit: in this case its content becomes even more ideologically concrete, and acquires a certain definiteness as regards objects and emotions. These new requirements serve to define, with great specificity, those who speak and those who write (in such cases, it

50. The horizon of "literary language" may be considerably narrowed down in other epochs—when one or another semi-literary genre works out a fixed and sharply differentiated canon (for example, the epistolary genre).

motivates itself in this way: "thus should every respectable person think, talk, and write," or "every refined and sensitive man does thus and so . . . ," etc.). In the latter instance, the "literariness" regulating the genres of ordinary everyday life (conversations, letters, diaries) cannot fail to exercise an influence—sometimes very profound—on the way we think in our actual lives, and even on our very life-styles, creating "literary people" and "literary deeds." And finally, there is great variety in the degree to which this category may be historically actualized and essential in the history of literature and literary language: it may be great, for instance, as in France in the seventeenth and eighteenth centuries, but it can also be negligible; thus, in other epochs, heteroglossia (even dialectological heteroglossia) spills over even into the high poetic genres. All of this—the nature and varying degrees of historical actuality—depends of course on the content of "literary language," on the force and durability of the cultural and political instantiation upon which it relies.

We are touching here only fleetingly on the extremely important category of the "general literariness of language." We are not concerned with its significance in literature in general or in the history of literary language, but only as it plays a role in the history of novelistic style. And its importance here is enormous: it has a direct significance in novels of the First Stylistic Line, and an indirect significance in novels of the Second Line.

Novels of the First Stylistic Line aspire to organize and stylistically order the heteroglossia of conversational language, as well as of written everyday and semiliterary genres. To a significant extent this impulse to order determines their relationship to heteroglossia. Novels of the Second Stylistic Line, however, transform this already organized and ennobled everyday and literary language into essential material for its own orchestration, and into people for whom this language is appropriate, that is, into "literary people" with their literary way of thinking and their literary ways of doing things—that is, such a novel transforms them into authentic characters.

An understanding of the stylistic essence of the First Line is impossible without taking into account the following extremely important consideration, namely the special relationship these novels have with conversational language and with life and everyday genres. Discourse in the novel is structured on an uninterrupted mutual interaction with the discourse of life. The chivalric romance in prose sets itself against the "low," "vulgar" heteroglossia of all areas of life and counterbalances to it its own specifically idealized, "ennobled" discourse. Vulgar, nonliterary discourse is saturated with low intentions and crude emotional expressions, oriented in a narrowly practical direction, overrun with petty philistine associations and reeks of specific contexts. The chivalric romance opposes to all this its own discourse, linked only with the highest and noblest associations, filled with references to lofty contexts (historical, literary, scholarly). Thus may the ennobled word—as distinct from the poetic word—replace the vulgar word in conversations, letters and other everyday genres just as a euphemism replaces a coarse expression, for it seeks to orient itself in the same sphere as real-life discourse.

Thus does chivalric romance become a vehicle for the *extrageneric literariness of language*—it aspires to provide norms for language in real life, to teach good style, *bon ton*, how to converse in society, how to write letters and so on. The influence of *Amadis* was very great in this respect. Special books such as *Treasures of Amadis* and *The Book of Compliments* were compiled that brought together models of conversations, letters, speeches and so forth extracted from the novel, and such books were very widely distributed and extremely influential throughout the entire seventeenth century. The chivalric romance provided a discourse proper to all possible situations and events in life, while at the same time everywhere opposing itself to vulgar discourse and its coarse ways.

Cervantes excelled in describing encounters between a discourse made respectable by the romance and vulgar discourse—in situations fundamental in both novels and life. In *Don Quixote* the internally polemical orientation of "respectable" discourse vis-à-vis heteroglossia unfolds in novelistic dialogues with Sancho, with other representatives of the heteroglot and coarse realities of life and in the movement of the novel's plot as well. The internal dialogic potential embedded in respectable discourse is thus actualized and brought to the surface—in dialogues and in plot movement—but, like every authentic manifestation of the dialogic principle in language—it does not exhaust itself completely in them, and is not resolved dramatically.

For the poetic word in the narrow sense, such a relationship to extraliterary heteroglossia is of course absolutely excluded. In our lived experience and in the genres of everyday life situations and everyday genres, poetic discourse cannot oppose itself to heteroglossia even indirectly, for it shares no immediate common ground with it. True, it may influence everyday genres and even conversational language, but it does so only indirectly.

To realize its task of stylistically organizing everyday language, it was of course necessary for the chivalric romance in prose to incorporate into its own structure a multitude of diverse genres from everyday life, as well as extraliterary ideological genres. The romance, like the Sophistic novel, came close to being a complete encyclopedia of the genres available in its time. From the point of view of their structure, all the inserted genres possessed a certain degree of completeness and self-sufficiency; for this reason they could easily detach themselves from the romance and still maintain their shape in isolation, as distinct models. Depending on the nature of the inserted genres, even the style of the romance (answering to only a minimum of generic requirements) might be somewhat modified—but in everything essential it remained single-imaged. Here one cannot even talk of generic languages in the strict sense: over the entire multi-imaged diversity of inserted genres there is stretched one "respectable" language, and this effectively turns everything into one single image.

The unity, or more precisely this single-imaged quality, of ennobled language is not sufficient unto itself: it is polemical and abstract. At its heart lies a certain *pose* of respectability, which it consistently assumes in all situations, vis-à-vis low reality. But this respectable pose, for all its unity and self-consistency, is purchased at the price of polemical abstraction and is therefore inert, static and moribund. In fact, the unity and relentless consistency of these novels is inevitable given their social disorientation and ideological rootlessness. The way of perceiving objects and expressions peculiar to this novelistic discourse is not the ever-changing world view of a living and mobile human being, one forever escaping into the infinity of real life; it is rather the restricted world view of a man trying to preserve one and the same immobile pose, someone whose movements are made not in order better to see, but quite the opposite—he moves so that he may turn *away* from, *not* notice, be distracted. This world view, filled not with real-life things but with verbal references to literary things and images, is polemically set against the brute heteroglossia of the real world and painstakingly (although in a deliberately polemical, and therefore tangible, way) cleansed of all possible associations with crude real life.

Representatives of the Second Stylistic Line (Rabelais, Cervantes and others) parodically reverse this device of avoidance; they develop, by means of comparisons, a series of deliberately crude associations, which have the effect of dragging what is being compared down to the dregs of an everyday gross reality congealed in prose, thereby destroying the lofty literary plane that had been achieved by polemical abstraction. Here heteroglossia avenges itself for having been excluded and made abstract (in, for instance, the speeches of Sancho Panza).[51]

For the Second Stylistic Line, the respectable language of the chivalric romance—with all its polemical abstractness—becomes only one of the participants in a dialogue of languages, it becomes the prosaic image of a language—most profoundly and fully instanced in Cervantes—capable of internally dialogic resistance to new authorial intentions; it is an image that is agitatedly double-voiced.

Toward the beginning of the seventeenth century, the First Stylistic Line of the novel begins to change somewhat: real-life historical forces begin to utilize abstract idealization and abstract polemics for the realization of tasks that are more concretely polemical and forensic. The social disorientation of the abstract romance of chivalry is replaced by the marked social and political orientation of the Baroque novel.

The pastoral novel already experiences its material and orients its stylization in a fundamentally different way. It is not only that the material is more freely treated;[52] its very functions change. Baldly stated, contemporary reality is still not the source for all that is incorporated into the alien material of the novel, but reality *is* clothed in that alien material; what is incorporated can, therefore, express itself in the material. The romance relation-

---

51. German literature is characterized by a certain partiality to this device, bringing high discourses low through a series of degrading comparisons and associations. Introduced into German literature by Wolfram von Eschenbach, this device in the fifteenth century determined the style of folk preachers such as Hillary von Kaisersberg, in the sixteenth century Fischart's style, in the seventeenth century the sermons of Abraham a Santa Clara and in the nineteenth century the novels of Hippel and Jean Paul.

52. This fact concerns the most important compositional achievements the pastoral novel made vis-à-vis the courtly romance: a great concentration of action, a greater finished quality to the whole, the development of a stylized landscape. One should also point out the introduction of mythology (classical mythology) and verse into prose.

ship toward material begins to be replaced by something completely different, by a Baroque relationship. A new formula is found for relating to material, a new mode for its artistic utilization, which we—again crudely—define as a re-clothing of surrounding reality in alien material, akin to enacting a sort of heroizing masquerade.[53] An era's sense of self becomes stronger and more intense, it begins to utilize a diversity of alien material for purposes of self-expression and self-representation. This new feeling toward material and the new mode of utilizing it is merely initiated in the pastoral novel; its scope in such novels is still too narrow, the historical forces of the epoch not yet sufficiently concentrated. There is an aspect of intimate-lyrical self-expression dominating these (what might be called) "chamber" novels.

This new mode of utilizing material is developed and realized to the fullest extent in the Baroque novel that deals with heroes from history. The era greedily sought heroically charged material from all ages, countries and cultures; a powerful sense of self is felt in these attempts to invest itself organically with every conceivable type of heroically charged material, regardless of its cultural-ideological source. Exoticism of every sort was felt to be desirable: oriental subjects were no less widespread than ancient or medieval subjects. To find oneself, to realize oneself in the alien, to heroize oneself and one's own struggle in alien material—such was the peculiar intensity of the Baroque novel. The Baroque feeling for the world, with its polarities, with the excessive tension of the contradictory unity permeating its historical material, squeezed out any trace of *internal* self-sufficiency, any internal resistance the alien cultural world (which had created this material) might offer; it transformed the world into an externally stylized shell for its own special content.[54]

The historical significance of the Baroque novel is enormous. Almost all categories of the modern novel have their origin in one or another of its aspects. The Baroque novel, heir to the entire preceding development of the novel and utilizing this heritage to

---

53. Characteristic here is the widespread phenomenon of the "dialogue of the dead"—a form that makes it possible to converse on one's own topics (contemporary and everyday themes) with sages, scholars and heroes of all countries and all eras.

54. There is a literal re-dressing of concrete persons from contemporary life in [Honoré d'Urfé's] *L'Astrée*.

the full (the Sophistic novel, *Amadis*, the pastoral novel), was able to unify in itself all those elements—problem, adventure, historical, psychological, social—that would later figure separately as independent categories of novel. The Baroque novel became in subsequent times an encyclopedia of source material, a source of novelistic motifs, plot positionings and situations. The majority of motifs in the modern novel that, from a comparative perspective, were derived from ancient or oriental sources found their way into the modern novel through the Baroque novel; almost all genealogical researches lead directly to it in the first instance and later, through it, to its own medieval and ancient sources (and further back, to the Orient itself).

We quite properly use the term *Prüfungsroman* for the Baroque novel. It is this [testing] aspect that makes it a culmination of the Sophistic novel, which was also a "novel of trial" (testing the fidelity and chastity of separated lovers). But in the Baroque novel it is the trial of the protagonist's heroism and fidelity, his all-round irreproachability, that serves to unify the novel's grand and exceedingly diverse material, and in a much more organic way. Everything in it is a touchstone, a means for testing all the sides and qualities of the hero, qualities required by the Baroque ideal of heroism. The idea of trial organizes the material throughout, at a deep and sustained level.

We must pause on this idea of trial, and on some of the other organizing ideas in the novel as genre.

The idea of testing the hero, of testing his discourse, may very well be the most fundamental organizing idea in the novel, one that radically distinguishes it from the epic. From the very beginning the epic hero has stood on the other side of trial; in the epic world, an atmosphere of doubt surrounding the hero's heroism is unthinkable.

The idea of trial permits a complex organization of diverse novelistic material around the hero. But the very content of the idea of trial may change fundamentally in different eras and among different social groups. In the Sophistic novel this idea, which had first coalesced in the rhetorical casuistry of the Second Sophistic, is expressed in a manner that is crudely formalistic and external (a psychological or ethical dimension is utterly lacking). This idea underwent a change in early Christian legend, saints' lives and confessional autobiographies, where it was usually united with the idea of crisis and rebirth (these are embryonic forms of the adventure-*cum*-confession novel of trial). The organizing idea of trial was given specific content in the enormous hagiographic literature of early Christians, and later in medieval lives, on the one hand by the Christian idea of martyrdom (trial by suffering and death) and on the other by the idea of temptation (trial by seduction).[55] Another variant on this same idea of trial organizes the material of the classical chivalric romance in verse, a variant that unites in itself both the features of trial characteristic of Greek romance (the testing of lovers' fidelity and valor) and those of Christian legend (trial by suffering and temptations). The same idea—although weakened and reduced—organizes the chivalric romance in prose, but it organizes such novels palely, externally, not penetrating to the core of the material. Ultimately in the Baroque novel, this idea elegantly unifies the most grand and diverse material with extraordinary compositional force.

As the novel continues to develop, the idea of trial preserves its overwhelming organizational significance, filling up with various ideological content depending on the era and all the while maintaining its links with tradition—but with now one, now another line of development predominating (ancient, hagiographical, Baroque). A special variant on the idea of the test, one extremely widespread in the nineteenth-century novel, was the testing of a hero's faithfulness to his calling, a testing of his genius and his "chosenness." Here first place belongs to the particular Romantic version of "chosenness" and the tests to which life puts it. A very important later variation of this "chosenness" motif is embodied in the Napoleonic parvenu of the French novel (the heroes of Stendhal and Balzac). In Zola the concept of "being singled out" is transformed into the concept of fitness for life, biological health, the adaptability of the individual; material in his novels is organized as a testing (with negative results) of the heroes' biological worth. Another variant might be a test determining whether or not a character has "genius" (this is often linked with the parallel test of an artist's fitness for life). Further variants of the nineteenth-century novel include: the testing of the strong personality who opposes himself, on one ground or another, to the com-

---

55. Thus the idea of trial organizes, with great elegance and consistency, the well-known old French poem "The Life of Alexis": in a similar vein we have in Russian the "Life" of Theodosius of the Caves.

munity, who seeks to attain complete self-sufficiency and a proud isolation, or who aspires to the role of a chosen leader; the testing of the moral reformer or amoralist, the trial of the Nietzschean man, of the emancipated woman and so forth—these are all very widespread organizing ideas in the European novel of the nineteenth and early twentieth century.[56] A special variant on the novel of trial would be the Russian novel testing the fitness and worth of an intellectual in society (the theme of the "superfluous man"), which in turn breaks down into a series of subcategories (from Pushkin up to the testing of intellectuals in the Revolution).

The idea of testing also has an enormous significance in the pure adventure novel. External evidence of just how productive this idea is may be seen in the fact that it permits one to connect, in the novel, a vivid and multi-faceted adventure quality with profound dilemmas and complex psychology. Everything depends on the ideological depth, the sociohistorical spirit peculiar to a given time and the forward movement of the idea of trial that becomes the content organizing the novel; insofar as the novel depends on these qualities, it may achieve its maximal breadth, depth and fullness and realize all its generic potential. The novel of pure adventure frequently reduces the potential of the novel as a genre to a minimum, but nevertheless a naked plot, brute adventure cannot in itself ever be the organizing force in a novel. On the contrary, we always uncover in any adventure the traces of some idea that had organized it earlier, some idea that had structured the body of the given plot and had animated it, as if it were its soul, but that in pure adventure novels has lost its ideological force, so the idea continues to flicker but only feebly. More often than not (but not always) the adventure plot is organized around just such a flickering, fading idea of a hero under test.

The modern European adventure novel stems from two fundamentally different sources. One type of adventure novel can be traced back to the high Baroque novel of trial (this is the dominant type of adventure novel), the other back to *Gil Blas* and even further to *Lazarillo*, that is, it is connected with the "picaresque novel." We find these same two types even in ancient times, represented by the Sophistic novel on the one hand and on the other

56. Those who represent every sort of fashionable idea and tendency undergo similar trials, which play a large role in the massive output of second-rate novelists.

by Petronius. The first basic type of adventure novel is organized, as in the Baroque novel, by one or another variation on the idea of testing, which, as a real ideological force, is flickering out and thus tending to externalization. Nevertheless, a novel of this type is more complex and richer than epics, Christian legends or Greek romances, for it is not severed completely from a certain degree of problematicalness and psychology: a blood kinship with the Baroque novel—*Amadis*, the chivalric romance and others— will always be detected in it.[57] Such is the English and American adventure novel (Defoe, Monk Lewis, Radcliffe, Walpole, Cooper, London and others); such also are the major categories of the French adventure novel and penny-dreadful. One observes fairly frequently a mixing of both types, but in such cases the first type (the novel of trial) is always the organizing source of the whole, as it is the stronger and more dominant. A Baroque piling-on of adventures in this type of novel is very marked: even in the construction of a penny-dreadful of the lowest, most primitive sort, it is possible to discern aspects that—via the Baroque novel and *Amadis*—lead us back to forms of early Christian biography, autobiography and legends of the Helleno-Roman world. Such a novel as the notorious *Rocambolle*[i] of Ponson du Terraille is full of the most ancient allusions. At the heart of its structure can dimly be felt forms of the Helleno-Roman novel of trial, with its crisis and rebirth (Apuleius and early Christian legends about the transformation of a sinner). We find in it a whole series of elements that can be traced back to the Baroque novel, to *Amadis* and further back to the chivalric romance in verse. At the same time elements of the second type (*Lazarillo, Gil Blas*) are also present in its structure, but the Baroque spirit is of course dominant in them.

A few words now about Dostoevsky. His novels are all sharply etched novels of trial. Without touching on the essence of the idiosyncratic idea of testing that lies at the heart of his structure,

57. It is true that this breadth is rarely to its advantage: in most cases the problematicalness and psychological material is trivialized. The second type is more precise and pure.

---

i. Reference is to the endless series by Ponson du Terraille (1829–1871), such as *Les Exploits de Rocambolle* (1859), *La Résurrection de Rocambolle* (1866) and so forth.

we will pause briefly on the historical traditions that have left their trace in these novels. Dostoevsky was linked to the Baroque novel by four strands: the English "sensational novel"[58] (Monk Lewis, Radcliffe, Walpole and others), the French socio-adventure novel exploring low life (Eugène Sue), Balzac's novels of trial and finally the German Romantics (primarily Hoffmann). But Dostoevsky was also linked directly with hagiographic literature and with Christian legends in their Orthodox forms, with their specific concept of trial. This is what gives organic unity to the adventures, confessions, problematicalness, saints' lives, crises and rebirths in his novels, that is, the whole complex that was already characteristic of the Helleno-Roman novel of trial (as far as we can judge from Apuleius, and from information that has come down to us on certain autobiographies and early Christian hagiographic legends).

A study of the Baroque novel, that form that had absorbed into itself such an enormous amount of material reflecting the genre's preceding development, has extraordinary significance for understanding the most important novel-types of the present day. Almost all lines of development lead back to it in the most immediate way, and, through it, further back into the Middle Ages, the Helleno-Roman world and the Orient.

In the eighteenth century Wieland, Wezel, Blankenburg and after them Goethe and the Romantics proclaimed, as a counterweight to the novel of trial, a new idea: the *Entwicklungsroman* and more particularly the *Bildungsroman*.

The idea of testing lacks within itself the necessary means to deal with a man's "becoming"; in several of its forms it knows crisis and rebirth, but it does not know development, becoming, a man's *gradual* formation. Testing begins with an already formed person and subjects him to a trial in the light of an ideal also already formed. The chivalric romance and in particular the Baroque novel are typical of this tendency to postulate directly the inborn and statically inert nobility of its heroes.

To this the modern novel opposes the process of a man's becoming, a certain duality, a lack of wholeness characteristic of living human beings, a mixture within the man of good and evil, strength and weakness. Life and its events no longer serve as a touchstone, a means for testing a ready-made character (or at best, as a factor triggering the development of an already pre-

58. The term was coined by W. Dibelius.

formed and predetermined hero)—now, life and its events, bathed in the light of becoming, reveal themselves as the hero's *experience*, as the school or environment that first forms and formulates the hero's character and world view. The idea of becoming and *Bildung* makes it possible to organize material around the hero in a new way and to uncover, in this material, completely new sides.

The theme of becoming and *Bildung* and the theme of testing are by no means mutually exclusive within the confines of the modern novel: on the contrary, they may enter into a profound and organic union. The greatest examples of the European novel organically combine in themselves both themes (this is especially true in the nineteenth century, when pure examples of the novel of trial or the *Entwicklungsroman* are relatively rare). Thus, even *Parzival* combines in itself the idea of testing (the idea that dominates) and the idea of becoming. The same must be said of the classic *Bildungsroman*, *Wilhelm Meister*: even in it, the idea of *Bildung* (which has already become dominant) is combined with the idea of trial.

The kind of novel created by Fielding and even more so by Sterne is likewise characterized by a union of both ideas, and here they are present in almost equal proportion. Under the influence of Fielding and Sterne, the continental type of *Bildungsroman* was created, represented by Wieland, Wezel, Hippel and Jean Paul; here the testing of an idealist or an eccentric does not result in a naked exposure of them as such in the novel, but rather facilitates their becoming more like real thinking people; in these novels life is not only a touchstone, but a school.

Of the many idiosyncratic variants that combine these two types of novel, we might point to Gottfried Keller's *Der grüne Heinrich*, which is organized around both themes. And Romain Rolland's *Jean-Christophe* is structured in an analogous manner.

The novel of trial and the *Entwicklungsroman* do not of course exhaust the ways material may be organized by the novel. Suffice it to point out the fundamentally new organizational ideas brought about by the structuring of a novel along biographical and autobiographical lines. In the course of their development, biography and autobiography worked out a series of forms determined by specific codes of organization—for example, using "valor and virtue" as the base on which to organize biographical material, or "deeds and labors," "successes/failures" and so on.

Let us return to the Baroque novel of trial, from which our present excursus has diverted us. What conditions govern discourse in this novel? And how does this discourse relate to heteroglossia?

Discourse in the Baroque novel is a *discourse of pathos*. In it a peculiarly novelistic pathos, quite unlike that found in poetry, was created (or more correctly, reaches its highest development). The Baroque novel was a seminal source for a particular kind of pathos, wherever its influence penetrated and wherever its traditions were retained, that is, primarily in the novel of trial (and in the testing element in novels of the mixed type).

Baroque pathos is determined by modes of *apologia*, and polemic. It is a prosaic pathos, one that continually senses the resistance offered by alien discourses, alien points of view; it is the kind of pathos associated with justification (self-justification) and accusation. The heroizing idealization found in Baroque novels is not epical, but rather of the kind familiar to chivalric romances: abstract, polemical and similar by and large to *apologias*. As distinct from chivalric romances, however, this idealization is deeply felt and is reinforced by social and cultural forces that actually exist and are self-aware. We must pause for a while on the unique nature of this novelistic pathos.

A discourse of pathos is fully sufficient to itself and to its object. Indeed, the speaker completely immerses himself in such a discourse, there is no distance, there are no reservations. A discourse of pathos has the appearance of directly intentional discourse.

Such is not always the case with pathos, however. A discourse of pathos may also be conditional, and may even be doubled, like double-voiced discourse. In the novel it is precisely as double-voiced that pathos almost inevitably occurs; in novels it does not have, and cannot have, any basis in reality, it must seek this support in other genres. Novelistic pathos does not have discourses that belong to it alone—it must borrow the discourses of others. When *authentic* pathos inheres in a subject, it can only be a poetic pathos.

Novelistic pathos always works in the novel to restore some *other* genre, genres that, in their own unmediated and pure form, have lost their own base in reality. In the novel a discourse of pathos is almost always a surrogate for some other genre that is no longer available to a given time or a given social force—such pathos is the discourse of a preacher who has lost his pulpit, a dreaded judge who no longer has any judicial or punitive powers, the prophet without a mission, the politician without political power, the believer without a church and so forth—everywhere, the discourse of pathos is connected with orientations and positions that are unavailable to the author as authentic expression for the seriousness and determination of his purpose, but which he must, *all the same*, conditionally reproduce by using his own discourse. All the means and forms of pathos that inhere in language—lexical, syntactical and compositional—are fused together with specific orientations and positions; they all achieve some degree of organizational power and involve a certain definite and well-formulated social representation of speakers. For the person writing the novel there is no language to express a purely individualized pathos: he must, against his will, mount the pulpit, assume the role of preacher, judge, etc. There is no pathos without threat, without profanation, promises, blessings and so forth.[59] In pathos-charged speech one cannot take the first step without first conferring on oneself some power, rank, position, etc. In this lies the "curse" of novelistic pathos when it is expressed directly. Therefore pathos in the novel (and in literature in general), if it is authentic, shies away from discourse that is *openly* emotional, not yet separated from its subject.

The discourse of pathos and the kind of representation it permits were born and shaped in a distanced image; they are organically linked with a hierarchically evaluated concept of the past. These forms of pathos are not found in familiar zones of contact with still-evolving contemporaneity—such pathos inevitably destroys zones of contact (as it does, for instance, in Gogol). It requires a hierarchically privileged position that is impossible in such a zone (if attempted, it can lead to false notes and straining for effect).

The apologetic and polemical pathos of the Baroque novel is organically combined with the specific Baroque idea of testing the hero, a hero who is ever constant and inherently irreproachable. In all important aspects there is no distance between hero and author; the verbal mass of the novel is all on a single plane, thus in all its aspects it is involved in heteroglossia to an equal

59. We are speaking, naturally, only about that discourse of pathos that relates in a polemical and forensic way to another's discourse, but not about the pathos of representation itself, the pathos inherent in the subject and that is itself therefore artistic and in no need of a specific conditioning.

degree and fails to incorporate this contradiction into its composition, leaving it, as it were, *outside* itself.

The Baroque novel unites in itself a great diversity of inserted genres. It also strives to become an encyclopedia of all the types of literary language of the epoch, even an encyclopedia of all possible types of knowledge and information (philosophical, historical, political, geographical, etc.). One could say that the furthest limit of the encyclopedia impulse fundamental for the First Stylistic Line is reached in the Baroque novel.[60]

In their further development, Baroque novels branch in two directions (the same two branches of development characterize the First Line as a whole): one branch continues the adventure-heroic aspect of the Baroque novel (Lewis, Radcliffe, Walpole and others), while the other branch, the seventeenth- and eighteenth-century novel that is in large part epistolary (La Fayette, Rousseau, Richardson and others), is characterized by psychology and pathos. We should add a few words about this latter type, since it has great stylistic significance for the subsequent history of the novel.

The Sentimental psychological novel is genetically connected with the inserted letter of the Baroque novel, with the epistolary expression of love. In the Baroque novel this kind of Sentimental emotion was only one aspect of a more general polemical and apologetic pathos, and a secondary aspect at that.

In Sentimental psychological novels, the discourse of pathos changes: it becomes associated with intimate situations and, losing the broad political and historical scope characteristic of the Baroque novel, combines with a didactic approach to the moral choices of everyday life and satisfies itself with the narrowly personal and family spheres of life. Pathos becomes associated exclusively with the kind of privacy found in one's own room. When this occurs, there is a change in the interaction between novelistic language and heteroglossia: their interaction becomes less mediated, and the purely everyday genres of the letter, the diary, casual conversations move to the fore. The didactic purpose behind this Sentimental pathos is tied to more concrete situations, descends to the depths of everyday life, its smallest details, to intimate relations between people and into the internal life of the individual person.

60. Especially in the German Baroque.

What emerges is a specific-temporal zone of Sentimental pathos associated with the intimacy of one's own room. This is the zone of the letter, the diary. Public-square and private-room zones of contact and familiarity ("proximities") are very different, as different, from this point of view, as are the palace and the private home, the temple (cathedral) and the more house-like Protestant church. It is not a matter of scale, but rather of a special organization of space (here parallels with architecture and painting could be drawn).

The Sentimental novel of pathos wherever it occurs is connected with fundamental change in the literary language, in the sense that literary language is brought closer to the conversational norm. But conversational language in such novels is still ordered and subjected to norms from the point of view of "literariness"; it becomes a unitary language for the direct expression of authorial intentions, and not merely one of the heteroglot languages orchestrating these intentions. As a unitary and authentic language of literature as well as life, one that is adequate to true intentions and true human expression, it is opposed both to the unordered and brute heteroglossia of life and to the archaic and conventional high literary genres.

The aspect of opposition to the old literary language and the correspondingly high poetic genres it sustained is of crucial importance in the Sentimental novel. While setting itself in opposition to the lowly and gross heteroglossia found in life—which is subject to being ordered and made respectable by Sentimentalism—Sentimentalism also opposes the quasi-elevated and false heteroglossia found in literary language, which is subject to exposure and invalidation by Sentimentalism and its discourse. But this orientation toward literary heteroglossia is polemical, the style and language being opposed is not introduced into the novel, but remains as its dialogizing background outside the work.

The essential aspects of Sentimental style are determined precisely by this opposition to a high heroizing pathos, a pathos that gives rise to abstract types. The finely detailed descriptions, the very deliberateness with which petty secondary everyday details are foregrounded, the tendency of the representation to present itself as an unmediated impression deriving from the object itself and finally a pathos occasioned by helplessness and weakness rather than by heroic strength, the deliberate narrowing-down of the conceptual horizon and the arena of a man's experience to his most immediate little micro-world (to his very own room)—all this is accounted for by the polemical opposition to a literary style in the process of being rejected.

In place of one conventionality, however, Sentimentalism creates another—and one similarly abstract, serving to draw attention away from other aspects of reality. A discourse made respectable by Sentimental pathos, one that attempts to replace the brute discourse of life, inevitably ends up in the same hopeless dialogic conflict with the actual heteroglossia of life, in the same unresolvable dialogized misunderstanding characteristic of the "respectable" discourse of Amadis, as present in the situations and dialogues of Don Quixote. The one-sided dialogism that is present in embedded form in Sentimental novels is made explicit in novels of the Second Stylistic Line, where Sentimental pathos, as one language among other languages, as one of many sides in the dialogue of languages surrounding a man and his world, takes on a parodic ring.[61]

Openly pathetic discourse did not, of course, cease to exist with the passing of the Baroque novel (with its pathos of heroism and terror) or with the passing of Sentimentalism (the private emotions one experiences in one's own room). It continued to live as one of the basic subcategories of direct authorial discourse in general, that is, the kind of discourse that expresses authorial intentions without refraction, unmediatedly and directly. Openly pathetic discourse continued to live, but it was never again the stylistic base for any of the important novel-types. The nature of openly pathetic discourse, wherever it has occurred, has remained unchanged: the speaker (the author) either assumes the conventionalized pose of judge, preacher, teacher and so forth, or his discourse makes a polemical appeal based on what is assumed to be a direct impression from the object or from life, one unencumbered by any ideological presuppositions. Thus in Tolstoy, for example, direct authorial discourse moves back and forth between polemical and unmediated extremes. His discourse is everywhere determined by the heteroglossia (literary *and* real-life)

61. In one generic form or another, in Fielding, Smollett and Sterne; in Germany, in Musäus, Wieland, Muller and others. In their artistic handling of the problem of Sentimental pathos (and the didactic approach) in its relationship to actual experience, all these authors follow the lead of Don Quixote, whose influence is decisively important. In Russia, cf. the role of Richardsonian language in the heteroglot orchestration of *Evgenij Onegin* (Tatiana in her country phase, and her mother, Madame Larina).

that dialogically—polemically or pedagogically—permeates discourse; for example, a representation that is direct and "unmediated" turns out to be in fact a highly polemical de-heroization of the Caucasus, of war and military exploits, even of nature itself.

Those who deny any artistic essence to the novel, who reduce novelistic discourse to a kind of rhetorical discourse that is only superficially ornamented with pseudo-poetic images, are primarily thinking of the First Stylistic Line of the novel, for on the surface it does indeed seem to support such a contention. It is true that at the outer limits of this line of development, novelistic discourse does not realize its unique potential, and often (although certainly not always) ends up as empty rhetoric or false poeticalness. But even here, in the First Line, novelistic discourse is nevertheless profoundly distinctive, radically distinct from the discourse of rhetoric and of poetry. This uniqueness is determined by the novel's fundamentally dialogic relationship to heteroglossia. Social stratification of language in the process of evolution is the basis for the stylistic shaping of discourse even in this First Line of the novel. The language of the novel is structured in uninterrupted dialogic interaction with the languages that surround it.

Poetry also comes upon language as stratified, language in the process of uninterrupted ideological evolution, already fragmented into "languages." And poetry also sees its own language surrounded by other languages, surrounded by literary and extraliterary heteroglossia. But poetry, striving for maximal purity, works in its own language *as if* that language were unitary, the only language, as if there were no heteroglossia outside it. Poetry behaves as if it lived in the heartland of its own language territory, and does not approach too closely the borders of this language, where it would inevitably be brought into dialogic contact with heteroglossia; poetry chooses not to look beyond the boundaries of its own language. If, during an epoch of language crises, the language of poetry *does* change, poetry immediately canonizes the new language as one that is unitary and singular, as if no other language existed.

Novelistic prose of the First Stylistic Line stands on the very borderline of its own language and is dialogically implicated in the surrounding heteroglossia, resonates with its most essential features and consequently participates in an ongoing dialogue of languages. The mode appropriate to its perception presumes precisely a background of heteroglossia, and the artistic meaning of prose of this kind can be uncovered only in a dialogic relation to it. This discourse is the expression of a language consciousness that has been profoundly relativized by heteroglossia and polyphony.

In the novel, literary language possesses an organ for perceiving the heterodox nature of its own speech. Heteroglossia-in-itself becomes, in the novel and thanks to the novel, heteroglossia-for-itself: languages are dialogically implicated *in* each other and begin to exist *for* each other (similar to exchanges in a dialogue). It is precisely thanks to the novel that languages are able to illuminate each other mutually; literary language becomes a dialogue of languages that both know about and understand each other.

Novels of the First Stylistic Line approach heteroglossia from above, it is as if they *descend* onto it (the Sentimental novel occupies a special position here, somewhere between heteroglossia and the high genres). Novels of the Second Line, on the contrary, approach heteroglossia from below: out of the heteroglot depths they rise to the highest spheres of literary language and overwhelm them. In both cases the starting point is the point of view heteroglossia takes toward literariness.

It is very difficult to speak of a clear-cut genetic distinction between the two lines, especially in the early stages of their development. We have already pointed out that the classic chivalric romance in verse is not completely comprehended by the framework of the First Line; von Eschenbach's *Parzival*, for instance, is already in fact a great example of a novel of the Second Line.

In the subsequent history of European prose, double-voiced discourse is worked out (as had been the case in ancient times) in the minor epic genres (*fabliaux*, *Schwänke*, minor parodic genres), out of the mainstream of the great chivalric romance. In such contexts are those basic types and subgenres of double-voiced discourse developed that later begin to determine style in great novels of the Second Type: the style of parodic discourse—ironic, comic *skaz* and so on—in all its degrees and nuances.

It is precisely here, on a small scale—in the minor low genres, on the itinerant stage, in public squares on market day, in street songs and jokes—that devices were first worked out for constructing images of a language, devices for coupling discourse with the image of a particular kind of speaker, devices for an objective exhibiting of discourse together with a specific kind of person and not as an expression in some depersonalized language understood by all in the same way: instead, we have exhibited a discourse characteristic or socially typical for a specific given kind of person—the language of a priest, a knight, a merchant, a peasant, a jurist and so on. Every discourse has its own selfish and biased proprietor; there are no words with meanings shared by all, no words "belonging to no one." This expresses what might be called the "philosophy of discourse" inherent in the satiric-realistic folk novella and other low parodic genres associated with jokesters. Moreover, the feeling for language at the heart of these genres is shot through with a profound distrust of human discourse as such. When we seek to understand a word, what matters is not the direct meaning the word gives to objects and emotions—this is the false front of the word; what matters is rather the actual and always self-interested *use* to which this meaning is put and the way it is expressed by the speaker, a use determined by the speaker's position (profession, social class, etc.) and by the concrete situation. *Who* speaks and under what conditions he speaks: this is what determines the word's actual meaning. All direct meanings and direct expressions are false, and this is especially true of emotional meanings and expressions.

We see the ground being prepared here for a radical scepticism toward any unmediated discourse and any straightforward seriousness, a scepticism bordering on rejection of the very possibility of having a straightforward discourse at all that would not be false. This finds its profoundest expression in works by (among others) Villon, Rabelais, Sorel and Scarron. Here too the ground is being prepared for that new dialogical category, verbal and effectual response to the lie of pathos, that has played such an extremely important role in the history of the European novel (and not only the novel)—the category of *gay deception*. Opposed to the *lie of pathos* accumulated in the language of all recognized and structured professions, social groups and classes, there is not straightforward truth (pathos of the same kind) but rather a gay and intelligent deception, a *lie* justified because it is directed precisely to *liars*. Opposed to the language of priests and monks, kings and seigneurs, knights and wealthy urban types, scholars and jurists—to the languages of all who hold power and who are well set up in life—there is the language of the merry rogue, wherever necessary parodically re-processing any pathos but always in such a way as to rob it of its power to harm, "distance it from the mouth" as it were, by means of a smile or a deception, mock its falsity and thus turn what was a lie into gay deception. Falsehood is illuminated by ironic consciousness and in the mouth of the happy rogue parodies itself.

Preceding and preparing the ground for the great novel forms of the Second Line is the unique cyclicity found in satiric and parodic novellas. We cannot here take up the problem of the cyclicity of such novelistic prose, its fundamental difference from cyclicity in the epic, the various ways for unifying novellas and other such aspects—all of which exceed the limits of stylistics.

Together with the image of the rogue (and often fusing with him) there appears the image of the *fool*—either of an actual simpleton or the image of the mask of a rogue. The naiveté of a simpleton who does not understand pathos (or who understands it in a distorted way, wrong side out), is counterposed to a false pathos, which together with gay deception has the effect of "making strange" any pretensions to lofty reality a discourse of pathos might have. This prosaic "estrangement" of the discourse of conventional pathos by means of an uncomprehending stupidity (simplicity, naiveté) had an enormous significance for the entire subsequent history of the novel. Even if the image of the fool (and the image of the rogue as well) loses its fundamental organizing role in the subsequent development of novelistic prose, nevertheless the very aspect of *not grasping* the conventions of society (the degree of society's conventionality), not understanding lofty pathos-charged labels, things and events—such incomprehension remains almost everywhere an essential ingredient of prose style. Either the prose writer represents a world through the words of a *narrator* who does not understand this world, does not acknowledge its poetic, scholarly or otherwise lofty and significant labels; or else the prose writer introduces a *character* who does not understand; or, finally, the direct style of the author himself involves a deliberate (polemical) failure to understand the habitual way of conceiving the world (this happens, for example, in Tolstoy). It is possible, of course, to make simultaneous use at all three levels of such failures to understand, such prosaic forms of stupidity.

Occasionally this failure to understand assumes a radical character and becomes the basic style-shaping factor of the novel (for example in Voltaire's *Candide*, in Stendhal, in Tolstoy)—but frequently an inability to grasp the conventional sense of the world is limited to specific languages or only to certain specific sides of life. This is the case, for instance, with Belkin as storyteller: the prosaic quality of his style is determined by his failure to understand the poetic weight of one or another aspect of the events he narrates: it is as if he lets slip all poetic potential and poetic effects; all the richest poetic aspects he recounts drily and tersely (deliberately so). Grinev is also just such a bad poet (it is not by accident that he writes bad poems). In Maxim Maximych's tale (*A Hero of Our Time*) it is Maximych's failure to understand Byronic language and Byronic pathos that is foregrounded.

The coupling of incomprehension with comprehension, of stupidity, simplicity and naiveté with intellect, is a widespread and highly typical phenomenon in novelistic prose. One could say that the aspect of incomprehension and of a specific sort of stupidity (a deliberate stupidity) is almost always, in one degree or another, a determining factor for novelistic prose of the Second Stylistic Line.

Stupidity (incomprehension) in the novel is always polemical: it interacts dialogically with an intelligence (a lofty pseudo intelligence) with which it polemicizes and whose mask it tears away. Stupidity, like gay deception and other novelistic categories, is a dialogic category, one that follows from the specific dialogism of novelistic discourse. For this reason stupidity (incomprehension) in the novel is always implicated in language, in the word: at its heart always lies a polemical failure to understand someone else's discourse, someone else's pathos-charged lie that has appropriated the world and aspires to conceptualize it, a polemical failure to understand generally accepted, canonized, inveterately false languages with their lofty labels for things and events: poetic language, scholarly and pedantic language, religious, political, judicial language and so forth. Such is the source of a multitude of different novelistic-dialogic situations or dialogic oppositions: the fool and the poet, the fool and the scholar-pedant, the fool and the moralist, the fool and the priest, the fool and the holy man, the fool and the representative of the law (the fool, he-who-fails-to-understand, in court, in the theater, at a scholarly conference, etc.), the fool and the politician and so forth. These manifold different situations are made broad use of in *Don Quixote* (especially the episode of Sancho's governorship, receptive ground for developing such situations); or—despite all the differences in style—in Tolstoy (the-man-who-fails-to-understand in various situations and institutions, such as Pierre on the battlefield,

Levin at the Elections of the Nobility, at the session of the City Duma, during Koznyshev's conversation with the philosophy professor, during the conversation with the economist and so forth; Nekhliudov at court, in the Senate and so on)—in all these, Tolstoy is reproducing time-honored traditional novelistic situations.

A fool introduced by the author for purposes of "making strange" the world of conventional pathos may himself, as a fool, be the object of the author's scorn. The author need not necessarily express a complete solidarity with such a character. Mocking these figures as fools may even become paramount. But the author needs the fool: by his very uncomprehending presence he makes strange the world of social conventionality. By representing stupidity, the novel teaches prose intelligence, prose wisdom. Regarding fools or regarding the world through the eyes of a fool, the novelist's eye is taught a sort of prose vision, the vision of a world confused by conventions of pathos and by falsity. A failure to understand languages that are otherwise generally accepted and that have the appearance of being universal teaches the novelist how to perceive them physically as *objects*, to see their relativity, to externalize them, to feel out their boundaries, that is, it teaches him how to expose and structure images of social languages.

We will not deal here with the manifold and various types of fools and failures to understand that have been worked out in the process of the novel's historical development. Each novel, each artistic trend will feature one or another aspect of stupidity or incomprehension and, depending on which aspect, will structure its image of the fool accordingly (for example, the cult of the child in Romantic literature, the eccentrics in Jean Paul). The estranged languages that accompany this stupidity and failure to understand are many and varied. Many and varied as well are the functions fulfilled by stupidity and failure to understand in the novel as a whole. The study of stupidity and incomprehension as well as the stylistic and compositional variations associated with them in their historical development constitute a basic (and extremely interesting) problem in the history of the novel.

Prose offers two responses to high pathos and to seriousness and conventionality of any sort: the gay deception of the rogue—a lie justified because directed to liars—and stupidity—also justified, as it is the failure to understand a lie. Between the rogue and the fool there emerges, as a unique coupling of the two, the image of the *clown*. He is a rogue who dons the mask of a fool in order to motivate distortions and shufflings of languages and labels, thus unmasking them by not understanding them. The clown is one of the most ancient of literature's images, and the clown's speech, determined by his specific social orientation (by his privileges as a clown) is one of the most ancient artistic forms of human discourse. In the novel, the stylistic functions of the clown, like those of the rogue and the fool, are completely determined by his relationship to heteroglossia (more precisely to its higher levels): the clown is the one who has the right to speak in otherwise unacceptable languages and the right to maliciously distort languages that *are* acceptable.

Thus the rogue's gay deception parodies high languages, the clown's malicious distortion of them, his turning them inside out and finally the fool's naive incomprehension of them—these three dialogic categories that had organized heteroglossia in the novel at the dawn of its history emerge in modern times with extraordinary surface clarity and are embodied in the symbolic images of the rogue, the clown and the fool. In their further development these categories are refined, differentiated, cut loose from their external and symbolically static images, but they continue to preserve their importance for organizing novel style. The distinctiveness of novelistic dialogues is determined by these categories, for the roots of such dialogues always reach deep down into the internal dialogic essence of language itself, that is, into the failure on the part of those speaking different languages to understand each other. For the organization of *dramatic* dialogues, on the contrary, these categories have only a secondary importance, for they lack the potential for being dramatically resolved. The rogue, the clown and the fool are the heroes of a series of episodes and adventures that is never resolved, and of dialogic oppositions that are unresolved as well. The prose cyclicity of novellas built around such images thus becomes possible. But it is precisely for this reason that drama cannot use such images. Pure drama strives toward a unitary language, one that is individualized merely through dramatic personae who speak it. Dramatic dialogue is determined by a collision between individuals who exist within the limits of a single world and a single unitary language.[62] To a certain extent comedy is an exception to this. Nev-

---

62. We are speaking, to be sure, of pure classical drama as expressing the ideal extreme of the genre. Contemporary realistic social drama may, of course, be heteroglot and multi-languaged.

ertheless it is significant that picaresque comedy has achieved nowhere near the same state of development as has the picaresque novel. The figure of Figaro is essentially the only great image produced by this type of comedy.[63]

The three categories we have outlined are of primary importance in understanding novel style. The rogue, the clown and the fool were first present in the very cradle of the modern European novel, and there left behind their foolscap and bells among the swaddling clothes. Our three categories are no less significant for understanding the prehistoric roots of prose thought, for grasping its links with folklore.

The image of the rogue determines the first powerful novel-form of the Second Line—the picaresque adventure novel. This novel's hero and his discourse can be understood in all its uniqueness only against the background of the high chivalric novel of trial, extraliterary rhetorical genres (biographical, confessional, sermon genres and others), and against the later background of the Baroque novel. The radical novelty and conceptual depth of the picaresque novel's hero (and the discourse peculiar to him) can be outlined with the necessary clarity only against this background.

The hero of such novels, the agent of gay deception, is located on the far side of any pathos—heroic or Sentimental—and located there deliberately and emphatically; his contra-pathetic nature is everywhere in evidence, beginning with his comic self-introduction and self-recommendation to the public (providing the·tone of the entire subsequent story) and ending with the finale. The hero is located beyond all these basically rhetorical categories that are at the heart of a hero's image in novels of trial: he is on the far side of any judgment, any defense or accusation, any self-justification or repentance. A radically new tone is given here to discourse about human beings, a tone alien to any pathos-charged seriousness.

As we said earlier, these pathos-charged categories wholly determine the hero's image in a novel of trial and the image of

63. We will not here take up the problem of comedy's influence on the novel, or the possible comedic origin of several variants on the rogue, the clown and the fool. Whatever the origin of these variants, in the novel their functions change, and under novelistic conditions completely new possibilities unfold for these images.

human beings in the majority of rhetorical genres: in biographies (glorification, *apologia*); in autobiographies (self-glorification, self-justification); in confessions (repentance); in judicial and political rhetoric (defense and accusation); in rhetorical satire (a pathos-charged exposure) and many others. The hero's defense, his *apologia*, his glorification or (on the contrary) the accusation against him, his exposure and so forth are the sole processes determining the way the hero's image is organized, how his features are selected, how they are linked, how the hero's image is brought into relation to actions and events. Such conceptions of the hero have at their heart a normative and static idea of human beings; it is a conception that excludes any hint, however slight, of essential becoming. Thus the hero can be evaluated only as *exclusively* positive or *exclusively* negative. Rhetorical-judicial categories predominate in the conception of human beings, which was definitive for the heroes of Sophistic novels, ancient biography and autobiography and later in chivalric romances, novels of trial and analogous rhetorical genres. The unity of a man and the coherence of his acts (his deeds) are of a rhetorical and legal character and therefore, viewed from a later psychological concept of the human personality, they appear external and merely formal. It is no accident that the Sophistic novel was born out of a utopian fantasy of the law having nothing to do with the actual legal and political life of rhetoricians. Rhetorical analyses and representations of "crime," "services rendered," "exploits," "political rectitude" and so forth provided the scheme for analyzing and representing human acts in the novel. This scheme was defined by the unity of the act and its categorical qualification. Such schemes were also at the heart of the representation of personality. Adventure, erotic and (primitively) psychological material was already gathering around this rhetorical-legal nucleus.

It is true that alongside this externally rhetorical approach to the unity of a human personality and its acts there existed as well a confessional, "repentant" approach to one's own self, an approach with its *own* scheme for structuring the image of a man and his acts (since the time of Augustine)—but this confessional idea of the interior man (and the corresponding structuring of his image) did not deeply influence chivalric romances or Baroque novels; it became significant only in modern times.

Against such a background what emerges first and most clearly is the negating work of the picaresque novel: the destruction of the rhetorical unity of personality, act and event. What is a "picaro"—Lazarillo, Gil Blas and the others? A criminal or an honest man, evil or good, cowardly or brave? Can one even talk about services rendered, about crimes, about exploits that create and define his profile? He stands beyond defense and accusation, beyond glorification or exposure, he knows neither repentance nor self-justification, he is not implicated in any norm, requirement, ideal; he is not all of one piece and is not consistent, if measured against the rhetorical unities of personality that were available. A human being is, as it were, emancipated here from all the entanglements of such conventional unities, he is neither defined nor comprehended by them; in fact, he can even laugh at them.

All the old links between a man and his act, between an event and those who participate in it, fall apart. A sharp gap now opens between a man and the external position he occupies—his rank, his public worth, his social class. All the high positions and symbols, spiritual as well as profane, with which men adorn themselves with such importance and hypocritical falsity are transformed into masks in the presence of the rogue, into costumes for a masquerade, into buffoonery. A reformulation and loosening-up of all these high symbols and positions, their radical re-accentuation, takes place in an atmosphere of gay deception.

The high languages, fused with specific occupations, are also subject to the same radical re-accentuation, as we have already pointed out.

The novel's discourse—like its hero—does not tie itself down to only one form among the "accentuating" unities available; it does not surrender itself to only one evaluating and accentuating system. Even in those places where novelistic discourse does not parody or laugh, it prefers to give the impression of a completely unaccented, dry, informative discourse.

As opposed to the hero of novels of trial and temptation, the hero of picaresque novels is faithful to nothing, he betrays everything—but he is nevertheless true to himself, to his *own* orientation, which scorns pathos and is full of scepticism. A new concept of human personality comes to fruition, one that is not rhetorical but not confessional either, still groping for a discourse of its own and preparing the ground for it. The picaresque novel does not yet orchestrate its own intentions in the precise sense of the word, but it does make essential preparations for this orchestration, freeing discourse from the heavy pathos that had oppressed it, from all moribund and false accents, and thus lightening up and to a certain extent emptying discourse. In this lies the significance of the type, one it shares with picaresque satiric and parodic novellas, and with the parodic epic and the corresponding cycles of novels built around the image of the clown and the fool.

All this prepared the way for the great exemplars of the novel of the Second Line—such as, for example, *Don Quixote*. In these great and seminal works the novelistic genre becomes what it really is, it unfolds in its fullest potential. In such works authentic double-voiced novelistic images fully ripen, now profoundly differentiated from poetic symbols, and become the unique thing they ultimately are. If in picaresque or comic parodic prose (in an atmosphere of gay liberating deception) a face distorted by false pathos is transformed into a half-mask, egregiously "artistic," then in these works, in the great novels of the Second Line, this half-mask is replaced by an authentic prose image, in art, of the face itself. Languages cease to be merely the object of a purely polemical or autotelic parodying: without losing their parodic coloration completely, they begin to assume the function of artistic representation, of a representation with value in its own right. The novel begins to make use of these languages, manners, genres; it forces all exhausted and used-up, all socially and ideologically alien and distant worlds to speak about themselves in their own language and in their own style—but the author builds a superstructure over these languages made up of his own intentions and accents, which then becomes dialogically linked with them. The author encases his own thought in the image of another's language without doing violence to the freedom of that language or to its own distinctive uniqueness. The hero's discourse about himself and about his world fuses organically, from the outside, with the author's discourse about him and his world. With such an internal fusion of two points of view, two intentions and two expressions in one discourse, the parodic essence of such a discourse takes on a peculiar character: the parodied language offers a living dialogic resistance to the parodying intentions of the other; an unresolved conversation begins to sound in the image itself; the image becomes an open, living, mutual interaction between worlds, points of view, accents. This makes it possible to re-accentuate the image, to adopt various attitudes toward the argument sounding within the image, to take various positions in this argument and, consequently, to vary the interpretations of the image itself. The image becomes polysemic, like a symbol. Thus are created the immortal novelistic images that live different lives in different epochs. The image of Don Quixote has been thus re-accentuated in a variety of ways in the later history of the novel and interpreted in different ways, for these re-accentuations and interpretations were an inevitable and organic further development of the image, a continuation of the unresolved argument embedded in it.

The internal dialogic quality of such images is connected with the general dialogic quality of all heteroglossia in the classic exemplars of the novel of the Second Stylistic Line. Here the dialogic nature of heteroglossia is revealed and actualized; languages become implicated in each other and mutually animate each other.[64] All fundamental authorial intentions are orchestrated, refracted at different angles through the heteroglot languages available in a given era. Only secondary, purely informative "stage-direction" aspects are given in direct authorial discourse. The language of the novel becomes an artistically organized system of languages.

In order to further and refine these distinctions between the First and Second Stylistic Lines, we will pause on two aspects that highlight their differing relationships to heteroglossia.

Novels of the First Line, as we have seen, incorporate a multitude of different semiliterary genres drawn from everyday life, and proceed to eliminate their brute heteroglossia, replacing it everywhere with a single-imaged, "ennobled" language. Such a novel was an encyclopedia not of languages, but of genres. It is true that all these genres were given together with a background of the appropriate heteroglot languages that served to dialogize them, the genres themselves being polemically rejected or purified in the process, but the heteroglot background itself remained outside the novel.

In the Second Stylistic Line we notice the same striving for a generic, encyclopedic comprehensiveness (although not in the same degree). It is enough to mention *Don Quixote*, so rich in in-

---

64. We have already said that it is here that the potential dialogism of ennobled language of the First Line is actualized, its polemic with brute heteroglossia.

serted genres. However, the function of inserted genres in novels of the Second Line undergoes a sharp change. They serve the basic purpose of introducing heteroglossia *into* the novel, of introducing an era's many and diverse languages. Extraliterary genres (the everyday genres, for example) are incorporated into the novel not in order to "ennoble" them, to "literarize" them, but for the sake of their very extraliterariness, for the sake of their potential for introducing nonliterary language (or even dialects) into the novel. It is precisely this very multiplicity of the era's languages that must be represented in the novel.

In novels of the Second Line there emerges the following imperative, one that was later often hailed as constitutive for the novel as a genre (in contrast to other epic genres) and usually formulated as: "the novel must be a full and comprehensive reflection of its era."

The imperative should be formulated differently: the novel must represent all the social and ideological voices of its era, that is, all the era's languages that have any claim to being significant; the novel must be a microcosm of heteroglossia.

Formulated in such a way, this imperative is in fact immanent to that conception of the novel motivating the creative development of the most important major modern novel types, beginning with *Don Quixote*. The imperative takes on new importance in the *Bildungsroman*, where the very idea of a man's becoming and developing—based on his own choices—makes necessary a generous and full representation of the social worlds, voices, languages of the era, among which the hero's becoming—the result of his testing and his choices—is accomplished. But it is not of course only the *Bildungsroman* that so radically needs this plentiful (almost exhaustive) supply of social languages. This requirement may be organically coupled with the most diverse orientations. For example, the novels of Eugène Sue strive to represent as fully as possible all social worlds.

At the heart of the novel's demand for an abundance of the social languages of its era, there lies a correctly perceived recognition of the essence of novelistic heteroglossia. A language is revealed in all its distinctiveness only when it is brought into relationship with other languages, entering with them into one single heteroglot unity of societal becoming. Every language in the novel is a point of view, a socio-ideological conceptual system of real social groups and their embodied representatives. Insofar as language is not perceived as a unique socio-ideological system it cannot be material for orchestration, it cannot become the image of a language. On the other hand, any point of view on the world fundamental to the novel must be a concrete, socially embodied point of view, not an abstract, purely semantic position; it must, consequently, have its own language with which it is organically united. A novel is constructed not on abstract differences in meaning nor on merely narrative collisions, but on concrete social speech diversity. Therefore even that abundance of embodied points of view to which the novel aspires is not a logical, systematic, purely semantic fullness with every possible point of view represented; no, it is a historical and concrete plenitude of actual social-historical languages that in a given era have entered into interaction, and belong to a single evolving contradictory unity. Against the dialogizing background of other languages of the era and in direct dialogic interaction with them (in direct dialogues) each language begins to sound differently than it would have sounded "on its own," as it were (without relating to others). Individual languages, their roles and their actual historical meaning are fully disclosed only within the totality of an era's heteroglossia, just as the definitive and final sense of an individual exchange in a dialogue is disclosed only when that dialogue is ended, when everyone has had his say, only, that is, in the context of the entire resolved conversation. Thus the language of *Amadis* in the mouth of Don Quixote fully reveals itself and the full complex of its historical meaning only within the whole dialogue of languages found in Cervantes' era.

Let us pass on to the second aspect, which also elucidates the difference between the First and the Second Line of development.

As a counterweight to "literariness," novels of the Second Line foreground a critique of literary discourse as such, and primarily novelistic discourse. This *auto-criticism of discourse* is one of the primary distinguishing features of the novel as a genre. Discourse is criticized in its relationship to reality: its attempt to faithfully reflect reality, to manage reality and to transpose it (the utopian pretenses of discourse), even to replace reality as a surrogate for it (the dream and the fantasy that replace life). Already in *Don Quixote* we have a literary, novelistic discourse being tested by life, by reality. And in its further development, the novel of the Second Line remains in large measure a novel that tests literary discourse. Such testing is divided into two types.

The first type concentrates the critique and trial of literary discourse around the hero—a "literary man," who looks at life through the eyes of literature and who tries to live "according to literature." *Don Quixote* and *Madame Bovary* are the best-known exemplars of this type, but the "literary man" and the testing of that literary discourse connected with him can be found in almost every major novel (to a greater or lesser extent these are the characters in Balzac, Dostoevsky, Turgenev, etc.); they differ from each other only in the relative weight accorded this feature in the novel as a whole.

The second type of testing introduces an author who is in the process of writing the novel (a "laying bare of the device," in the terminology of the Formalists), not however in the capacity of a character, but rather as the real author of the given work. Alongside the apparent novel there are fragments of a "novel about the novel" (the classic exemplar is, of course, *Tristram Shandy*).

Both these types of testing literary discourse may, moreover, be blended into one. Thus as early as *Don Quixote* we already have elements of a novel about a novel (the polemic of the author against the author of the projected second part). And the forms of testing literary discourse may be highly diverse (variations on the second type are especially numerous). Finally, we must emphasize in particular the varying degrees of parodying to which literary discourse is subjected. As a rule, the testing of discourse is coupled with its being parodied—but the degree of parody, as well as the degree of dialogic resistance of the parodied discourse, may be highly varied: from external and crude literary parody (where nothing more than parody is intended) to an almost complete solidarity with the parodied discourse ("romantic irony"); midway between these two extremes, that is, somewhere between literary parody and "romantic irony," stands *Don Quixote*, with its profound but cunningly balanced dialogism of parodying discourse. As an exception, we do find testing of literary discourse in the novel that completely lacks this parodying intention. An interesting recent example is M. Prishvin's *In the Land of Unfrightened Birds*.[j] In this novel the self-critique of literary discourse—a

---

j. Reference here is to *Žuravlinaja rodina* (1905), one of Mikhail Prishvin's (1873–1954) many celebrations of unspoiled nature. The title (literally, "Motherland of the Cranes") is also sometimes translated as *Among Friendly Birds*.

novel about a novel—develops into a philosophical novel devoid of parody on the topic of the creative process itself.

Thus the category of literariness characteristic of the First Line, with its dogmatic pretensions to lead a real life, is replaced, in novels of the Second Line, by a trial and self-critique of novelistic discourse.

Toward the beginning of the nineteenth century this sharp opposition between two stylistic lines of the novel comes to an end: the opposition between *Amadis* on the one hand and *Gargantua and Pantagruel* and *Don Quixote* on the other; between the high Baroque novel and *Simplicissimus*, the novels of Sorel, Scarron; between the chivalric romance on the one hand and the parodic epic, the satire novella, the picaresque novel on the other; between, finally, Rousseau and Richardson, and Fielding, Sterne, Jean Paul. It is of course possible to trace up to the present day a more-or-less pure development for both lines, but only off to the side of the mainstream of the modern novel. Any novel of any significance in the nineteenth and twentieth centuries is of a mixed character, although of course the Second Line dominates. It is characteristic that even in the pure novel of trial in the nineteenth century the Second Line dominates stylistically, even though aspects of the First Line are relatively strong in it. It could even be said that in the nineteenth century the distinctive features of the Second Line become the basic constitutive features for the novelistic genre as a whole. It was in the Second Line that novelistic discourse developed all its specific stylistic potential, unique to it alone. The Second Line opened up once and for all the possibilities embedded in the novel as a genre; in it the novel became what it in fact is.

What are the sociological presuppositions of novelistic discourse in the Second Stylistic Line? It was formed at a time when optimal conditions existed for the interaction and interanimation of languages, for the transmission of heteroglossia out of a state of "being in itself" (when languages do not acknowledge each other or are capable of ignoring each other) to a state of "being for itself" (when heteroglot languages mutually reveal each other's presence and begin to function for each other as dialogizing backgrounds). Languages of heteroglossia, like mirrors that face each other, each reflecting in its own way a piece, a tiny corner of the world, force us to guess at and grasp for a world behind their mutually reflecting aspects that is broader, more multi-leveled, containing more and varied horizons than would be available to a single language or a single mirror.

The era of the Renaissance and Protestantism, which destroyed the verbal and ideological centralization of the Middle Ages, was an era of great astronomical, mathematical and geographical discoveries, an era that destroyed the finitude and enclosed quality of the old universe, the finitude of mathematical quantity, which shifted the boundaries of the old geographical world—such an era could find adequate expression only through a Galilean language consciousness of the kind embodied in novelistic discourse of the Second Stylistic Line.

In conclusion, some methodological observations.

Traditional stylistics, acknowledging only a Ptolemaic language consciousness, is helpless when confronted with the authentic uniqueness of novelistic prose. Traditional stylistic categories cannot be applied to this prose, for they rely on the unity of language and on its unmediated equivalence of intentionality throughout. Thus the powerful style-shaping significance of another's discourse, of a mode of indirect, "qualified" speaking, has been neglected. This has led to a situation in which stylistic analysis of novel prose is replaced by linguistic description, usually neutral, of the language of a given work, or (even worse) of a given author.

But such a description of language taken by itself can offer nothing that will help understand novel style. Moreover, it is—as is the linguistic description of language in general—methodologically flawed, for in the novel there *is* no single language; there are rather languages, linked up with each other in a purely *stylistic* unity—not at all the same thing as a linguistic unity (the kind of situation where different dialects, coming together, shape a new dialectological unity).

The language of novels of the Second Line is not one language formed genetically out of the mixing of languages, but, as we have emphasized many times, is rather a unique artistic system of languages, all of which do not lie on the same plane. Even when we exclude character speech and inserted genres, authorial language itself still remains a stylistic system of languages: large portions of this speech will take their style (directly, parodically or ironically) from the languages of others, and this stylistic system is sprinkled with others' words, words not enclosed in quotation marks, *formally* belonging to authorial speech but clearly distanced from the mouth of the author by ironic, parodic, polemical or some other pre-existing "qualified" intonation. To relegate all these orchestrating and distancing discourses to the unitary vocabulary of a given author, to relegate the semantic and syntactic peculiarities of these orchestrating words and forms to the specific semantics and syntax of an author, that is, to perceive and describe everything as linguistic features belonging to some unitary authorial language, is just as absurd as blaming the language of the author for the grammatical mistakes he has employed to flesh out one of his characters. An authorial emphasis is present, of course, in all these orchestrating and distanced elements of language, and in the final analysis all these elements are determined by the author's artistic will—they are totally the author's artistic responsibility—but they do not belong to the author's *language*, nor do they occupy the same plane. From the point of view of methodology, it makes no sense to describe "*the* language of the novel"—because the very object of such a description, the novel's unitary language, simply does not exist.

What *is* present in the novel is an artistic *system* of languages, or more accurately a system of *images* of languages, and the real task of stylistic analysis consists in uncovering all the available orchestrating languages in the composition of the novel, grasping the precise degree of distancing that separates each language from its most immediate semantic instantiation in the work as a whole, and the varying angles of refraction of intentions within it, understanding their dialogic interrelationships and—finally— if there *is* direct authorial discourse, determining the heteroglot background outside the work that dialogizes it (for novels of the First Line, this final task is the primary one).

A resolution of these stylistic tasks necessitates first and foremost profound artistic and ideological penetration into the novel.[65] Only by such a penetration (reinforced, of course, by factual knowledge) can the artistic meaning of the whole be mastered and can we begin to sense how that artistic meaning is the source from which everything flows: the tiniest differences in distance between individual aspects of language and their most immediate

---

65. Such insight also involves a value judgment on the novel, one not only artistic in the narrow sense but also ideological—for there is no artistic understanding without evaluation.

semantic instantiation in the work, the most subtle nuances in the way an author accents various languages and their different aspects. No purely *linguistic* observations, however subtle, can ever uncover this movement and play of authorial intentions as they are at work among different languages and aspects of languages. Artistic and ideological penetration into the whole of the novel must at all times be guided by stylistic analysis. One must not forget during this process that the languages introduced into the novel are shaped into artistic images of languages (they are not raw linguistic data), and this shaping may be more or less artistic and successful, may more or less respond to the spirit and power of the languages that are being represented.

But, of course, artistic penetration by itself is not enough. Stylistic analysis encounters a whole series of difficulties, especially when it deals with works from distant times and alien languages, where our artistic perception cannot rely for support on a living feel for a language. In such a case (figuratively speaking) the entire language—as a consequence of our distance from it—seems to lie on one and the same plane; we cannot sense in it any three-dimensionality or any distinction between levels and distances. Here historico-linguistic research into the language systems and styles available to a given era (social, professional, generic, tendentious) will aid powerfully in re-creating a third dimension for the language of the novel, will help us to differentiate and find the proper distances within that language. But linguistic analysis is, of course, an indispensable support even when studying contemporary works.

But even this is not enough. A stylistic analysis of the novel cannot be productive outside a profound understanding of heteroglossia, an understanding of the dialogue of languages as it exists in a given era. But in order to understand such dialogue, or even to become aware initially that a dialogue is going on at all, mere knowledge of the linguistic and stylistic profile of the languages involved will be insufficient: what is needed is a profound understanding of each language's socio-ideological meaning and an exact knowledge of the social distribution and ordering of all the other ideological voices of the era.

An analysis of novel style confronts a unique difficulty in the fact that the processes of transformation (to which every language phenomenon is subject) occur at a very rapid rate of change: the process of *canonization*, and the process of *re-accentuation*.

When certain aspects of heteroglossia are incorporated into the language of a novel—for example, provincialism, characteristic professional and technical expressions and so forth—they may serve to orchestrate authorial intentions (consequently they are always distanced, "qualified"). But other aspects of heteroglossia, analogous to the first, may, at the given moment, already have lost their flavor of "belonging to another language"; they may already have been canonized by literary language, and are consequently sensed by the author as no longer within the system of provincial patois or professional jargon but as belonging rather to the system of literary language. It would be a gross mistake to ascribe to such aspects an orchestrating function: they either already lie on the same plane as the author's language or, in those cases where the author is not at one with contemporary literary language, they exist within a different orchestrating language (a literary, not provincial, language). In other instances it even becomes very difficult to decide what, for the author, has become an already canonized element of the literary language and in what he still senses heteroglossia. The more distant the work to be analyzed is from contemporary consciousness, the more serious this difficulty becomes. It is precisely in the most sharply heteroglot eras, when the collision and interaction of languages is especially intense and powerful, when heteroglossia washes over literary language from all sides (that is, in precisely those eras that most conduce to the novel) that aspects of heteroglossia are canonized with great ease and rapidly pass from one language system to another: from everyday life into literary language, from literary language into the language of everyday, from professional jargon into more general use, from one genre to another and so forth. In this intense struggle, boundaries are drawn with new sharpness and simultaneously erased with new ease; it is sometimes impossible to establish precisely where they have been erased or where certain of the warring parties have already crossed over into alien territory. All this gives rise to enormous difficulties for the analyst. In more stable eras languages are more conservative; canonization is accomplished more slowly, with more difficulty, and thus it can be easily traced. We should add, however, that the speed with which canonization is accomplished creates difficulties only in trivial matters, in the details of stylistic analysis (primarily in analyzing others' words scattered sporadically throughout authorial speech). For anyone who grasps the basic orchestrating languages and the basic lines of movement and play of intentions, canonization is no obstacle.

The second process—re-accentuation—is considerably more complicated and may fundamentally distort the way novel style is understood. This process has to do with the "feel" we have for distancing, and involves the tact with which an author assigns his accents, sometimes smudging and often completely destroying for us their finer nuances. We have already had occasion to point out that several types and variants of double-voiced discourse can, when being perceived, very easily lose their second voice and fuse with single-voiced direct speech. Thus a parodic quality (in those situations where it is not an end in itself, but is united with a representing function) may under certain circumstances be easily and quickly lost to perception, or be significantly weakened. We have already shown how parodied discourse, in an authentic prose image, can offer internal dialogic resistance to the parodying intentions. For the word is, after all, not a dead material object in the hands of an artist equipped with it; it is a *living* word and is therefore in all things true to *itself*; it may become anachronous and comic, it may reveal its narrowness and one-sidedness, but its meaning—once realized—can never be completely extinguished. And under changed conditions this meaning may emit bright new rays, burning away the reifying crust that had grown up around it and thus removing any real ground for a parodic accentuation, dimming or completely extinguishing such re-accentuation. In this process we must keep in mind the following peculiarity of every true prosaic image: authorial intentions move through it as if along a curve; the distances between discourse and intentions are always changing (in other words, the angle of refraction is always changing); a complete solidarity between the author and his discourse, a fusion of their voices, is only possible at the apexes of the curve. At the nadirs of the curve the opposite occurs: it is possible to have a full reification of the image (and consequently a gross parody on it), that is, it becomes possible to have an image deprived of any real dialogicality. A fusion of authorial intentions with the image may alternate abruptly with complete reification of an image, and this within the space of a short section of the work (in Pushkin, for instance, this can be seen in the author's relationship to Onegin's image and occasionally to Lensky's). The curve tracing the movement of authorial intentions may be more or less sharp, the prose image may be both less fraught and better balanced. Under changed conditions for perceiving an image, the curve may become less sharp and may even be stretched out into a straight line: the image then either becomes entirely or directly intentional, or (on the contrary) it may become purely reified and crudely parodic.

What conditions this re-accentuation of images and languages in the novel? It is a change in the background animating dialogue, that is, changes in the composition of heteroglossia. In an era when the dialogue of languages has experienced great change, the language of an image begins to sound in a different way, or is bathed in a different light, or is perceived against a different dialogizing background. In this new dialogue, a proper, direct intentionality in both the image and its discourse may be strengthened and deepened, or (on the contrary) may become completely reified (a comic image may become tragic, the one who had been unmasked may become the one who strips away mask and so on).

In re-accentuations of this kind there is no crude violation of the author's will. It can even be said that this process takes place *within the image itself*, i.e., not only in the changed conditions of perception. Such conditions merely actualize in an image a potential already available to it (it is true that while these conditions strengthen some possibilities, they weaken others). We could say with justification that in one respect the image has become better understood and better "heard" than ever before. In any case, a certain degree of incomprehension has been coupled here with a new and more profound comprehension.

Within certain limits the process of re-accentuation is unavoidable, legitimate and even productive. But these limits may easily be crossed when a work is distant from us and when we begin to perceive it against a background completely foreign to it. Perceived in such a way, it may be subjected to a re-accentuation that radically distorts it. Such has been the fate of many novels from previous eras. Especially dangerous is any vulgarizing that oversimplifies re-accentuation (which is cruder in all respects than that of the author and his time) and that turns a two-voiced image into one that is flat, single-voiced—into a stilted heroic image, a Sentimental and pathos-charged one, or (at the other extreme) into a primitively comic one. Such, for instance, is the primitive and philistine habit of taking "seriously" Lensky's image, or his parodic poem "Where, O where have you gone. . . ."; of such a sort would be a purely heroic interpretation (in the style of Marlinsky's heroes) of, for example, Pechorin.

The process of re-accentuation is enormously significant in the history of literature. Every age re-accentuates in its own way the works of its most immediate past. The historical life of classic works is in fact the uninterrupted process of their social and ideological re-accentuation. Thanks to the intentional potential embedded in them, such works have proved capable of uncovering in each era and against ever new dialogizing backgrounds ever newer aspects of meaning; their semantic content literally continues to grow, to further create out of itself. Likewise their influence on subsequent creative works inevitably includes re-accentuation. New images in literature are very often created through a re-accentuating of old images, by translating them from one accentual register to another (from the comic plane to the tragic, for instance, or the other way around).

Dibelius, in his books, offers interesting examples of just such a creation of new images by means of a re-accentuation of old ones. Professional and social-class types in the English novel—doctors, jurists, landowners—originally appeared in the comic genres, then later moved over into secondary comic planes of the novel as secondary reified characters, and only from there moved up into the higher levels where they were able to become the novel's major heroes. A basic method for transferring a character from the comic to a higher plane is to represent him in misfortune and suffering: sufferings serve to translate comic characters into another, higher register. Thus the traditionally comic image of the miser helps to establish hegemony for the new image of the capitalist, which is then raised to the tragic image of Dombey.

Of special importance is the re-accentuation of poetic images into prosaic ones, and vice-versa. In this way the parodic epic emerged during the Middle Ages, which played such a crucial role in preparing the way for the novel of the Second Stylistic Line (its parallel classical expression was Ariosto). Of great importance as well is the re-accentuation of images during their translation out of literature and into other art forms—into drama, opera, painting. The classic example is Tchaikovsky's rather considerable re-accentuation of *Evgenij Onegin*: it has had a powerful influence on the philistine perception of this novel's images, greatly weakening the quality of parody in them.[66]

66. This problem of double-voiced parodic and ironic discourse (more accurately, its analogues) in opera, in music, in choreography (parodic dances) is extremely interesting.

Such is the process of re-accentuation. We should recognize its great and seminal importance for the history of literature. In any objective stylistic study of novels from distant epochs it is necessary to take this process continually into consideration, and to rigorously coordinate the style under consideration with the background of heteroglossia, appropriate to the era, that dialogizes it. When this is done, the list of all subsequent re-accentuations of images in a given novel—say, the image of Don Quixote—takes on an enormous heuristic significance, deepening and broadening our artistic and ideological understanding of them. For, we repeat, great novelistic images continue to grow and develop even after the moment of their creation; they are capable of being creatively transformed in different eras, far distant from the day and hour of their original birth.

1934–1935

GLOSSARY

Bakhtin's technical vocabulary presents certain difficulties; while he does not use jargon, he does invest everyday words with special content. In the interests of a smooth translation we have rendered these words in a variety of ways; here we collect and summarize the terms most central to his theory.

The page numbers indicate where in the text useful illustrations or discussions of the concept occur.

ACCENT [*akcent*] [p. 5]
accentuation [*akcencuacija*]
accentuating system [*akcentnaja sistema*]
reaccentuation [*pereakcentuacija*]

An accent, stress or emphasis. Every language or discourse system accents—highlights and evaluates—its material in its own way, and this changes through time. The parallel with a language's stress system is not accidental, but it might be noted that as a rule Russian words have only one stress per word, and this is highly marked, so changes in stress can substantially alter the sound of a word in context.

ALIEN, other, another, someone else's [*čužoj*] [p. 43]

Čužoj is the opposite of *svoj* [one's own] and implies otherness—of place, point of view, possession or person. It does not (as does "alien" in English) imply any necessary estrangement or exoticism; it is simply that which someone has made his own, seen (or heard) from the point of view of an outsider. In Bakhtin's system, we are all *čužoj* to one another by definition: each of us has his or her own [*svoj*] language, point of view, conceptual system that to all others is *čužoj*. Being *čužoj* makes dialogue possible. The novel is that literary art form most indebted to *čuždost'* [otherness].

ARTISTIC GENRES [*xudožestvennye žanry*]
artistic-prose discourse [xudožestvenno-prozaičeskoe slovo]
[pp. 260–261]

artistic craftsmanship in prose

The opposite of "artistic" here is either extra-artistic [*vnex-udožestvennyj*] or *bytovoj* [everyday, casual, ordinary]. "Artistic" genres are those that are reworked to aesthetic purpose and can therefore be re-contextualized (a sonnet, a portrait, an art song); an "everyday genre" is a mode of expression that involves conventions (a personal letter, table talk, a chat over the back fence, throwing rice at weddings) but is of the *byt* [ordinary everyday life] and rooted in specific contexts. The project in "Discourse in the Novel" is precisely to establish a legitimate place for the novel in the artistic genres; novel theory, Bakhtin laments, too often presumes novel language to be a neutral medium, unreworked, or openly polemical, as in rhetoric.

ASSIMILATING during transmission [usvojajušaja peredača] [p. 341]

also, "simultaneous appropriation and transmission"

We communicate by crossing barriers: leaving our *svoj*, or making another's *čužoj* our own. Transmission of information is therefore always simultaneously an appropriation (or assimilation) of it. But there is always a gap between our own intentions and the words—which are always someone else's words—we speak to articulate them. The gap may be greater or smaller, however, depending on the "fit" between what we believe and what we are saying. If I am a believing Christian, how I recite the Lord's Prayer will indicate my closeness to the world view of the text. I assimilate its ideology while transmitting it. If I were a militant atheist, I would, in the ways I chose to speak it, indicate my *distance* from the prayer. I would dramatize nonassimilation of its "message" in my transmission.

AUTHORITATIVE DISCOURSE [*avtoritetnoe slovo*] [pp. 342ff.]

This is privileged language that approaches us from without; it is distanced, taboo, and permits no play with its framing context (Sacred Writ, for example). We recite it. It has great power over us, but only while in power; if ever dethroned it immediately becomes a dead thing, a relic. Opposed to it is *internally-persuasive discourse* [*vnutrenne-ubeditel'noe slovo*], which is more akin to retelling a text in one's own words, with one's own accents, gestures, modifications. Human coming-to-consciousness, in Bakhtin's view, is a constant struggle between these two types of discourse: an attempt to assimilate more into one's own system, and the simultaneous freeing of one's own discourse from the authoritative word, or from previous earlier persuasive words that have ceased to mean.

BELIEF SYSTEM [*krugozor*] [pp. 385–386]
also, conceptual system,
conceptual horizon

Literally in Russian "the circle of one's vision." Primary here is the fact that *krugozory* are all always highly specific, and the visual metaphor emphasizes this: what I see can never be what you see, if only (as Bakhtin put it in an early essay) because I can see what is behind your head. Every *čužoj* thus has its own *krugozor*. When the term is used on a global or societal scale we have rendered it as "belief system"; when it refers to the local vantage point of an individual, as "conceptual horizon."

CANONIZATION [*kanonizacija*]
canonic quality [*kanoničnost'*]

The tendency in every form to harden its generic skeleton and elevate the existing norms to a model that resists change. At the end of "Discourse in the Novel" (pp. 417ff.) Bakhtin discusses a special difficulty in novel theory, how to read properly the rapid transforming processes of *canonization* and of *re-accentuation*. Canonization is that process that blurs heteroglossia, that is, that facilitates a naive, single-voiced reading. It is no accident that the novel—that heteroglot genre—has no canon; it is, however, like all artistic genres subject to the pressures of canonization, which on a primitive level is merely the compulsion to repeat.

CENTRIPETAL—CENTRIFUGAL [*centrostremitel'nyj—centrobežnyj*] [pp. 272–273]

These are respectively the centralizing and decentralizing (or decentering) forces in any language or culture. The rulers and the high poetic genres of any era exercise a centripetal—a homogenizing and hierarchicizing—influence; the centrifugal (decrowning, dispersing) forces of the clown, mimic and rogue create alternative "degraded" genres down below. The novel, Bakhtin argues, is a de-normatizing and therefore centrifugal force.

CHRONOTOPE [*xronotop*]

Literally, "time-space." A unit of analysis for studying texts according to the ratio and nature of the temporal and spatial categories represented. The distinctiveness of this concept as opposed to most other uses of time and space in literary analysis lies in the fact that neither category is privileged; they are utterly interdependent. The chronotope is an optic for reading texts as x-rays of

the forces at work in the culture system from which they spring.
COMPLETED—finished, closed-off, finalized [*zaveršen*]
and its noun *zaveršennost'* [completedness, finalization]
its antonym *nezaveršennost'* [inconclusiveness, openendedness]

This implies not just completed, but capable of definitive finalization. Dialogue, for example, can be *zaveršen* (as in a dramatic dialogue)—it can be laid out in all its speaking parts, framed by an opening and a close. A dialogized word, on the other hand, can never be *zaveršeno*: the resonance or oscillation of possible meanings within it is not only not resolved, but must increase in complexity as it continues to live. Epic time is *zaveršeno*; novel-time, the present oriented toward the future, is always *nezaveršeno*.
CONTEMPORANEITY, contemporary life [*sovremennost'*] [pp. 18ff.]
also, contemporary reality

The Russian word implies a simultaneity of times—in past, present or future; for Bakhtin the concept is most productive when the two temporal simultaneities are that of author and created character, or of author and event. Epic occurs in an absolute past that could never have been *sovremennyj* to its author-bard or to its audience, regardless of when the related events had occurred in "real" historical time. The novel, in contrast, permits authorial- and reader-access to the artistically represented world.
DIALOGISM [*dialogizm*]

Dialogism is the characteristic epistemological mode of a world dominated by heteroglossia. Everything means, is understood, as a part of a greater whole—there is a constant interaction between meanings, all of which have the potential of conditioning others. Which will affect the other, how it will do so and in what degree is what is actually settled at the moment of utterance. This dialogic imperative, mandated by the pre-existence of the language world relative to any of its current inhabitants, insures that there can be no actual monologue. One may, like a primitive tribe that knows only its own limits, be deluded into thinking there is one language, or one may, as grammarians, certain political figures and normative framers of "literary languages" do, seek in a sophisticated way to achieve a unitary language. In both cases the unitariness is relative to the overpowering force of heteroglossia, and thus dialogism.
DIALOGUE [*dialog*] [pp. 411ff.]
dialogizing [*dialogujuščij*]
dialogized [*dialogizovannij*]

Dialogue and its various processes are central to Bakhtin's theory, and it is precisely as verbal process (participial modifiers) that their force is most accurately sensed. A word, discourse, language or culture undergoes "dialogization" when it becomes relativized, de-privileged, aware of competing definitions for the same things. Undialogized language is authoritative or absolute.

Dialogue may be external (between two different people) or internal (between an earlier and a later self). Jurij Lotman (in *The Structure of the Artistic Text*, tr. R. Vroon [Ann Arbor, 1977]), distinguishes these two types of dialogue as respectively spatial (A⟶B) and temporal (A⟶A') communication acts [p. 9].

DISCOURSE, word   [*slovo*]

The Russian word *slovo* covers much more territory than its English equivalent, signifying both an individual word and a method of using words [cf. the Greek *logos*] that presumes a type of authority. Thus the title of our final essay, "Discourse in the Novel," might also have been rendered "The Word in the Novel." We have opted for the broader term, because what interests Bakhtin is the sort of talk novelistic environments make possible, and how this type of talking threatens other more closed systems. Bakhtin at times uses discourse as it is sometimes used in the West—as a way to refer to the subdivisions determined by social and ideological differences within a single language (i.e., the discourse of American plumbers vs. that of American academics). But it is more often than not his more diffuse way of insisting on the primacy of speech, utterance, all *in praesentia* aspects of language.

DISPLAYED, exhibited   [*pokazannyj*]   [p. 322]

A word "displayed as a thing," reified, a word maximally deprived of authorial intention. It involves a manipulation of context in such a way that the word is stripped of those overtones that enable it to be perceived as natural. A word is *pokazano* when it is put in quotation marks, for instance.

"ENNOBLED DISCOURSE"

or "discourse made respectable" [*oblagorožennoe slovo*] [pp. 381–384]

A category of value located on the border between criteria for style and criteria for language. When discourse is "ennobled" it is elevated, made less accessible, more literary and better ordered. "Ennobled language" always presumes some privilege and exercises some social control.

EVALUATIVE, judgmental, valorized, axiological, value- [*cennostnyj*]

Evaluation never takes place in a void; to assign value means to assess and rank. Thus when Bakhtin (in "Epic and Novel") speaks of the epic past as a *cennostno-vremmenoj* [temporally valorized, or time-and-value] cateogory, he means to emphasize the fact that time, like all other sequences, is hierarchical along a good/bad axis as well as a before/after; the epic past is not only past, but good because it is past.

EVERYDAY LIFE [*byt*]

everyday genre [*bytovoj žanr*]

This is what ordinary people live, and their means for communicating with each other [*bytovye žanry*]—the private letter, the laundry note—are not considered artistic. They are, however, both conventionalized and canonized; indeed, all communication must take place against a certain minimum background of shared generic expectations.

GENRE [*žanr*]

In the most general terms, a horizon of expectations brought to bear on a certain class of text types. It is therefore a concept larger than literary genre (examples of everyday genres [*bytovye žanry*] would be the shopping list or telephone conventions). A genre both unifies and stratifies language [p. 288]. In these essays, however, the term is most frequently invoked to define the kind of formulae that have tended to limit literary discourse. The novel is seen as having a different relationship to genre, defining itself precisely by the degree to which it cannot be framed by pre-existing categories.

HETEROGLOSSIA [*raznorečie, raznorečivost'*] [p. 263]

The base condition governing the operation of meaning in any utterance. It is that which insures the primacy of context over text. At any given time, in any given place, there will be a set of conditions—social, historical, meteorological, physiological—that will insure that a word uttered in that place and at that time will have a meaning different than it would have under any other conditions; all utterances are heteroglot in that they are functions of a matrix of forces practically impossible to recoup, and therefore impossible to resolve. Heteroglossia is as close a conceptualization as is possible of that locus where centripetal and centrifugal forces collide; as such, it is that which a systematic linguistics must always suppress.

HYBRID [*gibrid*] [pp. 305ff.]
hybridization [*gibridizacija*] [pp. 358ff.]
    The mixing, within a single concrete utterance, of two or more different linguistic consciousnesses, often widely separated in time and social space. Along with dialogization of languages and pure dialogues, this is a major device for creating language-images in the novel. Novelistic hybrids are intentional [*nameren-nyj*] (unlike, say, naive mixing in everyday speech); their double-voicedness [*dvugolosnost'*] is not meant to resolve. Since hybrids can be read as belonging simultaneously to two or more systems, they cannot be isolated by formal grammatical means, by quotation marks (Bakhtin analyzes the hybrid constructions in Dickens' *Little Dorrit* [pp. 302ff.]). Hybridization is the peculiar mark of prose; poetry, and in particular poetic rhythm, tends to regiment and reduce multiple voices to a single voice [p. 298]. Double-voicedness in poetry, when it occurs, is of an essentially different sort [pp. 327–329].

IDEOLOGY [*ideologija*] [pp. 333–335]
ideologue [*ideolog*]
ideologeme [*ideologim*]
    This is not to be confused with its politically oriented English cognate. "Ideology" in Russian is simply an idea-system. But it is semiotic in the sense that it involves the concrete exchange of signs in society and in history. Every word/discourse betrays the ideology of its speaker; great novelistic heroes are those with the most coherent and individuated ideologies. Every speaker, therefore, is an ideologue and every utterance an ideologeme.

IMAGE OF A LANGUAGE [*obraz jazyka*] [p. 300]
    A central concept, but one difficult to conceptualize because few of the associations that cluster around either "image" or "language" are helpful in grasping what Bakhtin means in bringing them together. Images are what literature—preeminently the novel—uses; in selecting what is to be said, the overriding concern should be to highlight the ideological impulses behind an utterance rather than any local meaning an utterance might have when conceived as a mere linguistic expression.

INTERNALLY PERSUASIVE DISCOURSE [*vnutrenne-ubiditel'noe slovo*]
    cf. AUTHORITATIVE DISCOURSE, above.

INTERILLUMINATION, interanimation, mutual illumination [*vzaimnoosveščenie*]

The major relativizing force in de-privileging languages. When cultures are closed and deaf [*gluxoj*] to one another, each considers itself absolute; when one language sees itself in the light of another, "novelness" has arrived. With novelness, "two myths perish simultaneously: the myth of a language that presumes to be the only language, and the myth of a language that presumes to be completely unified" [p. 68].

We see here Bakhtin's fondness for vision metaphors (cf. "refraction," *krugozor*) as well as play with the Russian word *prosveščenie* [education, enlightenment], which comes about only in the light of another.

LANGUAGE   [*jazyk*]

Bakhtin seems to endorse that broad definition of language offered by Jurij Lotman in *The Structure of the Artistic Text*, "any communication system employing signs that are ordered in a particular manner" [p. 8]. With this in mind, Bakhtin differentiates between

ALIEN/OTHER/ANOTHER'S LANGUAGE   [*čužoj jazyk*]: a language not one's own, at any level.

SOCIAL LANGUAGE   [*social'nyj jazyk*]: a discourse peculiar to a specific stratum of society (professional, age group, etc.) within a given social system at a given time.

NATIONAL LANGUAGE   [*nacional'nyj jazyk*]: the traditional linguistic unities (English, Russian, French, etc.) with their coherent grammatical and semantic systems.

Jazyk is incorporated into compound nouns with the following equivalents:

HETEROGLOSSIA   [*raznorečie, raznojazyčie*]

OTHER-LANGUAGEDNESS   [*inojazyčie*]

POLYGLOSSIA   [*mnogojazyčie*]

MONOGLOSSIA   [*odnojazyčie*]

The distinction between *razno-* [hetero-] and *mnogo* [poly-] is the difference between type and quantity, but the two attributes are often used together.

ORCHESTRATION   [*orkestrovka*]

Bakhtin's most famous borrowing from musical terminology is the "polyphonic" novel, but orchestration is the means for achieving it. Music is the metaphor for moving from seeing (such as in "the novel is the encyclopedia of the life of the era") to *hearing* (as Bakhtin prefers to recast the definition, "the novel is the maximally complete register of all social voices of the era"). For

Bakhtin this is a crucial shift. In oral/aural arts, the "overtones" of a communication act individualize it. Within a novel perceived as a musical score, a single "horizontal" message (melody) can be harmonized vertically in a number of ways, and each of these scores with its fixed pitches can be further altered by giving the notes to different instruments. The possibilities of orchestration make any segment of text almost infinitely variable. The literary CHRONOTOPE (see above), with its great sensitivity to time [p. 86], finds a natural kinship with the overwhelmingly temporal art of music.

PENETRATION, insight [*proniknovenie*] [pp. 416–417]

Such blunt, often crudely material expressions are characteristic of Bakhtin's somewhat militarized language. Ideologies "battle it out in the arena of the utterance." Novelness "invades" privileged discourse. Boundaries between *svoj* and *čužoj* are "violated." Behind this aggressive talk is Bakhtin's concern that the reader feel the forces involved here as bodies, in concrete competition for limited supplies of authority and territory. A true "penetration" into the novel is more than a mere scholarly investigation of it: it is a sortie onto a battlefield, where victory belongs (but never for long) to the one who can best map the movement of hostile forces. These essays, written in the mid-1930s and early 1940s, perhaps reflect the general militarization of Soviet life and language during the prewar and war years. But such rhetoric is of course also impeccably Marxist—although Bakhtin, as it were, recoups the class struggle for epistemology.

PHILOSOPHEME [*filosofim*]

Any concept that is recognizably a unit of a philosophical system (cf. IDEOLOGEME).

POLYGLOSSIA [*mnogojazyčie*]

The simultaneous presence of two or more national languages interacting within a single cultural system (Bakhtin's two historical models are ancient Rome and the Renaissance).

PRECONDITIONED, qualified, "with reservations" [*ogovorennyj*] [p. 331]

cf. its noun *ogovorennost'* ("already bespoke quality")
ogovorka, a reservation [pp. 8–9]

The only un-preconditioned world was Eden, and since its Fall we have all spoken about the world in someone else's [*čužie*] words. The world of objects and meanings [*predmetno-smyslovoj mir*] in which we live is therefore highly relativized; Bakhtin's use of the term merely alludes to the encrustation of meanings bonded to any word or object.

PRINCIPLED, systematic, rigorous, regular [*principial'nyj*]

The Russian has no moral overtones as does its English equivalent, and bears some resemblance to what is meant today by structure: a "principled" solution is one that relates to a larger system, that presumes certain regularities or norms for itself. When Bakhtin complains that there has been no *principial'nyj* approach to the novel, he is referring not to the absence of a canon but to the absence of a minimal list of constitutive features.

REFRACTION [*perelom*] [pp. 299–300; 419ff.]

cf. the verb *prelomljat'sja*, to be refracted

In Bakhtin's ideal case, the poet writes in a directly intentional language, one that means what *he* wants it to mean, while the prose writer's intentions are of necessity "refracted" at various angles through already claimed territory. Authorial refraction is central to the light-ray metaphor Bakhtin uses to illustrate the complexity in reading a prose communication. Every word is like a ray of light on a trajectory to both an object and a receiver. Both paths are strewn with previous claims that slow up, distort, refract the intention of the word. A semantic "spectral dispersion" occurs, but not *within* the object (as would be the case with self-enclosed poetic tropes) but before the word reaches the object, in the "occupied territory" surrounding the object. In any novelistic prose one can trace—as Bakhtin does at length for *Little Dorrit* [pp. 302–307]—the "angle of refraction" of authorial discourse as it passes through various other voices, or voice- and character-zones. But there are other refracting media as well, including that mass of alien words present not in the object but in the consciousness of the listener.

REIFICATION, brute materiality [*ob"jektnost', ob"jektifikacija*]

cf. adj. *ob"jektnyj*, objectified, reified, "turned into a thing"

The process (rhetorically intended or historically caused) of stripping a word [*slovo*] of its "normal" contexts. This happens when a word is *pokazano* [exhibited].

SPEECH [*reč'*]

Character speech [*reči geroev*]: this refers not to the speeches of a character but to a manner of speaking specific to him.

Between the two traditional grammatical categories of DIRECT SPEECH [*prjamaja reč'*] and INDIRECT SPEECH [*kosvennaja reč'*]

Bakhtin posits an intermediate term, QUASI-DIRECT SPEECH [*ne-sobstevenno-prjamaja reč'*]. (This category is given very detailed treatment in chapter 4 of V. N. Vološinov's *Marxism and the Philosophy of Language* [tr. Matejka and Titunik, New York, 1973], pp. 141–159.) Quasi-direct speech involves discourse that is formally authorial, but that belongs in its "emotional structure" to a represented character, his "inner speech transmitted and regulated by the author" [p. 319, where the passage cited is an internal monologue of Nezhdanov's from Turgenev's *Virgin Soil*].

Quasi-direct speech is a threshold phenomenon, where authorial and character intentions are combined in a single intentional hybrid. Measuring the relative strength of these competing intentions is a major task of novel stylistics.

STRATIFICATION   [*rassloenie*]   [p. 289]

For Bakhtin this is a process, not a state. Languages are continually stratifying under pressure of the centrifugal force, whose project everywhere is to challenge fixed definitions. Represented characters in a novel exist in order to find, reject, redefine a stratum of their own; formal authors exist to coordinate these stratifying impulses.

Stratification destroys unity, but—as with our military metaphors discussed above (PENETRATION)—this is not a negative or negating process. It is cheerful war, the Tower of Babel as maypole. To create new strata is the express purpose of art, or as Lotman happily put it, "art is a magnificently organized generator of languages" (*Structure of the Artistic Text*, p. 4).

TENDENTIOUS, period-bound, belonging to a certain school or trend   [*napravlenčeskij*]

Tendentious language is a type of social language heavily influenced by the norms of a given literary school or period, i.e., the vocabulary and presuppositions shared at any given time by Naturalists, Neoclassicists and so forth.

UTTERANCE   [*vyskazivanie*]

Bakhtin's extension of what Saussure called the *parole* aspect of language (the speech act/utterance), but where utterance is made specifically social, historical, concrete and dialogized. See the numerous and excellent discussions of this in V. N. Vološinov, *Marxism and the Philosophy of Language*, as on pp. 40–41: "In the verbal medium, in each utterance, however trivial it may be, [a] living dialectical synthesis is constantly taking place between the psyche and ideology, between the inner and outer. In each speech act, subjective experience perishes in the objective fact of the enunciated word-utterance, and the enunciated word is subjectified in the act of responsive understanding in order to generate, sooner or later, a counterstatement."

VOICE [*golos, -glas*]

This is the speaking personality, the speaking consciousness. A voice always has a will or desire behind it, its own timbre and overtones. SINGLE-VOICED DISCOURSE [*edinogolosnoe slovo*] is the dream of poets; DOUBLE-VOICED DISCOURSE [*dvugolosnoe slovo*] the realm of the novel. At several points Bakhtin illustrates the difference between these categories by moving language-units from one plane to the other—for example, shifting a trope from the plane of poetry to the plane of prose [pp. 327ff.]: both poetic and prose tropes are ambiguous [in Russian, *dvusmyslennyj*, literally "double-meaninged"] but a poetic trope, while meaning more than one thing, is always only single-voiced. Prose tropes by contrast always contain more than one voice, and are therefore dialogized.

ZONE [*zona*]

character zones [*zony geroev*]

speech zones [*rečivye zony*]

Zones are both a territory and a sphere of influence. Intentions must pass through "zones" dominated by other [*čužoj*] characters, and are therefore refracted. A character's zone need not begin with his directly quoted speech but can begin far back in the text; the author can prepare the way for an autonomous voice by manipulating words ostensibly belonging to "neutral" authorial speech. This is a major device of comic style (see Bakhtin's analysis of *Little Dorrit* [pp. 302–307]).

In Bakhtin's view there are no zones belonging to no one, no "no-man's land." There are disputed zones, but never empty ones. A zone is the locus for hearing a voice; it is brought about *by* the voice.

INDEX